T0210784

Smart City Blueprint

The smart city movement, during the last decade and a half, advocated the built environment and digital technology convergence with the backing of institutional capital and government support. The commitment of a significant number of local governments across the globe, in terms of official smart city policies and initiatives, along with the constant push of global technology giants, has reinforced the popularity of this movement. This two-volume treatment on smart cities thoroughly explores and sheds light on the prominent elements of the smart city phenomenon and generates a smart city blueprint.

This first volume, with its 12 chapters, provides a sound understanding on the key foundations and growth directions of smart city frameworks, technologies, and platforms, with theoretical expansions, practical implications, and real-world case study lessons.

The second companion volume offers sophisticated perspectives on the key foundations and directions of smart city policies, communities, and urban futures, with theoretical expansions, practical implications, and real-world case study lessons.

This book is an invaluable reference source for urban policymakers, managers, planners, practitioners, and many others, particularly to benefit from it when tackling key urban and societal issues and planning for and delivering smart city solutions. Moreover, the book is also a rich and important repository for scholars and research and undergraduate students as it communicates the complex smart city phenomenon in an easy to digest form, by providing both the big picture view and specifics of each component of that view. It also appeals to local government agencies and smart city practitioners.

Tan Yigitcanlar is an eminent Australian researcher and author with international recognition and impact in the field of smart and sustainable city development. He is a Professor of Urban Studies and Planning at the School of Architecture and Built Environment, Queensland University of Technology, Brisbane, Australia.

Smart City Blueprint
Framework, Technology, Platform

Tan Yigitcanlar

CRC Press is an imprint of the
Taylor & Francis Group, an **informa** business

Designed cover image: Shutterstock

First edition published 2024
by CRC Press
2385 NW Executive Center Drive, Suite 320, Boca Raton FL 33431

and by CRC Press
4 Park Square, Milton Park, Abingdon, Oxon, OX14 4RN

CRC Press is an imprint of Taylor & Francis Group, LLC

Library of Congress Cataloging-in-Publication Data
Names: Yigitcanlar, Tan, author.
Title: Smart city blueprint : framework, technology, platform / Tan Yigitcanlar.
Description: First edition. | Boca Raton, FL : CRC Press, [2024]– |
Includes bibliographical references and index. |
Identifiers: LCCN 2023017883 (print) | LCCN 2023017884 (ebook) |
ISBN 9781032517179 (hbk) | ISBN 9781032517162 (pbk) | ISBN 9781003403630 (ebk)
Subjects: LCSH: Smart cities. | City planning. | Urban policy.
Classification: LCC TD159.4 .Y55 2024 (print) | LCC TD159.4 (ebook) |
DDC 307.1/216–dc23/eng/20230422
LC record available at https://lccn.loc.gov/2023017883
LC ebook record available at https://lccn.loc.gov/2023017884

ISBN: 978-1-032-51717-9 (hbk)
ISBN: 978-1-032-51716-2 (pbk)
ISBN: 978-1-003-40363-0 (ebk)

DOI: 10.1201/9781003403630

Typeset in Times New Roman
by Newgen Publishing UK

This book is dedicated to the following four beloved, beautiful, and brilliant women that have shaped my life: Cahide, Susan, Ela, Selin

Contents

PART 3
Smart City Platform   231

Foreword

The idea of the smart city is largely coincident with the massive miniaturisation of computers and their networking that has proceeded apace, particularly since the Millennium. When everybody has immediate access to their own personal computer, be it a hand-held device, a tablet, a laptop, or anything larger, there emerge countless possibilities that these devices can be used to enable us to do things in much more efficient, faster, and possibly more intelligent ways than we did manually in the past. Although miniaturisation has dominated the evolution of computing from the very beginning in the middle of the last century, it was not until the early 2000s that enough critical mass was reached to enable everyone to have access to a small machine. Moreover it took developments in parallel in terms of communications technologies to reach the point where millions of machines could suddenly be networked and used interactively with digital connectivity becoming global. Although a definite date cannot be fixed, the sea change was extremely rapid, with many of these possibilities coming together in the development of the smart phone, in particular the iPhone. By 2010, much of this interactivity had come to pass and we had entered the world of "big data", software platforms, and new organisational structures built around digital technologies.

To a very large extent, this transformation to a world of total connectivity has also changed the nature of computing itself through its software. By far the dominant software types now running on millions of computers (including all mobile devices) are much smaller and accessible than the technical and scientific software of the late 20th century. Apps, for example, now dominate computing and many smaller more routine tasks are now computable. In this sense, the smart city is now dominated by millions of small-scale applications but with considerable power due to their ability to connect with one another. The ability to link up hardware, which is multiplying ever faster, has established the preconditions for the development of platforms that specialise in providing new forms of service—mobility as a service being a particularly well-defined applications domain where travel is provided and costed on demand. Uber, for example, is the quintessential application but there are an increasing number of variants which are continually being adapted to new ways of living and moving within cities. Retailing of course has also moved online and is increasingly the way we acquire or at least order material products.

Many of these themes are organised by Yigitcanlar in two foci which define his blueprint for the smart city. The first of these in Volume 1 covers these as "Framework, Technology, Platform" where the notion of how the smart city can increase sustainability and thence engender a city's "transformation readiness", that is, the ability of a city to embrace new technologies, practices, and behaviours which are heavily influenced by new digital data, methods, and models. Many of the examples in the book are drawn from Yigitcanlar's own experience of city planning and development in Australia where he emphasises how innovation, sustainability, and governance are reflected in the IoT (Internet of Things), with AI (artificial intelligence), and autonomous vehicle technology being the most popular contemporary technologies. These new methods and approaches have evolved to support the idea of many different urban behaviours as a service, where energy, mobility, and a variety of procedures and protocols are collected together into wider organisational forms where the whole city is regarded as a platform.

The smart city can be approached from many angles, and it is a virtue of these two volumes that the author goes well beyond mere technical notions, embracing multiple threads that characterise different attributes of the traditional city and thence the smart city. Into this context again over the last decade has come the advent of a new form of AI and in the first volume, Yigitcanlar exhibits a somewhat sceptical perspective on such intelligence. At the beginning of computing in the 1950s, there was great excitement that computers could be considered to be akin to digital brains and like the human brain could be programmed to produce the same sorts of problem-solving that we as humans engage in. In fact, the view was that this kind of AI that might be programmed into computers could lead to super-intelligent machines. Of course, no such future could ever be realised and the field of AI fell into its nuclear winter where it was widely discredited in the 1970s and 1980s. But with successive miniaturisation and the evolution of machines that could generate big data in real time, a new form of weak AI emerged where the focus was not on trying to program computers to act like human brains but to use them to figure out significant patterns in data that could be used intelligently. This is the world of machine learning where bigger and bigger quantities of data can be used to provide new types of application that are speeding up many routine but nevertheless highly complicated tasks. In fact, Yigitcanlar sketches ways in which AI and the smart cities paradigm in general might be developed to address current grand challenges such as climate change, green policies, more comfortable transport, a range of improvements to routine services in cities, and of course more generally increasing productivity in the post-industrial economy.

In the second volume, the focus is much more on how policies that reflect the smart city concept are formulated and implemented as well as ways in which various policies involve community engagement and citizen participation demonstrate how ambiguous and ill-defined the concept might be. His aim is to generate a number of different perspectives on smart cities ranging from smart new towns like Masdar in the UAE and Songdo in the Seoul suburbs to much more organically developing smart information technologies in the services that places like Amsterdam have developed. In fact, many of the examples he develops in this book reveal considerable dissent over what constitutes not only the smart city but policies that are manifestly smart. There are many different pathways to the "smart city" and these enrich the discussion of how one develops appropriate blueprints for future cities that are more sustainable and equitable as well as more efficient than cities that do not overtly aim to develop such intelligence. The last section of the second volume deals with community engagement, and the relationship to local and municipal governance. The entire nexus of smart technologies and traditional organisational practices and processes that aim to develop the smart city is fraught with difficulties and Yigitcanlar concludes his blueprint with some of the conundrums associated with realising smart city policies and how they might evolve and adapt to the wider goals facing the future city, such as those pertaining to the UN's sustainable development goals.

What is good about this book is that Yigitcanlar weaves organisational, behavioural, and planning practices into platforms that enable smart technologies to be effectively developed. And to do this, he does not mince his words concerning the difficulties of ensuring this integration but also the great opportunities that are available in future cities if we tenaciously grasp the changes that confront our long-term urban futures in an intrinsically digital world.

Michael Batty
Centre for Advanced Spatial Analysis
University College London, UK

Preface

No or inadequately regulated urbanisation and industrialisation practices since the beginning of the industrial revolution in the 1850s have resulted in climate change, environmental degradation, and unsustainable development worldwide with immense negative externalities on our cities, societies, and the planet. During the last couple of decades, the concept of the smart city has become a hot topic among urban policy circles, and today more and more cities are channelling their planning and development energy, strategies, and investments for becoming a smart locale—to somehow tackle the negative externalities.

Nevertheless, the smart city concept is neither new, nor always had the same emphasis. In the 1800s, this concept was used for the first time and referred to the efficiency and self-governance of cities in the western USA. In the 1960s, the modern smart city concept was referred to as smart urban growth management, and relevant strategies were introduced to avoid sprawling development and concentrating growth in compact walkable urban centres. Vancouver is one of the best practices for such smart growth management.

In the 1990s, the smart city concept emphasised technology-based innovation in the planning, development, operation, and management of cities. Nonetheless, some cities laid the foundations of this technocentric approach much earlier. For example, in the 1970s, Los Angeles created the first urban big data project, and in the early 1990s, Amsterdam built its virtual digital city. The conception of the last boom of the smart city dates to 2008, which was due to a strong push of major global technology, development, and consultancy firms—including CISCO, IBM, KPMG—as a business strategy to survive the global financial crisis (GFC).

This has led to the emergence of a corporate sector driven sociotechnical imaginary of the smart city movement. The best practice—e.g., Songdo, Masdar City, Gujarat International Finance Tec-City, Hudson Yards, Jurong Lake District, Amsterdam, City Verve, Barcelona, Tel Aviv—of this movement followed different pathways for their smart city transformation.

The first wave of the contemporary smart city emerged as a response of global technology, development, and consultancy firms to the GFC and perceived cities as enterprises that need the state-of-the-art digital technologies and infrastructures and an innovation culture to become internationally competitive. The meaning of "smart" in the smart city has shifted from a pre-GFC emphasis on sustainability and climate change to a post-GFC engagement with entrepreneurship and platformization.

In that perspective, smart city is widely conceptualised as the convergence of digital technology and the built environment, institutional capital, and government support over long periods of time. An example of this would be public–private partnership in initiatives for convergence of blockchain and artificial intelligence (AI) in the Internet of Things (IoT) network for smart precinct development.

Despite some success examples and progress, this smart city perspective has proved insufficiently nimble to respond to shifting public attitudes about the ethics of urban technology and the governance of large-scale urban development. The most obvious example of the inadequacy of the existing algorithmic approach to smart cities is the termination of Sidewalk Labs' signature smart city development in Toronto waterfront.

The COVID-19 pandemic accelerated digital transformation efforts across the globe that have provided an invaluable opportunity for technology companies. Now, urban tech is on the rise, as venture investors move in with much more focused short-term plays. This is leading to the creation of the second wave of the smart city that is producing a global supply chain of smart city solutions and an emerging urban innovation industry for delivery. On the one hand, it is also cultivating the emergence of the global urban innovation industry, moving from standalone solutions to standardised frameworks/systems/processes that produce novel/bespoke/tailored solutions. On the other hand, this poses risks of urban innovation industry following the business-as-usual of laissez faire ruthless capitalist practices for smart city (trans)formation, resulting in unsustainable outcomes.

During a debate at the Harvard Museum of Natural History, in the early days of the smart city movement in 2009, American sociobiologist Edward O. Wilson underlined the real problem of humanity as follows: "We have Palaeolithic emotions, medieval institutions, and god-like technology". Now, hence, we need to figure out how we are going to utilise existing and emerging powerful technologies, such as AI, wisely in our cities and societies.

The consolidated smart city concept advocates, developed by exclusively technocentric solution sceptic scholars, the emerging global urban innovation industry to adopt a responsible innovation practice for smart city (trans)formation, delivering accountable, ethical, frugal, sustainable, and trustworthy outcomes—and also forming a most needed responsible urban innovation industry and skilled and informed policymakers and planners to support the efforts in building sustainable and liveable futures for all.

Against this backdrop, this first volume of the Smart City Blueprint book (Smart City Blueprint: Framework, Technology, Platform) thoroughly explores and sheds light on the prominent elements of the smart city phenomenon and generates insights into a smart city blueprint. This first volume, with its dozen chapters, provides a sound understanding on the key foundations and growth directions of smart city frameworks, technologies, and platforms, with theoretical expansions, practical implications, and real-world case study lessons. This first volume is accompanied by the second volume titled Smart City Blueprint: Policy, Community, Futures.

This book is also part of the author's book trilogy on smart cities—i.e., *Technology and the City: Systems, Applications, and Implications* (2016), *Smart City Blueprint: Framework, Technology, Platform* (2023), and *Smart City Blueprint: Policy, Community, Futures* (2023). The books in the trilogy are invaluable reference sources for urban policymakers, managers, planners, and practitioners, and many others, particularly to benefit from it when tackling key urban and societal issues and planning for and delivering smart city solutions. Moreover, these books also form a rich and important repository for scholars and higher degree research and undergraduate students as they communicate the complex smart city phenomenon in an easy to digest form, by providing both the big picture view and specifics of each component of that view, and hence offering a smart city blueprint.

The volume *Smart City Blueprint: Framework, Technology, Platform* is structured under three main parts and elaborated briefly as below:

Part 1, Smart City Framework: This part of the book concentrates on providing a clear understanding on the key foundations of smart cities' conceptual and practice dimensions. These foundations include multidimensional perspective, smartness and sustainability, and transformation readiness.

Part 2, Smart City Technology: This part of the book concentrates on providing a clear understanding on the technocentric aspects of smart cities. These aspects include what these technologies are, how they are perceived and utilised in cities, how cities can get smarter with the responsible use of these technologies, how urban artificial intelligences can support smart city and sustainable development goals, why such intelligence should be green, and how these technologies are utilised for smart urban mobility.

Part 3, Smart City Platform: This part of the book concentrates on providing a clear understanding on the platforms that help in operationalising smart city functions. These platforms include mobile energy as a service, mobility as a service, urban management platform, and city as a platform.

Author

 **Tan Yigitcanlar** is an eminent Australian researcher with international recognition and impact in the field of urban studies and planning. He is a Professor of Urban Studies and Planning at the School of Architecture and Built Environment, Queensland University of Technology, Brisbane, Australia. Along with this post, he holds the following positions: Honorary Professor at the School of Technology, Federal University of Santa Catarina, Florianopolis, Brazil; Director of the Australia-Brazil Smart City Research and Practice Network; Lead of QUT Smart City Research Group; and Co-Director of QUT City 4.0 Lab. He is a member of the Australian Research Council College of Experts.

He has been responsible for research, teaching, training, and capacity-building programs in the fields of urban studies and planning in esteemed Australian, Brazilian, Finnish, Japanese, and Turkish universities. His research aims to address contemporary urban planning and development challenges—that are economic, societal, spatial, governance, or technology related in nature. The main foci of his research interests, within the broad field of urban studies and planning, are clustered around the following three interdisciplinary themes:

- *Smart Technologies, Communities, Cities, and Urbanism*—e.g., examining the disruptive externalities and beneficial impacts of urban technologies and digital transformation of urban services and infrastructures on our cities and societies.
- *Sustainable and Resilient Cities, Communities, and Urban Ecosystems*—e.g., exploring the urban and environmental dynamics and challenges to determine strategies for planning and designing sustainable, resilient, responsive, healthy, and liveable natural and built urban environments.
- *Knowledge-Based Development of Cities and Innovation Districts*—e.g., scrutinising the impacts of global knowledge and innovation economy on our cities and societies, and developing strategies for space and place making for knowledge-based activities in cities.

He has been providing research consultancy services to all tier governments (i.e., federal, state, local)—along with for international corporations, and non-governmental organisations—in Australia and overseas. These services have helped government and industry form their key strategies, become more resilient, and better prepared for the emerging disruptive conditions. He has received over $4 million funding from research consultancy projects and national competitive grant programs.

He is the lead Editor-in-Chief of Elsevier Smart Cities Book Series and carries out senior editorial positions in the following 11 high-impact journals: *Sustainable Cities and Society, Cities, Land Use Policy, Journal of Urban Technology, Sustainability, Journal of Open Innovation: Technology, Market, and Complexity, Journal of Knowledge Management, Knowledge Management Research and Practice, Global Journal of Environmental Science and Management, International Journal of Information Management,* and *Measuring Business Excellence.*

He undertook the Chairman role of the annual Knowledge Cities World Summit series between 2007 and 2019. Under this brand, he organised 12 international conferences in the following locations: Monterrey (Mexico); Shenzhen (China); Melbourne (Australia); Bento Gonçalves (Brazil); Matera (Italy); Istanbul (Turkey); Tallinn (Estonia); Daegu (Korea); Vienna (Austria); Arequipa (Peru); Tenerife (Spain); and Florianopolis (Brazil). He also contributed to the organisation of over two-dozen other international conferences in various capacities. He has also delivered over 70 keynote and invited talks at prestigious international academic conferences and national industry events.

He has disseminated his research findings extensively, including over 300 articles published in high-impact journals, and the following 24 key reference books published by the esteemed international publishing houses:

- *Innovation District Planning* (CRC Press, 2024)
- *Smart City Blueprint: Framework, Technology, Platform* (Routledge, 2023)
- *Smart City Blueprint: Policy, Community, Futures* (Routledge, 2023)
- *Companion of Creativity and the Built Environments* (Routledge, 2023)
- *Internet of Things for Smart Environments and Applications* (MDPI, 2023)
- *Urban Analytics with Social Media Data* (CRC Press, 2022)
- *Distributed Computing and Artificial Intelligence* (Springer, 2022)
- *State of the Art and Future Perspectives in Smart and Sustainable Urban Development* (MDPI, 2022)
- *Sustainable Mobility and Transport* (MDPI, 2022)
- *Reviews and Perspectives on Smart and Sustainable Metropolitan and Regional Cities* (MDPI, 2021)
- *Smart Cities and Innovative Urban Technologies* (Routledge, 2021)
- *Approaches, Advances and Applications in Sustainable Development of Smart Cities* (MDPI, 2020)
- *Geographies of Disruption* (Springer, 2019)
- *Planning, Development and Management of Sustainable Cities* (MDPI, 2019)

- *Urban Knowledge and Innovation Spaces* (Routledge, 2018)
- *Technology and the City* (Routledge, 2016)
- *Knowledge and the City* (Routledge, 2014)
- *Sustainable Urban Water Environment* (Edward Elgar, 2014)
- *Building Prosperous Knowledge Cites* (Edward Elgar, 2012)
- *Knowledge-Based Development for Cities and Societies* (IGI Global, 2010)
- *Sustainable Urban and Regional Infrastructure Development* (IGI Global, 2010)
- *Rethinking Sustainable Development* (IGI Global, 2010)
- *Knowledge-Based Urban Development* (IGI Global, 2008)
- *Creative Urban Regions* (IGI Global, 2008)

His research outputs have been widely cited and influenced urban policy, practice, and research internationally. His research was cited over 20,000 times, resulting in an h-index of over 80 (Google Scholars).According to the 2022 Science-wide Author Databases of Standardised Citation Indicators, amongst urban and regional planning scholars, he is ranked #1 in Australia and a top-10 ranked researcher worldwide. He was also recognised as an "Australian Research Superstar" in the Social Sciences Category at the Australian's 2020 Research Special Report.

Part 1

Smart City Framework

This part of the book concentrates on providing a clear understanding on the key foundations of smart cities' conceptual and practice dimensions. These foundations include multidimensional perspective, smartness and sustainability, and transformation readiness.

DOI: 10.1201/9781003403630-1

1 Multidimensional Perspective

1.1 Introduction

Improper and deliberate human activities pushed the planet into the Anthropocene epoch—characterised by significant impacts on geology, ecosystems, and climate change (Smith & Zeder, 2013; Dizdaroglu & Yigitcanlar, 2014). Despite representing only about 2% of the geographic space and accommodating over 50% of the world's population, cities today produce 80% of greenhouse gas (GHG) emissions and consume 80% of the world's resources (Ioppolo et al., 2014, 2016; La Greca & Martinico, 2016; Arbolino et al., 2017, 2018). A heavy reliance on non-renewable resources increases GHG emissions, including a vast amount of carbon-dioxide (CO_2) responsible for global warming (Yigitcanlar et al., 2007; Mahbub et al., 2011; Goonetilleke et al., 2014; Szopik-Depczyńska et al., 2017).

At the dawn of the catastrophic global climate change era, "smart cities" came to the scene as a potential panacea to, somehow, reverse or ease the impacts of negative urbanisation, industrialisation, and consumerism practices (Wiig, 2015; Taamallah et al., 2017; Trindade et al., 2017). Although the initial rationale for smart city developments was mostly related to environmental concerns, the practice, unfortunately, indicates that only marginal attention is paid to these concerns. Current practice is mostly unidimensional with technology at the core (Yigitcanlar, 2016). This unidimensional focus is a result of, as well as points to, a number of challenges that smart city practice will have to overcome. These are briefly elaborated below.

Firstly, the fourth industrial revolution (Industry 4.0) helps leading global cities to advance their innovation edges, and hence, further secure their global hub status in innovation and knowledge generation (Edvardsson et al., 2016; Yigitcanlar et al., 2016; Pancholi et al., 2019). Subsequently, cities that are falling behind have started to strategise their economic development to increase abilities in fostering, attracting, and retaining innovation activities (Millar & Choi, 2010; Holland, 2015; Yigitcanlar et al., 2017; Pancholi et al., 2019). The smart cities agenda in many cities—e.g., Amsterdam, Vienna—goes together with these knowledge-based economic development efforts (Sarimin & Yigitcanlar, 2012; Carrillo et al., 2014; Esmaeilpoorarabi et al., 2016, 2018). Today, smart cities are seen as the hubs of

DOI: 10.1201/9781003403630-2

technological innovation—e.g., San Francisco, Seoul—(urban areas generate 93% of the world's patented inventions) rather than cities of sustainable development.

Secondly, smart city projects, nonetheless, are big and expensive capital investments—supposed to drive societal and environmental transformations—thus they very hard to properly deliver. Current practice is highly ad hoc in nature in transforming cities and societies into truly smart ones. For example, after over a decade of investment, Songdo City (Korea)—widely referred to as the world's first smart city—is still a "work in progress" project without achieving any concrete desired outcomes (Yigitcanlar & Lee, 2014). This ad hoc approach makes smart city practice highly risky to accurately identify, produce, and/or meet desired socio-spatial outcomes.

Next, Hoon & Hawken (2018, p. 1) underline the monocentric focus on technology of the present smart city practice by stating:

> Current discourse on smart cities is obsessed with technological capability and development. Global rankings reduce cities to a one-dimensional business model and series of metrics. If the term "smart city" is to have any enduring value, technology must be used to develop a city's unique cultural identity and quality of life for the future.

The comprehension of smart cities in current practice carries a risk of leading to a long-term trend toward increasing dependency on technology, and negligence of socio-spatial issues (Yigitcanlar, 2016).

Fourthly, the popularity of the smart cities agenda is mainly an outcome of the aggressive promotion/push of major global technology, development, and consultancy firms and their programs—e.g., KPMG and CISCO's partnership in smart cities, IBM's Smarter Planet, and Smarter Cities Challenge initiatives (Alizadeh, 2017). While smart city sceptics have raised their concerns about the ongoing global craze on this new city brand (Kunzmann, 2014; Anthopoulos, 2017; Grossi & Pianezzi, 2017), many governments across the globe are still jumping on the smart cities bandwagon by turning a blind eye to these warnings (Caragliu et al., 2011; Townsend, 2013).

Lastly, there are too many smart city definitions/conceptualisations—focusing on separate aspects of drivers or outcomes—in the rapidly growing literature. These are coined by scholars and commercial, government, and international organisations and most are vague or inchoate in conception (Dameri, 2013). However, due to the infancy, interdisciplinary nature, or generally poor conceptualisation, there is not a commonly agreed definition of smart cities. This is due to the lack of a sound and/ or common conceptual understanding. Scholars, practitioners, and organisations have developed frameworks that suit their own practical perspectives—rather than (in general) a generic framework outlining the complexities and links of various dimensions of smart cities in a comprehensive and at the same time simple way.

Against this backdrop, this chapter aims to address the broad conceptualisation and multidimensionality issues through developing a better understanding of the smart cities notion—in terms of identifying the key development drivers and desired outcomes, and placing them under a multidimensional framework. This would, in turn, help urban administrators and smart city practitioners better grasp the smart city notion and assist them in undertaking necessary actions to utilise the smart city drivers to achieve the desired outcomes. The methodological approach adopted in this research includes a systematic but at the same time critical review of the interdisciplinary literature on smart cities focusing on conceptual analysis to develop a multidimensional framework. By developing such a framework, this study contributes to the efforts of a few other scholars, who have developed multi-dimensional conceptualisations and frameworks, and expands the understanding beyond a mostly monocentric focus of the current common smart city practice.

1.2 Literature Background

1.2.1 Origin and Definition

In recent years, the development of smart cities is at the forefront of the urban discourse due to the rapid urbanisation rate and associated socioeconomic, environmental, and governance challenges, along with the global innovation leadership challenge (Belanche et al., 2016). Nevertheless, the concept of a smart city is not new. The term was first coined in the mid-1800s to describe new cities of the American West that were efficient and self-governed. However, it has its contemporary origins in the "smart growth" movement of the 1990s—referencing sustainable urbanisation (Eger, 2009; Albino et al., 2015; Susanti et al., 2016).

Since the 1990s, the smart city concept has evolved to mean almost any form of technology-based innovation in the planning, development, operation, and management of cities, for example, the deployment of smart mobility solutions to combat urban traffic challenges (Yigitcanlar et al., 2008a; Harrison & Donnelly, 2011; Battarra et al., 2016). With the offerings of digital technologies and online urban planning opportunities, this concept increased its popularity among the urban technocrats (Yigitcanlar, 2005, 2006; Aina, 2017; Pettit et al., 2018).

Although originating from the smart growth movement, a smart city can be, sometimes mistakenly, termed in other jargons. These include sustainable city (Bulkeley & Betsill, 2005), digital city (Aurigi, 2005), intelligent city (Komninos, 2008), ubiquitous city (Lee et al., 2008), techno-centric city (Willis & Aurigi, 2017), creative city (Baum et al., 2009), and knowledge city (Yigitcanlar et al., 2008b). However, the notion of a smart city is not equivalent to these city brands; although smart cities carry some of the common characteristics of other city brands or their conceptualisations. For example, an intelligent city is not equivalent to the notion of a smart city, instead it focuses on only either a single aspect of the smart city field (e.g., ICT) or on other less closely related issues (e.g., resilient city). These branding variations have occurred as a result of different interpretations of what an ideal city should be like, and which policies these cities utilise to sustain growth, and address socio-spatial inequalities of resources (Chang et al., 2018). However, after the increasing popularity of the smart city phenomenon, in recent years many cities across the globe have incorporated the "smart" tag in their brands. For instance, Songdo was initially branded as a "ubiquitous city", but the new brand is now a "compact smart city".

Over the last two decades, the pace of globalisation has accelerated number of large multinational corporations' focus on the lucrative smart urban technology and engineering solutions. IBM, Cisco, Microsoft, Hitachi, Samsung, LG, Siemens, ARUP, KPMG, and a number of national telecommunication companies—e.g., Alcatel, KT Corporation—are among the front-runners of the industry that led the expansion of the smart cities movement, and technology deployment across the global cities (Yigitcanlar, 2016). Moreover, today various technology and car manufacturing companies—e.g., Google, Uber, Volvo, Tesla, Audi, BMW, Mercedes-Benz, Nissan to name a few—also joined the smart cities bandwagon with their smart mobility solutions of autonomous vehicles or driverless cars (Shladover, 2018). The global market for smart city solutions and services is expected to grow from $40.1 billion in 2017 to 94.2 billion by 2026.

After two decades since the commencement of contemporary conceptualisation and practice of the smart cities notion, it is still in its infancy (Alizadeh, 2017; Praharaj et al., 2018). Unparalleled with its raising popularity, there is no commonly agreed definition of smart cities, and what they represent in the international economic order. A selection of the most popular definitions of smart cities—based on Lara et al. (2016) and Mora et al.'s (2017) studies—is presented in Table 1.1. The fast-growing literature on smart cities comes from the streams of academic, commercial, and (inter)national organisations researching into and practicing smart cities. These groups have a different take on the concept as they see it from different lenses, such as disciplinary, practice- or conceptualisation-orientation, and domain-orientation—e.g., technology, economy, society, environment, governance (Yigitcanlar, 2017).

1.2.2 Technology

The original intention or rationale, as devised from the smart growth movement, was predominantly to provide environmental sustainability (Dizdaroglu et al., 2012). Today, smart city projects seem to pay more attention to providing economic development and quality-of-life outcomes using the capabilities of modern technologies (Afzalan et al., 2017)—perhaps as, in the short run, these are more profitable and relatively easier tasks to deliver (Hollands, 2008). In other words, during the last decade the smart city concept became a buzz word predominantly for techno-centric urbanisation with the recognition of flexible and mobile means of production and innovation (Neirotti et al., 2014).

A bibliometric analysis, undertaken by Mora et al. (2017), underlines that smart cities are a fast-growing topic of scientific enquiry. However, much of the knowledge generated about them is singularly technological in nature—thus, lacking social intelligence, cultural artefacts, and environmental attributes. Similarly, Angelidou (2017) identified the characteristics of smart cities from the literature and checked these characteristics in 15 smart cities best practices. This study found that most smart city strategies are focused on the role of technology in improving

Table 1.1 Definition and primary theme of smart cities (derived from Lara et al., 2016; Mora et al., 2017)

Literature	Definition	Theme
Lara et al. (2016)	A community that systematically promotes the overall wellbeing of all its members, and flexible enough to proactively and sustainably become an increasingly better place to live, work, and play.	Community, wellbeing, sustainability, liveability
Yigitcanlar (2016)	An ideal form to build the sustainable cities of the 21st century, in the case that a balanced and sustainable view on economic, societal, environmental, and institutional development is realised.	Sustainability, productivity, governance, community
Piro et al. (2014)	A city that intends to be an urban environment which, supported by pervasive ICT systems, is able to offer advanced and innovative services to citizens in order to improve their overall quality of life.	Technology, liveability, policy
Alkandari et al. (2012)	A city that uses a smart system characterised by the interaction between infrastructure, capital, behaviours, and cultures, achieved through their integration.	Technology, productivity, community, governance
Lazaroiu & Roscia (2012)	A city that represents the future challenge, a city model where the technology is in service to the person and to his economic and social life quality improvement.	Technology, prosperity, liveability, wellbeing
Schaffers et al. (2012)	A safe, secure, environmentally green, and efficient urban centre of the future with advanced infrastructures such as sensors, electronics, and networks to stimulate sustainable economic growth and a high quality of life.	Technology, productivity, liveability, sustainability
Caragliu et al. (2011)	A city that is smart when investments in human and social capital and traditional transport and modern ICT infrastructure fuel sustainable economic growth and a high quality of life, with the wise management of natural resources, through participatory governance.	Community, technology, liveability, sustainability, governance, policy, accessibility
Gonzalez & Rossi (2011)	A public administration or authority that delivers or aims to a set of new-generation services and infrastructure, based on information and communication technologies.	Governance, policy, technology
Hernandez-Munoz et al. (2011)	A city that represents an extraordinary rich ecosystem to promote the generation of massive deployments of city-scale applications and services for a large number of activity sectors.	Technology, governance
Nam & Pardo (2011)	A humane city that has multiple opportunities to exploit its human potential and lead a creative life.	Community, wellbeing, productivity
Zhao (2011)	A city that improves the quality of life, including ecological, cultural, political, institutional, social, and economic components without leaving a burden on future generations.	Liveability, governance, sustainability, community, productivity

(Continued)

Table 1.1 (Continued)

Literature	Definition	Theme
Belissent et al. (2010)	A city that uses ICTs to make the critical infrastructure components and services of a city—administration, education, healthcare, public safety, real estate, transportation, and utilities—more aware, interactive, and efficient.	Technology, accessibility, liveability, governance
Eger (2009)	A particular idea of local community, one where city governments, enterprises, and residents use ICTs to reinvent and reinforce the community's role in the new service economy, create jobs locally and improve the quality of community life.	Community, governance, technology, liveability, productivity
Paskaleva (2009)	A city that takes advantages of the opportunities offered by ICT in increasing local prosperity and competitiveness—an approach that implies integrated urban development involving multi-actor, multi-sector, and multi-level perspectives.	Productivity, technology, policy
Rios (2008)	A city that gives inspiration, shares culture, knowledge, and life, a city that motivates its inhabitants to create and flourish in their own lives—it is an admired city, a vessel to intelligence, but ultimately an incubator of empowered spaces.	Community, liveability, productivity
Giffinger et al. (2007)	A city performing well in a forward-looking way in economy, people, governance, mobility, environment, and living built on the smart combination of endowments and activities of self-decisive, independent, and aware citizens.	Community, governance, accessibility, technology, productivity, policy
Partridge (2004)	A city that actively embraces new technologies seeking to be a more open society where technology makes it easier for people to have their say, gain access to services, and stay in touch with what is happening around them, simply and cheaply.	Technology, community, accessibility, liveability
Odendaal (2003)	A city that capitalises on the opportunities presented by ICTs in promoting its prosperity and influence.	it
Bowerman et al. (2000)	A city that monitors and integrates conditions of all of its critical infrastructures including roads, bridges, tunnels, rails, subways, airports, seaports, communications, water, power, even major buildings, can better optimise its resources, plan its preventive maintenance activities, and monitor security aspects while maximising services to its citizens.	Policy, governance, accessibility, liveability
Hall et al. (2000)	An urban centre of the future, made safe, secure environmentally green, and efficient because all structures—whether for power, water, transportation, etc. are designed, constructed, and maintained making use of advanced, integrated materials, sensors, electronics, and networks which are interfaced with computerised systems comprised of databases, tracking, and decision-making algorithms	Sustainability, technology, governance

the functionality of urban systems and advancing knowledge transfer and innovation networks.

Smart cities' primary focus being exclusive to technology has been heavily criticised by a number of scholars. For instance, Yigitcanlar & Lee's (2014, p. 112) research on the Korean context revealed that smart cities

> are typically prone to problems related to the lack of social infrastructure, market restrictions, political quagmires and vested financial interests. Such cities have been built from the perspective of technical computing with an emphasis on supply-side technology, which has put in place advance technologies with impressive budgets. However, through such a computing-driven approach, social and cultural aspects have been neglected and absent from discussions of the design of cities, which have emphasised physical aspects and industry portfolios and veered off from the idea of a knowledge culture.

The darker side of smart cities—particularly the extreme dependency on technology, and on corporations dominating technology and related services—is mentioned in the literature as threatening. As stated by Kunzmann (2014, p. 17),

> sooner or later society will not manage any more to live without the ICT-based services. Like addicts, or chronically sick patients who are extremely suffering from the lack of some substance, respectively the medicine they are relying on, citizens will become sick, if the access to smart ICT services will be cut-off. They will soon forget how to survive in cities, once smart ICT technologies are not available anymore. The concentration processes, which characterize the global market of smart technologies, are threatening.

1.2.3 Economy

One of the main reasons behind the increasing popularity of the smart cities notion across local governments is the economic premise of such development to the city. In their recent study, Caragliu & Del Bo (2018b, p. 81) found that "smart city policy intensity is associated with a better urban economic performance. Moreover, instrumenting smart policies with smart urban characteristics suggests that the causality direction goes from policy intensity to growth, and not vice versa".

There is, however, conflation of smart cities and creative class (or innovation) economies, which tends to reflect policies that support amenities that benefit persons in higher socioeconomic groups rather than focus on broadening economic gains to a more inclusive population. This issue is also elaborated by Costa & Oliveira (2017), highlighting the need for a humane approach where technology is responsive to the needs, skills, and interests of users, respecting their diversity and individuality. They state that

> a smart city is in general associated with technology: sensors, cameras, fast internet connections, and control centres. While useful, technology should not

be the central focus. A humane smart city addresses first people and their needs. Then comes technology and only in direct connection with these needs. The point here is to raise the right questions. Rather than needing a solution to traffic jams, we need a solution to the mobility of the people who today are trapped in the chaotic jams.

(p. 228)

1.2.4 Society

Smart cities face the risk of social exclusion and gentrification. For instance, as part of the Abu Dhabi government's long-term development agenda of Vision 2030— targeting a move from petro-urbanism to smart urbanism—the idea behind Masdar smart city was to build the future of a sustainable living model for all (Yigitcanlar, 2016). Despite the frequent presence of the concepts of social justice and equity along with social sustainability in the vision, the city only reserves a small area for underprivileged groups. This indicates that the project is not as socially sustainable as it is claimed to be (Cugurullo, 2013). This issue is also evident in many other smart city initiatives—e.g., gentrification in Brooklyn, Los Angeles, the Bay Area in the US, and Toronto in Canada (Bronstein, 2009; Abbruzzese, 2017).

Although the Tianjin smart city project received attention for its environmental sustainability, and eco-technologies, it is criticised due to its design, and lack of recognition of the complex web of socio-cultural and economic processes, which link the lived environment of the city to its environmental characteristics (Yigitcanlar, 2016). On that very point, Wong (2011) argues that the city lacks a human scale with giant blocks that are about four times the size of a typical block in Manhattan and which make pedestrian and bike journeys difficult. As for Caprotti (2014), one of the critical issues in Tianjin is the internal social resilience and the emergence of new communities. Moreover, Caprotti (2014) highlights that the projects need to consider not only the high-tech, new urban environments materialised as smart cities, but also the production and reproduction of large, often transient populations of low-paid workers that build the city and who form the "new urban poor", forming "worker cities" on the edges of flagship smart and sustainable urban projects.

As a solution to societal challenges, Caragliu & Del Bo (2012, p. 97) highlight the importance of "space-specific characteristics in shaping the economic effect of smart urban qualities, providing grounding to place-based public policies that account for local characteristics". In other words, the incorporation of local communities and actors in a place-based decision-making process to build the development on endogenous assets is an integral element of forming prosperous, sustainable, and smart cities (Pancholi et al., 2018).

1.2.5 Environment

The limited environmental aspects of smart city projects—despite their promise— are highly criticised. For example, Songdo, the Korean model smart city, was subjected to strong opposition from environmentalist groups, both local and international. According to Shwayri (2013, p. 53), this smart city is

> built on the destruction of precious wetlands, home to some of the rarest species on the planet, causing the disappearance of some. Once reclaimed, its developers have pursued sustainable building practices, applying guidelines and materials that promote efficient energy use, and recycling 75% of construction waste.

The impact of this smart city project on the local natural ecosystem is evident (Ko et al., 2011). The relationship between the concepts of smart and sustainable is currently a hot topic of academic debate as smart cities tend to fail to keep their sustainability promises (Ahvenniemi et al., 2017). In their investigation into 15 UK cities, Yigitcanlar & Kamruzzaman (2018) find no clear evidence that a smart city policy leads to the sustainability of cities.

Likewise, as stated by Cugurullo (2016, p. 2429),

> the way sustainability is expressed in Masdar city associates environmentalism with consumerism. The environmental attention of the developers is put almost exclusively on CO_2 whose reduction can be capitalised through the development and commercialisation of clean technologies designed to decrease the carbon emissions of urban environments. As a result of this profit-driven selection of environmental targets, a plethora of other important themes (ecosystem services in particular) are cut off because they are perceived as unattractive from an economic perspective. More problematically, the extreme reliance on technology as the solution to global environmental problems reiterates the very origin of those environmental problems.

As a solution to environmental challenges, Martin et al. (2018, p. 1) suggest that "the potential to empower and include citizens represents the key to unlocking forms of smart-sustainable urban development that emphasise environmental protection and social equity, rather than merely reinforcing neoliberal forms of urban development".

1.2.6 Governance

In terms of smart city development governance, the top-down state-led process with no or minimal public participation in Northeast Asia is heavily criticised. Particularly referring to the Songdo, Yujiapu, and Lingang smart city initiatives, Kim (2014, p. 352) states that these state-led mega projects

> are devoid of the planners' consciousness of the "social". Instead, the technological paradigm, an abstract and utopian view of social diversity and codified images of nature (symbolized in the colour green) are viscerally reinvented to benefit the privileged few and commoditized under the tyranny of environmental emergency. After a century, for those who do not necessarily align their interests

with the majority urbanites or for those who rarely make themselves available for the contesting, dynamic and spontaneous construction of everyday urban spaces, these colossal modernist schemes stand as a testimony to the burgeoning urban fantasies in Northeast Asia.

As a solution to governance challenges, Deakin (2013, 2014) advocates a "triple helix model" approach—public–private–academia partnership—to overcome the governance and development limitations. Additionally, Bolivar (2018, p. 57) analyses the public value creation in smart cities and finds that

public value creation surpasses the capacities, capabilities, and reaches of their traditional institutions and their classical processes of governing, and therefore new and innovative forms of governance are needed to meet it. This way, the creation of public value under the context of the smart cities is based on smart urban collaboration, which promotes the use of new technologies to adopt a more participative model of governance.

1.2.7 Drivers

The interdisciplinary literature highlights a number of smart city drivers. According to Kunzmann (2014) these drivers are: (a) technology—smart city technology makes life in the city easier, more convenient, and more secure; (b) community—beneficiary of smart city services, and decider of which problems to be tackled; (c) policy—enabler of smart city initiatives and taking measures to minimise the negative impacts of smart city disruption. Almost identical to these drivers, Nam & Prado (2011) conceptualise the drivers of smart cities as: (a) technology; (b) people; and (c) institutions. They state that given the connection between these drivers, "a city is smart when investments in human/social capital and ICT infrastructure fuel sustainable growth and enhance a quality of life, through participatory governance" (p. 286).

1.2.8 Desired Outcomes

After placing 10 cities—Abu Dhabi, Amsterdam, Auckland, Barcelona, Brisbane, Incheon, Istanbul, Rio de Janeiro, San Francisco, Tianjin—under the smart cities microscope, Yigitcanlar (2016) advocates the need for smart city projects to generate desired outcomes, in economic, societal, environmental, and governance terms, in a sustainable and balanced manner. Yigitcanlar (2016) suggests the following for a successful smart city transformation:

- *Economic development in smart cities:* We need to give our cities the capability of developing their technologies unique to their own developmental problems and needs. This in turn contributes to the establishment of a local innovation economy and prosperity that is a central element of smart cities;

- *Sociocultural development in smart cities:* We need to develop our cities wired with smart urban technologies not only exclusive to urban elites, but also inclusive to those less fortunate. This in turn helps in establishing socioeconomic equality which is an essential element of smart cities;
- *Spatial (urban and environmental) development in smart cities:* We need to reform our cities by adopting sustainable urban development principles—e.g., minimising urban footprint, limiting emissions, establishing urban farms. This in turn helps in generating ecological sustainability that is a critical element of smart cities;
- *Institutional development in smart cities:* We need to equip our cities with highly dynamic mechanisms to better plan their growth and manage their day-to-day operational challenges. This in turn helps in performing appropriate planning, development, and management practices that are a core element of smart cities.

1.2.9 Frameworks

Scholars highlight that the challenges of smart city practice might be due to limited conceptualisation of the smart cities phenomenon—particularly the limited number of multidimensional framework developments is an issue (Harrison & Donnelly, 2011; Nam & Pardo, 2011; Yigitcanlar, 2016). Although there seems to be, so far, a few multidimensional smart city definitions and frameworks developed (e.g., Caragliu et al., 2011; Fernandez-Anez et al., 2018), not many of them adequately addressed the abovementioned balanced and sustainable approach.

For instance, amongst the existing frameworks, perhaps the best known one is the EU's smart city wheel. According to this wheel, smart cities can be characterised by having: smart economy (e.g., productivity), smart people (e.g., community with high social and human capitals), smart governance (e.g., good governance and policy), smart mobility (e.g., transport and technology accessibility), smart environment (e.g., sustainability), and smart living (e.g., liveability and wellbeing) (EU, 2014). Despite covering all primary smart city domains and serving as a model to integrate smart city practice areas, this popular wheel is far from being a comprehensive framework—as it lacks underlining relationships among the smart city domains. However, it serves a noble purpose particularly in emphasising a holistic view for moving smart city projects' focus beyond the technology realm.

Additionally, Angelidou (2015) conceptualise a smart city based on four major forces, namely: (a) urban futures; (b) knowledge and innovation economy; (c) technology push; and (d) application pull. While these driving forces are highly relevant, this framework is highly abstract to be easily adopted in a local smart city planning context. Similarly, Kummitha & Crutzen (2017) propose a framework, consisting of four elements—(a) restrictive; (b) reflective; (c) rationalistic; and (d) critical—to critically analyse various stages in the development of the smart cities field. This framework, rather, focuses on how smart cities differ in their meanings, intentions, and offerings.

1.2.10 Knowledge Gaps

Despite the heavy criticisms of smart city sceptics of this type of urban form and development practice, as presented above, there is a general sense among the scholars that rethinking our cities' planning and development paradigms and processes in the age of digital disruption and climate change is a good thing (Yigitcanlar, 2009; Caragliu & Del Bo, 2018a). Nevertheless, this still requires a clear definition and elaboration of: (a) What a smart city is; (b) What their key drivers and desired outcomes are; and (c) How the smart city paradigm can be conceptualised. This necessity, despite a few multidimensional definition and framework examples (e.g., Caragliu et al., 2011; Fernandez-Anez et al., 2018), calls for further investigation to synthesise a new framework for smart cities. This forms the rationale of the current chapter.

1.3 Methodology

This research applies a systematic review of the literature to achieve the research aim—following the procedures suggested by Bask & Rajahonka (2017).

Firstly, a research plan involving the research aim, keywords, and a set of inclusion and exclusion criteria was developed. The research aim was framed to explore links among various aspects of smart cities and to develop a framework. As the keyword, we decided to use "smart cities". We identified the inclusion criteria as peer-reviewed research articles in the English language. An online search was conducted using a university library search engine—Queensland University of Technology—that connects to 393 different databases, including ScienceDirect, Scopus, Web of Science, Wiley online library, and a directory of open access journals. We excluded edited or authored books, conference proceedings, journal editorials, articles in languages other than English, grey literature such as government or industry reports, and non-academic research. The search included only peer-reviewed and full-text journal articles available online.

Secondly, the search was conducted in January 2018 for journal articles published between January 2000 and January 2018. Although there were some articles predating 2000, due to the negligible numbers and limited relevance, the review focused on the post-2000 articles. Several thematic searches were specified through a combination of multiple keywords. The keywords used in all thematic searches were directed to the title of the articles. The resultant search items were initially checked by reading the abstract, and then by reading the full text in order to verify the scope against the research aim.

Thirdly, the initial thematic search was conducted using the keywords "smart cities", "framework", and "model" to identify articles that contain smart cities frameworks—the keyword "model" was included to broaden the coverage of the search. The Boolean search line was: ((TitleCombined:("smart cities")) AND ((TitleCombined:(framework)) OR (model))). The search resulted in 105 papers, which were reduced to 33 articles after checking their abstracts, and further reduced to 26 articles after reading their full texts.

Then, we undertook a conceptual analysis to determine new keywords—or general themes or broad concepts or key elements—using the selected 26 full-text articles by following the methodological steps as suggested by Jabareen (2008). These steps were: (a) recognition of similarities or patterns amongst the general themes; (b) synthesisation of general themes; and (c) formation of a multidimensional framework. As a result of the abovementioned conceptual analysis steps, we determined three general themes—i.e., "community", "technology", "policy"—from the literature as the main areas that drive smart cities development. These drivers are placed at the inner middle-ring of the proposed framework (see Figure 1.1). These three themes (or drivers) were then used as keywords to further search the smart city literature.

The second thematic search was conducted using the keywords "smart cities", "community", and "society" to identify articles on the community aspects of smart cities—the keyword "society" was included to broaden the coverage of the search. The following Boolean search line was performed: ((TitleCombined:("smart cities")) AND ((TitleCombined:(community)) OR (society))). The search resulted in 366 papers, which were reduced to 48 articles after checking their abstracts, and further reduced to 14 articles after reading their full texts.

Next, we conducted another search in the database using a combination of the keywords "smart cities", "technology", and "innovation" to identify articles on the technology aspects of smart cities—the keyword "innovation" was included to broaden the coverage. For this, the following Boolean search was conducted: ((TitleCombined:("smart cities")) AND ((TitleCombined:(technology)) OR (innovation))). This search resulted in 433 papers, which were screened through by reading their abstracts (resulting in 36 articles) and then their full texts (resulting in 25 articles).

The final thematic search was conducted using a combination of the keywords "smart cities", "policy", and "plan" to identify articles on the policy aspects of smart cities—the keyword "plan" was included to broaden the coverage of the search. The Boolean search line was: ((TitleCombined:("smart cities")) AND ((TitleCombined:(policy)) OR (plan))). The search resulted in 302 papers. We went through their abstracts and limited the selection to 15 articles. After reading their full texts, the final selection was reduced to 13 journal articles.

As a result, 78 journal articles fulfilled our selection criteria (out of 1,206 articles), and these papers were then read, reviewed, and analysed. We categorised the reviewed papers according to themes—i.e., "framework", "community", "technology", "policy". We undertook a conceptual analysis to determine the new concepts/themes or framework elements related to the outcomes of smart cities by following the aforementioned methodological steps. The analysis produced six new subthemes—i.e., "productivity", "sustainability", "accessibility", "wellbeing", "liveability", "governance"—from the literature that are then considered as desired outcomes of smart cities. These desired outcomes are placed at the outer middle-ring of the proposed framework (see Figure 1.1).

We subsequently extracted data from the reviewed papers in tables, formulated according to the four themes—i.e., framework, community, technology, policy

(Tables 1.2–1.5). Each table contained the following information against each of the selected articles: author(s), year of publication, title of the article, name of the journal, framework, and desired outcome (or subtheme).

We then discussed and linked up the individual findings of each theme and subtheme into one. Some reviewed papers were discarded at this stage as they did not directly match with issues relevant to specific themes of smart cities. This helped us to better understand the conceptual/thematic issues relating to smart cities—based on themes (smart city drivers) and subthemes (smart city desired outcomes).

The final stage of the review process was to write up and present our findings in the format of a literature review chapter. In this process, some other relevant papers, which do not fulfil the pre-determined selection criteria, are also included as supporting material to better appreciate the background context, and discuss the findings—e.g., books, book chapters, conference papers, government policy documents, and online reports. With these, the total number of the reviewed and cited references is increased to 192.

1.4 Results

1.4.1 General Observations

An initial review on how smart cities are defined has shown that there is no consensus on what a smart city is. The provided 20 popular definitions (Table 1.1) revealed that the technology perspective is the dominant feature of smart cities. Different conceptualisations include other features—e.g., community, policy, productivity, sustainability, accessibility, wellbeing, liveability, governance—but not in a single definition. This is mainly due to disciplinary and sectoral perspective differences, and the infancy of the smart cities concept and practice in the 2000s and 2010s.

In reviewing the literature on smart cities, the selected 78 academic papers (out of 1,206 articles abstracts that were read) are assembled under four broad categories—as explained in the methodology section. These are: (a) smart city frameworks—containing 26 articles; (b) smart city and community—14 articles; (c) smart city and technology—25 articles; and (d) smart city and policy—13 articles. In looking at the distribution of the papers, it can be stated that framework development and technology aspects have a larger coverage than community and policy aspects.

The reviewed literature, in all categories, illustrates that research on smart cities is mostly limited to developed countries of Europe, North America, Oceania, and Southeast Asia—although there were some papers focusing on the cities of emerging economies such as Brazil. This finding shows parallels with the smart city initiatives taking place in the major cities of the world. For example, a recent smart city ranking exercise has placed the following cities at the top of the list—New York, London, Paris, San Francisco, Boston, Amsterdam, Chicago, Seoul, Geneva, Sydney (IESE, 2016). According to another smart city ranking, the top-10 cities are: Copenhagen, Singapore, Stockholm, Zurich, Boston, Tokyo, San Francisco, Amsterdam, Geneva, Melbourne (EasyPark Group, 2017).

The earliest study of smart cities in reviewed publications—in four categories—only dates back to 2012 (Walravens, 2012). Although there were studies prior to 2012 on smart cities—for instance Bowerman et al. (2000) and Hall et al. (2000)—Walravens's (2012) paper was the earliest one that satisfied the selection criteria as applied in this research. Almost two-thirds of the papers were published in 2016 and later (64%), which indicates an exponential growth trend of research on this topic during the last couple of years.

1.4.2 Smart City Frameworks

Amongst the 78 reviewed literature pieces, 26 had a framework focus. Most of those papers used a framework approach to develop a component of a smart city, rather than having a holistic approach to conceptualise and develop smart cities. Only 17 presented or proposed a framework on a smart city or a feature of it. Among the articles outlining a framework, four had a broader smart city focus, four contained a technology framework, two provided service provision frameworks, two showed business model and integration frameworks, and the remaining five contained transport procurement, public participation, and management frameworks. The desired smart city outcomes are varied in these frameworks due to their specific focus, but most of them had (good) "governance" as a desired outcome. A summary of the literature on smart cities with a framework focus is presented in Table 1.2.

Table 1.2 Literature on smart cities with a framework focus

Literature	Year	Framework	Outcome
Kousiouris et al.	2018	N/A	N/A
Meijer & Thaens	2018	N/A	Sustainability, liveability
Bhide	2017	N/A	Productivity, liveability, accessibility
Chen et al.	2017	N/A	Sustainability, wellbeing
Fernandez-Anez et al.	2018	Smart cities framework	Sustainability, liveability, governance, accessibility, wellbeing, productivity
Khan et al.	2017	Smart city secure service provisioning framework	Sustainability
Liu et al.	2017	Smart city technology framework	Governance
Pierce et al.	2017	N/A	Sustainability
Romão et al.	2018	Conceptual model for smart city local-visitor interests	Sustainability, liveability, accessibility, productivity
Anthopoulos & Reddick	2016	N/A	Governance

(*Continued*)

Table 1.2 (Continued)

Literature	Year	Framework	Outcome
Brooks & Schrubbe	2016	N/A	Governance
Damurski	2016	Smart city integrated planning framework	Governance
Fassam et al.	2016	Smart city transport procurement framework	Productivity, liveability, accessibility
Joshi et al.	2016	Smart cities framework	Sustainability, liveability, governance, productivity
Puiu et al.	2016	Smart city technology framework	N/A
Villanueva et al.	2016	N/A	N/A
Zhang et al.	2016	N/A	N/A
Aamir et al.	2014	Smart city management framework	Productivity, governance, sustainability
Cano et al.	2014	Smart city public participation framework	Governance
Errichiello & Marasco	2014	Smart cities framework	Governance
Jin et al.	2014	Smart city technology framework	N/A
Khan et al.	2014	Smart city citizen services framework	Governance
Lee et al.	2014	Smart city analysis framework	Sustainability, wellbeing, liveability, productivity
Sanchez et al.	2013	Smart city platform framework	Governance
Vlacheas et al.	2013	Smart city technology framework	Governance
Walravens	2012	Smart city business model framework	Governance

One of the frameworks with broader smart city focus has adopted the EU's smart cities framework to explore innovation networks in the development of smart city services (Errichello & Marasco, 2014). The second one, by Lee et al. (2014), was a smart city analysis framework, which includes the following dimensions: (a) urban openness; (b) service innovation; (c) partnerships formation; (d) urban pro-activeness; (e) smart city infrastructure integration; and (f) smart city governance. The third one, by Joshi et al. (2016), identified six significant pillars for developing a smart city framework: (a) social; (b) management; (c) economic; (d) legal; (e) technology; and (f) sustainability. The last framework, by Fernandez-Anez et al. (2018), sees a smart city as an integrated and multidimensional system, and attempts to link three main issues: (a) the key role of governance and stakeholders' involvement; (b) the importance of displaying a comprehensive vision of smart city projects and dimensions; and (c) the understanding of a smart city as a

Table 1.3 Literature on smart cities with a community focus

Literature	Year	Framework	Outcome
Beretta	2018	N/A	Sustainability, wellbeing
Cowley et al.	2018	N/A	Liveability, wellbeing
Damiani et al.	2017	N/A	Liveability, wellbeing
Deakin & Reid	2017	N/A	Liveability
Kaika	2017	N/A	Sustainability, liveability, accessibility
Joss et al.	2017	Smart city standards	Sustainability, liveability, wellbeing
Marsal-Llacuna	2017	N/A	Liveability
Smith	2017	N/A	Liveability
Garau et al.	2016	N/A	Sustainability, wellbeing, liveability
Granier & Kudo	2016	N/A	Liveability, accessibility, governance
Ianuale et al.	2016	Smart cities taxonomy	N/A
Lara et al.	2016	Smart city domains	Liveability, wellbeing
Snow et al.	2016	N/A	Sustainability, liveability, productivity
Chichernea	2015	Smart city model	Productivity, liveability, sustainability

tool to tackle urban challenges. While these frameworks made contributions to the smart city conceptualisation, they have limitations in providing a solid and widely acknowledged conceptual framework with a big picture view of smart cities.

1.4.3 Smart City and Community

From the reviewed 78 smart city literature works, only 14 had a community focus. A limited number of research on the community aspect of smart cities rings alarm bells, and indicates the negligence of considering local communities as the key player in smart city development. Despite this, most of the papers raised the issue of the critical importance of local communities for the formation of smart cities, and some suggested ways to achieve this. For example, Beretta (2018) discusses the social implications of eco-innovations in the context of smart cities. Amongst the reviewed papers, four developed or adopted various frameworks, including smart city frameworks with specific interest on standards, taxonomies, domains, and models. The only paper that had a generic smart city model, or framework, was Chichernea's (2015) study. However, this model was based on the EU's smart city wheel. The desired smart city outcomes in these literature works varied, but almost all included "liveability" and "wellbeing". A summary of the literature on smart cities with a community focus is presented in Table 1.3.

1.4.4 Smart City and Technology

From the reviewed 78 articles, 25 had a technology focus. This area of smart city research seems to be the one that generated the greatest portion of academic writings. Of these 25 papers, seven used or proposed a framework. These frameworks mostly focused on smart city technology architecture, technology taxonomy, or technology roadmap. However, there was a framework that covered the broader or generic smart city conceptualisation aspect. Sun et al. (2016) propose a framework that views a smart city as being based on technology, humans, and organisation, and service relationships among them. While the framework provided a big overview by bringing technology, human (or community), and organisation (or policy) aspects of smart cities together, it remains too coarse, and also shared an economy perspective focus.

Desired smart city outcomes in the reviewed literature on smart city technology are diverse, without a concentration on specific outcome item. This is an indication of large number of smart city technologies and their numerous application areas. A summary of the literature on smart cities with a technology focus is presented in Table 1.4.

Table 1.4 Literature on smart cities with a technology focus

Literature	Year	Framework	Outcome
Abella et al.	2017	N/A	Productivity
Branchi et al.	2017	N/A	N/A
He et al.	2017a	N/A	N/A
He et al.	2017b	N/A	N/A
Hui et al.	2017	Smart city technology architecture	Liveability
Hung & Peng	2017	N/A	Sustainability
Marek et al.	2017	N/A	Sustainability, liveability
McFarlane & Söderström	2017	N/A	Wellbeing
Petrolo et al.	2017	N/A	Sustainability, wellbeing, liveability
Tucker et al.	2017	N/A	Sustainability, liveability, accessibility
Yacoob et al.	2017	Technology taxonomy smart cities	N/A
Pollio	2016	N/A	Productivity
Sun et al.	2016	Smart city conceptual framework	Productivity
D'Aquin	2015	N/A	N/A
Khorov et al.	2015	N/A	N/A
Lynggaard & Skouby	2015	N/A	Liveability
Popescu	2015	N/A	Productivity
Stratigea et al.	2015	Smart city methodological framework	Governance
Orlowski	2014	N/A	N/A
Paroutis et al.	2014	Smart city strategic view	Productivity
Viitanen & Kingston	2014	N/A	Sustainability, wellbeing
Wang et al.	2014	N/A	Productivity
Wenge et al.	2014	Smart city technology architecture	Liveability
Lee et al.	2013	Smart city technology roadmap	Sustainability, liveability
Sidawi & Deakin	2013	N/A	Wellbeing

1.4.5 Smart City and Policy

Despite some of the eminent smart city scholars indicating the critical importance of policies in transforming cities into smart ones (e.g., Caragliu & Del Bo, 2012), from the reviewed 78 smart city articles, only 13 had a policy focus. This is a surprising finding as one would hope that in such a popular area there would be plenty of research to inform national, regional, and local policy and decision-making processes. This indicates the existence of a major gap in the policy domain of smart cities research—and possibly has undesired implications for the practice. Reviewed papers looked at different policy aspects of smart cities ranging from accessibility and mobility issues to digital infrastructure planning, from developing public participatory mechanisms to urban governance, and from development planning to urban sustainability policies. The desired smart city outcomes in the smart city policy-related literature vary, with "sustainability" and "liveability" being the most common outcome items. A summary of the literature on smart cities with a policy focus is presented in Table 1.5.

Among these papers only two presented a smart city framework. The paper by Castelnovo et al. (2016) proposes a smart city governance assessment framework. The framework comprises five key evaluation dimensions: (a) community building and management; (b) vision and strategy formulation; (c) public value generation; (d) asset management; and (e) economic and financial sustainability. The framework measures how city governance performs in pursuing sustainable and participatory public value generation, while the intersections of the five dimensions

Table 1.5 Literature on smart cities with a policy focus

Literature	Year	Framework	Outcome
Kourtit et al.	2017	N/A	Sustainability, liveability
Pinna et al.	2017	N/A	Accessibility
Trindade et al.	2017	N/A	Sustainability
Caragliu & Del Bo	2016	N/A	Sustainability, liveability
Castelnovo et al.	2016	Smart city governance framework	Governance
Glasmeier & Nebiolo	2016	N/A	Sustainability, liveability, wellbeing
Marsal-Llacuna & Segal	2016	Smart city subsystem collaboration framework	Governance
Crivello	2015	N/A	Accessibility, liveability, wellbeing
Syvajarvi et al.	2015	N/A	Governance
Wiig	2015	N/A	Sustainability, liveability, productivity, governance
Yigitcanlar	2015	N/A	Sustainability, liveability, productivity, governance
Angelidou	2014	N/A	Sustainability, liveability
Sivarajah et al.	2014	N/A	Governance

define four perspectives from which to assess smart city governance. The other study, by Marsal-Llacuna & Segal (2017), proposes a smart city subsystem collaboration framework to coordinate complex smart city governance tasks. While both frameworks are found useful in improving the governance dimension of smart cities, they are not equipped to form an overarching framework.

1.5 Discussion

Many cities across the globe have become very keen on smart city recognition and jumped on the bandwagon to apply this concept. Planners, practitioners, politicians, and urban administrators eagerly used smart cities as jargon in their day-to-day tasks. Many cities have claimed to be smart cities—or at least they declared themselves as smart (Anthopoulos, 2017). The analysis reported in this chapter reveals that even though the movement of smart cities is a hot topic in urban development circles, it is a largely uncharted territory of research and practice, particularly from the conceptual viewpoint.

As stated by Harrison & Donnelly (2011, p. 6),

> the current ad hoc approaches of smart cities to the improvement of cities are reminiscent of pre-scientific medicine. They may do good, but we have little detailed understanding of why. Smart cities is a field in want of a good theoretical base.

Surely as the smart city practice becomes more common, the concept will eventually mature. This was the case for other concepts, for instance sustainable cities (Jabareen, 2008). However, the delay in the conceptualisation is highly likely to result in inefficient policies, poor investment decisions, and an inability to properly address the urbanisation challenges in a timely and adequate manner.

Besides, the current hype around smart cities tends to be mostly technocratic, beyond speculation, there is no strong evidence to suggest that a smart city can provide genuine answers to a number of complex problems cities face today. As underlined by Mora et al. (2017, p. 20), "the knowledge necessary to understand the process of building effective smart cities in the real-world has not yet been produced, nor the tools for supporting the actors involved in this activity". The desired outcomes from the smart city initiatives must be identified and articulated at the initial stage of the planning process. However, the planning process is not clearly stated in the smart city initiatives (Yigitcanlar, 2016)—for a good reason, there is no widely accepted sound smart cities framework. The messiness of outcomes is due, in part, to a lack of clarity about what are we trying to measure and plan for in the first instance.

Ensuring liveable conditions within the context of such rapid urban population growth worldwide, while considering sustainable and balanced development, requires a deeper understanding of the smart city phenomenon. The body of work reviewed in this chapter provides evidence that so far the attention has been focused on the smart city drivers (e.g., technology, community, policy) in the literature. However, coordinated actions to identify and achieve desired outcomes such as economy (e.g., productivity), society (e.g., liveability, wellbeing), environment (e.g., sustainability, accessibility), and governance (e.g., transparent and participatory policymaking and governance) are more or less neglected.

After analysing the existing smart city frameworks in the academic literature, the findings suggest that smart cities and their development have not been adequately conceptualised yet—although there are some highly promising recent attempts such as that by Fernandez-Anez et al. (2018). Existing frameworks have some limitations in advancing our understanding of the smart city phenomenon—either inadequate or not widely promoted, accepted, or adopted. There is, hence, room for the development of new smart city frameworks. At the conceptual level, to develop a thorough understanding, theoretically and practically, of designing smart cities for sustainable and balanced growth, this study proposes a smart city development framework, as a system of systems (see McLoughlin, 1969)—by intertwining smart city drivers with desired outcomes. The proposed framework—that builds on the reviewed key smart city characteristics—is illustrated in Figure 1.1 and elaborated as follows.

First, the framework conceptualises a smart city as a balanced and sustainable development. The framework adopts an input–process–output (IPO) model

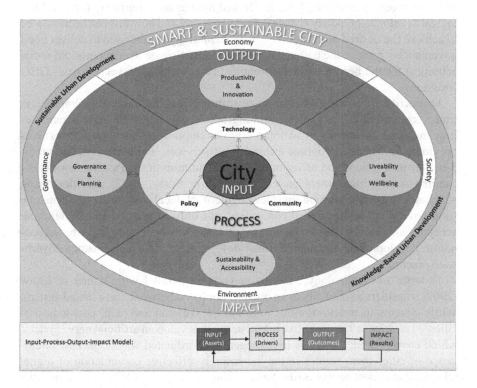

Figure 1.1 Multidimensional smart city framework.

logic with a "systems view" (Fincher, 1972; Chadwick, 2013). In this IPO model, the "city" itself—as the "asset"—is the "input"; the three "drivers" (community, technology, policy) form the "process"; and the "desired outcomes" (productivity, sustainability, accessibility, wellbeing, liveability, governance) constitute the "output". Given the IPO model works effectively and efficiently, "output" eventually transforms the city ("input") into a smart city. In a diagrammatic representation, the framework places the four fundamental development domains at the most outer-ring of the framework diagram—i.e., "economy", "society", "environment", "governance"—suggesting a quadruple bottom line approach (Teriman, 2009). Then, desired outcomes (output) from a smart city project are placed at the outer middle-ring of the framework—i.e., "productivity", "sustainability", "accessibility", "wellbeing", "liveability", "governance". Lastly, the inner middle-ring is allocated to the key smart city drivers (process)—i.e., "community", "technology", "policy". In the inner-ring, "(smart) city" is located as the key asset (input) (Figure 1.1).

The internal logic of the framework is that there is a chain of causal links starting with the drivers through desired outcomes to sustainable urban development—initially originated from the assets-base of the city. The description of the causal links from drivers to sustainable urban development is a complex task which is broken down into individual elements (e.g., desired outcomes and overall sustainability outcomes). A driving force is denoted here as an opportunity (new technological development, policy changes) for a smart city and how this can be translated to achieve the desired outcomes (e.g., new technology can be used to deliver good governance—remove the barriers of distance to participate in economic and social activities) for the benefit of the environment (e.g., reduced travel decreases GHG emissions).

Distinctive from many other smart city approaches, the framework emphasises smart "communities" as the essential ingredient of smart cities and determines it as the most critical driver of smart city development. This approach involves providing access to appropriate technologies, services, and platforms, and modifying the perceptions and behaviours of local communities via various awareness campaigns and engagement projects (Hughes & Spray, 2002). Additionally, it advocates the customisation and development of local and culturally sensitive solutions by the residents and companies, not only to provide locally tailored/accepted solutions, but also make contributions to the local knowledge-based economic development, sustainable urban development, and participatory governance practices.

In terms of "technology", this framework, in parallel with Kanter & Litow (2009), considers a smart city as an organic whole—a network and a linked system. While systems in industrial cities were mostly skeleton and skin, post-industrial cities—i.e., smart cities—are like organisms that develop an artificial nerve system, which enables them to behave in intelligently coordinated ways. The new intelligence of cities then, resides in the increasingly effective combination of digital telecommunication networks (the nerves), ubiquitously embedded intelligence (the brains), sensors and tags (the sensory organs), and software (the knowledge and cognitive competence). However, in this perspective technology is only seen as a "mean"—not an "end"—to achieve the desired outcomes.

The proposed framework highlights the "policy" context as vital to the understanding of the use of technology in appropriate ways (Aurigi, 2006). Hence, an innovative local government stresses the change in policies because a government cannot innovate without a normative drive addressed in policy. Whereas innovation in technology for a smart city can be relatively easily observed and broadly agreed upon, subsequent changes in the policy context are more ambiguous. The policy context characterises institutional and non-technical urban issues and creates conditions enabling smart and sustainable urban development.

Besides the abovementioned drivers—i.e., "community", "technology", "policy"—the comprehensive conceptual view of the framework focuses on finding ways to achieve desired outcomes in the development domains—i.e., "economy", "society", "environment", "governance". Smart city desired outcomes—i.e., "productivity", "sustainability", "accessibility", "wellbeing", "liveability", "governance"—play a critical role in determining the performance of smart cities. An analysis of the 20 popular definitions and their reference documents——based on Lara et al. (2016) and Mora et al.'s (2017) studies—also confirmed these desired outcomes (Table 1.1). There is also a vast literature on each of these outcomes, thus, rather than elaborating them here, we highlight the crucial importance of integration of these desired smart city outcomes with the mentioned smart city drivers—while the framework emphasises this integration or in other words intertwining.

The proposed multidimensional framework—the first of its kind in bringing the key smart city drivers and outcomes under the same roof—may not be an ultimate solution to the conceptualisation issue, even though it contributes to the theorisation and better practice of smart cities along with guiding the development of sustainable smart cities. However, in the absence or a limited supply of sound smart city frameworks, the proposed framework is a step towards making scholars, urban administrators, and smart city practitioners think about linking smart city drivers and outcomes in an effective way under an approach that advocates balanced and sustainable development.

1.6 Conclusion

Smart cities are a global phenomenon today, as there are well over 250 smart city projects underway across 178 cities around the world—for example, India alone hosts 100 of those projects (Praharaj et al., 2018). Despite the high-level popularity of the smart cities concept and practice, there is no consensus on what a smart city is, what the key smart city drivers and desired outcomes are, or how the smart city paradigm can be conceptualised. Furthermore, scholars seem to have not reached a conclusion on whether a smart city is an urban model or a corporate business plan (Yigitcanlar & Lee, 2014; Rosati & Conti, 2016).

This chapter has placed smart city literature under the microscope of a systematic review and conceptual analysis to address the smart city development issue. The literature review findings have revealed that apart from limited suitable definitions (e.g., Caragliu et al., 2011), smart cities have not been adequately conceptualised, and most of the existing conceptual frameworks have limitations to advance our understanding on the smart city phenomenon or have potential but have not been widely adopted yet (e.g., Fernandez-Anez et al., 2018). The analysis finds that smart city policies are not extensively covered in the literature, which comes as no surprise. This is mainly due to the infancy of the field—naturally it takes time to accumulate evidence on smart city programs. In this instance, the role of scholars, however, is to generate guiding principles and frameworks to inform public and/or private decision-making circles for competent smart city policy and practice to take place. For that very reason, this study develops a new multidimensional smart cities framework.

The analysis findings revealed a number of generic (sub)themes clustered under smart city drivers and desired outcomes. Intertwining these (sub)themes helped us to assemble a new multidimensional smart city framework. This research contributes to both the theory and practice of smart cities. It contributes to the theory by intertwining smart city drivers and desired outcomes in a novel way under a new framework. This will encourage/attract smart city researchers to undertake investigations into the planning and development processes (input–process–output mechanisms) of the claimed smart cities, and evaluate their performances, and come up with consolidated versions of the framework put forward in this chapter. It contributes to the practice of smart cities by providing guiding principles—such as balanced and sustainable development, technology as a mean not an end, and desired outcomes to be clearly identified and articulated at the initial stage of the smart city planning process—for urban administrators and smart city practitioners. The approach presented also highlights the importance of focusing on the assets–drivers–outcomes trio to better plan smart city development and then monitor/evaluate the progress (Yigitcanlar et al., 2018).

Acknowledgements

This chapter, with permission from the copyright holder, is a reproduced version of the following journal article: Yigitcanlar, T., Kamruzzaman, M., Buys, L., Ioppolo, G., Sabatini-Marques, J., Costa, E., & Yun, J. (2018). Understanding 'smart cities': Intertwining development drivers with desired outcomes in a multidimensional framework. *Cities*, 81, 145–160.

References

Aamir, M., Uqaili, M., Amir, S., Chowdhry, B., Rafique, F., Poncela, J. (2014). Framework for analysis of power system operation in smart cities. *Wireless Personal Communications, 76*(3), 399–408.

Abbruzzese, T. (2017). Build Toronto (not social housing). In: Keil, R., Hamel, P., Boudreau, J., Kipfer, S. *Governing cities through regions* (pp. 143–172). Waterloo, Wilfrid Laurier University Press.

Abella, A., Ortiz-de-Urbina-Criado, M., De-Pablos-Heredero, C. (2017). A model for the analysis of data-driven innovation and value generation in smart cities' ecosystems. *Cities, 64*, 47–53.

Afzalan, N., Sanchez, T., Evans-Cowley, J. (2017). Creating smarter cities. *Cities, 67,* 21–30.

Ahvenniemi, H., Huovila, A., Pinto-Seppä, I., Airaksinen, M. (2017). What are the differences between sustainable and smart cities? *Cities, 60,* 234–245.

Aina, Y. (2017). Achieving smart sustainable cities with GeoICT support. *Cities, 71,* 49–58.

Albino, V., Berardi, U., Dangelico, R. (2015). Smart cities. *Journal of Urban Technology, 22*(1), 3–21.

Alizadeh, T. (2017). An investigation of IBM's smarter cites challenge: what do participating cities want? *Cities, 63,* 70–80.

Alkandari, A., Alnasheet, M., Alshaikhli, I. (2012). Smart cities. *Journal of Advanced Computer Science and Technology Research, 2*(2), 79–90.

Angelidou, M. (2014). Smart city policies. *Cities, 41,* S3–S11.

Angelidou, M. (2015). Smart cities. *Cities, 47,* 95–106.

Angelidou, M. (2017). The role of smart city characteristics in the plans of fifteen cities. *Journal of Urban Technology, 24*(4), 3–28.

Anthopoulos, L. (2017). Smart utopia vs smart reality. *Cities, 63,* 128–148.

Anthopoulos, L., Reddick, C. (2016). Understanding electronic government research and smart city: a framework and empirical evidence. *Information Polity, 21*(1), 99–117.

Arbolino, R., Carlucci, F., Cira, A., Ioppolo, G., Yigitcanlar, T. (2017). Efficiency of the EU regulation on greenhouse gas emissions in Italy. *Ecological Indicators, 81*(1), 115–123.

Arbolino, R., Carlucci, F., Cira, A., Yigitcanlar, T., Ioppolo, G. (2018). Mitigating regional disparities through microfinancing. *Land Use Policy, 70*(1), 281–288.

Aurigi, A. (2005). *Making the digital city.* London, Ashgate.

Aurigi, A. (2006). New technologies, yet same dilemmas? *Journal of Urban Technology, 13*(3), 5–28.

Bask, A., Rajahonka, M. (2017). The role of environmental sustainability in the freight transport mode choice. *International Journal of Physical Distribution & Logistics Management, 47,* 560–602.

Battarra, R., Gargiulo, C., Pappalardo, G., Boiano, D., Oliva, J. (2016). Planning in the era of information and communication technologies. *Cities, 59,* 1–7.

Baum, S., O'Connor, K., Yigitcanlar, T. (2009). The implications of creative industries for regional outcomes. *International Journal of Foresight and Innovation Policy, 5*(1–3), 44–64.

Belanche, D., Casaló, L., Orús, C. (2016). City attachment and use of urban services. *Cities, 50,* 75–81.

Belissent, J. (2010). *Getting clever about smart cities.* Cambridge, Forrester.

Beretta, I. (2018). The social effects of eco-innovations in Italian smart cities. *Cities, 72,* 115–121.

Bhide, V. (2017). Smart cities. *Institute of Transportation Engineers Journal, 87*(7), 26–29.

Bolivar, M. (2018). Governance models and outcomes to foster public value creation in smart cities. *Scienze Regionali, 17*(1), 57–80.

Bowerman, B., Braverman, J., Taylor, J., Todosow, H., Wimmersperg, U. (2000). The vision of a smart city. In 2nd International Life Extension Technology Workshop. Paris.

Branchi, P., Fernandez-Valdivielso, C., Matias, I. (2017). An analysis matrix for the assessment of smart city technologies. *Systems, 5*(1), 8.

Bronstein, Z. (2009). Industry and the smart city. *Dissent, 56*(3), 27–34.

Brooks, B., Schrubbe, A. (2016). The need for a digitally inclusive smart city governance framework. *UMKC Law Review, 85,* 943.

Bulkeley, H., Betsill, M. (2005). Rethinking sustainable cities. *Environmental Politics, 14*(1), 42–63.

Cano, J., Hernandez, R., Ros, S. (2014). Distributed framework for electronic democracy in smart cities. *Computer, 47*(10), 65–71.

Caprotti, F. (2014). Critical research on eco-cities? *Cities, 36*(1), 10–17.

Caragliu, A., Del Bo, C. (2012). Smartness and European urban performance. *Innovation: The European Journal of Social Science Research, 25*(2), 97–113.

Caragliu, A., Del Bo, C. (2016). Do smart cities invest in smarter policies? *Social Science Computer Review, 34*(6), 657–672.

Caragliu, A., Del Bo, C. (2018a). Smart cities: is it just a fad? *Scienze Regionali, 17*(1), 7–14.

Caragliu, A., Del Bo, C. (2018b). The economics of smart city policies. *Scienze Regionali, 17*(1), 81–104.

Caragliu, A., Del Bo, C., Nijkamp, P. (2011). Smart cities in Europe. *Journal of Urban Technology, 18*(2), 65–82.

Carrillo, F., Yigitcanlar, T., García, B., Lönnqvist, A. (2014). *Knowledge and the city.* New York, Routledge.

Castelnovo, W., Misuraca, G., Savoldelli, A. (2016). Smart cities governance. *Social Science Computer Review, 34*(6), 724–739.

Chadwick, G. (2013). *A systems view of planning.* New York, Elsevier.

Chang, D., Sabatini-Marques, J., da Costa, E., Selig, P., Yigitcanlar, T. (2018). Knowledge-based, smart and sustainable cities. *Journal of Open Innovation: Technology, Market, and Complexity, 4*, 5.

Chen, L., Ho, Y., Lee, H., Wu, H., Liu, H., Hsieh, H., Lung, S. (2017). An open framework for participatory PM2.5 monitoring in smart cities. *IEEE Access, 5*, 14441–14454.

Chichernea, V. (2015). Smart cities communities and smart ICT platform. *Journal of Information Systems & Operations Management, 1*, 11.

Costa, E., Oliveira, Á. (2017). Humane smart cities. In: Frodeman, R., Klein, J., Pacheco, R. (Eds.). *The Oxford handbook of interdisciplinarity* pp. (228–240), Oxford, Oxford University Press.

Cowley, R., Joss, S., Dayot, Y. (2018). The smart city and its publics. *Urban Research & Practice, 11*(1), 53–77.

Crivello, S. (2015). Urban policy mobilities. *European Planning Studies, 23*(5), 909–921.

Cugurullo, F. (2013). How to build a sandcastle. *Journal of Urban Technology, 20*(1), 23–37.

Cugurullo, F. (2016). Urban eco-modernisation and the policy context of new eco-city projects. *Urban Studies, 53*(11), 2417–2433.

D'Aquin, M., Davies, J., Motta, E. (2015). Smart cities' data. *IEEE Internet Computing, 19*(6), 66–70.

Dameri, R.P. (2013). Searching for smart city definition. *International Journal of Computers & Technology, 11*(5), 2544–2551.

Damiani, E., Kowalczyk, R., Parr, G. (2017). Extending the outreach. *ACM Transactions on Internet Technology, 18*(1), 1.

Damurski, L. (2016). Smart city, integrated planning, and multilevel governance: a conceptual framework for e-planning in Europe. *International Journal of E-Planning Research, 5*(4), 41–53.

Deakin, M. (2013). *Smart cities.* New York, Routledge.

Deakin, M. (2014). Smart cities. *Triple Helix, 1*(1), 7.

Deakin, M., Reid, A. (2017). The embedded intelligence of smart cities. *International Journal of Public Administration in the Digital Age, 4*(4), 62–74.

Dizdaroglu, D., Yigitcanlar, T. (2014). A parcel-scale assessment tool to measure sustainability through urban ecosystem components. *Ecological Indicators, 41*(1), 115–130.

Dizdaroglu, D., Yigitcanlar, T., Dawes, L. (2012). A micro-level indexing model for assessing urban ecosystem sustainability. *Smart and Sustainable Built Environment, 1*(3), 291–315.

EasyPark Group. (2017). 2017 Smart Cities Index. Accessed on 17 January 2018 from https://easyparkgroup.com/smart-cities-index.

Edvardsson, I., Yigitcanlar, T., Pancholi, S. (2016). Knowledge city research and practice under the microscope. *Knowledge Management Research & Practice, 14*(4), 537–564.

Eger, J. (2009). Smart growth, smart cities, and the crisis at the pump a worldwide phenomenon. *Journal of E-Government Policy and Regulation, 32*(1), 47–53.

Errichiello, L., Marasco, A. (2014). Open service innovation in smart cities. *Advanced Engineering Forum, 11*, 115–124.

Esmaeilpoorarabi, N., Yigitcanlar, T., Guaralda, M. (2016). Place quality and urban competitiveness symbiosis? *International Journal of Knowledge-Based Development, 7*(1), 4–21.

Esmaeilpoorarabi, N., Yigitcanlar, T., Guaralda, M. (2018). Place quality in innovation clusters. *Cities, 74*(1), 156–168.

EU (2014). *Mapping smart cities in the EU*. Brussels, European Union Directorate General for Internal Policies.

Fassam, L., Copsey, S., Gough, A. (2016). Network Northamptonshire. *International Journal of Advanced Logistics, 5*(3–4), 117–124.

Fernandez-Anez, V., Fernández-Güell, J. M., Giffinger, R. (2018). Smart city implementation and discourses: An integrated conceptual model. The case of Vienna. *Cities, 78*, 4–16.

Fincher, C. (1972). Planning models and paradigms in higher education. *The Journal of Higher Education, 43*(9), 754–767.

Garau, C., Zamperlin, P., Balletto, G. (2016). Reconsidering the Geddesian concepts of community and space through the paradigm of smart cities. *Sustainability, 8*(10), 985.

Giffinger, R., Fertner, C., Kramar, H., Kalasek, R., Pichler-Milanovic, N., Meijers, E. (2007). *Smart cities*. Vienna, Vienna University of Technology.

Glasmeier, A., Nebiolo, M. (2016). Thinking about smart cities. *Sustainability, 8*(11), 1122.

Goonetilleke, A., Yigitcanlar, T., Ayoko, G., Egodawatta, P. (2014). *Sustainable urban water environment*. London, Edward Elgar.

González, J., Rossi, A. (2011). New trends for smart cities. Accessed from http://opencities.net/sites/opencities.net/files/content-files/repository/D2.2.21%20New%20trends%20for%20Smart%20Cities.pdf.

Granier, B., Kudo, H. (2016). How are citizens involved in smart cities? *Information Polity, 21*(1), 61–76.

Grossi, G., Pianezzi, D. (2017). Smart cities. *Cities, 69*, 79–85.

Hall, R., Bowerman, B., Braverman, J., Taylor, J., Todosow, H., Von Wimmersperg, U. (2000). *The vision of a smart city*. Upton, Brookhaven National Lab.

Han, H., Hawken, S. (2018). Innovation and identity in next-generation smart cities. *City, Culture and Society, 12*(1), 1–4.

Harrison, C., Donnelly, I. (2011). A theory of smart cities. In: Proceedings of the 55th Annual Meeting of the ISSS-2011, Hull, UK.

He, H., Cui, L., Zhou, F., Wang, D. (2017a). Distributed proxy cache technology based on autonomic computing in smart cities. *Future Generation Computer Systems, 76*, 370–383.

He, K., Weng, J., Mao, Y., Yuan, H. (2017b). Anonymous identity-based broadcast encryption technology for smart city information system. *Personal and Ubiquitous Computing, 21*(5), 841–853.

Hernandez-Munoz, J., Vercher, J., Muñoz, L., Galache, J., Presser, M., Gómez, L., Pettersson, J. (2011). Smart cities at the forefront of the future internet. In: Domingue, J., Galis, A., Gavras, A., Zahariadis, T., Lambert, D., Cleary, F., Schaffers, H. *The Future Internet Assembly.* Berlin, Springer.

Holland, B. (2015). Typologies of national urban policy. *Cities, 48,* 125–129.

Hollands, R. (2008). Will the real smart city please stand up? *City, 12*(3), 303–320.

Hughes, C., Spray, R. (2002). Smart communities and smart growth-maximising benefits for the corporation. *Journal of Corporate Real Estate, 4*(3), 207–214.

Hui, T., Sherratt, R., Sánchez, D. (2017). Major requirements for building smart homes in smart cities based on internet of things technologies. *Future Generation Computer Systems, 76,* 358–369.

Hung, P., Peng, K. (2017). Green-energy, water-autonomous greenhouse system. *International Review for Spatial Planning and Sustainable Development, 5*(1), 55–70.

Ianuale, N., Schiavon, D., Capobianco, E. (2016). Smart cities, big data, and communities: reasoning from the viewpoint of attractors. *IEEE Access, 4,* 41–47.

IESE. (2016). *IESE Cities in Motion Index.* Navarra, University of Navarra.

Ioppolo, G., Heijungs, R., Cucurachi, S., Salomone, R., Kleijn, R. (2014). Urban metabolism. In: Salomone, R., Saija, G. *Pathways to Environmental Sustainability,* Berlin, Springer.

Ioppolo, S., Cucurachi, S., Salomone, R., Saija, G., Shi, L. (2016). Sustainable local development and environmental governance. *Sustainability, 8*(2), 180.

Jabareen, Y. (2008). A new conceptual framework for sustainable development. *Environment, Development and Sustainability, 10*(2), 179–192.

Jin, J., Gubbi, J., Marusic, S., Palaniswami, M. (2014). An information framework for creating a smart city through internet of things. *IEEE Internet of Things Journal, 1*(2), 112–121.

Joshi, S., Saxena, S., Godbole, T. (2016). Developing smart cities. *Procedia Computer Science, 93,* 902–909.

Joss, S., Cook, M., Dayot, Y. (2017). Smart cities. *Journal of Urban Technology, 24*(4), 29–49.

Kaika, M. (2017). Don't call me resilient again! *Environment and Urbanization, 29*(1), 89–102.

Kanter, R., Litow, S. (2009). *Informed and Interconnected.* Boston, Harvard Business School.

Khan, Z., Kiani, S., Soomro, K. (2014). A framework for cloud-based context-aware information services for citizens in smart cities. *Journal of Cloud Computing, 3*(1), 14.

Khan, Z., Pervez, Z., Abbasi, A. (2017). Towards a secure service provisioning framework in a smart city environment. *Future Generation Computer Systems, 77,* 112–135.

Khorov, E., Lyakhov, A., Krotov, A., Guschin, A. (2015). A survey on IEEE 802.11ah. *Computer Communications, 58,* 53–69.

Kim, J. (2014). Making cities global. *Planning Perspectives, 29*(3), 329–356.

Ko, Y., Schubert, D., Hester, R. (2011). A conflict of greens. *Environment, 53*(3), 3–17.

Komninos, N. (2008). *Intelligent Cities and Globalisation of Innovation Networks.* New York, Routledge.

Kourtit, K., Nijkamp, P., Steenbruggen, J. (2017). The significance of digital data systems for smart city policy. *Socio-Economic Planning Sciences, 58,* 13–21.

Kousiouris, G., Akbar, A., Sancho, J., Ta-shma, P., Psychas, A., Kyriazis, D., Varvarigou, T. (2018). An integrated information lifecycle management framework for exploiting social network data. *Future Generation Computer Systems, 78*, 516–530.

Kummitha, R., Crutzen, N. (2017). How do we understand smart cities? *Cities, 67*, 43–52.

Kunzmann K. (2014). Smart cities. *Crios, 1*, 9–20.

La Greca, P., Martinico, F. (2016). Energy and spatial planning. In: Papa, R., Fistola, R. *Smart Energy in the Smart City*. Berlin, Springer.

Lara, A., Costa, E., Furlani, T., Yigitcanlar, T. (2016). Smartness that matters. *Journal of Open Innovation: Technology, Market, and Complexity, 2*, 8.

Lazaroiu, G., Roscia, M. (2012). Definition methodology for the smart cities model. *Energy, 20*(1), 326–335.

Lee, J., Hancock, M., Hu, M. (2014). Towards an effective framework for building smart cities. *Technological Forecasting & Social Change, 89*, 80–99.

Lee, J., Phaal, R., Lee, S. (2013). An integrated service-device-technology roadmap for smart city development. *Technological Forecasting & Social Change, 80*(2), 286–306.

Lee, S., Yigitcanlar, T., Han, J., Leem, Y.T. (2008). Ubiquitous urban infrastructure. *Innovation, 10*(2–3), 282–292.

Liu, X., Heller, A., Nielsen, P. (2017). CITIESData. *Knowledge and Information Systems, 53*, 699–722.

Lynggaard, P., Skouby, K. (2015). Deploying 5G-technologies in smart city and smart home wireless sensor networks with interferences. *Wireless Personal Communications, 81*(4), 1399–1413.

Mahbub, P., Goonetilleke, A., Ayoko, G., Egodawatta, P., Yigitcanlar, T. (2011). Analysis of build-up of heavy metals and volatile organics on urban roads in Gold Coast, Australia. *Water Science and Technology, 63*(9), 2077–2085.

Marek, L., Campbell, M., Bui, L. (2017). Shaking for innovation. *Cities, 63*, 41–50.Marsal-Llacuna, M. (2017). Building universal socio-cultural indicators for standardizing the safeguarding of citizens' rights in smart cities. *Social Indicators Research, 130*(2), 563–579.

Marsal-Llacuna, M., Segal, M. (2016). The intelligenter method (I) for making "smarter" city projects and plans. *Cities, 55*, 127–138.

Martin, C. J., Evans, J., Karvonen, A. (2018). Smart and sustainable? Five tensions in the visions and practices of the smart-sustainable city in Europe and North America. *Technological Forecasting and Social Change, 133*, 269–278.

McFarlane, C., Söderström, O. (2017). On alternative smart cities. *City*, 1–17.

McLoughlin, J. (1969). *Urban and regional planning*. London, Faber and Faber.

Meijer, A., Thaens, M. (2018). Urban technological innovation. *Urban Affairs Review, 54*(2), 363–387.

Millar, C., Ju Choi, C. (2010). Development and knowledge resources. *Journal of Knowledge Management, 14*(5), 759–776.

Mora, L., Bolici, R., Deakin, M. (2017). The first two decades of smart-city research. *Journal of Urban Technology, 24*(1), 3–27.

Nam, T., Pardo, T. (2011). Conceptualizing smart city with dimensions of technology, people, and institutions. In: 12th Annual International Digital Government Research Conference.

Neirotti, P., De Marco, A., Cagliano, A., Mangano, G., Scorrano, F. (2014). Current trends in smart city initiatives. *Cities, 38*, 25–36.

Odendaal, N. (2003). Information and communication technology and local governance. *Computers, Environment and Urban Systems, 27*(6), 585–607.

Orłowski, C. (2014). Rule-based model for selecting integration technologies for smart cities systems. *Cybernetics and Systems, 45*(2), 136–145.

Pancholi, S., Yigitcanlar, T., Guaralda, M. (2018). Societal integration that matters: place making experience of Macquarie Park Innovation District, Sydney. *City, Culture and Society, 13*, 13–21.

Pancholi, S., Yigitcanlar, T., Guaralda, M. (2019). Place making for innovation and knowledge-intensive activities: The Australian experience. *Technological Forecasting and Social Change, 146*, 616–625.

Paroutis, S., Bennett, M., Heracleous, L. (2014). A strategic view on smart city technology. *Technological Forecasting & Social Change, 89*, 262–272.

Partridge, H. (2004). Developing a human perspective to the digital divide in the smart city. In: ALIA 2004 Biennial Conference.

Paskaleva, K. (2009). Enabling the smart city. *International Journal of Innovation and Regional Development, 1*(4), 405–422.

Petrolo, R., Loscri, V., Mitton, N. (2017). Towards a smart city based on cloud of things, a survey on the smart city vision and paradigms. *Transactions on Emerging Telecommunications Technologies, 28*(1), 1–12.

Pettit, C., Bakelmun, A., Lieske, S., Glackin, S., Thomson, G., Shearer, H., Newman, P. (2018). Planning support systems for smart cities. *City, Culture and Society, 12*(1), 13–24.

Pierce, P., Ricciardi, F., Zardini, A. (2017). Smart cities as organizational fields. *Sustainability, 9*(9), 1506.

Pinna, F., Masala, F., Garau, C. (2017). Urban policies and mobility trends in Italian smart cities. *Sustainability, 9*(4), 494.

Piro, G., Cianci, I., Grieco, L.A., Boggia, G., Camarda, P. (2014). Information centric services in smart cities. *Journal of Systems and Software, 88*(1), 169–188.

Pollio, A. (2016). Technologies of austerity urbanism. *Urban Geography, 37*(4), 514–534.

Popescu, G.H. (2015). The economic value of smart city technology. *Economics, Management and Financial Markets, 10*(4), 76.

Praharaj, S., Han, J., Hawken, S. (2018). Urban innovation through policy integration. *City, Culture and Society, 12*(1), 35–43.

Puiu, D., Barnaghi, P., Toenjes, R., Kümper, D., Ali, M., Mileo, A., Gao, F. (2016). Citypulse. *IEEE Access, 4*, 1086–1108.

Rios, P. (2008). Creating the smart city. Accessed from https://archive.udmercy.edu/handle/10429/393.

Romão, J., Kourtit, K., Neuts, B., Nijkamp, P. (2018). The smart city as a common place for tourists and residents: A structural analysis of the determinants of urban attractiveness. *Cities, 78*, 67–75.

Rosati, U., Conti, S. (2016). What is a smart city project? *Procedia-Social and Behavioral Sciences, 223*, 968–973.

Sanchez, L., Elicegui, I., Cuesta, J., Muñoz, L., Lanza, J. (2013). Integration of utilities infrastructures in a future internet enabled smart city framework. *Sensors, 13*(11), 14438–14465.

Sarimin, M., Yigitcanlar, T. (2012). Towards a comprehensive and integrated knowledge-based urban development model. *International Journal of Knowledge-Based Development, 3*(2), 175–192.

Schaffers, H., Komninos, N., Tsarchopoulos, P., Pallot, M., Trousse, B., Posio, E., Carter, D. (2012). Landscape and roadmap of future internet and smart cities. Accessed from https://hal.inria.fr/hal-00769715/document.

Shladover, S. (2018). Connected and automated vehicle systems: Introduction and overview. *Journal of Intelligent Transportation Systems, 22*(3), 190–200.

Shwayri, S. (2013). A model Korean ubiquitous eco-city? *Journal of Urban Technology, 20*(1), 39–55.

Sidawi, B., Deakin, M. (2013). Diabetes, built environments and (un)healthy lifestyles. *Smart and Sustainable Built Environment, 2*(3), 311–323.

Sivarajah, U., Lee, H., Irani, Z., Weerakkody, V. (2014). Fostering smart cities through ICT driven policy-making. *International Journal of Electronic Government Research, 10*(3), 1–18.

Smith, B., Zeder, M. (2013). The onset of the Anthropocene. *Anthropocene, 4*, 8–13.

Smith, E. (2017). Smart cities and communities. *Institute of Transportation Engineers Journal, 87*(2), 36–38.

Snow, C., Håkonsson, D., Obel, B. (2016). A smart city is a collaborative community. *California Management Review, 59*(1), 92–108.

Stratigea, A., Papadopoulou, C., Panagiotopoulou, M. (2015). Tools and technologies for planning the development of smart cities. *Journal of Urban Technology, 22*(2), 43–62.

Sun, J., Yan, J., Zhang, K. (2016). Blockchain-based sharing services. *Financial Innovation, 2*(1), 26.

Susanti, R., Soetomo, S., Buchori, I., Brotosunaryo, P. (2016). Smart growth, smart city and density. *Procedia-Social and Behavioral Sciences, 227*, 194–201.

Syväjärvi, A., Kivivirta, V., Stenvall, J., Laitinen, I. (2015). Digitalization and information management in smart city government. *International Journal of Innovation in the Digital Economy, 6*(4), 1–15.

Szopik-Depczyńska, K., Cheba, K., Bąk, I., Kiba-Janiak, M., Saniuk, S., Dembińska, I., Ioppolo, G. (2017). The application of relative taxonomy to the study of disproportions in the area of sustainable development of the European Union. *Land Use Policy, 68*(1), 481–491.

Taamallah, A., Khemaja, M., Faiz, S. (2017). Strategy ontology construction and learning. *International Journal of Knowledge-Based Development, 8*(3), 206–228.

Teriman, S., Yigitcanlar, T., Mayere, S. (2009). Sustainable urban development. In Goonetilleke, A. *The Second Infrastructure Theme Postgraduate Conference Proceedings*.

Townsend, A. (2013). *Smart Cities*. New York, WW Norton & Company.

Trindade, E., Hinnig, M., Costa, E., Sabatini-Marques, J., Bastos, R., Yigitcanlar, T. (2017). Sustainable development of smart cities. *Journal of Open Innovation, 3*, 11.

Tucker, R., Ruffini, M., Valcarenghi, L., Campelo, D., Simeonidou, D., Du, L., Bourg, K. (2017). Connected OFcity. *Journal of Optical Communications and Networking, 9*(2), A245–A255.

Viitanen, J., Kingston, R. (2014). Smart cities and green growth. *Environment and Planning A, 46*(4), 803–819.

Villanueva, F.J., Aguirre, C., Rubio, A., Villa, D., Santofimia, M., López, J. (2016). Data stream visualization framework for smart cities. *Soft Computing, 20*(5), 1671–1681.

Vlacheas, P., Giaffreda, R., Stavroulaki, V., Kelaidonis, D., Foteinos, V., Poulios, G., Moessner, K. (2013). Enabling smart cities through a cognitive management framework for the internet of things. *IEEE Communications Magazine, 51*(6), 102–111.

Walravens, N. (2012). Mobile business and the smart city. *Journal of Theoretical and Applied Electronic Commerce Research, 7*(3), 121–135.

Wang, L., Ruan, P., Li, S. (2014). Effects of information technology on rural economic development from the perspective of smart city. *Applied Mechanics and Materials, 668*, 1466–1469.

Wenge, R., Zhang, X., Dave, C., Chao, L., Hao, S. (2014). Smart city architecture. *China Communications, 11*(3), 56–69.

Wiig, A. (2015). IBM's smart city as techno-utopian policy mobility. *City, 19*(2–3), 258–273.

Willis, K., Aurigi, A. (2017). *Digital and Smart Cities.* New York, Routledge.

Wong, T. (2011). Eco-cities in China. In: Wong, T., Yuen, B., *Eco-city Planning.* Berlin, Springer.

Yaqoob, I., Hashem, I., Mehmood, Y., Gani, A., Mokhtar, S., Guizani, S. (2017). Enabling communication technologies for smart cities. *IEEE Communications Magazine, 55*(1), 112–120.

Yigitcanlar, T. (2005). Is Australia ready to move planning to online mode? *Australian Planner, 42*(2), 42–51.

Yigitcanlar, T. (2006). Australian local governments' practice and prospects with online planning. *URISA Journal, 18*(2), 7–17.

Yigitcanlar, T. (2009). Planning for smart urban ecosystems. *Theoretical and Empirical Researches in Urban Management, 4*(3), 5–21.

Yigitcanlar, T. (2015). Smart cities. *Australian Planner, 52,* 27–34.

Yigitcanlar, T. (2016). *Technology and the City.* Routledge, New York.

Yigitcanlar, T. (2017). Smart cities in the making. *International Journal of Knowledge-Based Development, 8*(3), 201–205.

Yigitcanlar, T., Dodson, J., Gleeson, B., Sipe, N. (2007). Travel self-containment in master planned estates: analysis of recent Australian trends. *Urban Policy and Research, 25*(1), 129–149.

Yigitcanlar, T., Edvardsson, I.R., Johannesson, H., Kamruzzaman, M., Ioppolo, G., Pancholi, S. (2017). Knowledge-based development dynamics in less favoured regions. *European Planning Studies, 25*(12), 2272–2292.

Yigitcanlar, T., Fabian, L., Coiacetto, E. (2008a). Challenges to urban transport sustainability and smart transport in a tourist city. *Open Transportation Journal, 1,* 19–36.

Yigitcanlar, T., Guaralda, M., Taboada, M., Pancholi, S. (2016). Place making for knowledge generation and innovation. *Journal of Urban Technology, 23*(1), 115–146.

Yigitcanlar, T., Kamruzzaman, M. (2018). Does smart city policy lead to sustainability of cities? *Land Use Policy, 73*(1), 49–58.

Yigitcanlar, T., Lee, S. (2014). Korean ubiquitous-eco-city. *Technological Forecasting and Social Change, 89,* 100–114.

Yigitcanlar, T., Velibeyoglu, K., Martinez-Fernandez, C. (2008b). Rising knowledge cities. *Journal of Knowledge Management, 12*(5), 8–20.

Yigitcanlar, T., Kamruzzaman, M., Buys, L., Ioppolo, G., Sabatini-Marques, J., Costa, E., Yun, J. (2018). Understanding 'smart cities': Intertwining development drivers with desired outcomes in a multidimensional framework. *Cities,* 81, 145–160.

Zhang, N., Chen, H., Chen, X., Chen, J. (2016). Semantic framework of internet of things for smart cities: case studies. *Sensors, 16*(9), 1501.

Zhao, J. (2011). *Towards Sustainable Cities in China.* Berlin, Springer.

2 Smart and Sustainable

2.1 Introduction

Urban growth is taking place on an unprecedented scale globally and its externalities on the environment and society are evident (Goonetilleke et al., 2014; Arbolino et al., 2017; Kamruzzaman et al., 2018). Without exception, all parts of the world, today, are confronted with various environmental and/or socioeconomic crises (Kamruzzaman et al., 2015; Moore, 2017; Kamruzzaman et al., 2018). For instance, an increasing number and intensity of natural disasters, climate change, biodiversity loss, ecosystem destruction, regional disparities, socioeconomic inequity, and knowledge and digital divides are some of them (Didsbury, 2004; Caprotti, 2014). Besides, large number of megacities around the world are creating urban management quagmires for their administrations (Madon & Sahay, 2001; Teriman et al., 2009). These crises are mainly caused by rapid population growth; and a net total growth of consumption of natural resources, combined with vigorous industrialisation, urbanisation, mobilisation, globalisation, agricultural intensification, and excessive consumption-driven lifestyles (Epstein & Buhovac, 2014; Yigitcanlar & Dizdaroglu, 2015; Yigitcanlar & Teriman, 2015).

The Anthropocene is known as the era of geological time during which human activity is considered to have the dominant influence on the environment, climate, and ecology of the Earth (Lewis, 2015; Derickson, 2018). In the Anthropocene, urban and environmental issues induced by the above crises (e.g., environmental pollution, biodiversity loss, resources shortage, traffic congestion, socioeconomic inequities) have become highly problematic for urban administrations to handle (Mahbub et al., 2011; Dizdaroglu et al., 2012; Wu et al., 2018). At this dire strait, technology is seen as a potential saviour (Yigitcanlar, 2009; Paroutis et al., 2014; van den Buuse & Kolk, 2019). The rapid advancements in information and communication technologies (ICTs) gave urban administrators a hope that the impacts of global-scale environmental and socioeconomic crises can possibly be eased with the aid of technologies—such as achieving cities' climate targets by lowering energy use and greenhouse gas emissions (Lee et al., 2008; Rice & Martin, 2020). The need for cities to reap the benefits of smart urban technologies is widely

DOI: 10.1201/9781003403630-3

advocated, due to the recent rapid progress in the technology innovation domain generating feasible technology solutions for cities (Hollands, 2008; Söderström et al., 2014).

The potential of these technologies in providing effective instruments for the development of model cities of the century has made smart cities a highly attractive notion for urban administrators and planners (Bibri, 2018a; Macke et al., 2018). Consequently, the smart city model has been promoted as a suitable instrument to manage urban and environmental challenges (Meijer & Bolívar, 2016; Wu et al., 2018). However, there are various views in the literature on what a smart city is or what makes a city smart (see Table 2.1). In theory, smart cities should contribute to the formation of high-quality, healthy, and regenerative built environments modelled around the circular economy and with a net positive impact on the natural environment (Angelidou, 2014; Heo et al., 2014; Birkeland, 2002, 2014). However, technology alone cannot be a panacea to all of the development ills. Cities can only be considered smart when they invest in the growth of human, social, and environmental capitals that generate sustainable urban development (Caragliu et al., 2011; Kourtit & Nijkamp, 2012; Carrillo et al., 2014). It is argued that only this holistic view can help in building truly smart cities (Ibrahim et al., 2015; Yigitcanlar, 2015; Alizadeh & Irajifar, 2018; Foth, 2018).

Today, the smart cities notion has become a global phenomenon and movement; where its promise is to enable us to use resources in cities in more efficient ways, to make public transport more attractive, and to provide planners and decision-makers with data to allocate resources more accurately (Townsend, 2013). The shift in the smart city discourse is evident in national-level (e.g., South Korea, Australia, India, USA) as well as in city-level policies and initiatives (e.g., Amsterdam, San Francisco, Seoul, Vienna) (Cugurullo, 2016; Foth, 2017; Cowley et al., 2018). There are, presently, hundreds of smart city initiatives underway across the world, large populations are affected by them, and substantial resources are dedicated to these projects (Monfaredzadeh & Berardi, 2015; Praharaj et al., 2018). While some of these projects are incorporating dimensions beyond technology, there is little evidence in practice that sustainability targets are achieved in cities claiming to be smart cities in order to move the smart city notion closer to the goal of a sustainable city (Yigitcanlar & Kamruzzaman, 2018, 2019).

On the one hand, advocates see smart cities as a promise for a new and sustainable urban future, providing technological solutions to our urban challenges and changing how we manage and live in cities. In contrast, critics view smart cities as another form of neoliberal urban entrepreneurialism, in pursuit of old-fashioned growth agendas. A mere focus on efficiency gains is not going to bring true sustainability to our cities. Keeping these two conflicting views in mind, some scholars also reconceptualise smart cities as "smart sustainable cities" and offer transformation roadmaps to guide urban administrators, managers, and planners in understanding the essential stages and components to be considered during the transformation journey (Ibrahim et al., 2017, 2018).

Against this backdrop, this chapter aims to address the research question of whether cities can become smart without being sustainable. The methodological approach of this investigation includes the systematic selection of relevant academic articles from the smart city literature.

2.2 Literature Background

Cities are human-dominated living organisms that perform the most dramatic manifestations of human activities (Dizdaroglu & Yigitcanlar, 2014, 2016). According to Yigitcanlar & Kamruzzaman (2015, p. 14677), human activities "degrade natural habitats, simplify species composition, disrupt hydrological systems, and modify energy flow and nutrient cycling". Sustainable urban development practices, thus, are critical to dealing with these problems adequately (Perveen et al., 2017a; Arbolino et al., 2018a, 2018b). Sustainable urban development requires an interlinked triad comprising economy, society and nature that facilitates the establishment of a socioeconomic system that does not harm the natural world (Dur et al., 2014; Dur & Yigitcanlar, 2015; Ioppolo et al., 2019).

As stated by Fu & Zhang (2017, p. 113),

it has become common practice to contrive a city concept for transforming our cities into a more sustainable urban form. The salience of these terms has been mutually reinforced whenever it is advocated in policy discourse or seriously elaborated in the academic field. To date, a multitude of city concepts intending to depict a more sustainable and prosperous urban future have been contrived and debated. Of these concepts, the "smart city" and "sustainable city" are the most outstanding and persistent [ones].

The smart city notion, initially, was a spin off concept originating from the smart growth movement in the 1990s, which basically advocates planning strategies to address sprawl development and associated environmental "externalities" (Downs, 2005; Perveen et al., 2017b, 2019). Despite its original sustainable urban development roots, the smart city concept has become popular following a speech by Samuel J. Palmisano, then IBM Chairman, President and CEO, on "A Smarter Planet: The Next Leadership Agenda" on 12 November 2008 (Söderström et al., 2014). Consequently, as argued by Yigitcanlar et al. (2018a, p. 2), it has evolved to mean

almost any form of technology-based innovation in the planning, development, operation and management of cities, for example, the deployment of smart mobility solutions to combat urban traffic challenges. ...With the offerings of digital technologies and online urban planning opportunities, this concept increased its popularity among the urban technocrats.

As stated by Ibrahim et al. (2018, p. 530), "there is neither a single template for framing the [smart city] concept, nor a one-size-fits-all definition for it... Depending on the lens or viewpoint taken, there exist various definitions and dimensions of the concept". This is to say there is, however, no consensus established so far on what a smart city is and what its main domains and dimensions are. A collection of popular smart city definitions can be found in Table 2.1. The reason for not having a common smart city definition is elaborated by Yigitcanlar et al. (2018a, p. 3) as

> the fast-growing literature on smart cities comes from the streams of academic, commercial, and (inter)national organisations researching on and practicing smart cities. These groups have a different take on the concept as they see it from different lenses such as disciplinary, practice—or conceptualisation-orientation, and domain-orientation, e.g., technology, economy, society, environment, governance.

Table 2.1 Selection of broad smart city definitions and domains, sorted by year of publication (derived from Yigitcanlar et al., 2018a)

Literature	*Definition*	*Domain*
Yigitcanlar et al. (2018a)	An ideal model to build the cities of the 21st century, in the case, its practice involves a system of systems approach and a sustainable and balanced view on the economic, societal, environmental, and institutional development domains	Community, policy, technology, productivity, innovation, liveability, wellbeing, sustainability, accessibility, governance, planning
Lara et al. (2016)	A community that systematically promotes the overall wellbeing for all its members, and flexible enough to proactively and sustainably become an increasingly better place to live, work and play	Community, wellbeing, sustainability, liveability
Yigitcanlar (2016)	An ideal form to build the sustainable cities of the 21st century, in the case that a balanced and sustainable view on economic, societal, environmental, and institutional development is realised	Sustainability, productivity, governance, community
ITU (2014)	An innovative city that uses ICTs and other means to improve quality of life, efficiency of urban operation and services, and competitiveness, while ensuring that it meets the needs of present and future generations with respect to economic, social, and environmental aspects	Technology, productivity, innovation, community, liveability, wellbeing, sustainability
Piro et al. (2014)	A city that intends as an urban environment which, supported by pervasive ICT systems, can offer advanced and innovative services to citizens to improve the overall quality of their life	Technology, liveability, policy

Table 2.1 (Continued)

Literature	Definition	Domain
Alkandari et al. (2012)	A city that uses a smart system characterised by the interaction between infrastructure, capital, behaviours, and cultures, achieved through their integration	Technology, productivity, community, governance
Lazaroiu & Roscia (2012)	A city that represents the future challenge, a city model where the technology is in service to the person and to his economic and social life quality improvement	Technology, prosperity, liveability, wellbeing
Schaffers et al. (2012)	A safe, secure environmentally green, and efficient urban centre of the future with advanced infrastructures such as sensors, electronics, and networks to stimulate sustainable economic growth and a high quality of life	Technology, productivity, liveability, sustainability
Caragliu et al. (2011)	A city that is smart when investments in human and social capital and traditional transport and modern ICT infrastructure fuel sustainable economic growth and a high quality of life, with a wise management of natural resources, through participatory governance	Community, technology, liveability, sustainability, governance, policy, accessibility
Gonzalez & Rossi (2011)	A public administration or authority that delivers or aims to a set of new generation services and infrastructure, based on information and communication technologies	Governance, policy, technology
Hernandez-Munoz et al. (2011)	A city that represents an extraordinary rich ecosystem to promote the generation of massive deployments of city-scale applications and services for large number of activity sectors	Technology, governance
Nam & Pardo (2011)	A humane city that has multiple opportunities to exploit its human potential and lead a creative life	Community, wellbeing, productivity
Zhao (2011)	A city that improves the quality of life, including ecological, cultural, political, institutional, social, and economic components without leaving a burden on future generations	Liveability, governance, sustainability, community, productivity
Belissent et al. (2010)	A city that uses ICTs to make the critical infrastructure components and services of a city—administration, education, healthcare, public safety, real estate, transportation, and utilities—more aware, interactive, and efficient	Technology, accessibility, liveability, governance
Eger (2009)	A particular idea of local community, one where city governments, enterprises and residents use ICTs to reinvent and reinforce the community's role in the new service economy, create jobs locally and improve the quality of community life	Community, governance, technology, liveability, productivity

(Continued)

Table 2.1 (Continued)

Literature	Definition	Domain
Paskaleva (2009)	A city that takes advantages of the opportunities offered by ICT in increasing local prosperity and competitiveness—an approach that implies integrated urban development involving multi-actor, multi-sector and multi-level perspectives	Productivity, technology, policy
Rios (2008)	A city that gives inspiration, shares culture, knowledge, and life, a city that motivates its inhabitants to create and flourish in their own lives—it is an admired city, a vessel to intelligence, but ultimately an incubator of empowered spaces	Community, liveability, productivity
Giffinger et al. (2007)	A city well performing in a forward-looking way in economy, people, governance, mobility, environment, and living built on the smart combination of endowments and activities of self-decisive, independent, and aware citizens	Community, governance, accessibility, technology, productivity, policy
Partridge (2004)	A city that actively embraces new technologies seeking to be a more open society where technology makes easier for people to have their say, gain access to services and to stay in touch with what is happening around them, simply and cheaply	Technology, community, accessibility, liveability
Odendaal (2003)	A city that capitalises on the opportunities presented by ICTs in promoting its prosperity and influence	Technology, productivity
Bowerman et al. (2000)	A city that monitors and integrates conditions of all its critical infrastructures including roads, bridges, tunnels, rails, subways, airports, seaports, communications, water, power, even major buildings, can better optimise its resources, plan its preventive maintenance activities, and monitor security aspects while maximising services to its citizens	Policy, governance, accessibility, liveability
Hall et al. (2000)	An urban centre of the future, made safe, secure environmentally green, and efficient because all structures—whether for power, water, transportation, etc. are designed, constructed, and maintained making use of advanced, integrated materials, sensors, electronics, and networks which are interfaced with computerised systems comprised of databases, tracking, and decision-making algorithms	Sustainability, technology, governance

Additionally, while there are a variety of smart city dimensions proposed, one of the most popular sets is the one used in the EU's smart city wheel (EU, 2014)—i.e., smart economy, smart people, smart governance, smart mobility, smart environment, and smart living (Giffinger et al., 2007).

This study adopts the following smart city definition derived from Yigitcanlar et al. (2018a, 2019a): *The smart city is an urban locality functioning as a healthy system of systems with sustainable and knowledge-based development activities to generate desired outcomes for all humans and non-humans.* The rationale for the adoption is that while offering comprehensive conceptualisation, it also provides a practical process with analytical elements. This definition envisages the smart city as a system of systems targeting a sustainable and knowledge-based development view (see Yigitcanlar, 2012; Yigitcanlar & Bulu, 2015). This view suggests interconnecting assets, drivers, outcomes, and results strategically to realise the potential in our cities to become smart and sustainable. In this perspective, assets are the inputs or resources of a city that its development is situated on; driving forces are denoted as processes or opportunities for the smart city formation; desired outcomes are the outputs or achievements to realise sustainable urban development to benefit both society and the environment; results are the impacts that transform a city into a smart city (Yigitcanlar & Kamruzzaman, 2014; Yigitcanlar et al., 2018a, 2019a). This multidimensional conceptual view is illustrated in Figure 2.1.

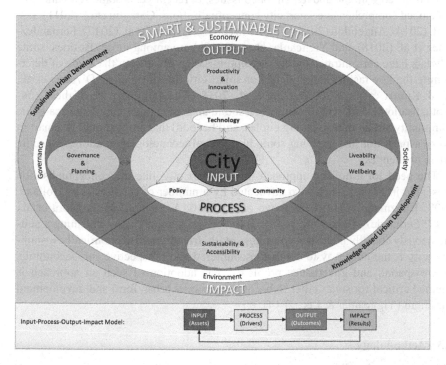

Figure 2.1 A multidimensional smart city framework (derived from Yigitcanlar et al., 2018a, 2018c).

From the urban environmental sustainability point of view, some scholars, such as Wachsmuth and Angelo (2018, p. 2), see smart cities as "a distinctive pairing of high-tech environmental strategies with traditionally green interventions such as parks and gardens" also including vertical and roof-top ones. Others see smart cities as zero- or low-carbon localities emitting none to low greenhouse gases as a result of the application of smart green technologies (Kim, 2018) or even achieving a net positive impact (Birkeland 2002, 2014). Some scholars, such as Bibri and Krogstie (2017a) and Bonato and Orsini (2018), argue that smart and sustainable cities should adopt a circular economy model.

According to Bibri (2018b, p. 47), the smart city model should

> strive to maximise efficiency of energy and material resources, create a zero-waste system, support renewable energy production and consumption, promote carbon-neutrality and reduce pollution, decrease transport needs and encourage walking and cycling, provide efficient and sustainable transport, preserve ecosystems, emphasize design scalability and spatial proximity, and promote liveability and sustainable community.

This is to say, the focus of truly smart cities should be well beyond technological innovations and technical quick fixes (see Taamallah et al., 2017).

Concerned with the abovementioned issues, in recent years some scholars have developed comprehensive smart city conceptualisations. Caragliu et al. (2011), Lee et al. (2014), Angelidou (2015), Foth et al. (2015), Ibrahim et al. (2017), Fernandez-Anez et al. (2018), and Yigitcanlar et al. (2018a) are among those. Besides, some scholars have concentrated on the conceptualisation issue from the angle of determining the key factors and policies for smart city transformation (D'Auria et al., 2018; Kumar et al., 2020; Myeong et al., 2018). The main purpose of these conceptualisation works is to disseminate a sound understanding (among the academic community, urban policymaking circles, and beyond) that cities should be smart in every aspect, not just applying some hip or cool technologies to address specific urban challenges.

The need for a holistic approach to the smart city, like the conceptualisation presented in Figure 2.1, is also advocated by a number of scholars (i.e., Holland, 2008; Kunzmann, 2014; Castelnovo et al., 2016; Angelidou, 2017; Mora et al., 2017; Fernandez-Anez et al., 2018). These scholars argue that establishing a simultaneously socially inclusive, environmentally friendly, and economically sustainable city is the only way to combat encountered and prospective socioeconomic, enviro-spatial, and governance problems. The adoption of such an approach is deemed critical for smart cities to become the model urban form and development paradigm (Yigitcanlar & Lee, 2014).

2.3 Methodology

This study undertakes a systematic literature review to address the research question of: *Can cities become smart without being sustainable?* This distinguishes our study from other recent systematic reviews of the smart city literature such as Ingwersen and Serrano-López (2018), who omitted key smart city scholars and did not incorporate a post-anthropocentric notion of sustainability concerns in their assessment. Our study adopts a three-stage procedure as the methodologic approach. Highlighted by Bask and Rajahonka, (2017, p. 562),

[Stage 1] Planning stage contains objectives and review protocol for a systematic review, defining sources and procedures for literature searches. [Stage 2] Conducting the review stage contains descriptive and structural analysis. [Stage 3] Reporting and dissemination stage contains analysis and synthesis of the results according to the established objectives.

In Stage 1 (planning stage), a research plan involving the research aim and question, keywords, and a set of inclusion and exclusion criteria was developed. The research aim was framed to identify the links between the smart city and urban sustainability literatures to address the research question of whether cities can become smart without actually being sustainable. Therefore, "smart cities", "sustainable cities", "urban smartness", and "urban sustainability" were selected as the search keywords. The inclusion criteria were determined as academic journal articles, available online in full text and published in English, that are relevant to the research aim; meaning selection of the articles that relate to and help address the research aim and question. The exclusion criteria were determined as publications other than those mentioned in the inclusion criteria. The search was conducted using the following databases: Scopus, ScienceDirect, Web of Science, Directory of Open Access Journals, and Wiley Online Library.

In Stage 2 (conducting the review stage), the search task of the relevant articles was undertaken in June 2018. No starting publication date was introduced in the search, where the end date was when the search was conducted, in June 2018. The following keywords were used in the search to identify articles that contain smart and sustainable aspects of cities: "smart", "smartness", "sustainable", "sustainability", "city", "cities", and "urban". The query string used for database searches was: (("smart" OR "smartness") AND ("sustainable" OR "sustainability") AND ("city" OR "cities" OR "urban")). The keywords were directed to the titles and abstracts of the searched articles. The abstracts of the selected articles were read. In the case that abstracts were found relevant, the full texts were read to decide whether to include the article in the review pool. Initially, the search returned a total of 423 articles. All of these were "eye-balled" for consistency and accuracy of the keyword search (see Yin, 1994). After evaluating the abstracts against the research aim and also removing duplicates, this figure was reduced to 92 articles. The full texts of these initially screened articles were then read against the research aim. This resulted in the selection of the final 35 articles. Finally, these 35 articles were re-read, reviewed, categorised and analysed. This literature selection procedure is illustrated in Figure 2.2.

The study relies on a descriptive rather than statistical analysis of results. Qualitative techniques of pattern matching and explanation building have been

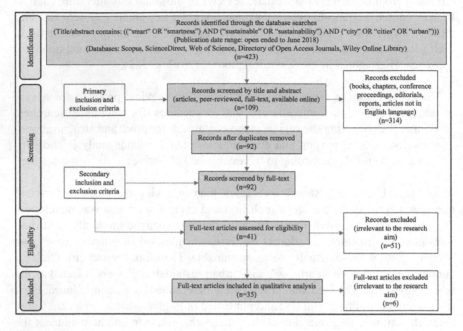

Figure 2.2 Literature selection procedure.

adopted to descriptively categorise the journal articles under specific categories (Yin, 2015). In this regard, pattern matching refers to scanning for commonalities and disparities in which an eye-balling technique is sufficiently convincing to draw a conclusion or categorisation (Yin, 1994). The categorisation of the reviewed literature under specific themes is done in four steps. The selection criteria for the formulation of categories are listed in Table 2.2. Firstly, the key critiques and challenges raised in the reviewed materials were tabulated; highlighting the major challenges and critiques raised on the sustainability of smart cities. Secondly, the most important themes to best categorise the reviewed literature, in relation to the research aim, were determined. Then, these themes were cross-checked with the other review studies, identified critiques and challenges on the investigated topic (e.g., Ahvenniemi et al., 2017; Mora et al., 2017, 2019; D'Auria et al., 2018; Komninos & Mora, 2018) to verify or reconsider the common themes. Following this, the categorisation was amended and finalised under the three themes, which are *technocentricity*, *practice complexity*, and *ad-hoc conceptualisation* of smart cities, and presented in Tables 2.3 to 2.5. However, a possible bias in allocation of articles under specific categories should be noted; as some of the papers' coverage extended beyond the allocated category.

In Stage 3 (reporting and dissemination stage), the work focused on writing up and presenting our findings in the format of a literature review chapter. At the write-up stage, other publications on the topic were also incorporated as additional

Table 2.2 Selection criteria for the formulation of categories

---

Selection criteria

Determine the key critiques and challenges of smart cities by using the eye-balling technique in the selected literature

Detect the issues relating to the sustainable development of smart cities and the smart–sustainable dichotomy among them

Identify the issues with negative impact, cautions, or warnings on the sustainable development of smart cities among them

Group the identified key issues with similarities to form broader potential categories containing an adequate number of literature pieces

Shortlist the categories and crosscheck the reliability of these categories with the other published smart city literature

Reconsider the shortlisted categories by going through the selected and reviewed literature one more time

Confirm the selection and classification of the categories and finalise the formulation of categories

Place the reviewed literature pieces under the determined categories

---

supporting literature evidence to better analyse the topic and elaborate the overall findings. With the inclusion of additional literature identified—including the seminal literary works that have not been a part of the selected databases—by the authors and peer reviewers, the total number of reviewed, cited, and quoted references was increased to 170 literature pieces.

2.4 Results

2.4.1 General Observations

The descriptive analysis of the selected 35 literature pieces was commenced by classifying them according to their publication year. This classification disclosed that during the last couple of years the attention given to the topic has increased dramatically. Close to half of the articles (n=16; 45.7%) were published in 2018, a little over a quarter of them (n=10; 28.6%) were in 2017, and slightly more than a quarter of them (n=9; 25.7%) were in 2016 or earlier (the earliest being 2013). These figures show parallels to other review works stating the increase in the smart city literature over the last few years (Neirotti et al., 2014; Mora et al., 2017; Ingwersen & Serrano-Lopez, 2018; Komninos & Mora, 2018).

In terms of the affiliations of the authors, most of the leading countries in the smart and sustainable cities discourse are from the North American, European, and Oceanian contexts. However, some South East Asian cities, particularly from Singapore and South Korea, are commonly referred to among the best practice examples in the field. This finding is in line with Yigitcanlar (2016), who underlines the growing interest from Western countries in establishing environmentally sustainable smart cities. In terms of the journals these articles are published in, with six articles, *Sustainable Cities and Society* comes first. This is followed by four articles in the *Journal of Cleaner Production*, and then three articles each in *Cities* and *Technological Forecasting and Social Change*. More than one-third of them (13 articles) were published in urban-studies-focused journals, another slightly over one-third (12 articles) in environmental-studies-focused journals, over one-fifth (eight articles) in science- and technology-studies-focused journals, and two of them in transport-studies-focused journals. We acknowledge a risk of bias in our selection strategy, which focuses only on journals, whereas the technology, engineering, and design fields often publish cutting-edge works in prestigious conference proceedings.

After carefully reviewing the selected 35 papers, they were categorised under three groups based on the main critiques provided on the challenges of achieving sustainability outcomes and limitations of smart cities. The reviewed literature was categorised into the following: (a) technocentricity of smart cities (11 papers)—highlighting issues around the heavily technology-centred conceptualisation and practice of smart cities; (b) practice complexity of smart cities (12 papers)—highlighting issues around the highly difficult or even unmanageable complexities impacting the smart city practice; and (c) ad-hoc conceptualisation of smart cities (12 papers). It is important to note that although these papers are assigned to a single category, many of them also relate to other categories. The results of our analysis are presented under the three categories in the following sections. The specific limitations of smart cities to achieve the sustainability outcome raised in the reviewed literature are also listed in Tables 2.3–2.5.

2.4.2 Heavy Technocentricity of Smart Cities

Almost one-third (32%) of the reviewed papers include some degree of criticism of the heavy technocentricity of the smart city notion and/or practice (Table 2.3). Heavy technocentricity refers to the technology obsession or dominance that prioritises technology-based solutions and neglects solutions that have nothing to do with technology.

Sustainable urban development is a multifaceted phenomenon and environmental sustainability is its most intricate aspect (Goodland, 1995; Moldan et al., 2012; Arbolino et al., 2018c). As for Balducci and Ferrara (2018, p. 395),

> environmental sustainability is fundamental in a world where resources are increasingly scarce: in smart cities any kind of exploitation (from energy to commodity) must ensure safe and renewable energy use. In smart cities, vehicle traffic is obviously managed dynamically and in real-time with constant exchange of information between flow management (traffic lights, car parks, public transport) and drivers who have traffic information, car seats available, saving time and fuel and contributing to the reduction of road congestion and emissions.

Table 2.3 Heavy technocentricity problem of smart cities, sorted by year of publication

Literature	Challenge	Critique
Deakin & Reid (2018)	Seeing sustainability solutions in smart cities predominantly through the technology lens	Under-gridding the sustainability of smart city districts with smart technologies as energy-efficient/low-carbon zones, where inclusive growth strategy is not resilient enough, does not generate an opportunity for the ecological footprint to stabilise the transition towards the post-carbon economy of a climate-neutral adaptation
Macke et al. (2018)	Issues around the technologies for sustainability used in smart cities hampering achieving desired outcomes	Sustainability dimension of a smart city project involves the adoption of smart technologies in order to mitigate environment impacts and implement policies of natural ecosystem regeneration. However, these technologies are not simple, integrated, cost-effective, and resource-efficient
Marsal-Llacuna (2019)	Poor sustainability execution in smart cities due to heavy focus on technologic solutions	Smart city practice lacks successful execution of urban planning through technology-based interventions to achieve sustainable outcomes due to a mismatch between policy and practice
Noy & Givoni (2018)	Sector-driven different views on what smart and sustainable are and should be, practice has a dominant techno-centric view	There is a mismatch in the practice between interpretation and understanding of what is "smart" and what is "sustainable". It is clear that the concern of technology firms is primarily with commercial considerations and that their appreciation of what it takes to advance towards a more sustainable transport system is lacking
Dall'O et al. (2017)	Lack of a beyond-technology approach that is needed for smart cities to deliver sustainable outcomes	Technological innovation is to be considered a positive addition and it must not remain the only goal of the evolution of smart cities. The goal should rather be sustainability in its environmental, social, and economic components
Stratigea et al. (2017)	Too much technology focus and not enough holistic approaches to deliver sustainability	Smart city concept has limitations in achieving sustainability; resulting in a shift from a technology-driven to a more holistic approach by means of integrating city attributes in pursuing smart and sustainable development
Trindade et al. (2017)	Lack of convincing policy and practice commitment to sustainable urban development in smart cities due to techno-centric view	Although a smart city is conceptualised as a city that uses technology to generate environmental gains and sustainable outcomes, smart cities do not showcase a strong commitment to sustainable urban development goals

(Continued)

Table 2.3 (Continued)

Literature	Challenge	Critique
Niaros (2016)	Environmental sustainability, both in theory and practice, is only loosely associated with the smart cities notion and projects	A "commons-based approach" is needed to link socio-environmental aspects more strongly with the smart cities theory and practice; the demand-driven production system established in the commons-oriented smart city reduces consumption of ICTs and utilises the existing conditions in the city to allow for more sustainable outcomes
Ramaswami et al. (2016)	Smart city practice with too much technology focus not being able to incorporate multisectoral, multi-scalar and social-ecological-infrastructural systems adequately	To achieve the full potential of smart cities, discussions must move beyond technology and data to envision cities as multisectoral, multi-scalar, social-ecological-infrastructural systems with diverse actors, priorities, and solutions
De Jong et al. (2015)	Smart city practice that is techno-centric not delivering concrete environmental sustainability outcomes	The smart city category is relatively weakly related to the sustainable city category—it is also not immediately obvious what concrete environmental progress can be expected from large-scale technology-centric smart city development activities
Herrschel (2013)	The techno-centric view limiting smart cities to moderate conflicting and competing goals of competitiveness and sustainability	In the case smart city concept is seen beyond a techno-centric point-of-view, smart city regionalism can serve as a vehicle for negotiation between the conflicting and competing goals of competitiveness and sustainability

In the context of smart cities, an intelligent transport system (ITS) enables efficiency in the management of the transport system and generates smart mobility (Garau et al., 2016). In order to achieve smart mobility, electric and autonomous vehicles are seen as an integral part of future smart cities (Firnkorn & Müller, 2015; Lim & Taeihagh, 2018). However, technology cannot create urban smartness alone; the real urban smartness comes from citizens and urban administrators and policymakers directly (Morse, 2014).

The abovementioned view finds increasing support in the academic smart city literature. For instance, according to Han and Hawken (2018, p. 1),

current discourse on smart cities is obsessed with technological capability and development. Global rankings reduce cities to a one-dimensional business model and series of metrics. If the term smart city is to have any enduring value, technology must be used to develop a city's unique cultural identity and quality of life for the future.

Likewise, Costa and Oliveira (2017) and Almeida et al. (2018) highlight the importance of consolidated smart city policies (moving beyond the technology obsession) to generate clear results for the sustainability of both society and the environment.

Some scholars blame the business nature of the smart city practice for the smart city agenda at the global scale (Yigitcanlar et al., 2018b). Major engineering, construction, technology, and consultancy firms (e.g., AT&T, CISCO, Ericsson, Google, Hitachi, Huawei, IBM, Intel, KPMG, McKinsey, Microsoft, Oracle, Schneider Electric, Siemens, Toshiba) play a leading role in the formation of smart city agendas and policies, which poses a risk of conflict of interest (Wiig, 2015; Alizadeh, 2017). On that very point, Noy and Givoni (2018, p. 13) state that private smart city

> business actors are expected, even required, to be concerned primarily with the commercial goals of their companies and with profitability. However, it becomes a problem if these same actors and companies are the ones who set the agenda, drive and largely determine transport policy and planning and are the ones who lead public transport policy and research institutions.

Further dwelling on the mainly technocentric perspective of smart cities, scholars highlight the need for the urban smartness issue to be considered beyond technological innovation (i.e., Herrschel, 2013; Haarstad, 2017; Dall'O et al., 2017; Balducci & Ferrara, 2018; Yigitcanlar & Kamruzzaman, 2018). For example, according to Haarstad (2017), the current smart city agendas are driven mostly by the concerns for economic growth and innovation rather than by environmental sustainability. The smartness agenda of cities pursuing smart city formation is, thus, bound up with the aim of fostering innovation and competitiveness in the knowledge economy. This misconception on the urban smartness issue is also causing ill-informed investment of the limited public funds in many cities.

Another important issue highlighted in the reviewed literature concentrates on the complexity, integration, cost-effectiveness, and resource efficiency of smart city technologies (Macke et al., 2018). Fortunately, many local policymakers are aware of these issues (at least the cost issue), although they still remain reluctant to implement large-scale smart city projects. Beyond the initial investment cost, many urban administrators are concerned with the future update and upgrade requirements that might make them dependent to technology solution companies for a very long time (Yigitcanlar, 2016). This is referred to as a "vendor lock-in" (Kitchin, 2014). Most people regularly update their computers, smart mobile devices, and smart TVs for security and new functionality purposes.

Furthermore, "planned obsolescence" causes these devices not to function properly after a certain period of time, requiring consumers to replace or upgrade them

(Satyro et al., 2018). The prospect of installing millions of Internet of Things (IoT) sensors and devices across a city that eventually all require replacement due to planned obsolescence worries many sensible urban administrators who shy away from such investments (Rathore et al., 2016; Silva et al., 2018b). Nevertheless, the point is not omitting sensing technologies to collect useful data to inform better decision-making. It is rather stating that not so carefully planned technology investments could risk the best use of taxpayers' money. The planned obsolescence issue also contributes to growing problems of rare earth metal depletion, an inability to trace and avoid conflict resources in smart city and IoT supply chains, and an ever-increasing amount of e-waste being exported and dumped in places such as Accra in Ghana and Guangdong Province of China.

While smart city sceptics rightfully argue that many solutions to urban problems have nothing to do with technology, such as plans, policies, and regulations, they also advocate the importance of smart mentality over smart technology; thus, cities must reap the benefits of the appropriate technology opportunities without becoming obsessed with them (Kunzmann, 2014; Vanolo, 2014). Keeping this in mind, our review of the literature in this category raises an important question: *What are the appropriate technologies and the right amount of technocentrism to bring sustainability to our cities?*

2.4.3 Practice Complexity of Smart Cities

Slightly over one-third (34%) of the reviewed papers mainly raised issues around the challenges coming from the practice complexity of smart cities (Table 2.4).

Cities are a highly complex (meaning sophisticated, intricate, and complicated) system of systems; involving various economic, societal, environmental, governance, and technical systems and their sub-systems (Albeverio et al., 2007). Managing complexity (meaning analysing and optimising all involved systems and subsystems) in cities has always been a major challenge for urban policymakers, managers, and planners, and it requires a holistic approach that can comfortably deal with these entanglements (Batty, 2009). Throughout history, cities have always endured long periods of socioeconomic and environmental changes and challenges. Speculation prevails that the forthcoming changes in the age of the Anthropocene will be even greater than ever before (Derickson, 2018; Stewart et al., 2018). Moreover, as historical trends reveal, the complexity of urban systems will increase over time due to rapid urbanisation and population increases (Colding et al., 2020). Hence, a sustainable urban development pathway, to establish smart and sustainable cities, is the only way to support socioeconomic development and withstand environmental changes and challenges, while securing a healthy and prosperous environment for humans and non-humans (Yigitcanlar et al., 2015; Foth, 2017).

An investigation of the literature by Jepson and Edwards (2010) found the three most common development approaches that are directly associated with sustainable urban development. These are new urbanism, ecological city (eco-city), and smart growth. Up until the recent smart city movement, smart growth and new

Table 2.4 Practice complexity problem of smart cities, sorted by year of publication

Literature	Challenge	Critique
Ibrahim et al. (2018)	Complexity of sustainability being mostly ignored in smart city planning	Smart sustainable city transformation is a continuous, long-term, complex, and complicated process that requires radical changes to be introduced—to be planned effectively and efficiently, a thorough high-level overview roadmap of needed aspects to be considered during a transformation process is required
Lyons (2018)	Not delivering social and environmental sustainability due to misalignment of smart city development goals	Smart city notion comes with a caution, as large corporations are exerting significant influence in pursuit of goals that may not strongly align with those of urban planners concerned with social and environmental sustainability
Silva et al. (2018)	Smart city implementation challenges to deliver sustainability	Implementation of sustainable smart cities is challenged throughout design, implementation, and operation stages—cost, heterogeneity among devices, enormous data collection and analysis, information security, and sustainability are the key challenges
Yigitcanlar & Kamruzzaman (2018a)	Gaps between policy and practice limiting sustainability achievements in smart cities	Smart city policy does not generate clear sustainable urban development outcomes despite their claims
Zawieska & Pieriegud (2018)	Delivering sustainability being challenging as it requires major investment and behavioural change in smart cities	Meeting the greenhouse gas emission reduction targets set by the European Union is highly challenging for smart cities, as these cities are required to establish an in-depth transformation of their transport and energy sectors
Anthopoulos (2017)	Sustainability not being seen as a compulsory component of smart cities in the techno-centric approach	In the current techno-centric practice, for cities to be self-claimed as smart the fundamental requirements include them having: a smart agenda; open data; services or apps; smart infrastructure—where the critical sustainability issue is not seen as a requirement
Haarstad (2017)	Lack of enough attention to sustainability in the smartness agendas of cities	The smart city agenda is driven more by concerns for economic growth and innovation rather than by environmental sustainability per se as the smartness agenda is bound up with the aim of fostering innovation and competitiveness in the knowledge economy

(Continued)

Table 2.4 (Continued)

Literature	Challenge	Critique
Hara et al. (2016)	Lack of key performance evaluation in place in smart city initiatives to measure sustainability progress	Smart city practice fails to produce triple-bottom-line sustainability; additionally, development and application of comprehensive key performance indicators are also absent in the practice
Marsal-Llacuna et al. (2015)	Lack of holistic smart city sustainability progress and performance monitoring and assessment measures in place	Progress and performance of smart city practice are not monitored adequately, which might be a contributing factor for their under-performance in the sustainability domain
Monfaredzadeh & Berardi (2015)	Smart cities mostly being only concerned about pockets of the natural environment surrounded in the built environment open for human use and interaction	Sustainable city systems emphasise more environmental issues in comparison to smart city systems that focus more on people and living; smart city systems mainly focus on the virtual and human/built environment rather than the natural one
Yigitcanlar (2015)	Smart city practice failing to produce either concrete or promising sustainable urban development outcomes	Smart city practice encounters major challenges in the shaping up of the built environment that produces prosperous and sustainable urban futures for all citizens
Yigitcanlar & Lee (2014)	Failure of the smart city practice is not only limited to sustainable outcomes in the environmental but also economic, societal, and governance areas	Smart city practice has failed to produce its promised sustainable development outcomes, not only in built and natural environmental areas but also economic, societal, and governance domains

urbanism were relatively mainstream, particularly in North America. This was mainly due to the integration of these two approaches into the planning strategies of some North American cities. The eco-city model has been less influential in many parts of the world, particularly in Europe, Oceania, and South East Asia (Jepson & Edwards, 2010).

With the rise of the smart city notion, cities that adopt the abovementioned three development approaches started to embrace technology as part of the solution or as the pivotal driver of development (Silva et al., 2017, 2020). However, the confusion about what a smart city is generates an issue, particularly for urban policymakers. Likewise, such confusion is evident in the academic literature as well. A possible reason for that might be the word "smart" (as there are many ways of perceiving the smartness of a city) (Lara et al., 2016). Some scholars perceive "smart" in the smart city the same as in "smart growth", that is, a development that provides an opportunity to implement some of the historic concerns of urban sustainability advocates (Alexander & Tomalty, 2002). Others interpret "smart" to mean digital or intelligent cities (Komninos, 2013; Kitchin, 2014) that connect innovation strategies and digital growth strategies for establishing smart environments and sustainable economic growth (Komninos, 2016). While the former is more environmentally sound, the latter is fiscally more prudent, at least in the short term.

A recent empirical study by Yigitcanlar and Kamruzzaman (2018) revealed that there is little evidence that sustainability targets are achieved in cities that are recognised as or claim to be smart cities. Despite the clear empirical evidence, research by Noy and Givoni (2018) found that the prevalent belief amongst technology firms is still that smart technology developments alone, for example, connected and autonomous driving technologies, can lead to sustainability, especially in the transport area. Noy and Givoni (2018) raised this issue as a real concern for the planning and development of smart cities. Unfortunately, complexities involved in developing truly smart cities are pushing policymakers to opt for short-term wins by implementing blackbox technology solutions promoted by technology companies.

The practice complexity of smart cities is evident (Colding et al., 2020). Although applying "complexity science" to achieve urban sustainability is, theoretically, plausible (UNU-IAS, 2017); most urban administrators ignore (or are not even aware of) the smart city complexities and challenges in the policy- and plan-making processes and during their implementation stages (Ibrahim et al., 2018). Some urban administrators are mindful and somehow incorporate strong policies and actions to combat unsustainable development (Fernandez-Anez et al., 2018). However, in many cases, either strong policies and plans are not implemented in practice (Silva et al., 2018a), or there are no adequate performance assessment measures to evaluate the outcomes, so they cannot be improved easily (Marsal-Llacuna et al., 2015; Hara et al., 2016).

Furthermore, as stated by Colding et al. (2020, p. 7), "whether the [smart city] model is a new panacea for urban sustainability or instead opens up for a future of unmanageable complexity is an open question that deserves more debate". Keeping this view in mind, our review of the literature in this category raises another important question: *Will the future city models be able to manage the currently unmanageable complexity of our cities?*

2.4.4 Ad-hoc Conceptualisation of Smart Cities

Slightly over one-third (34%) of the reviewed papers raised the issue of a lack of sound smart city conceptualisations (Table 2.5).

The lack of progress towards smart and sustainable cities is not only limited to the issues around heavy technocentricity and practice complexity of smart cities.

Table 2.5 Ad-hoc conceptualisation problem of smart cities, sorted by year of publication

Literature	Challenge	Critique
Balducci & Ferrara (2018)	Sustainability being seen only as an ancillary issue to smart cities	Environmental dimension, in the smart city practice, is often not explicitly treated but interrelated to the others as a strategic component to promote quality of life and urban sustainability
Bibri (2018a)	No systems thinking placed in smart city to address environmental sustainability challenges	Smart city does not adopt systems thinking perspective to provide novel solutions for addressing environmental and socioeconomic challenges pertaining to sustainability
Chang et al. (2018)	Incapability of delivering sustainability as smart city being highly ad-hoc in nature	Smart city practice is ad-hoc in nature and lacks a knowledge-based urban development perspective to generate desired sustainable outcomes
Colding et al. (2020)	Misconception of the sustainability concept in the smart city context	Smart cities are often uncritically launched as a sustainable way of developing cities—instead of a new panacea for urban sustainability, the smart city model could open up a future of unmanageable complexity
Cugurullo (2018)	Fragmented nature and conceptualisation of smart cities hampering sustainability achievements in these cities	Smart city is a fragmented city made of disconnected and often incongruous pieces of urban fabric with serious limitations in addressing issues of sustainability
Martin et al. (2018)	Variance between what a smart city should be and its current sustainable development practice generates inconsistencies	There are tensions between smart cities and goals of sustainable urban development—reinforcing neoliberal economic growth; focusing on affluent populations; disempowering citizens; neglecting environmental protection; failing to challenge consumerist cultures
Yigitcanlar et al. (2018a)	Sustainability being perceived only ancillary to a smart city due to lack of a widely accepted holistic conceptualisation	Sustainable urban development principles are not necessarily placed at the heart of current smart city practice
Ahvenniemi et al. (2017)	Lack of a widely accepted conceptualisation of smart and sustainable cities	The current large gap between smart city and sustainable city frameworks suggest that there is a need for developing smart city frameworks further or re-defining or re-conceptualising the smart city concept

Table 2.5 (Continued)

Literature	Challenge	Critique
Bibri & Krogstie (2017a)	Smart cities failing to deliver sustainability due to various reasons mainly driven from misconceptualisation	Smart city practice has shortcomings, difficulties, uncertainties, paradoxes, and fallacies in relation to sustainable urban form
Bibri & Krogstie (2017b)	Smart cities lack holistic approaches, subsequently they fail to address the sustainability challenge	Smart city practice needs to be reoriented in a more environmentally sustainable direction, as it cannot, as currently practiced, solve the complex environmental problems placed in the agenda of smart sustainable cities as a holistic approach to urban development
Colding & Barthel (2017)	Misconceptualised smart city practice may contribute to the deterioration of human and nature relations	The practice of smart city solutions may affect the autonomy of urban governance, personal integrity, and how it may affect the resilience of infrastructures that provide inhabitants with basic needs, such as food, energy, and water security; moreover, smart city developments may change human–nature relations
Mundoli et al. (2017)	Poor conceptualisation and delivery of urban ecosystem approach in smart cities	Smart is a catchy prefix for cities, but sustainability and equity are enduring qualities—developing both ecologically and socio-culturally smart cities requires reconceptualisation of the notion to move towards a multi-faceted use-value of urban ecosystems

Martin et al. (2018) highlight a much more prominent issue: the clear tension between aspirations of smart cities and goals of sustainable urban development. These goals include the 17 Sustainable Development Goals (SDGs)—identified by the United Nations (UN) in 2015 as part of the 2030 Agenda—to shape international efforts to promote a sustainable, peaceful, and equitable world. Figure 2.3 lists the SDGs, where each goal is also accompanied by a set of more specific targets with indicators to measure progress (see www.un.org/sustainabledevelopm ent). Besides these goals being critical for smart cities, the Intergovernmental Panel on Climate Change's recent report also underlines the prominent role of sustainable development for the planet and people (IPCC, 2018, p. 45): "The global transformation that would be needed to limit warming to 1.5°C requires enabling conditions that reflect the links, synergies and trade-offs between mitigation, adaptation and sustainable development."

Consistent with this view, the smart city practice reinforces neoliberal economic growth, focuses on affluent populations, disempowers citizens, neglects

Figure 2.3 Sustainable development goals (www.un.org/sustainabledevelopment).

environmental protection, and fails to challenge or provide real alternatives to the prevailing consumerist culture. One of the reasons for this limitation is that as smart cities evolved from various concepts originating from academia, governments, global corporations, and international organisations, there has been no agreement whatsoever on what smart cities precisely are (Letaifa, 2015).

The vision of smart cities, today, has been forcefully introduced into urban policies in many countries (Vanola, 2014). While in theory smart is seen as inclusive of the sustainability goals, in practice, the smart and sustainable notions have often been used merely as window-dressing or reduced to ancillary aspects (Serbanica & Constantin, 2017; Balducci & Ferrara, 2018). Heavy technocentrism has, in many countries, distorted what a smart city should look like. In smart city projects, rather than producing new visions for the "good city", the focus has shifted to mainly generating technocentric solutions for cities. This shift, so far, has proved at best to be not effective (Herrschel, 2013; Stratigea et al., 2017) and at worst to be producing dystopian city futures (Vanolo, 2016; Mattern, 2017).

This is due to the challenges caused by the artificial smart vs. sustainable dichotomy. These challenges were highlighted in the reviewed literature. They include short-termism vs. long-term gains, elitist vs. inclusive, profit-driven vs. equilibrium-driven, business-friendly vs. environmentally friendly, carbon economy vs. climate-neutral economy, materialism vs. dematerialism, and so on. Addressing these challenges through sound smart city conceptualisation (e.g., Yigitcanlar et al., 2018a) and urban policy and discourse will help in formulating the right direction to establish smart and sustainable cities. This can also lead to the formation of the long-awaited model cities that are truly smart, sustainable, and inclusive.

The ad-hoc smart city conceptualisation issue is heavily criticised in the reviewed literature. For instance, Bibri (2018a) pointed out the reason for smart cities not being able to address environmental and socioeconomic challenges pertaining to sustainability is due to an absence of systems-thinking. Smart city frameworks not adopting a knowledge-based urban development perspective to generate desired sustainable outcomes is also raised as a conceptualisation weakness (Chang et al., 2018). Likewise, Ahvenniemi et al. (2017) emphasised the need for developing smart city frameworks further by re-defining and re-conceptualising the concept. Furthermore, Mundoli et al. (2017) argued that smart should be more than a catchy prefix for cities like the "smart phone", hence, reconceptualisation of the smart city notion to move towards a multi-faceted use-value of urban ecosystems is an urgent necessity.

In addition to the emerging comprehensive views on smart city conceptualisa-tion as discussed in Section 2.1, it is also useful to highlight the meta-principles as stated by Ramaswami et al. (2016, p. 940) that "focus attention on the [higher-order] systems-level decisions that society faces to transition toward a smart, sustainable, and healthy urban future". Advocated by Ramaswami et al. (2016, p. 941), these meta-principles for developing smart, sustainable, and healthy cities include to:

(a) Focus on providing and innovating basic infrastructure for all; (b) Pursue dynamic multisector and multi-scalar urban health improvements, with attention to inequities; (c) Concentrate on urban form and multisector syner-gies for resource efficiency; (d) Recognise diverse strategies for resource effi-ciency in different city types; (e) Integrate high and vernacular technologies; (f) Apply transboundary systems analysis to inform decisions about localised versus larger-scale infrastructure; (g) Recognise coevolution of infrastructures and institutions; (h) Create capacity and transparent infrastructure governance across sectors and scales.

Lastly, the review of the literature in this category, particularly in light of the abovementioned smart and sustainable city meta-principles, also brings the following important question to mind: *Are self-claimed comprehensive smart city conceptualisations comprehensive enough to be able to tackle the unsustainable development problems of our cities?*

2.5 Findings and Discussion

This chapter has studied whether cities can become smart without actually being sus-tainable, and the answer based on our review is clear: No, they cannot. The reviewed 35 literature pieces highlighted the limitations of the prevailing understanding on what a smart city is and what enables its successful and sustainable development. This creates a major urban policy dilemma for urban policymakers; adopting an ad-hoc technology solution approach to generate palliative remedies vs. a holistic sustainable development approach to generate long-lasting solutions. Moreover, it is still not clear what smart cities can offer as solutions to the global environmental challenges. Norman (2018, p. 2) advocates that

a key driver for smarter cities is planning for the impacts of climate change and the expected increase in urban heat island effects and extreme events (droughts, floods and coastal storms). In this context, the policy of smart cities has the potential to make a major contribution.

The smart city practice, however, should not be predominantly relying on technology as a saviour to achieve sustainable outcomes. Technology solutions are needed to support the systems and processes that allow the city to achieve sustainable urban development. Nonetheless, urban smartness is beyond technological smartness. The smartness of urban leaders, policymakers, technocrats, and residents along with the smartness of policies developed and actions put into practice matter more.

The findings of our systematic literature review provide strong evidence to justify this study's hypothesis: Cities *cannot* be truly smart without being sustainable. In line with Yigitcanlar et al. (2018a), our study finds that the development of smart and sustainable cities can only be accomplished through inclusive and sustainable growth using a healthy mixture of smart people, policies, and technologies. In terms of urban policy, the findings are in line with Jepson and Edwards' (2010, p. 420) suggestion:

policies that encourage the replacement of non-renewable energy and other resources, the protection of open space (particularly in relation to biological and natural processes, assets and services), the use of "appropriate" technologies, the reduction and natural assimilation of waste, and local economic and functional self-reliance

are required to be in place for a healthy smart and sustainable city transformation (see Joss, 2015). Beyond these, a good urban policy should also include deliberate considerations and actions on the issues of accessibility, mobility, education, health, quality of life, and overall urban services and operations. Furthermore, the chapter argues, in line with Norman (2018, p. 2), that "the concurrent global trends of urbanisation and climate change will require very smart and innovative solutions. However, it will take a lot more than a smart cities agenda to provide a more sustainable urban future" for our cities and societies.

An urban paradigm worth highlighting, which only recently started to emerge in the smart city discourse and appears to be promising to bring about genuinely smart and sustainable cities, is the *post-anthropocentric city* or *more-than-human city* (Abrams, 1996; Haraway, 2016; Franklin, 2017; Heitlinger et al., 2018; Foth, 2017; Foth & Caldwell, 2018; Yigitcanlar et al., 2019a). While this systematic review found a notable emphasis in the smart city discourse calling for participation and engagement, which aim to increase the involvement of diverse and often marginalised citizens, a human-centred approach to smart cities comes with its own set of problems. Drawing attention to the fallacy of human exceptionalism and anthropocentrism, some scholars have started to move away from the predominant view that urban space is separate from nature and designed primarily for humans and just humans (DiSalvo & Lukens, 2011; Forlano, 2016, 2017; Luusua et al., 2017). Anderson (2003) calls for cities to be problematised, where people, in entering distinctively non-natural relations (political, legal, and so on) realise their full humanity among a set of relations that are absent in the wholly natural lives of other living things. Informed by science and technology studies, critical geography, urban planning, and interaction design, these authors call for a "more-than-human" approach to smart cities (involving biophilia, mutualism, and cohabitation) (Foth, 2017; Houston et al., 2017; Smith et al., 2017; Heitlinger et al., 2018). By considering new ways to appreciate and cater for our broader ecological entanglements with plants, animals, and the environment at large, a more-than-human perspective to the design and development of smart cities appears highly imperative to pursue in conjunction with a circular economic model.

The study also generated a number of insights along with new research questions about potential opportunities with respect to identified challenges.

Firstly, to address the heavy technocentricity of smart cities, it is important for smart cities to involve a more specific approach based on the use of technology that complements other planning models, such as smart growth, new urbanism, and strategic urban planning. Besides, as De Wijs et al. (2016, p. 424) claim, "technologies are not yet completely developed, and concerns about the 'loss' of personal privacy are holding back the widespread and advanced use of data supplied technologies". Moreover, technology does not necessarily need to be new to be effective, and particularly in the global south context, the most effective solutions often involve retrofitting as well as innovative uses of existing and relatively inexpensive technology. In this instance the question of "what the appropriate technologies and the right amount of technology to bring sustainability to our cities are" is critical to address.

Secondly, to address the practice complexity of smart cities, it is important to engage complexity science offerings to the urban policymaking process. However, at the same time the trends of "rapid population growth, growth of consumption of natural resources, vigorous industrialisation, urbanisation, mobilisation, globalisation, agricultural intensification and excessive consumption-driven lifestyles" are the main contributors to the increasing complexity that need to be urgently resolved. In this instance the question of "whether the future city models will be able to manage the currently unmanageable complexity of our cities" is vital to answer.

Thirdly, to address the ad-hoc conceptualisation of smart cities, it is important to establish a commonly agreed definition and comprehensive conceptualisation of smart cities. However, the focus perhaps needs to be beyond the smart city concept. We need to start thinking of and conceptualising the "post-anthropocentric city" that will bring genuine sustainability and planetary health expectations and aspirations for all (humans and non-humans). In this instance the question of "whether self-claimed comprehensive smart city conceptualisations are comprehensive enough to be able to tackle the unsustainable development problems of our cities" is important to address.

Finally, in addition to the above raised ones, the following questions are also worth concentrating on (Yigitcanlar et al., 2019a): *Will urban scholars, planners, designers and activists be able to convince urban policymakers and the general public of the need for a post-anthropocentric urban turnaround? If yes, how will the actors (public, private, and academic sectors jointly along with communities) pave the way for post-anthropocentric cities and more-than-human futures?*

The special report from the Intergovernmental Panel on Climate Change has provided clear scientific evidence that we have to start creating our low-carbon future today without any further delay—we have only 12 years left to act on climate change (IPCC, 2018). In theory, the smart and sustainable city poses an opportunity to create such a future. In practice this can be achieved only by successfully linking the two school of thoughts—i.e., technocentric and envirocentric views—and creating a uniformed post-anthropocentric urbanism view. Nevertheless, in the transformation journey of our cities towards smart and sustainable ones, the Theory of Change (Ibrahim et al., 2017) and Ecological Human Settlement Theory could pave the way.

The systematic review and critique of work on smart and sustainable cities reported in this chapter provide a useful reference for scholars and practitioners in related research communities and the necessary material to inform urban administrators, policymakers, and planners on the major challenges in developing smart and sustainable cities. These challenges include, but are not limited to, the inability of the policies to: (a) abstain from the heavy technocentrism obsession, due to the aggressive promotion of technology solutions by the industry; (b) tackle the core and long-term problems, including the sustainability issue, adequately, due to the complexities involved in the urban planning, development, and management practices; and (c) achieve desired planning and practice outcomes, due to the lack of comprehensive conceptualisations (and frameworks) that uncovers the big picture view and brings together the essential elements (e.g., theories, concepts, domains, approaches) that matter most.

2.6 Conclusion

The study at hand addressed the research question of "whether cities can become smart without actually being sustainable" by investigating the links between the smart city and urban sustainability literatures. The results pointed out an expectation in the reviewed academic literature for cities to become sustainable first to be considered truly smart. The study identified three major weaknesses or challenges of smart cities in delivering sustainable outcomes. These are heavy technocentricity, practice complexity, and ad-hoc conceptualisation of smart cities.

This chapter contributes to the efforts in not only raising awareness in the academic and policy circles for better configuration and application of the smart and sustainable city notion, but also advocates urban administrators, managers, and planners to adopt a post-anthropocentric approach in urban policy making for the development of truly smart and sustainable cities. The study, hence, can serve as a base to stimulate prospective research and further critical debates on this topic to promote the development of truly smart and sustainable cities and the post-anthropocentric urbanism practice.

In addition to the efforts of addressing the questions raised in this chapter, our prospective research will continue to focus on two fronts. The first will be conducted thorough conceptual explorations and empirical case investigations into smart and sustainable cities of today's Anthropocene. We have already started this work in media architecture (Foth & Caldwell, 2018). The second one will be reimagining the ideal 21st-century city to produce a consolidated understanding of the nature and key characteristics of the post-Anthropocene urbanism that will create the truly smart and sustainable cities—or more-than-human cities—of tomorrow. We have also started this work in conceptualising post-anthropocentric urbanism (Yigitcanlar et al., 2019, 2019a).

Acknowledgements

This chapter, with permission from the copyright holder, is a reproduced version of the following journal article: Yigitcanlar, T., Kamruzzaman, M., Foth, M., Sabatini-Marques, J., Costa, E., & Ioppolo, G. (2019). Can cities become smart without being sustainable? A systematic review of the literature. *Sustainable Cities and Society*, 45, 348–365.

References

Abrams, D. (1996). *The Spell of the Sensuous*. New York: Vintage Books.
Ahvenniemi, H., Huovila, A., Pinto-Seppä, I., Airaksinen, M. (2017). What are the differences between sustainable and smart cities? *Cities*, *60*, 234–245.
Albeverio, S., Andrey, D., Giordano, P., Vancheri, A. (2007). *The Dynamics of Complex Urban Systems*. Springer.
Alexander, D., Tomalty, R. (2002). Smart growth and sustainable development. *Local Environment*, *7*, 397–409.
Alizadeh, T. (2017). An investigation of IBM's smarter cites challenge. *Cities*, *63*, 70–80.
Alizadeh, T., Irajifar, L. (2018). Gold Coast smart city strategy. *International Journal of Knowledge-Based Development*, *9*, 153–173.
Alkandri, A., Alnasheet, M., Alshekhly, I. (2012). Smart cities: a survey. *Journal of Advanced Computer Science and Technology Research*, *2*(2), 79–90.
Almeida, V., Doneda, D., Costa, E. (2018). Humane smart cities. *IEEE Internet Computing*, *22*, 91–95.
Anderson, K. (2003). White natures. *Transactions of the Institute of British Geographers*, *28*, 422–441.
Angelidou, M. (2014). Smart city policies. *Cities*, *41*, 3–11.
Angelidou, M. (2015). Smart cities. *Cities*, *47*, 95–106.
Angelidou, M. (2017). The role of smart city characteristics in the plans of fifteen cities. *Journal of Urban Technology*, *24*, 3–28.

Anthopoulos, L. (2017). Smart utopia vs smart reality. *Cities, 63*, 128–148.

Arbolino, R., Carlucci, F., Cirà, A., Ioppolo, G., Yigitcanlar, T. (2017). Efficiency of the EU regulation on greenhouse gas emissions in Italy. *Ecological Indicators, 81*, 115–123.

Arbolino, R., Carlucci, F., Simone, L., Yigitcanlar, T., Ioppolo, G. (2018a). The policy diffusion of environmental performance in the European countries. *Ecological Indicators, 89*, 130–138.

Arbolino, R., Carlucci, F., Simone, L., Yigitcanlar, T., Ioppolo, G. (2018b). Towards a sustainable industrial ecology. *Journal of Cleaner Production, 178*, 220–236.

Arbolino, R., De Simone, L., Yigitcanlar, T., Ioppolo, G. (2018c). Facilitating solid biomass production planning. *Journal of Cleaner Production, 181*, 819–828.

Balducci, F., Ferrara, A. (2018). Using urban environmental policy data to understand the domains of smartness. *Ecological Indicators, 89*, 386–396.

Bask, A., Rajahonka, M. (2017). The role of environmental sustainability in the freight transport mode choice. *International Journal of Physical Distribution & Logistics Management, 47*, 560–602.

Batty M. (2009). Cities as complex systems. In Meyers, R. (Eds.) *Encyclopedia of Complexity and Systems Science* (pp. 1041–1071). New York: Springer.

Bélissent, J. (2010). Getting clever about smart cities: New opportunities require new business models. *Forrester Research, 3*, 1–31.

Bibri, S. (2018a). A foundational framework for smart sustainable city development. *Sustainable Cities and Society, 38*, 758–794.

Bibri, S. (2018b). *Smart Sustainable Cities of the Future*. Cham: Springer.

Bibri, S., Krogstie, J. (2017a). Smart sustainable cities of the future. *Sustainable Cities and Society, 31*, 183–212.

Bibri, S., Krogstie, J. (2017b). On the social shaping dimensions of smart sustainable cities. *Sustainable Cities and Society, 29*, 219–246.

Birkeland, J. (2002). *Design for Sustainability*. London: Routledge.

Birkeland, J. (2014). Positive development and assessment. *Smart and Sustainable Built Environment, 3*, 4–22.

Bonato, D., Orsini, R. (2018). Urban circular economy. In: Clark, W. (ed.) *Sustainable Cities and Communities Design Handbook*. Oxford: Butterworth-Heinemann.

Bowerman, B., Braverman, J., Taylor, J., Todosow, H., Von Wimmersperg, U. (2000, September). The vision of a smart city. In: *2nd International Life Extension Technology Workshop, Paris* (Vol. 28, No. 7).

Caprotti, F. (2014). Eco-urbanism and the eco-city, or, denying the right to the city? *Antipode, 46*, 1285–1303.

Caragliu, A., Del Bo, C., Nijkamp, P. (2011). Smart cities in Europe. *Journal of Urban Technology, 18*, 65–82.

Carrillo, J., Yigitcanlar, T., Garcia, B., Lonnqvist, A. (2014). *Knowledge and the City*. New York: Routledge.

Castelnovo, W., Misuraca, G., Savoldelli, A. (2016). Smart cities governance. *Social Science Computer Review, 34*, 724–739.

Chang, D., Sabatini-Marques, J., da Costa, E., Selig, P., Yigitcanlar, T. (2018). Knowledge-based, smart and sustainable cities. *Journal of Open Innovation, 4*, 5.

Colding, J., Barthel, S. (2017). An urban ecology critique on the "smart city" model. *Journal of Cleaner Production, 164*, 95–101.

Colding, J., Colding, M., Barthel, S. (2020). The smart city model: A new panacea for urban sustainability or unmanageable complexity?. *Environment and Planning B: Urban Analytics and City Science, 47*(1), 179–187.

Costa, E., Oliveira, A. (2017). Humane smart cities. In: Frodeman, R., Klein, J., Pacheco, R. (eds.) *The Oxford Handbook of Interdisciplinarity.* Oxford: Oxford University Press.

Cowley, R., Joss, S., Dayot, Y. (2018). The smart city and its publics. *Urban Research & Practice, 11*, 53–77.

Cugurullo, F. (2016). Urban eco-modernisation and the policy context of new eco-city projects. *Urban Studies, 53*, 2417–2433.

Cugurullo, F. (2018). Exposing smart cities and eco-cities. *Environment and Planning A, 50*, 73–92.

D'Auria, A., Tregua, M., Vallejo-Martos, M. (2018). Modern conceptions of cities as smart and sustainable and their commonalities. *Sustainability, 10.* 2642.

Dall'O, G., Bruni, E., Panza, A., Sarto, L., Khayatian, F. (2017). Evaluation of cities' smartness by means of indicators for small and medium cities and communities. *Sustainable Cities and Society, 34*, 193–202.

De Jong, M., Joss, S., Schraven, D., Zhan, C., Weijnen, M. (2015). Sustainable–smart–resilient–low carbon–eco–knowledge cities. *Journal of Cleaner Production, 109*, 25–38.

De Wijs, L., Witte, P., Geertman, S. (2016). How smart is smart? *Innovation, 29*, 424–441.

Deakin, M., Reid, A. (2018). Smart cities. *Journal of Cleaner Production, 173*, 39–48.

Derickson, K. (2018). Urban geography III. *Progress in Human Geography, 42*, 425–435.

Didsbury, H. (2004). *Thinking Creatively in Turbulent Times.* Bethesda: World Future Society.

DiSalvo, C., Lukens, J. (2011). Nonanthropocentrism and the non-human in design. In Foth, M., Forlano, L., Satchell, C., Gibbs, M., Donath, J. (ed.) *From Social Butterfly to Engaged Citizen Urban Informatics, Social Media, Ubiquitous Computing, and Mobile Technology to Support Citizen Engagement.* Cambridge: MIT Press.

Dizdaroglu, D., Yigitcanlar, T. (2014). A parcel-scale assessment tool to measure sustainability through urban ecosystem components. *Ecological Indicators, 41*, 115–130.

Dizdaroglu, D., Yigitcanlar, T. (2016). Integrating urban ecosystem sustainability assessment into policy-making. *Journal of Environmental Planning and Management, 59*, 1982–2006.

Dizdaroglu, D., Yigitcanlar, T., Dawes, L. (2012). A micro-level indexing model for assessing urban ecosystem sustainability. *Smart and Sustainable Built Environment, 1*, 291–315.

Downs, A. (2005). Smart growth. *Journal of the American Planning Association, 71*, 367–378.

Dur, F., Yigitcanlar, T. (2015). Assessing land-use and transport integration via a spatial composite indexing model. *International Journal of Environmental Science and Technology, 12*, 803–816.

Dur, F., Yigitcanlar, T., Bunker, J. (2014). A spatial-indexing model for measuring neighbourhood-level land-use and transport integration. *Environment and Planning B, 41*, 792–812.

Eger, J. M. (2009). Smart growth, smart cities, and the crisis at the pump a worldwide phenomenon. *I-WAYS-The Journal of E-Government Policy and Regulation, 32*(1), 47–53.

Epstein, M., Buhovac, A. (2014). *Making Sustainability Work.* San Francisco: Berrett-Koehler.

EU (2014). *Mapping Smart Cities in the EU.* Brussels: European Union.

Fernandez-Anez, V., Fernández-Güell, J., Giffinger, R. (2018). Smart city implementation and discourses. *Cities, 78,* 4–16.

Firnkorn, J., Müller, M. (2015). Free-floating electric carsharing-fleets in smart cities. *Environmental Science & Policy, 45,* 30–40.

Forlano, L. (2016). Decentering the human in the design of collaborative cities. *Design Issues, 32,* 42–54.

Forlano, L. (2017). Posthumanism and design. *Journal of Design, Economics, and Innovation, 3,* 16–29.Foth, M. (2017). The next urban paradigm. *IT-Information Technology, 59,* 259–262.

Foth, M. (2018). Participatory urban informatics. *Smart and Sustainable Built Environment, 7,* 4–19.

Foth, M., Brynskov, M., Ojala, T. (2015). *Citizen's Right to the Digital City* Singapore: Springer.

Foth, M., Caldwell, G. (2018). More-than-human media architecture. In: *Proceedings of the Media Architecture Biennale.*

Franklin, A. (2017). The more-than-human city. *The Sociological Review, 65,* 202–217.

Fu, Y., Zhang, X. (2017). Trajectory of urban sustainability concepts. *Cities, 60,* 113–123.

Garau, C., Masala, F., Pinna, F. (2016). Cagliari and smart urban mobility. *Cities, 56,* 35–46.

Giffinger, R., Fertner, C., Kramar, H., Kalasek, R., Pichler-Milanović, N., Meijers, E. (2007). *Smart Cities.* Vienna: Vienna University of Technology.

González, J. A., Rossi, A. (2011). New trends for smart cities, open innovation mechanism in smart cities. *European Commission with the ICT Policy Support Programme, 270896.*

Goodland, R. (1995). The concept of environmental sustainability. *Annual Review of Ecology and Systematics, 26,* 1–24.

Goonetilleke, A., Yigitcanlar, T., Ayoko, G., Egodawatta, P. (2014). *Sustainable Urban Water Environment.* Cheltenham: Edward Elgar.

Haarstad, H. (2017). Constructing the sustainable city. *Journal of Environmental Policy & Planning, 19,* 423–437.

Hall, R. E., Bowerman, B., Braverman, J., Taylor, J., Todosow, H., Von Wimmersperg, U. (2000). *The Vision of a Smart City* (No. BNL-67902; 04042). Brookhaven National Lab.(BNL), Upton, NY (United States).

Han, H., Hawken, S. (2018). Innovation and identity in next-generation smart cities. *City, Culture and Society, 12,* 1–4.

Hara, M., Nagao, T., Hannoe, S., Nakamura, J. (2016). New key performance indicators for a smart sustainable city. *Sustainability, 8,* 206.

Haraway, D. (2016). *Staying with the Trouble.* Durham: Duke University Press.

Heitlinger, S., Foth, M., Clarke, R., DiSalvo, C., Light, A., Forlano, L. (2018). Avoiding ecocidal smart cities. In: *Proceedings of the 15th Participatory Design Conference,* Vol. 2. ACM, New York.

Heo, T., Kim, K., Kim, H., Lee, C., Ryu, J., Leem, Y., Jun, J., Pyo, C., Ypp, S., Ko, J. (2014). Escaping from ancient Rome. *Transactions on Emerging Telecommunications Technologies, 25,* 109–119.

Hernández-Muñoz, J. M., Vercher, J. B., Muñoz, L., Galache, J. A., Presser, M., Gómez, L. A. H., Pettersson, J. (2011, May). Smart cities at the forefront of the future internet. In: *Future Internet Assembly* (pp. 447–462).

Herrschel, T. (2013). Competitiveness and sustainability. *Urban Studies, 50,* 2332–2348.

Hollands, R. (2008). Will the real smart city stand up. *City, 12,* 302–320.

Houston, D., Hillier, J., MacCallum, D., Steele, W., Byrne, J. (2017). Make kin, not cities! *Planning Theory, 17*, 190–212.

Ibrahim, M., Adams, C., El-Zaart, A. (2015). Paving the way to smart sustainable cities. *Journal of Information Systems and Technology Management, 12*, 559–576.

Ibrahim, M., El-Zaart, A., Adams, C. (2017). Theory of change for the transformation towards smart sustainable cities. In: *IEEE Sensors Networks Smart and Emerging Technologies Proceedings.*

Ibrahim, M., El-Zaart, A., Adams, C. (2018). Smart sustainable cities roadmap. *Sustainable Cities and Society, 37*, 530–540.

Ingwersen, P., Serrano-López, A. E. (2018). Smart city research 1990–2016. *Scientometrics, 117*, 1205–1236.

Ioppolo, G., Cucurachi, S., Salomone, R., Shi, L., Yigitcanlar, T. (2019). Integrating strategic environmental assessment and material flow accounting: a novel approach for moving towards sustainable urban futures. *The International Journal of Life Cycle Assessment, 24*, 1269–1284.

IPCC (2018). *Special Report on Global Warming of 1.5°C.* Incheon: Intergovernmental Panel on Climate Change (IPCC).

ITU (2014). *Smart Sustainable Cities Analysis of Definitions.* Geneva: ITU.

Jepson, E., Edwards, M. (2010). How possible is sustainable urban development? *Planning Practice & Research, 25*, 417–437.

Joss, S. (2015). *Sustainable Cities.* London: Palgrave Macmillan.

Kamruzzaman, M., Deilami, K., Yigitcanlar, T. (2018). Investigating the urban heat island effect of transit-oriented development in Brisbane. *Journal of Transport Geography, 66*, 116–124.

Kamruzzaman, M., Hine, J., Yigitcanlar, T. (2015). Investigating the link between carbon dioxide emissions and transport-related social exclusion in rural Northern Ireland. *International Journal of Environmental Science and Technology, 12*, 3463–3478.

Kim, K. (2018). *Low-Carbon Smart Cities.* Cham: Springer.

Kitchin, R. (2014). The real-time city? *GeoJournal, 79*, 1–14.

Komninos, N. (2013). *Intelligent Cities.* New York: Routledge.

Komninos, N. (2016). Smart environments and smart growth. *International Journal of Knowledge-Based Development, 7*, 240–263.

Komninos, N., Mora, L. (2018). Exploring the big picture of smart city research. *Scienze Regionali: Italian Journal of Regional Science, 1*, 15–38.

Kourtit, K., Nijkamp, P. (2012). Smart cities in the innovation age. *Innovation: The European Journal of Social Science Research, 25*, 93–95.

Kumar, H., Singh, M. K., Gupta, M. P., Madaan, J. (2020). Moving towards smart cities: Solutions that lead to the Smart City Transformation Framework. *Technological Forecasting and Social Change, 153*, 119281.

Kunzmann, K. (2014). Smart cities. *Crios, Critica Degli Ordinamenti Spaziali, 1/2014*, 9–20.

Lara, A., Costa E., Furlani, T., Yigitcanlar, T. (2016). Smartness that matters. *Journal of Open Innovation, 2*, 8.

Lazaroiu, G. C., Roscia, M. (2012). Definition methodology for the smart cities model. *Energy, 47*(1), 326–332.

Lee, J., Hancock, M., Hu, M. (2014). Towards an effective framework for building smart cities. *Technological Forecasting and Social Change, 89*, 80–99.

Lee, S., Yigitcanlar, T., Hoon, H., Taik, L. (2008). Ubiquitous urban infrastructure. *Innovation, 10*, 282–292.

Letaifa, S. (2015). How to strategize smart cities. *Journal of Business Research, 68,* 1414–1419.

Lewis, S., Maslin, M. (2015). A transparent framework for defining the Anthropocene epoch. *The Anthropocene Review, 2,* 128–146.

Lim, H., Taeihagh, A. (2018). Autonomous vehicles for smart and sustainable cities. *Energies, 11,* 1062.

Luusua, A., Ylipulli, J., Rönkkö, E. (2017). Nonanthropocentric design and smart cities in the Anthropocene. *Information Technology, 59,* 295–304.

Lyons, G. (2018). Getting smart about urban mobility. *Transportation Research Part A, 115,* 4–14.

Macke, J., Casagrande, R., Sarate, J., Silva, K. (2018). Smart city and quality of life. *Journal of Cleaner Production, 182,* 717–726.

Madon, S., Sahay, S. (2001). Urbanisation and megacities in developing countries. In: Avgerou, C., Walsham, G. (eds.) *Information Technology in Context.* Ashgate.

Mahbub, P., Goonetilleke, A., Ayoko, G., Egodawatta, P., Yigitcanlar, T. (2011). Analysis of build-up of heavy metals and volatile organics on urban roads in Gold Coast, Australia. *Water Science & Technology, 63,* 2077–2085.

Marsal-Llacuna, M. L. (2019). How to succeed in implementing (smart) sustainable urban Agendas: "keep cities smart, make communities intelligent". *Environment, Development and Sustainability, 21*(4), 1977–1998.

Marsal-Llacuna, M. L., Colomer-Llinàs, J., Meléndez-Frigola, J. (2015). Lessons in urban monitoring taken from sustainable and livable cities to better address the smart cities initiative. *Technological Forecasting and Social Change, 90,* 611–622.

Martin, C., Evans, J., Karvonen, A. (2018). Smart and sustainable? *Technological Forecasting and Social Change, 133,* 269–278.

Mattern, S. (2017). A city is not a computer. *Places Journal.* https://doi.org/10.22269/170207.

Meijer, A., Bolívar, M. (2016). Governing the smart city. *International Review of Administrative Sciences, 82,* 392–408.

Moldan, B., Janoušková, S., Hák, T. (2012). How to understand and measure environmental sustainability. *Ecological Indicators, 17,* 4–13.

Monfaredzadeh, T., Berardi, U. (2015). Beneath the smart city. *International Journal of Sustainable Building Technology and Urban Development, 6,* 140–156.

Moore, J. (2017). The capitalocene. *Journal of Peasant Studies, 44,* 594–630.

Mora, L., Bolici, R., Deakin, M. (2017). The first two decades of smart-city research. *Journal of Urban Technology, 24,* 3–27.

Mora, L., Deakin, M., Reid, A. (2019). Strategic principles for smart city development: A multiple case study analysis of European best practices. *Technological Forecasting and Social Change, 142,* 70–97.

Morse, S. (2014). *Smart Communities.* San Francisco: Wiley & Sons.

Mundoli, S., Unnikrishnan, H., Nagendra, H. (2017). The "sustainable" in smart cities. *Decision, 44,* 103–120.

Myeong, S., Jung, Y., Lee, E. (2018). A study on determinant factors in smart city development. *Sustainability, 10,* 1–17.

Nam, T., Pardo, T. A. (2011, June). Conceptualizing smart city with dimensions of technology, people, and institutions. In *Proceedings of the 12th Annual International Digital Government Research Conference: Digital Government Innovation in Challenging Times* (pp. 282–291).

Neirotti, P., De Marco, A., Cagliano, A., Mangano, G., Scorrano, F. (2014). Current trends in smart city initiatives. *Cities, 38*, 25–36.

Niaros, V. (2016). Introducing a taxonomy of the smart city. *Communication, Capitalism & Critique, 14*, 51–61.

Norman, B. (2018). Are autonomous cities our urban future? *Nature Communications, 9*, 2111.

Noy, K., Givoni, M. (2018). Is 'smart mobility' sustainable? *Sustainability, 10*, 422.

Odendaal, N. (2003). Information and communication technology and local governance: Understanding the difference between cities in developed and emerging economies. *Computers, Environment and Urban Systems, 27*(6), 585–607.

Paroutis, S., Bennett, M., Heracleous, L. (2014). A strategic view on smart city technology. *Technological Forecasting and Social Change, 89*, 262–272.

Partridge, H. L. (2004). Developing a human perspective to the digital divide in the 'smart city'. In: *Australian Library and Information Association Biennial Conference.*

Paskaleva, K. A. (2009). Enabling the smart city: The progress of city e-governance in Europe. *International Journal of Innovation and Regional Development, 1*(4), 405–422.

Perveen, S., Kamruzzaman, M., Yigitcanlar, T. (2017a). Developing policy scenarios for sustainable urban growth management. *Sustainability, 9*, 1787.

Perveen, S., Kamruzzaman, M., Yigitcanlar, T. (2019). What to assess to model the transport impacts of urban growth? A Delphi approach to examine the space–time suitability of transport indicators. *International Journal of Sustainable Transportation, 13*(8), 597–613.

Perveen, S., Yigitcanlar, T., Kamruzzaman, M., Hayes, J. (2017b). Evaluating transport externalities of urban growth. *International Journal of Environmental Science and Technology, 14*, 663–678.

Piro, G., Cianci, I., Grieco, L. A., Boggia, G., Camarda, P. (2014). Information centric services in smart cities. *Journal of Systems and Software, 88*, 169–188.

Praharaj, S., Han, J., Hawken, S. (2018). Urban innovation through policy integration. *City, Culture and Society, 12*, 35–43.

Ramaswami, A., Russell, A., Culligan, P., Sharma, K., Kumar, E. (2016). Meta-principles for developing smart, sustainable, and healthy cities. *Science, 352*, 940–943.

Rathore, M., Ahmad, A., Paul, A., Rho, S. (2016). Urban planning and building smart cities based on the internet of things using big data analytics. *Computer Networks, 101*, 63–80.

Rice, J., Martin, N. (2020). Smart infrastructure technologies: Crowdsourcing future development and benefits for Australian communities. *Technological Forecasting and Social Change, 153*, 119256.

Rios, P. (2008). *Creating "the smart city"*. Available at http://dspace.udmercy.edu:8080/dspace/bitstream/10429/20/ 1/2008_rios_smart.pdf.

Satyro, W., Sacomano, J., Contador, J., Telles, R. (2018). Planned obsolescence or planned resource depletion? *Journal of Cleaner Production, 195*, 744–752.

Schaffers, H., Komninos, N., Tsarchopoulos, P., Pallot, M., Trousse, B., Posio, E., ... Carter, D. (2012). Landscape and roadmap of future internet and smart cities. Accessed on 27 May 2018 from https://hal.inria.fr/hal-00769715/document.

Serbanica, C., Constantin, D. (2017). Sustainable cities in central and eastern European countries. *Habitat International, 68*, 55–63.

Silva, B. N., Khan, M., Han, K. (2017). Big data analytics embedded smart city architecture for performance enhancement. *Wireless Communications and Mobile Computing, 9429676*, 1–12.

Silva, B. N., Khan, M., Han, K. (2018a). Towards sustainable smart cities: A review of trends, architectures, components, and open challenges in smart cities. *Sustainable Cities and Society, 38*, 697–713.

Silva, B. N., Khan, M., Han, K. (2018b). Internet of things. *IETE Technical Review, 35*, 205–220.

Silva, B. N., Khan, M., Han, K. (2020). Integration of Big Data analytics embedded smart city architecture with RESTful web of things for efficient service provision and energy management. *Future Generation Computer Systems, 107*, 975–987.

Smith, N., Bardzell, S., Bardzell, J. (2017). Designing for cohabitation. In: *Proceedings of the 2017 CHI Conference on Human Factors in Computing Systems*.

Söderström, O., Paasche, T., Klauser, F. (2014). Smart cities as corporate storytelling. *City, 18*, 307–320.

Stewart, I., Kennedy, C., Facchini, A., Mele, R. (2018). The electric city as a solution to sustainable urban development. *Journal of Urban Technology, 25*, 3–20.

Stratigea, A., Leka, A., Panagiotopoulou, M. (2017). In search of indicators for assessing smart and sustainable cities and communities' performance. *International Journal of E-Planning Research, 6*, 43–73.

Taamallah, A., Khemaja, M., Faiz, S. (2017). Strategy ontology construction and learning. *International Journal of Knowledge-Based Development, 8*, 206–228.

Teriman, S., Yigitcanlar, T., Mayere, S. (2009). Urban sustainability and growth management in South-East Asian city-regions. *Planning Malaysia Journal, 7*, 47–68.

Townsend, A. (2013). *Smart Cities*. New York: WW Norton.

Trindade, E., Hinnig, M.P., da Costa, E., Marques, J., Bastos, R., Yigitcanlar, T. (2017). Sustainable development of smart cities. *Journal of Open Innovation, 3*, 11.

UNU-IAS (2017). *Sustainable Smart Cities*. Tokyo: United Nations University.

van den Buuse, D., Kolk, A. (2019). An exploration of smart city approaches by international ICT firms. *Technological Forecasting and Social Change, 142*, 220–234.

Vanolo, A. (2014). Smartmentality. *Urban Studies, 51*, 883–898.

Vanolo, A. (2016). Is there anybody out there? *Futures, 82*, 26–36.

Wachsmuth, D., Angelo, H. (2018). Green and gray. *Annals of the American Association of Geographers, 108*, 1038–1056.

Wiig, A. (2015). IBM's smart city as techno-utopian policy mobility. *City, 19*, 258–273.

Wu, Y., Zhang, W., Shen, J., Mo, Z., Peng, Y. (2018). Smart city with Chinese characteristics against the background of big data. *Journal of Cleaner Production, 173*, 60–66.

Yigitcanlar, T. (2009). Planning for smart urban ecosystems. *Theoretical and Empirical Researches in Urban Management, 4*, 5–21.

Yigitcanlar, T. (2015). Smart cities. *Australian Planner, 52*, 27–34.

Yigitcanlar, T. (2016). *Technology and the city*. New York: Routledge.

Yigitcanlar, T., Bulu, M. (2015). Dubaization of Istanbul. *Environment and Planning A, 47*, 89–107.

Yigitcanlar, T., Dizdaroglu, D. (2015). Ecological approaches in planning for sustainable cities. *Global Journal of Environmental Science and Management, 1*, 159–188.

Yigitcanlar, T., Dur, D., Dizdaroglu, D. (2015). Towards prosperous sustainable cities. *Habitat International, 45*, 36–46.

Yigitcanlar, T., Foth, M., Kamruzzaman, M. (2019). Towards post-anthropocentric cities: Reconceptualizing smart cities to evade urban ecocide. *Journal of Urban Technology, 26*(2), 147–152.

Yigitcanlar, T., Kamruzzaman, M. (2014). Investigating the interplay between transport, land use and the environment. *International Journal of Environmental Science and Technology, 11*, 2121–2132.

Yigitcanlar, T., Kamruzzaman, M., (2015). Planning, development and management of sustainable cities. *Sustainability, 7*, 14677–14688.

Yigitcanlar, T., Kamruzzaman, M. (2018). Does smart city policy lead to sustainability of cities? *Land Use Policy, 73*, 49–58.

Yigitcanlar, T., Kamruzzaman, M. (2019). Smart cities and mobility: Does the smartness of Australian cities lead to sustainable commuting patterns?. *Journal of Urban Technology, 26*(2), 21–46.

Yigitcanlar, T., Kamruzzaman, M., Buys, L., Ioppolo, G., Sabatini-Marques, J., Costa, E., Yun, J. (2018a). Understanding 'smart cities'. *Cities, 81,* 145–160.

Yigitcanlar, T., Kamruzzaman, M., Buys, L., Perveen, S. (2018b). *Smart Cities of the Sunshine State: Status of Queensland's Local Government Areas.* Accessed from https://eprints.qut.edu.au/118349.

Yigitcanlar, T., Lee, S. (2014). Korean ubiquitous-eco-city. *Technological Forecasting and Social Change, 89,* 100–114.

Yigitcanlar, T., Metaxiotis, K., Carrillo, F. (2012). *Building Prosperous Knowledge Cities.* Cheltenham: Edward Elgar.

Yigitcanlar, T., Teriman, S. (2015). Rethinking sustainable urban development. *International Journal of Environmental Science and Technology, 12*, 341–352.Yin, R. (1994). Discovering the future of the case study. *Evaluation Practice, 15,* 283–290.

Yigitcanlar, T., Kamruzzaman, M., Foth, M., Sabatini-Marques, J., Costa, E., Ioppolo, G. (2019a). Can cities become smart without being sustainable? A systematic review of the literature. *Sustainable Cities and Society, 45*, 348–365.

Yin, R. (2015). *Qualitative Research from Start to Finish.* London: Guilford.

Zawieska, J., Pieriegud, J. (2018). Smart city as a tool for sustainable mobility and transport decarbonisation. *Transport Policy, 63*, 39–50.

Zhao, J. (2011). *Towards Sustainable Cities in China: Analysis and Assessment of some Chinese Cities in 2008.* Springer Science & Business Media.

3   Transformation Readiness

3.1 Introduction

At present, over 55% of the world's 7.7 billion human population is housed in urban areas, where this figure is expected to increase to over 70% by the end of the century (Sotto et al., 2019). Many countries today have already exceeded this projected global urbanisation level—e.g., Australia with 86% (Zhang, 2016). These rapid population and urbanisation trends are not only accelerating global natural resource and environmental depletion, along with food, water, and energy insecurity, but they are also worsening socioeconomic inequity, and making our cities almost ungovernable (Yigitcanlar et al., 2020a).

During the last decade—to be precise since IBM's 2008 A Smarter Planet Agenda—as a solution to some of the urbanisation challenges, a new city blueprint or brand is proposed: so called the "smart city" (Söderström et al., 2014). Initially, a smart city was defined as a city that employs digital data and technology to create efficiencies for boosting economic development, enhancing quality of life, and improving the sustainability of the city (Mora et al., 2017).

With the increasing popularity of this city brand, city administrations across the globe have started to consider or develop various strategies and initiatives for a smart city transformation (Fernandez-Anez et al., 2018). Nonetheless, besides a limited number of best practices, many cities have either failed or experienced a financial roadblock due to the heavy technocentric view of this city brand (Yigitcanlar et al., 2019b). Subsequently, it was comprehended that digital data and technology are not the only key ingredients for the making of smart cities (Yigitcanlar et al., 2019a; Araral, 2020).

In fact, increased technological reliance could bring new policy challenges related to data management, privacy, security (Vandercruysse et al., 2020), and accessibility to digital technology and infrastructure (Yigitcanlar et al., 2020b). These could further complicate city governance where economic, social, and environmental challenges related to health care, employment, financial and resource management, air and water quality, social equity, housing (Bunders & Varró, 2019), and mobility (Butler et al., 2020) persist.

Most recently, a more holistic perspective to smart cities has begun to emerge, and these cities are conceptualised as "urban localities functioning as a robust

DOI: 10.1201/9781003403630-4

system of systems with sustainable practices—supported by community, technology and policy—to generate desired outcomes and futures for all humans and non-humans" (Yigitcanlar, 2021, p. 89). The study at hand adopts this smart city definition as this renewed perspective emphasises urban smartness not only in terms of technology, but also other key factors that determine the smart city transformation readiness (Yigitcanlar et al., 2020b). While this perspective provides endogenous city assets, community engagement, and good governance and policy as examples of factors complementing technology, it does not detail what the specific factors that make localities smart are.

Whilst there are some literature pieces offering insights into how to go beyond the technocentric smart city development (Desouza et al., 2019) or what the pathways to the making of prosperous smart cities are (Noori et al., 2020a), the factors affecting urban smartness are still an understudied area of research. Besides, there is limited empirical evidence in the literature on what the exact factors of urban smartness—a key indicator for smart city transformation readiness—are.

Although the use of information and communication technology (ICT) is classified as a requirement for transforming traditional cities into smarter ones, others highlight the necessity of taking into consideration other non-ICT-related factors throughout the transformation process. This includes proximity to major infrastructure, e.g., distance to international and domestic airports, seaports, and state capital city (Yigitcanlar et al., 2022), labour productivity (Richter et al., 2015), cultural diversity (Lombardi et al., 2012), remoteness value (Yigitcanlar & Kamruzzaman, 2019), population density (Susanti et al., 2016), and unemployment level (Ivars-Baidal et al., 2021). These indicators are classified by this study as independent variables, where smart city performance is the dependent variable.

To address this gap in the knowledge and literature, the study at hand conducts an empirical investigation that places Australian local government areas under the smart city microscope to statistically evaluate, through a multiple regression analysis, the key factors affecting their urban smartness levels—a proxy for smart city transformation readiness.

3.2 Literature Background

The literature on smart cities is vast (Batty et al., 2012; Albino et al., 2015; Silva et al., 2018). To date, scholars have tackled various issues when it comes to planning (Batty, 2013; Rathore et al., 2016), designing (Heo et al., 2014; Barns, 2018; Cledou et al., 2018), and governing (Castelnovo et al., 2016) smart cities. Much of this work has focused on deploying a wide assortment of ICTs to capture, analyse, visualise, and act on data from a wide assortment of entities that traverse and are fixed within our cities (Hashem et al., 2016; Allam & Dhunny, 2019).

There has also been work on devising smarter policies to encourage citizen engagement (Desouza & Bhagwatwar, 2012), co-creation of innovation (Desouza & Bhagwatwar, 2014; Cho et al., 2021), and more collaborative and transparent governance (Meijer & Bolívar, 2016; Brauneis & Goodman, 2018). Making a city smarter requires careful investment considerations, where multiple competing demands and scarce resources compete for attention. Research to date has uncovered varying trajectories for cities (and communities), when embarking on smart city projects (Desouza et al., 2021).

While the research on smart cities continues to grow, there is limited work to date on how to measure the smartness of a city. For instance, Anthopoulos et al. (2015) compared various smart city modelling and benchmarking tools. Carli et al. (2013) developed a conceptual framework on smart city performance indicators that focused on two dimensions. The first dimension contains two components that represent various key elements of a city's functioning and health. One consisting of the city's physical infrastructure, urban assets, and environmental conditions, while the other incorporates citizen satisfaction and wellbeing. The second dimension is made up of three layers that signify how data are collected to monitor and evaluate the components in the first dimension. The three layers are traditional tools, data sensing and mining of the physical infrastructure, and data sensing and mining tools of social infrastructure.

Similarly, Priano and Guerra (2014) compared various approaches to measure a city's smartness and proposed a framework that has three levels. The first level focuses on identifying the problem, solution, and indicators that a smart city project is aimed at. The second level outlines the scope of the smart city project (e.g., street, district, city-wide). The third level is an assessment of the residents of the city. Dameri (2017) outlined a five-step process employed when building a smart city dashboard. The process begins with an understanding of the smart city value chain, followed by choosing performance indicators, designing the dashboard, implementing the dashboard, and then scaling and sustaining it over time.

Moreover, a study by Huovila et al. (2019) identified indicator standards on smart cities set by international organisations—namely, the European Committee for Standardization (CEN), European Committee for Electrotechnical Standardization (CENELEC), European Telecommunications Standards Institute (ETSI), International Standardization Organization (ISO), International Telecommunication Union (ITU) and the United Nation's (UN) Sustainable Development Goal 11+ monitoring framework. In total, including duplicates, 413 indicators are identified by these organisations (see Huovila et al., 2019).

The literature on smart cities also refers to a number of non-ICT related indicators (or factors) in relation to smart city transformation readiness. These indicators are listed in Table 3.1, elaborated below, and are classified by this study as independent variables, where smart city performance is the dependent variable.

First, locational centrality for smart cities—in line with the Central Place Theory—is deemed to be an opportunity for cities, as cities that are reaping the benefits of metropolitan offerings are more advantageous in the provision of required amenities and services for their residents and visitors (Romao et al., 2018; Kummitha, 2020; Didenko et al., 2021). The location of the city in regional or metropolitan contexts was not included in any of the abovementioned international smart city indicators and standards. Nonetheless, the studies suggest centrality and connectivity as critical aspects of cities for providing quality of living to citizens as "remoteness" and tyranny of distance risk the provision of all required

Table 3.1 Non-ICT-related smart city transformation readiness indicators

Indicator	Description	Literature
Remoteness value	Access value to a range of services, some of which are available in smaller and others in larger centres	Brown et al., 1999; Keane & Beer, 2000; Yigitcanlar & Kamruzzaman, 2019
Proximity to major infrastructure	Proximity to international and domestic airports, main passenger/import/export seaports, capital city, and top-ranked universities	Dowling et al., 2021; Tulumello & Iapaolo, 2022; Yigitcanlar et al., 2022
Population density	Number of individuals per unit geographic area—e.g., city/local government area	Susanti et al., 2016; Ali-Haidery et al., 2018; Kummitha, 2018
Unemployment level	Number of unemployed people as a percentage of the labour force	Wiig, 2016; Mwaniki et al., 2017; Ivars-Baidal et al., 2021
Labour productivity	Worker skills, technological change, management practices, and changes in other inputs	Shapiro, 2006; Richter et al., 2015; Hongli et al., 2021
Cultural diversity	People with different ethnic and religious backgrounds and languages spoken at home	Florida & Gaters, 2002; Lombardi et al., 2012; Sulyova & Vodak, 2020

amenities and services (Brown et al., 1999; Keane & Beer, 2000; Yigitcanlar & Kamruzzaman, 2019).

Second, when such locational positioning is coupled with close "proximity to major infrastructure"—such as international and domestic airports, main passenger/import/export seaports, capital city and top-ranked universities—smart city transformation could be much easier (Dowling et al., 2021; Tulumello & Iapaolo, 2022; Yigitcanlar et al., 2022). This indicator is also among the International Standardization Organization's (ISO 37120:2018) indicators.

Third, medium to high "population density" is another indicator, that offers the desired level of infrastructure or service patronage, and hence contributes to the frugality of the smart city investment (Susanti et al., 2016; Ali-Haidery et al., 2018; Kummitha, 2018). Medium to high population densities also offer more sustainable solutions by avoiding urban sprawl, and in the case of smart and sustainable design solutions involved even mitigate the urban heat island effects (Kamruzzaman et al., 2018). This indicator is also among the European Telecommunications Standards Institute's (ETSI TS 103 463:2017) indicators.

Fourth, along with these indicators, decreased a "unemployment level" that creates employment opportunities for all—not only for the knowledge workers but also service industry workers—boosts economic conditions that increase the receptivity of the smart city agenda (Wiig, 2016; Mwaniki et al., 2017; Ivars-Baidal et al., 2021). This indicator is also among the International Standardization Organization's (ISO 37120:2018) indicators.

Fifth, likewise, high-level "labour productivity" along with creativity and innovation capabilities generate the ideal economic conditions for a city to achieve its smart city aspirations (Shapiro, 2006; Richter et al., 2015; Hongli et al., 2021). This indicator is also among the International Telecommunication Union's (ITU-T Y.4903:2016) indicators.

Sixth, another critical indicator is "cultural diversity", generally measured by place of birth or language spoken at home. When a location is culturally diverse, it offers an idyllic high tolerance and vibrant social environment, particularly for the creative class of knowledge workers (Florida & Gaters, 2002; Lombardi et al., 2012; Sulyova & Vodak, 2020). This indicator only indirectly relates to the International Standardization Organization's (ISO/DIS 37122:2018) indicators. Instead of using mother tongue language diversity, the relevant ISO indicator concerns professional proficiency in foreign languages. While the research on smart cities continues to grow at an astounding rate, the research focused on smart city transformation readiness, performance indicators, and performance is still at an embryonic stage (Achmad et al., 2018). As illustrated above, while there have been a few attempts to design frameworks for smart city transformation readiness and performance evaluations (Noori et al., 2020b), many of these efforts have been either: (a) small pilots (i.e., testing the framework in a single city); (b) conceptual in nature (i.e., framework proposed with no reliable implementation or validation); or (c) just the provision of a collection of indicators and standards. Hence, there is a need for prospective empirical investigations to identify the key factors affecting smart city transformation readiness.

3.3 Methodology

In a nutshell, our methodological approach can be summarised as follows. First, we calculated the smart city performance of case study Australian local government areas (LGAs) through "the smart city performance indexing" approach. Then, by using the index score (overall LGA performance score) as the dependent variable, we undertook a statistical investigation (multiple regression analysis) to determine which factors are significant in affecting smart city transformation readiness. The independent variables are derived from the smart city literature (see Section 2). Below, this methodological approach is elaborated further.

The rationale behind the selection of Australia (Figure 3.1) as the testbed includes having: (a) a national and numerous local smart city strategies in place to increase the smartness and competitiveness of cities; (b) prioritised public-funded infrastructure development to boost urban productivity, accessibility, liveability, and sustainability; and (c) best practice cases that rank several Australian cities among the top global smart cities (Joss et al., 2019; Yigitcanlar et al., 2021b).

To test the influence of key factors on smart city transformation readiness, as a first step, we collected data on the key factors by focusing on Australian LGAs. Out of 563 LGAs, 180 (all in "greater capital city statistical areas" [GCCSAs] and out-side GCCSAs with over 50,000 population) are selected—these house over 85% of the Australian population. Using ESRI ArcGIS Pro and census data obtained from the Australian Bureau of Statistics (ABS) a map has been created to show the distribution of the LGAs selected for this study (Figure 3.1). In light of the litera-ture findings (see Section 2), potential factors for smart city transformation readi-ness were identified as: (a) cultural diversity (as in language and country of birth diversity); (b) high population density; (c) low remoteness level; (d) high labour productivity levels; (e) low unemployment; and (e) close distance to international airport, domestic airport, seaport, state capital city, and global university.

Firstly, data associated with diversity in language spoken at home, and total percentage of population born overseas were obtained from census data collected by the ABS in 2016 (www.abs.gov.au/census). In addition, population density and remoteness were also calculated from the ABS data. Population density is calculated by dividing the 2016 population against the total area of the LGA. For level of remoteness, data obtained by ABS showing five classes of remoteness based on a "measure of relative access to services"—this is entered into ESRI ArcGIS Pro software. As the boundaries of the remoteness classes were not commensurate with

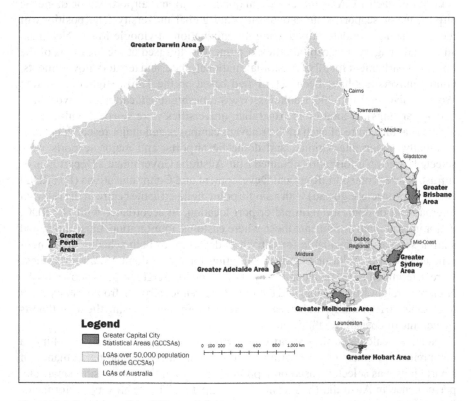

Figure 3.1 Location of the 180 case LGAs.

the LGA boundaries, each LGA was assigned a ranking based on its location relative to the class of remoteness that was most common. LGAs where a majority of their area overlapped with the "Major cities Australia" class received a ranking of "1"; "Inner regional Australia" areas received a ranking of "2"; "Outer regional Australia" areas received a ranking of "3"; and "Remote Australia" areas received a ranking of "4". None of the 180 LGAs analysed in this study were in areas classed as "Very remote Australia".

Secondly, labour productivity and unemployment data were obtained from the National Institute of Economic and Industry Research (NIEIR) (https://nieir.com. au). The NIEIR calculates unemployment based on information received from the Australian Department of Employment. The latest available data were dated for the financial year 2017–2018. Labour productivity, on the other hand, is a measure of "Gross Regional Product" (GRP) divided by the average number of persons employed for the four quarters of the financial year—in this instance 2017–2018. GRP is a calculation of industry value by the NIEIR using a range of data sources including ABS, tax office, and welfare data. GRP is equivalent to "Gross Domestic Product" (GDP), with the exception that it is measured at a local, rather than national level.

Thirdly, using GIS software, a distance in kilometres was calculated from the centroid of each LGA to the closest major international airport, major domestic airport, major seaport, state capital city, and global university. The positions of these features were determined using a combination of Google Maps, Nearmap, and aerial imagery. For capital cities, a point was digitised at the locations of the houses of parliament for all of Australia's national, state, and territory governments. Global universities have been determined based on the Times Higher Education World University Top-200 Rankings (www.timeshighereducation.com/world-uni versity-rankings). A total of 11 Australian universities were selected with a point digitised at the centre of each of the relevant campuses and major research centres.

Finally, major international and domestic airports, and major seaports were selected based on information obtained from Australia Government's Department of Infrastructure, Transport, Regional Development and Communications (DITRDC) (www.infrastructure.gov.au) with a single point digitised at the centre of the relevant international or domestic terminal or port location. In accordance with DITRDC, major international airports are those where customs, immigration, biosecurity, and similar services are available for entry and departure to both scheduled and non-scheduled flights. With no standard definition for major domestic airports, these were determined based on a combination of the major freight airports shown on the National Freight Routes Map, and the top-20 passenger airports from January 2009 to October 2019. Finally, major seaports were determined by using the top-10 ports by volume of coastal freight discharged.

Next, we calculated the "smart city performance" score for each city. First, a comprehensive smart city performance index that calculates the performance of smart cities was selected based on a previous study applied to measure smart city performance in Australia (Yigitcanlar et al., 2020c). The smart city performance index is made up of one composite indicator, divided into four categories, and four indicator areas which each include four indicators. The model contains a total of 16 indicators. Table 3.2 shows the structure of the index, the rationale, and identifies data sources. These 16 indicators are selected from a large pool of smart cities indicators and standards set by regional and international organisations—e.g., CEN, CENELEC, ETSI, ISO, ITU, and UN.

Once the raw indicator values were obtained and input into the model a "min-max normalisation" calculation was completed to normalise the data on a scale range between 0 and 1. This process of normalising the raw indicator values was calculated as follows:

$$Inew = \frac{Iraw - Imin}{Imax - Imin}$$
(Eq. 1)

Where I corresponds to the indicator value; *new*, *raw*, *min*, and *max* subscripts, respectively, denote normalised (transformed), original, minimum, and maximum scores of each indicator.

For example, the normalised value (I_{new}) of the median income indicator for Sydney City LGA is calculated as follows. First, the highest median income indicator value is identified as I_{min} that is \$89,795 (Peppermint Grove LGA). Second, the lowest median income indicator value is identified as I_{max} that is \$13,732 (Murrindindi Shire LGA). Next, Sydney City LGA's median income is identified as I_{raw} \$53,393. Then, Sydney City LGA's median income normalised value (I_{new}) is determined by executing Eq. 1 as follows: (53393 – 13732)/(89795 – 13732) = 0.52.

Within each indicator area, the four normalised indicator values were averaged to illustrate the smart city performance within each of these four indictor areas (i.e., Productivity & Innovation, Liveability & Wellbeing, Sustainability & Accessibility, and Governance & Planning). Since there is one indicator area for each indicator category, the resulting value also represents the smart city performance of each of the indicator categories (i.e., economy, society, environment, and governance). Finally, the overall smart city performance is calculated by averaging each of the four indicator category values to determine the composite indicator value.

Here our approach is to determine the smart city performance levels of LGAs, and through statistical modelling identify the key factors that actually affect smart city transformation readiness of the investigated LGAs. In order to achieve this, we, through a multiple regression analysis, identified the key factors affecting urban smartness levels—a proxy for smart city transformation readiness. We chose to conduct a multiple regression analysis, because it allows to predict a single dependent variable from the knowledge of multiple independent variables (Hair et al., 2019). Our regression model followed the following equation (Bordens & Abbott, 2018):

$$\hat{Y} = b_1 X_1 + \cdots b_n X_n + constant$$
(Eq. 2)

Table 3.2 Smart city performance index

Indicator category	Indicator area	Indicator	Description	Rationale	Data source	International standard
Economy	Productivity & Innovation	• Economic Productivity	• Median income ($)	• Smart cities are claimed to be prosperous locations for the generation of wealth and disposable household income (Kumar & Dahiya, 2017)	ABS	ETSI TS 103 463:2017
		• Labour Force Participation	• Percentage of population within the labour force	• Smart cities provide increased employment opportunities in knowledge and service sectors (Schatz & Johnson, 2007)	ABS	ITU-T Y.4903 2016
		• Innovation Industries	• Percentage of knowledge intensive industries	• Innovation industries form the economic core of smart cities (Zyiaris, 2013)	ABS	ETSI TS 103 463:2017
		• Talent Pool	• Percentage of knowledge workers in population	• Highly educated workers are the backbone of smart cities in stimulating economic growth and vibrancy (Betz et al., 2016)	ABS	ISO/DIS 37122:2018
Society	Liveability & Wellbeing	• Health Status	• Percentage of population with private medical insurance	• Smart cities develop and implement policies to increase health conditions of their residents (Solanas et al., 2014)	ABS	ISO/DIS 37122:2018
		• Safety and Security	• Number of offences per 100,000 people, per year	• Digital security, health security, and infrastructure and personal safety are integral elements of smart cities (De Marco et al., 2015)	ABS	ETSI TS 103 463:2017

		Housing Affordability	Percentage of households where cost of rent is less than 30% of total household income	Housing affordability is a critical element facilitating the varied skill sets that support sustainable innovation economy of smart cities (Katz & Wagner, 2014)	ABS	ETSI TS 103 463:2017
		Socioeconomic Progress	Percentage of low-income individuals	Smart economy of smart cities should be socially inclusive to address the urban inequity issue (Makushkin et al., 2016)	ABS	ISO 37120:2018
Environment	Sustainability & Accessibility	Sustainable Commuting	Percentage of public transport commuters	Smart cities aim to develop innovative services for sustainable transport and mobility (Zawieska & Pieriegud, 2018)	ABS	ISO 37120:2018
		Sustainable Vehicles	Percentage of electric or hybrid electric private vehicles	Mobility strategies of smart cities promote cleaner mobility options (Oldenbroek et al., 2017)	ABS	ISO/DIS 37122:2018
		Sustainable Energy	Households with solar power and hot water installed (per 100,000 people)	In realising the energy supply of a smart city, it is essential to maximise the use of renewable energy sources (Kylili & Fokaides, 2015)	ABS	ISO/DIS 37122:2018
		Sustainable Buildings	Number of buildings with a 4+ score under the National Australia Built Environment Rating System (NABERS) (per 100,000 people)	Smart cities contain buildings that are designed, built, and utilised to consume less energy, and facilitate efficient building operation (To et al., 2018)	ABS	ISO/DIS 37122:2018

(Continued)

Table 3.2 (Continued)

Indicator category	Indicator area	Indicator	Description	Rationale	Data source	International standard
Governance	Governance & Planning	• Local Government Dispersion	• Urban sprawl index calculation	• Controlling urban sprawl and promoting sustainable growth are among the common smart city policies (Lombardi et al., 2012)	ABS	ETSI TS 103 463:2017
		• Public Wi-Fi	• Number of free Wi-Fi locations (per 100,000 people)	• Smart cities offer public Wi-Fi networks to increase the connectivity and access to smart services (Ylipulli et al., 2014)	Local councils	ETSI TS 103 463:2017
		• Broadband Internet	• Percentage of total areas covered by the National Broadband Network (NBN)	• World-class broadband provides opportunities for inclusion in the innovation economy that is the core economic activity of smart cities (Sutherland, 2017)	DITRDC	ITU-T Y.4903 2016
		• Smart City Policy	• Smart City Policy = 2; Smart City Policy in discussion = 1; No Smart City Policy = 0	• A well-formulised smart city policy is necessary to establish a shared democratic approach to engage leaderships from local institutions and to prioritise local issues (Praharaj & Han, 2019)	Local councils	ETSI TS 103 463:2017

where $\hat{Y}$ is the predicted criterion score of our dependent variable, b is the regression weight associated with the predictors, X is the value of the predictors, and *constant* is the y-intercept of the regression line. We draw on an example by Hair et al. (2019) to illustrate how to use this equation for a multiple regression analysis using real data. In the example, the purpose is to predict the number of credit cards used in families, where the dependent variable is the number of credit cards used and the predictors are family size and family income. Including the data in the regression equation, the example is producing using the following prediction equation: $\hat{Y} = 0.63X_1 + 0.216\ X_2 + 0.482$, where $\hat{Y}$ is the predicted number of credit cards used, 0.63 is the regression weight associated with the predictor family size (change in number of credit cards used associated with a unit change in family size), X_1 is the value of the predictor family size, 0.216 is the regression weight associated with the predictor family income (change in number of credit cards used associated with a unit change in family income), X_2 is the value of the predictor family income, and 0.482 is the constant number of credit cards independent of family size and income. Including the values of the first row of the data (family size = 2; family income = 14 [in thousands]), we receive a value of 4.76 for the multiple regression prediction, therefore, the prediction error is –0.76 (4 [actual number of credit cards used] – 4.76 [multiple regression prediction]) and the prediction error squared is 0.58. The sum of all prediction error squared leads to a total of 3.04 (see Hair et al., 2019 for the complete set of the data for this example), which leads to an R^2 of 0.86 (22.0 [total prediction error] – 3.04 = 18.96; 18.96/22.0 = 0.86).

We followed Hair et al.'s (2019) consideration of three primary issues regarding the suitability of multiple regression: (a) appropriateness of the research problem; (b) specification of a statistical relationship; and (c) selection of the dependent and independent variables. We found the multiple regression analysis to be suitable for analysing our research problem of how smart city transformation readiness is determined. We specified the statistical relationship by measuring associations representing the degree of relationship between dependent and independent variables. We selected the smart city transformation readiness score as the dependent variable and the identified key factors as predictors to estimate the coefficients of the underlying relationship.

3.4 Results

Based on this statistical analysis model used and the data basis including the data on the key factors and the smart city transformation readiness score, we conducted a multiple regression analysis using IBM SPSS Statistics software. To ensure statistical robustness, we analysed the following assumptions in multiple regression analysis: multicollinearity among the independent variables, multivariate normality, homoscedasticity, and the linearity of the relationship between dependent and independent variables (Hair et al., 2019).

To identify independent variables that are highly correlated with each other, we tested for multicollinearity by computing a correlation matrix and calculating the "variance inflation factor" (VIF). We computed a matrix of Pearson's bivariate correlations among all variables and identified two correlations that indicated a magnitude of coefficients that were more than the threshold of 0.80: the correlation between "total born overseas" and "language diversity" ($r = 0.894$, $p < 0.01$), and the correlation between "distance to university" and "distance to seaport" ($r = 0.955$, $p < 0.01$). A calculation of collinearity statistics helped us to detect two factors with high VIF values, i.e., "distance to university" (VIF = 40.01) and "total born overseas" (VIF = 9.126), which were above the threshold VIF value of 5. Thus, we removed both factors from the regression equation. The results of the correlation analysis can be found in the correlation matrix in Table 3.3.

For the analysis of multivariate normality, we examined the errors between observed and predicted values. As shown in Figure 3.2a, the residuals of the regression are normally distributed. This is confirmed by the values of skewness and kurtosis, which are within the threshold range between –1 and 1 (skewness = –0.267, kurtosis = 0.575). Further, the absolute value of skewness is below three times the standard error of skewness, which is $0.181 \times 3 = 0.543$, and the absolute value of kurtosis is below three times the standard error of kurtosis, which is $0.360 \times 3 = 1.08$. In addition, we ran the Shapiro-Wilks test and the Kolmogorov-Smirnov test to calculate the level of significance for the differences from a normal distribution (Hair et al., 2019). Our calculation produced a significance value of 0.759 for the Shapiro-Wilks test and a significance value of 0.200 for the Kolmogorov-Smirnov test, both exceeding the threshold level of 0.05, which indicated that there is no statistically significant difference between our dependent variable and the normal distribution. Therefore, we can presume that the smart city transformation readiness values are normally distributed. Multivariate normality is further supported by the normal probability plot in Figure 3.2b, which shows that the errors between observed and predicted values fall along the diagonal with no substantial or systematic departures. Thus, our analysis supports a normal distribution of the residuals of the regression.

To examine the constancy of the residuals across values of the independent variables, we extracted a scatterplot, which showed no pattern of increasing or decreasing residuals (Figure 3.3). This finding indicates the homoscedasticity of residuals.

For the last assumption of the multiple linear regression, we analysed the linearity of the relationship between dependent and independent variables. Figure 3.4 shows a linear relationship in a scatterplot.

After all statistical assumptions have been met, we continued with the multiple regression analysis. Table 3.4 shows the results of the multiple regression analysis.

The results show that population density ($\beta = 0.383$, $p < 0.001$), unemployment level ($\beta = -0.285$, $p < 0.001$), distance to domestic airport ($\beta = -0.211$, $p < 0.001$), and labour productivity ($\beta = 0.183$, $p < 0.001$) are highly significant factors predicting smart city transformation readiness. Further, we identified a significant effect of remoteness value ($\beta = -0.168$, $p < 0.05$). All other factors had t-values below 1.96, denoting significance error probability levels above 0.05, which were considered not significant. We determined the change of R^2 by running the

Table 3.3 Correlation matrix

	SCR	INT	DOM	SEA	SCC	REM	POP	UNEMP	PROD	LANG
SCR	1									
INT	-.400**	1								
DOM	-.499**	.653**	1							
SEA	-.066	.113	.074	1						
SCC	-.369**	.497**	.253**	.234**	1					
REM	.494**	-.566**	-.492**	-.450**	-.611**	1				
POP	.676**	-.414**	-.423**	-.187*	-.345**	.577**	1			
UNEMP	-.541**	.214**	.228**	-.038	.225**	-.140	-.328**	1		
PROD	.552**	-.280**	-.322**	.081	-.278**	.265**	.457**	-.350**	1	
LANG	.314**	-.408**	-.402**	-.136	-.341**	.541**	.554**	.021	.159*	1

Notes: SCR = smart city transformation readiness, INT = distance to international airport, DOM = distance to domestic airport, SEA = distance to seaport, SCC = distance to state capital city, REM = remoteness value, POP = population density, UNEMP = unemployment level, PROD = labour productivity, LANG = language diversity. * Denotes significance level of $p < 0.05$ (two-tailed). ** Denotes significance level of $p < 0.01$ (two-tailed).

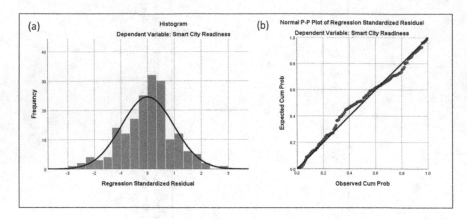

Figure 3.2 Analysis of multivariate normality.

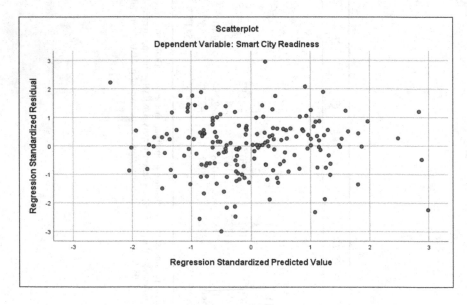

Figure 3.3 Scatterplot testing homoscedasticity.

regression analysis again and excluding the factors that have no significant impact on the dependent variable. The R^2 value slightly decreased (R^2_{excl} = 0.650) and the adjusted R^2 value went marginally down as well (adjusted R^2_{excl} = 0.639).

3.5 Discussion

The results of the analysis revealed the following key factors that determine 65% of smart city transformation readiness: (a) close distance to domestic airport; (b) low

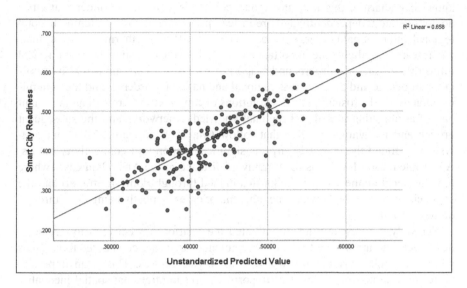

Figure 3.4 Scatterplot testing linearity.

Table 3.4 Results of multiple regression analysis

Effect	R^2	Adjusted R^2	Path coefficient	t-value	Sig.	VIF
Smart city transformation readiness	0.658	0.640				
(Constant)				14.811	.000	
Distance to international airport			.095[n.s.]	1.408	.161	2.270
Distance to domestic airport			−.211***	−3.280	.001	2.066
Distance to seaport			.063[n.s.]	1.192	.235	1.394
Distance to state capital city			−.050[n.s.]	−.808	.420	1.898
Remoteness value			−.168*	−2.124	.035	3.121
Population density			.383***	5.676	.000	2.268
Unemployment level			−.285***	−5.499	.000	1.335
Labour productivity			.183***	3.355	.001	1.472
Language diversity			−.067[n.s.]	−1.090	.277	1.852

*** $p < 0.001$; ** $p < 0.01$; * $p < 0.05$; [n.s.] = not significant

remoteness value; (c) high population density; (d) low unemployment level; and (e) high labour productivity. The relationship and impact of these factors on urban smartness are further discussed below.

Firstly, the relationship between a local government's distance to international and domestic airports, seaports, and state capital cities, and urban smartness highlights the importance of well-established international and interregional connectivity for the development of smarter cities. Given that a key element of urban smartness relates to a city's ability to encourage and foster innovation and knowledge sharing, this indicator (connectivity) is a useful reminder that cities do not operate independently and are instead part of a network stretching beyond regional and national borders (Tranos & Gertner, 2012). Furthermore, while smart city research highlights the importance of ICT, this research suggests that physical infrastructure such as airports and seaports—which facilitate the actual transportation of people and goods across regional and national borders—and the communication networks fostered in the institutions of capital cities, are still an important part of establishing global and regional knowledge networks and the subsequent growth and innovation benefits that follow (Mayer & Cowell, 2014). Our analysis only found the domestic airports significant among all connectivity modes. A possible reason for this is the tyranny of distance in the Australian case (where most physical connectivity is being maintained through domestic travel) and the smart city connectivity between the other major cities is mostly being done through domestic flights.

Secondly, the research has highlighted the relationship between low remoteness levels and urban smartness. Low remoteness areas are considered those areas which have relatively unfettered access to service centres. This is an important indicator (remoteness) because it supports the presumption that spatial inequality is not entirely dependent on the goods and services a city produces, but also on the social infrastructure contained within—i.e., the actual spaces and facilities where residents can access social services including education, arts, culture, and other recreational places (Mora et al., 2017). In fact, increased accessibility to social services has been linked to increased quality of life by actively supporting community participation and connectedness among a wide range of sociodemographic groups (Davern et al., 2017). This, in turn, could contribute to smart city transformation readiness as previous research has shown a direct link between social participation, connectedness, and the following: (a) public health—as residents are more likely to have easy access to beneficial services including medical, exercise, and leisure facilities (Davern et al., 2017); (b) perception of safety and fear of crime— which has been shown to be reduced, when residents are able to recognise their neighbours or when they feel a part of their community (Crank et al., 2003); and (c) innovation—that has been shown to thrive in regions which support human and social capital—particularly through enhanced active and passive learning opportunities (Fernandez-Anez et al., 2018).

Thirdly, the research has highlighted the relationship between high population density and urban smartness. This is an important indicator (density) because it highlights the benefits of population density for creating more vibrant, innovative, productive, and sustainable communities. In fact, research has shown that areas with a population density of between 50 to 150 persons per hectare tend to make more efficient use of limited resources—particularly with regard to infrastructure provision, travel distance, and overall energy consumption (Lohrey & Creutzig, 2016). Furthermore, given the greater concentration of residents and businesses there is a greater variety of expertise within the community, which lends itself to the spread of knowledge and the creation of more entrepreneurial and innovative businesses (Carlino et al., 2007). Knowledge sharing, innovation, and sustainable environmental outcomes are critical components for the development of smart cities (Yigitcanlar et al., 2019c).

Fourthly, the research has highlighted the relationship between low unemployment levels and urban smartness. This is an important indicator (employment) of economic growth and a common theme of smart city development and, in fact, many smart initiatives seek to generate new employment by encouraging industrial development, innovation, and attracting new enterprises (Zygiaris, 2013). This research provides a link between smart city transformation readiness and low unemployment, while also highlighting the following: (a) do smart city initiatives create low unemployment—as highlighted by other research, which showed that increased innovation and entrepreneurship seen in "smart" urban areas was not certainly a result of necessity (i.e., high unemployment), but rather the opportunities afforded by good smart city initiatives (Barba-Sánchez et al., 2019); or (b) is low unemployment a prerequisite for the implementation of smart city initiatives (meaning it is an advantage for the transformation process, and if this requirement is not met there is a need to find solutions and initiatives to lower it)? We anticipate both aspects to be relevant—i.e., low unemployment creates the opportunities, and economic certainty and prosperity to facilitate smart city initiatives, with these initiatives further contributing to job growth. Hence, while localities with low unemployment levels might be advantageous places for smart city transformation, smart city transformation processes of other localities should aim at lowering the unemployment rate through considering this goal as a high priority at the beginning of the process.

Fifthly, the research has highlighted the relationship between high labour productivity and urban smartness. This is an important indicator (productivity) because it provides a link between urban smartness and the actual economic output of a city. This is likely a critical factor, because the cities need budget and resources to implement smart city initiatives. Subsequently, while human and social capital continue to remain an important element of smart city development, the actual economic output of a city, or the physical capital it produces, is critical for its success. This aligns with previous research, which links urban wealth measures such as GDP and GRP to model urban smartness (Lombardi et al., 2012).

In fact, for a smart city to be truly sustainable, addressing these complex and often integrated challenges remains paramount. This study has ranked urban smartness of 180 of the largest and most urban LGAs within Australia and determined that the highest ranking (or "smartest") cities often share key characteristics such as connectivity, low remoteness, high population density, low unemployment, and high productivity. Based on these results, four key policy directions have been developed to help policymakers and planners better transition towards increased urban smartness, these include: (a) establish networks; (b) improve physical and social infrastructure; (c) increase population density; and (d) encourage innovations and employment options. These directions should be considered a guide for developing clear and simple policy objectives aimed at improving urban smartness and sustainability within the local, regional, and national contexts.

Given the above findings, the key takeaway message for city administrators and other decision-makers—while embracing digital technology and fostering innovation that are important tools for smart cities—is not to ignore the existing economic, environmental, social, and governance challenges. Along with this, the following actions to improve smart city transformation readiness are recommended.

- *Establish Networks:* Cities should look beyond their boundaries to establish business and communication networks. While the development of actual physical infrastructure such as airports may be an unrealistic expectation for many cities; urban policy and planning efforts could instead focus on developing strong transportation links to such infrastructure that is supported by high-speed internet. This could help facilitate both the physical movement of people and goods, in addition to the communication channels that foster international trade and relationships. A recent example which could assist with passenger connectivity to major airports relates to the concept of mobility-as-a-service (MaaS) (Butler et al., 2021). This service—which is reliant on good-quality wireless networks such as 5G—aims to integrate both public and private transport offerings so that they can be accessed on-demand through a single interface, or app. Where existing airports are serviced by high occupancy transit services MaaS can use the various transport modes available in a city—including existing airport shuttle services—to provide users with the most suitable transportation options depending on need or pre-existing constraints. In doing so, these services can make use of existing transportation infrastructure by providing suitable first- and last-mile connections to existing public transportation nodes. Such an innovative service could improve smart city transformation readiness by providing a more sustainable transport option that is cheaper, faster, and more comfortable than existing options (Merkert & Beck, 2020).
- *Improve Physical and Social Infrastructure:* While those cities in remote locations have significant disadvantages, they can still look into improving not only their physical capital—that is an important indicator of urban smartness—but also look to improve human and social capital by increasing the accessibility and diversity of social infrastructure within their city. Urban policy and planning strategies that are successful in balancing community needs and providing the necessary mixture of social infrastructure such as libraries, community centres, and education and sporting facilities can help improve smart city transformation readiness by facilitating community participation and connectiveness which has been shown to improve the wellbeing and liveability of residents. Nonetheless, planning and strategy are key to ensure cities have the required social infrastructure in place to benefit a community (Alizadeh & Irajifar, 2018). For instance, different social infrastructures may serve catchments at a different scale—a university would have a larger service catchment than a community centre—therefore, strategic planning would need to be undertaken at both a regional and local level (Wear, 2016).
- *Increase Density:* Encouraging density is an important urban planning policy. While recent events associated with the COVID-19 pandemic have increased

discussion of a new era of suburbanisation, encouraging density remains an important planning tool primarily as a means of containing urban sprawl and sparing ecologically and agriculturally significant land from development (Kunzmann, 2020). Furthermore, density can improve smart city transformation readiness by increasing the efficiency and sustainable development potential of cities, in addition to its demonstrated potential to increase knowledge sharing and innovation. Cities should look to infill development and transit-oriented planning strategies to encourage density and mixed-use development close to existing transportation nodes. Strategies such as these could contribute to smart city development by maximising the use of existing infrastructure within cities while limiting urban sprawl (Newman & Kenworthy, 1996).

- *Encourage Innovation and Employment Opportunities:* The literature highlights the importance of encouraging innovation and entrepreneurship for the development of smart cities (Ritcher et al., 2015). Increased innovation can contribute to smart city transformation readiness by encouraging cutting-edge technology and ideas, stimulating business growth, and creating employment opportunities, (Katz & Wagner, 2014). Some of the methods of encouraging innovation have been identified above, including increasing population density, encouraging diversity, improving social infrastructure, and establishing inter-regional and international networks. Other examples including: (a) encourage business start-up to foster new ideas; (b) create collaborative working spaces to promote communication and knowledge sharing; and (c) develop dedicated innovation districts where similar and complement industries and firms can gather and share ideas and resources (Millar & Choi, 2010; Katz & Wagner, 2014).

3.6 Conclusion

This chapter has conducted a thorough investigation of the salient factors that determine urban smartness or, in other words, smart city transformation readiness in Australia. It has provided several recommendations that draw on our findings for cities to consider as they continue their smart city transformation trajectories. This chapter opens several avenues for future research.

First, future research is needed to examine the trade-offs that cities must make when considering various investment options to increase their level of smartness. Making the appropriate trade-off choices given the current conditions of a city and the examination of their existing Achilles' heels are critical to ensure that one engages in responsible innovation.

Second, given the current COVID-19 pandemic environment and the associated dynamics that have followed (e.g., working-from-home, physical distance practices), some of the key determinants need to be examined. For example, how the changing nature of density and the diminishing need to be physically present within concentrated hubs (e.g., central business districts—CBDs) impact our cities, and how cities will revise their smart city transformation efforts accordingly. In a similar vein, the need to connect various stakeholders in the city using ICTs, and the need to create online platforms for citizen engagement, co-creation, and even civic action will impact the nature of physical spaces and planned investments in them.

Third, while the present study analysed the Australian context, comparative work is needed to look at factors that might vary across countries. Especially, it is important to compare factors between countries where there are significant national-level plans and investments in creating smarter cities (e.g., India, China, Korea) with countries where the impetus is more organic and bottom-up (e.g., Brazil, Italy, the UK).

In conclusion, cities will continue to invest significant resources to continue to make themselves smarter and advance the goals of making themselves more resilient, sustainable, and liveable. In this regard, the study at hand contributes to our understanding of the key determinants of urban smartness, and generates insights to inform urban policymakers, managers, and planners on their policy, planning, and practice decisions concerning smart cities (Yigitcanlar et al., 2022a).

Acknowledgements

This chapter, with permission from the copyright holder, is a reproduced version of the following journal article: Yigitcanlar, T., Degirmenci, K., Butler, L., & Desouza, K. (2022). What are the key factors affecting smart city transformation readiness? Evidence from Australian cities. *Cities*, 120, 103434.

References

Achmad, K., Nugroho, L., Djunaedi, A. (2018). Smart city readiness based on smart city council's readiness framework. *International Journal of Electrical & Computer Engineering, 8*, 271–279.

Albino, V., Berardi, U., Dangelico, R. (2015). Smart cities. *Journal of Urban Technology, 22*, 3–21.

Ali-Haidery, S., Ullah, H., Khan, N., Fatima, K., Rizvi, S., Kwon, S. (2020). Role of big data in the development of smart city by analyzing the density of residents in Shanghai. *Electronics, 9*, 837.

Alizadeh, T., Irajifar, L. (2018). Gold Coast smart city strategy. *International Journal of Knowledge-Based Development, 9*, 153–173.

Allam, Z., Dhunny, Z. (2019). On bigdata, artificial intelligence and smart cities. *Cities, 89*, 80–91.

Anthopoulos, L., Janssen, M., Weerakkody, V. (2015). Comparing smart cities with different modeling approaches. In: *24th International Conference on WorldWideWeb*.

Araral, E. (2020). Why do cities adopt smart technologies? *Cities, 106*, 102873.

Barba-Sánchez, V., Arias-Antúnez, E., Orozco-Barbosa, L. (2019). Smart cities as a source for entrepreneurial opportunities. *Technological Forecasting and Social Change, 148*, 119713.

Barns, S. (2018). Smart cities and urban data platforms. *City, Culture and Society, 12*, 5–12.

Batty, M. (2013). Big data, smart cities and city planning. *Dialogues in Human Geography, 3*, 274–279.

Batty, M., Axhausen, K., Giannotti, F., Pozdnoukhov, A., Bazzani, A., Wachowicz, M., Portugali, Y. (2012). Smart cities of the future. *European Physical Journal, 214*, 481–518.

Betz, M.R., Partridge, M., Fallah, B. (2016). Smart cities and attracting knowledge workers. *Papers in Regional Science, 95*, 819–841.

Bordens, K., Abbott, B. (2018). *Research design and methods*. McGraw-Hill.

Brauneis, R., Goodman, E. (2018). Algorithmic transparency for the smart city. *Yale Journal of Law & Technology, 20*, 103.

Brown, W., Young, A., Byles, J. (1999). Tyranny of distance? *Australian Journal of Rural Health, 7*, 148–154.

Bunders, D., Varró, K. (2019). Problematizing data-driven urban practices. *Cities, 93*, 145–152.

Butler, L., Yigitcanlar, T. Paz, A. (2020). Smart urban mobility innovations. *IEEE Access, 8*, 196034–196049.

Butler, L., Yigitcanlar, T., Paz, A. (2021). Barriers and risks of Mobility-as-a-Service adoption in cities. *Cities, 109*, 103036.

Carli, R., Dotoli, M., Pellegrino, R., Ranieri, L. (2013). Measuring and managing the smartness of cities. In: *IEEE International Conference on Systems, Man, and Cybernetics*.

Carlino, G., Chatterjee, S., Hunt, R. (2007) Urban density and the rate of invention. *Journal of Urban Economics, 61*, 389–419.

Castelnovo, W., Misuraca, G., Savoldelli, A. (2016). Smart cities governance. *Social Science Computer Review, 34*, 724–739.

Cho, S., Mossberger, K., Swindell, D., Selby, J. (2021). Experimenting with public engagement platforms in local government. *Urban Affairs Review, 57*(3), 763–793.

Cledou, G., Estevez, E., Barbosa, L. (2018). A taxonomy for planning and designing smart mobility services. *Government Information Quarterly, 35*, 61–76.

Crank, J., Giacomazzi, A. Heck, C. (2003). Fear of crime in a nonurban setting. *Journal of Criminal Justice, 31*, 249–263.

Dameri, R. (2017). Urban smart dashboard. In: *Smart city implementation*. Cham: Springer.

Davern, M., Gunn, L., Whitzman, C., Higgs, C., Giles-Corti, B., Simons, K., Villanueva, K., Mavoa, S., Roberts, R. Badland. H. (2017) Using spatial measures to test a conceptual model of social infrastructure that supports health and wellbeing. *Cities & Health, 1*, 194–209.

De Marco, A., Mangano, G., Zenezini, G. (2015). Digital dashboards for smart city governance. *Journal of Computer and Communications, 3*, 144–152.

Desouza, K., Bhagwatwar, A. (2012). Citizen apps to solve complex urban problems. *Journal of Urban Technology, 19*, 107–136.

Desouza, K., Bhagwatwar, A. (2014). Technology-enabled participatory platforms for civic engagement. *Journal of Urban Technology, 21*, 25–50.

Desouza, K., Hunter, M., Jacop, B., Yigitcanlar, T. (2021). Pathways to the making of prosperous smart cities. *Journal of Urban Technology, 27*, 3–32

DeSouza, K., Hunter, M., Yigitcanlar, T. (2019). Under the hood. *Public Management, 12*, 30–35.

Didenko, N., Skripnuk, D., Kulik, S., Kosinski, E. (2021). Smart city concept for settlements in the Arctic zone of the Russian Federation. *Earth and Environmental Science, 625*, 012003.

Dowling, R., McGuirk, P., Maalsen, S., Sadowski, J. (2021). How smart cities are made: A priori, ad hoc and post hoc drivers of smart city implementation in Sydney, Australia. *Urban Studies, 58*(16), 3299–3315.

Fernandez-Anez, V., Fernández-Güell, J., Giffinger, R. (2018). Smart city implementation and discourses. *Cities, 78*, 4–16.

Florida, R., Gates, G. (2002). Technology and tolerance. *Brookings Review, 20*, 32–36.

Hair, J., Black, W., Babin, B., Anderson, R. (2019). *Multivariate data analysis*. Hampshire: Cengage.

Hashem, I., Chang, V., Anuar, N., Adewole, K., Yaqoob, I., Gani, A., Chiroma, H. (2016). The role of big data in smart city. *International Journal of Information Management, 36*, 748–758.

Heo, T., Kim, K., Kim, H., Lee, C., Ryu, J., Leem, Y., Ko, J. (2014). Escaping from ancient Rome! *Transactions on Emerging Telecommunications Technologies, 25*, 109–119.

Hongli, J., Pengcheng, J., Dong, W., Jiahui, W. (2021). Can smart city construction facilitate green total factor productivity? *Sustainable Cities and Society, 69*, 102809.

Huovila, A., Bosch, P., Airaksinen, M. (2019). Comparative analysis of standardized indicators for Smart sustainable cities. *Cities, 89*, 141–153.

Ivars-Baidal, J.A., Celdrán-Bernabeu, M.A., Femenia-Serra, F., Perles-Ribes, J.F., Giner-Sánchez, D. (2021). Measuring the progress of smart destinations. *Journal of Destination Marketing & Management, 19*, 100531.

Joss, S., Sengers, F., Schraven, D., Caprotti, F., Dayot, Y. (2019). The smart city as global discourse. *Journal of Urban Technology, 26*, 3–34.

Kamruzzaman, M., Deilami, K., Yigitcanlar, T. (2018). Investigating the urban heat island effect of transit oriented development in Brisbane. *Journal of Transport Geography, 66*, 116–124.

Katz, B., Wagner, J. (2014) *The rise of innovation districts*. Brookings Institution.

Keane, R., Beer, A. (2000). Population decline and service provision in regional Australia. *People and Place, 8*, 69–76.

Kumar, T., Dahiya, B. (2017). Smart economy in smart cities. In: *Smart economy in smart cities*. Springer.

Kummitha, R. (2018). Entrepreneurial urbanism and technological panacea. *Technological Forecasting and Social Change, 137*, 330–339.

Kummitha, R. (2020). Why distance matters. *Technological Forecasting and Social Change, 157*, 120087.

Kunzmann, K. (2020). Smart cities after Covid-19. *disP–The Planning Review, 56*, 20–31.

Kylili, A., Fokaides, P. (2015). European smart cities. *Sustainable Cities and Society, 15*, 86–95.

Lohrey, S., Creutzig, F. (2016). A sustainability window of urban form. *Transportation Research Part D, 45*, 96–111.

Lombardi, P., Giordano, S., Farouh, H., Yousef, W. (2012). Modelling the smart city performance. *Innovation, 25*, 137–149.

Makushkin, S., Kirillov, A., Novikov, V., Shaizhanov, M., Seidina, M. (2016). Role of inclusion smart city concept as a factor in improving the socio-economic performance of the territory. *International Journal of Economics and Financial Issues, 6*, 152–156.

Mayer, H., Cowell, M. (2014). Capital cities as knowledge hubs. In: *Hub cities in the knowledge economy*. Routledge.

Meijer, A., Bolívar, M. (2016). Governing the smart city. *International Review of Administrative Sciences, 82*, 392–408.

Merkert, R., Beck, M. (2020). Can a strategy of integrated air-bus services create a value proposition for regional aviation management? *Transportation Research Part A, 132*, 527–539.

Millar, C., Choi, C. (2010). Development and knowledge resources: a conceptual analysis. *Journal of Knowledge Management, 14*, 759–776

Mora, L., Bolici, R., Deakin, M. (2017). The first two decades of smart-city research. *Journal of Urban Technology, 24*, 3–27.

Mwaniki, D., Kinyanjui, M., Opiyo, R. (2017). Towards smart economic development in Nairobi. In: *Smart economy in smart cities*. Springer.

Newman, P., Kenworthy, J. (1996). The land use-transport connection. *Land Use Policy, 13*, 1–22.

Noori, N., Hoppe, T., Jong, M. (2020a). Classifying pathways for smart city development. *Sustainability, 12*, 4030.

Noori, N., Jong, M., Hoppe, T. (2020b). Towards an integrated framework to measure smart city readiness. *Smart Cities, 3*, 676–704.

Oldenbroek, V., Verhoef, L., Van Wijk, A. (2017). Fuel cell electric vehicle as a power plant. *International Journal of Hydrogen Energy, 42*, 8166–8196.

Praharaj, S., Han, H. (2019). Cutting through the clutter of smart city definitions. *City, Culture and Society, 18*, 100289.

Priano, F., Guerra, C. (2014). A framework for measuring smart cities. In: *15th Annual International Conference on Digital Government Research.*

Rathore, M.M., Ahmad, A., Paul, A., Rho, S. (2016). Urban planning and building smart cities based on the internet of things using big data analytics. *Computer Networks, 101*, 63–80.

Richter, C., Kraus, S., Syrjä, P. (2015). The smart city as an opportunity for entrepreneurship. *International Journal of Entrepreneurial Venturing, 7*, 211–226.

Romao, J., Kourtit, K., Neuts, B., Nijkamp, P. (2018). The smart city as a common place for tourists and residents. *Cities, 78*, 67–75.

Schatz, L., Johnson, L.C. (2007). Smart city north. *Work Organisation, Labour and Globalisation, 1*, 116–130.

Shapiro, J. (2006). Smart cities. *The Review of Economics and Statistics, 88*, 324–335.

Silva, B., Khan, M., Han, K. (2018). Towards sustainable smart cities. *Sustainable Cities and Society, 38*, 697–713.

Söderström, O., Paasche, T., Klauser, F. (2014). Smart cities as corporate storytelling. *City, 18*, 307–320.

Solanas, A., Patsakis, C., Conti, M., Vlachos, I. S., Ramos, V., Falcone, F., Martinez-Balleste, A. (2014). Smart health. *IEEE Communications Magazine, 52*, 74–81.

Sotto, D., Philippi, A., Yigitcanlar, T., Kamruzzaman, M. (2019). Aligning urban policy with climate action in the global south. *Energies, 12*, 3418.

Sulyova, D., Vodak, J. (2020). The impact of cultural aspects on building the smart city approach. *Sustainability, 12*, 9463.

Susanti, R., Soetomo, S., Buchori, I., Brotosunaryo, P. (2016). Smart growth, smart city and density. *Procedia-Social and Behavioral Sciences, 227*, 194–201.

Sutherland, E. (2017). World-class broadband. *Digital Policy, Regulation and Governance, 19*, 189–209.

To, W., Lai, L., Lam, K., Chung, A. (2018). Perceived importance of smart and sustainable building features from the users' perspective. *Smart Cities, 1*, 163–175.

Tranos, E., Gertner, D. (2012). Smart networked cities? *Innovation, 25*, 175–190.

Tulumello, S., Iapaolo, F. (2022). Policing the future, disrupting urban policy today. Predictive policing, smart city, and urban policy in Memphis (TN). *Urban Geography, 43*(3), 448–469.

Vandercruysse, L., Buts, C., Dooms, M. (2020). A typology of smart city services. *Cities, 104*, 102731.

Wear, A. (2016) Planning, funding and delivering social infrastructure in Australia's outer suburban growth areas. *Urban Policy and Research, 34*, 284–297.

Wiig, A. (2016). The empty rhetoric of the smart city. *Urban Geography, 37*, 535–553.

Yigitcanlar, T. (2021). Smart city beyond efficiency. *Housing Policy Debate, 31*, 88–92.

Yigitcanlar, T., Butler, L., Windle, E., Desouza, K., Mehmood, R., Corchado, J. (2020a). Can building artificially intelligent cities safeguard humanity from natural disasters, pandemics, and other catastrophes? *Sensors, 20*, 2988.

Yigitcanlar, T., Desouza, K., Butler, L., Roozkhosh, F. (2020b). Contributions and risks of artificial intelligence in building smarter cities. *Energies, 13*, 1473.

Yigitcanlar, T., Foth, M., Kamruzzaman, M. (2019a). Towards post-anthropocentric cities. *Journal of Urban Technology, 26*, 147–152

Yigitcanlar, T., Hoon, M., Kamruzzaman, M., Ioppolo, G., Sabatini-Marques, J. (2019b). The making of smart cities. *Land Use Policy, 88*, 104187.

Yigitcanlar, T., Kamruzzaman, M. (2019). Smart cities and mobility. *Journal of Urban Technology, 26*, 21–46.

Yigitcanlar, T., Kamruzzaman, M., Foth, M., Sabatini-Marques, J., Costa, E., Ioppolo, G. (2019c). Can cities become smart without being sustainable? *Sustainable Cities and Society, 45*, 348–365

Yigitcanlar, T., Kankanamge, N., Butler, L., Vella, K., Desouza, K. (2020c). *Smart cities down under*. Queensland University of Technology, Australia.

Yigitcanlar, T., Kankanamge, N., Inkinen, T., Butler, L., Preston, A., Rezayee, M., ... Senevirathne, M. (2022). Pandemic vulnerability knowledge visualisation for strategic decision-making: A COVID-19 index for government response in Australia. *Management decision, 60*(4), 893–915.

Yigitcanlar, T., Kankanamge, N., Inkinen, T., Butler, L., Preston, A., Rezayee, M., ... Senevirathne, M. (2021a). Pandemic vulnerability knowledge visualisation for strategic decision-making. *Management Decision*. https://doi.org/10.1108/MD-11-2020–1527.

Yigitcanlar, T., Kankanamge, N., Vella, K. (2021b). How are smart city concepts and technologies perceived and utilized? *Journal of Urban Technology, 28*, 135–154.

Yigitcanlar, T., Degirmenci, K., Butler, L., Desouza, K. (2022a). What are the key factors affecting smart city transformation readiness? Evidence from Australian cities. *Cities*, 120, 103434.

Ylipulli, J., Suopajärvi, T., Ojala, T., Kostakos, V., Kukka, H. (2014). Municipal WiFi and interactive displays. *Technological Forecasting and Social Change, 89*, 145–160.

Zawieska, J., Pieriegud, J. (2018). Smart city as a tool for sustainable mobility and transport decarbonisation. *Transport Policy, 63*, 39–50.

Zhang, X. (2016). The trends, promises and challenges of urbanisation in the world. *Habitat International, 54*, 241–252.

Zygiaris, S. (2013). Smart city reference model. *Journal of the Knowledge Economy, 4*, 217–231.

Part 2

Smart City Technology

This part of the book concentrates on providing a clear understanding on the technocentric aspects of smart cities. These aspects include what these technologies are, how they are perceived and utilised in cities, how cities can get smarter with the responsible use of these technologies, how urban artificial intelligences can support smart city and sustainable development goals, why such intelligence should be green, and how these technologies are utilised for smart urban mobility.

DOI: 10.1201/9781003403630-5

4　Perception and Utilisation

4.1 Introduction

At the dawn of global socioeconomic and environmental crises, the utilisation of smart city technologies is seen by many city administrations as a popular avenue to achieve desired urbanisation outcomes (Albino et al., 2015; Komninos, 2016). A smart city can be described as an urban locality that employs digital data and technology to create efficiencies for boosting economic development, enhancing quality of life, and improving the sustainability of the city (Bibri, 2019). Today, many cities are developing sound smart city strategies, and turning them into official local policies (Townsend, 2013). Successful approaches and practices are emerging in London, San Francisco, Singapore, Stockholm, Toronto, Vienna, and in a few other cities (Yigitcanlar & Kamruzzaman, 2018).

Despite the emergence of good smart city policy practices, our knowledge and understanding about how smart city concepts and technologies are perceived and utilised in cities is very limited (Mah et al., 2012). For instance, the literature does not provide clear answers to the following questions: Which smart city concepts and technologies are currently trending? What are the relationships between popular smart city concepts and technologies? What are the official smart city policies that influence the perception and utilisation of smart city concepts and technologies? The answers to these questions will inform policymakers and planners in shaping their future policy agendas—e.g., improving the quality and implementation of smart city policies.

To address this gap in the literature, the chapter evaluates "how relevant smart city concepts and technologies are perceived and utilised" in cities. This investigation is undertaken through a case study analysis. Australian cities are selected as the testbed—as they are among the early and successful adopters of smart city technologies (Pettit et al., 2018). The study provides a snapshot of community perceptions on smart city concepts and technologies with the objective to inform smart city policymaking.

The methodological approach adopted in this study utilises a novel approach—instead of traditional survey and interview techniques. Thanks to the proliferation of social media platforms, capturing and evaluating community perceptions has become much easier (Williamson & Ruming, 2020). Social media motivates

DOI: 10.1201/9781003403630-6

people to express their thoughts, criticisms, and reflections in the form of social media posts (Kankanamge et al., 2020). By commenting, sharing, and responding to such posts, people create trending topics in social media networks—and some go viral (Dufty, 2016). Thus, in this study, trending smart city concepts and technologies are identified and analysed through the social media analysis of geo-located Twitter messages (tweets).

There are two different types of locations associated with a tweet: (a) geo-tagged tweets that give the exact longitude and latitude information of the sender; and (b) geo-located tweets that give the area name of the sender's location—e.g., Sydney. In this study, initially geo-tagged tweets were intended to be used, but as there was a very limited number of them, instead both geo-tagged and geo-located tweets are used. As the numbers of geo-tagged tweets were marginal (n=64), in this study we refer to the combined set of geo-tagged and geo-located tweets as "geo-located" (n=3,073). The systematic geo-located Twitter analytics method—containing descriptive, content, policy, and spatial analyses—is used to harvest community perceptions expressed as tweets on smart city-related concepts and technologies.

4.2 Literature Background

The urbanisation rate across the globe has been growing exponentially (Arbolino et al., 2017). Urbanisation, when practiced as densification, can have positive consequences in making the urban footprint smaller. Nonetheless, when urbanisation is coupled with overpopulation, excessive consumerism, and fossil fuel energy dependency, its consequences become catastrophic for natural systems (Mysterud, 2017; Arbolino et al., 2018). If these issues are not addressed, the challenges of greenhouse gas emissions, climate change, resource scarcity, housing affordability, and food security will become even more acute, threatening our existence on the planet (Zhang et al., 2013; Yigitcanlar et al., 2019b).

Along with sustainability issues, high urbanisation levels put heightened pressures on urban infrastructure, amenity and service delivery, and governance of cities (Grossi & Pianezzi, 2017; Mora et al., 2017). Housing large populations in cities—particularly in megacities of over 10 million residents—adds further to the already significant challenges facing urban administrations (Ersoy, 2017). This has led city authorities to search for innovative methods and mechanisms, such as smart and sustainable infrastructures to deliver urban services with increased efficiency (Mora et al., 2019).

In recent years, urban policymakers and technocrats have been adopting technology-centric solutions (such as autonomous vehicles, Internet of Things, artificial intelligence, smart poles, digital twins, blockchain, bigdata, robotics, open data) to urban development and management more than ever (Söderström et al., 2014; Faisal et al., 2019; Yigitcanlar et al., 2019d). Technocentric urban management approaches, which are a part of the "smart cities" agenda, have become mainstream in many local governments (Caragliu et al., 2011; Praharaj et al., 2018). The digital data and technology utilisation aspect of smart cities is widely recognised as their distinctive characteristic in boosting economic growth, enriching living conditions, and maintaining environmental sustainability (Winden & Buuse, 2017; Joss et al., 2019).

The popularity of smart cities has increased rapidly due to their offerings of the digitalisation of cities (Yigitcanlar, 2009; Aina, 2017). Paradoxically, the extreme reliance on technology has also created drawbacks. Scholars argue that this dependency on technology solutions could become a threat soon. According to Kunzmann (2014, p. 9), "there is a darker side of smart city that is not so much the access to this technology, but rather the extreme dependency on technology, and on corporations dominating technology and related services".

There are various conceptual smart city frameworks developed so far. For instance, Giffinger and Pichler-Milanović's (2007) put together the following key dimensions in a smart city framework comprising smart environment, people, economy, living, mobility, and governance. This framework was adopted by the European Union. There are few other smart city frameworks. The most notable ones are developed by Errichiello and Marasco (2014), Fernandez-Anez et al. (2017), and Yigitcanlar (2018). These frameworks aimed at providing a clearer view on how the smart city idea can be best operationalised to deliver desired outcomes.

In general, smart city frameworks can be grouped under two categories. The first category is the conceptual frameworks that encompass theories, typologies, features, and strategies for understanding smart cities. They provide the big picture view (De-Jong et al., 2015). The second category is the practical frameworks that contain processes, planning mechanisms, and performance evaluation tools for transforming cities into smart cities. They provide sectoral, specific application area, or practical perspectives (Aina, 2017).

There is not any widely accepted generic smart city framework—either conceptual or practical (Deakin & Reid, 2018). Increasing numbers of local governments have also developed their own smart policy frameworks. To name a few, the following cities have fully fledged official smart city government policies: Belfast, Brussels, Greenwich, London, Newcastle, Nottingham, Ottawa, San Francisco, San Jose, Singapore, Stockholm, Toronto, Vienna, and Western Sydney (Yigitcanlar et al., 2019a).

Each of these official smart city strategies has their own unique features, and their common elements. Some of them adopted smart city frameworks developed by scholars. For instance, Giffinger and Pichler-Milanović's (2007) framework was adopted in the smart city policy of the City of Newcastle (Australia). Some others formed their own—e.g., Vienna. Despite the popularity of smart cities policy/practice; how relevant concepts and technologies are being perceived and utilised is still an understudied area of research (Alizadeh, 2015; Komninos et al., 2019).

4.3 Methodology

4.3.1 Case Study

The research selected Australian cities as the case study context. Table 4.1 shows the 2016 population of Australian states and territories—for the sake of

Table 4.1 Australian state and territory populations

State/Territory	Population
New South Wales (NSW)	7,480,228
Victoria (VIC)	5,926,624
Queensland (QLD)	4,703,193
Western Australia (WA)	2,474,410
South Australia (SA)	1,676,653
Tasmania (TAS)	509,965
Australian Capital Territory (ACT)	397,397
Northern Territory (NT)	228,833

simplification, territories will also be referred to as states in the rest of this chapter. The case selection was done due to the following reasons: (a) Australian cities are among the early adopters of smart city technologies (Yigitcanlar, 2018; Yigitcanlar & Kamruzzaman, 2019); (b) Australian cities are listed among the reputable global smart cities (Anthopoulos, 2017); (c) the Australian Government introduced a smart city policy in 2016; (d) at present, more than 50 large-scale smart city projects across the country are in progress—e.g., Parramatta City Council's smart warning system for flooded roads; Logan City Council's smart urban irrigation system; Cairns Regional Council's smart climate responsive neighbourhoods; and Monash City Council's i-Sense Oakleigh smart connected precinct.

4.3.2 Data

In recent years, social media channels have been frequently used as key data sources in academic studies. The following can be given as examples: (a) determining post-disaster damage levels in smart cities (Kankanamge et al., 2020); (b) evaluating community perceptions, through opinion mining, on smart city projects (Alizadeh et al., 2019); (c) calculating home–work travel metrics as a smart urban mobility measure (Osorio-Arjona et al., 2019); and (d) assessing the impact of smart tourism policies (Brandt et al., 2017). Despite increasing numbers of studies, the use of social media content and analytic techniques in relation to smart city concepts and technologies remains an understudied area of research.

This research adopted an analysis framework introduced by Fan and Gordon (2014) to conduct social media data analysis. Social media has altered our modes of work and life, has received attention from multiple fields (Kane, 2017), and there is also an increasing trend toward social media as a source of big data in urban research (Ciuccarelli et al., 2014). The systematic geo-located Twitter analysis framework the study used contains three analysis stages—i.e., "capture", "understand", and "present" (Figure 4.1).

The first stage of the framework involves "capturing" social media information. This study selected Twitter as a potential social media platform. Nonetheless, Twitter has certain merits and limitations. The main merits include: (a) Twitter is the fastest

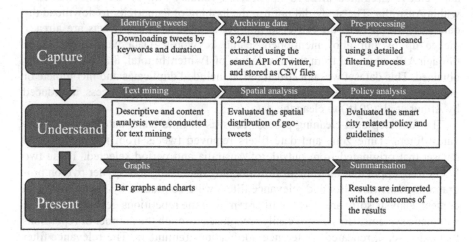

Figure 4.1 Systematic geo-located Twitter analysis framework (Fan & Gordon, 2014).

growing social media microblogging service; (b) researchers and practitioners can use a free Twitter "application programming interface" (API) to conduct analysis based on their interests; (c) as opposed to Facebook and Instagram, Twitter data are considered as "open data", which provides succinct real-time data to public (Dufty, 2016); (d) search and streaming APIs of Twitter allow researchers to write queries and download information under certain keywords and/or hashtags (Guan & Chen, 2014); and (e) analysing Twitter data is a novel method of harvesting dispersed community knowledge (Kankanamge et al., 2019b).

The main limitation is the restricted API-based data accessibility, where APIs provide access to only 1% of publicly available Twitter data. From this sample, only around 10% is either geo-located or geo-tagged (Cebeillac & Rault, 2016). Even from geo-located and geo-tagged tweets, geo-tagged tweets are becoming even harder to collect. This is due to not sharing personal mobile location information and ethical barriers as such information consists of the exact latitude and longitude information.

For instance, from the collected data for this analysis, only 64 tweets contained geo-tagged information. This is due to geo-tagged information often being collected through data providers, as geo-tagged tweets often become available during crisis periods and it is challenging for individuals to capture this information (Kankanamge et al., 2020). As another limitation, Lin and Cromley (2015) highlighted the bias of the age group for the Twitter data. Despite these limitations, there is an increasing number of studies that use tweets as the main data source (Brandt et al., 2017; Yuan & Liu, 2018).

In this study, Twitter data were collected for the most recent full year—i.e., 2018. The data-capturing process started with the identification of keywords. Accordingly, the study downloaded tweets with the keywords of "smart", "city", and "cities" circulated in 2018—between 1 January and 31 December 2018—within Australia. The study did not use the hashtag of #smartcity to download the data as it would limit the retrieved number of tweets. These tweets are already picked up by our abovementioned search keywords. Data were downloaded through APIs obtained from the developers of Twitter. In total, 8,241 tweets were obtained. This dataset was not structured; it included duplicates and incomplete or unusable tweets. The study adopted the four-step data-cleaning process, introduced by Arthur et al. (2018) to clean the data.

The four-step data-cleaning process consists of time zone, date, bot, and relevance filters. Time zone and date filters removed tweets from the downloaded dataset that originated from outside of Australia and period selected. These two filters were applied at the time of downloading data using the Spyder python programming software. Bot and relevance filters were conducted by using Nvivo—a content analysis software. The bot filter removed the repetitions generated through automatic systems. Bots can be easily recognised through the number of repetitions that exist—e.g., repeated conference notifications/reminders. The relevance filter was conducted manually by closely inspecting tweets, which are used with a different meaning—e.g., smart people. From the downloaded 8,241 tweets, only 3,073 qualified to be used in the study. Figure 4.2 presents the selection criteria, and types of analyses.

The second stage of the framework involved "understanding" what tweets say/communicate. Four different, but intertwining, analyses were used to understand tweets. They were descriptive, content, network, and policy analyses.

The last stage of the framework involved "presenting" outcomes of the abovementioned analyses. It adopted appropriate visualising techniques such as graphs and maps for an easy communication of the results.

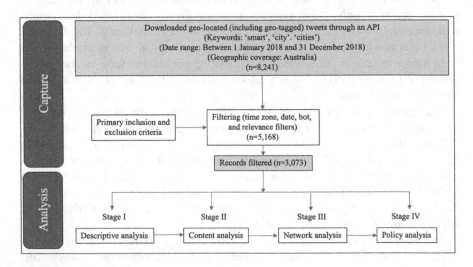

Figure 4.2 Tweet selection criteria for analysis.

4.3.3 Descriptive Analysis

Twitter data contain various information, such as "created_date", "user-screen name", "user-name", "text", "photo/video", and "user-location". The study used a descriptive analysis (DA) to deliver a broader view about the captured data. This study focused on three descriptive statistics, namely Twitter statistics, user analysis, and web-link (URL) analysis. Identifying prominent hashtags are especially useful for urban planners as tweets reflect the emotive and evaluative perceptions of the citizens. Twitter statistics provided information about the number of active users, number of retweets, and number of hashtags used. The study considered all "retweets" as new tweets with the related location of the retweet sender. This information acted as a gateway for many other inline analyses, such as content analysis and spatial analysis.

4.3.4 Content Analysis

Tweets are informal in nature, and consist of lay language, acronyms, URLs, photos, videos, and ideograms. They also contain people's opinions. Analysing tweets is a sensitive and significant task. Word frequency analysis was the initial point for the content analysis. Word frequency analysis identified the popular concepts and technologies, and then the co-occurrence of words helped in determining the linkages among the concepts and technologies. Popular concepts and technologies reflect both hidden and dispersed community knowledge around smart cities.

The study also conducted a spatial analysis to complement the content analysis. For the analysis, we used the location information collected in tweets to categorise the main themes of the analysis by their locations. We categorised the most popular concepts and technologies into themes based on the origin of tweets (i.e., city and state) using co-occurrence frequencies of words. This presented a snapshot of the most popular concepts and technologies for each state.

4.3.5 Network Analysis

This research used a network analysis to present the association between concepts and technologies and their popularity (centrality). Different metrics can be used in network theory to interpret the strength and topology of a network. We used nodes (concepts and technologies) and edges (relationships between these concepts and technologies) as the key elements of the network. Nodes and edges help in interpreting the network topology. The network topology represents a layout of nodes and edges created based on the co-occurrence of concepts and technologies in tweets and retweets.

Two types of network analysis emerged through the network theory. These analyses were centrality and community-level analyses. First, centrality analysis considered the significance of each node compared to adjacent nodes. Second, community-level analysis explored network-level characteristics such as density. This represents all the possible connections between all the nodes. This study used centrality analysis to identify the association between popular concepts and technologies.

4.3.6 Policy Analysis

Through a policy analysis, the study evaluated prevailing smart city strategies and planning policies. This aimed to understand processes behind the development of planning policies, and the role of strategies in developing the concepts that were identified through descriptive and content analyses. This analysis connects social media data with numerous smart city policies developed and introduced in Australia. It helps in better comprehension of how smart city policies are perceived by the public, and how these policies influenced public perceptions. Exploring both policy and perception dimensions provides policymakers with essential information for consolidating existing policies or developing new effective, efficient, and feasible ones.

4.4 Results

4.4.1 What Are the Trending Smart City Concepts and Technologies?

Of the 3,073 usable tweets, 1,179 (38%) were original, and 1,894 (62%) were retweeted, reflecting the highly interactive nature of users. All Twitter discussions developed in total 28 hashtags. The hashtag analysis identified (excluding #smartcities and #smartcity) 16 key hashtags among them as the most strongly associated ones with the smart city domain. These were: #autonomousvehicle; #transport; #5G; #sustainability; #mobility; #internet-of-things; #energy; #innovation; #governance; #artificialintelligence; #blockchain; #bigdata; #robotics; #opendata; #waste; #startups.

Trending hashtags were: #IoT, #AI, #opendata, #robotics, #bigdata, #autonomous, #automation, #automative, #autonomousvehicle, #driverless, #selfdriving, #5G, #blockchain. Tweets with these hashtags captured views on incorporating novel, innovative, and advance technologies to shape smart cities. Other popular hashtags were: #cybersecurity, #android, #traffic, #software, #digitalbuiltaustralia, #austech, #sustainability, #ausbiz. Tweets with these hashtags concentrated on smart city strategies with an economy and mobility focus. The temporal variation of hashtag usage is significant to the study. For instance, tweet numbers increased substantially between September and October 2018 due to the Smart Cities Week Australia 2018 event in Sydney. The event hashtags such as #SCW and #SCWAus were frequently circulated during this period.

In total, 1,090 users contributed to create the dataset of 3,073 tweets. A total of 69% of the tweets were circulated by individual users, and 31% by institutions. However, 75% of the top-20 most active users were institutional users. These organisations include technology firms, research centres, not-for-profit organisations, and conference organisers. The number of tweets of the most active users ranged between 20 and 150 tweets per year. In terms of followers these organisations had more followers than individuals, meaning they naturally had wider outreach. Yet, it would not be correct to interpret this as their dominance in communicating opinions, as individual user tweets were more than double in quantity than institutional ones.

There were 176 tweets with informative URLs in the dataset. Most of them contained links to blogs, discussion sites, articles, and conference websites that talk about the smart city movement in Australia and overseas. Hot topics discussed included Melbourne's high-tech vision; driverless cars and national autonomous vehicle law; cyber security; smarter irrigation management solutions; and smart waste management systems.

4.4.2 What Are the Relationships between Smart City Concepts and Technologies?

Tweets obtained from each state were categorised separately (Figure 4.3). The states with the highest number of smart city tweets were NSW (1,372), VIC (710), QLD (432), ACT (371), and SA (103). WA (60) and TAS (25) had the lowest number of tweets. The national capital Canberra is in the Australian Capital Territory (ACT). The city houses almost all of the Federal authorities, and naturally the key national policy issues, including smart cities and technologies, are widely discussed in the city. Interestingly, most of the analysed tweets consist of scholarly discussions that evaluate the smart city notion under different concepts and technologies. Tweets discussed included: Launching robotics roadmaps for automation adoption; Lake Macquarie

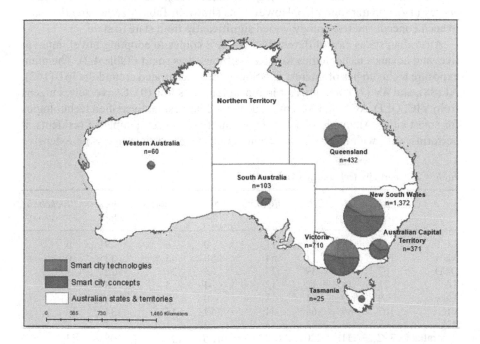

Figure 4.3 Spatial distribution of tweets.

smart city network project; and Tesla's power wall batteries project for smart energy management systems. Twitter provided a user-centric online media/platform to express individual and institutional views on the projects. Institutional tweets on policies and projects helped the information to be circulated widely. This, in return, motivated or provoked individuals to reflect their responses. For instance, 28 individuals have retweeted posts related to Lake Macquarie Smart City Network with their own comments included. This has ultimately developed a thought-provoking discussion thread related to the project by individuals expressing their concerns or endorsements.

To evaluate the intellectual value of such tweets, the study conducted a word count analysis to identify the frequently used concepts and technologies. When the tweets consisted of more concepts such as innovation and sustainability, they were classified as "tweets on smart city concepts", and when the tweets discussed technologies such as AI and IoT, they were classified as "tweets on smart city technologies". In a situation where tweets equally discussed both concepts and technologies, they were classified under both categories. Further, tweets which generally commented on smart cities without referring to any technology or concept, e.g., Enjoying the life in a smart city of Australia, were ignored.

Finally, the study identified 16 themes that acted as the basis for most of the tweets. Across Australia the most referred-to technologies were: Internet of Things (IoT) (392); artificial intelligence (AI) (231); autonomous vehicle (AV) (220); big data (152); 5G (126); robotics (123); open data (108); and blockchain (53). These technologies were discussed in relation to key concepts such as: innovation (423); sustainability (413); start-ups (269); governance (255); mobility (97); waste (82); energy (19); and transport (13). However, as shown in Table 4.2, the attention paid to each concept and technology varied significantly from state to state.

Australian states have different foci when it comes to adopting novel, innovative, and advance technologies for making their cities smart (Table 4.2). The main exposure technologies of interest in NSW were concentrated around the IoT (162), AI (88), and AV (71); and interest in blockchain was low (0). Conversely, citizens from VIC, QLD, ACT, and SA have a dispersed interest in diversified technologies for smart cities. Although ACT has a comparatively lower number of residents, it performs well, with a considerable number of tweets. This reflects the extensive

Table 4.2 Smart city technology tweets by states

	IoT	AI	AV	Big Data	5G	Robotics	Open Data	Blockchain
ACT	27	15	27	11	9	6	9	6
NSW	162	88	71	54	58	45	32	0
QLD	67	41	39	27	6	21	22	11
SA	21	18	12	12	4	5	8	4
TAS	9	0	1	1	0	0	1	1
VIC	103	66	68	44	47	45	34	30
WA	3	3	2	3	2	1	2	1
Australia	392	231	220	152	126	123	108	53

Table 4.3 Smart city concept tweets by states

	Innovation	Sustainability	Start-ups	Governance	Mobility	Waste	Energy	Transport
ACT	54	40	14	23	10	12	10	10
NSW	213	140	145	125	44	46	2	4
QLD	30	50	17	31	15	11	2	2
SA	16	6	4	14	5	2	2	0
TAS	5	5	2	7	0	0	0	0
VIC	82	207	88	60	28	19	7	0
WA	11	1	5	6	3	0	1	3
Australia	423	413	269	255	97	82	19	13

Table 4.4 Most active (top-10) cities in smart city tweets

City	Number of tweets and retweets	Population weighted rank
Sydney (NSW)	1,339	1
Melbourne (VIC)	696	3
Brisbane (QLD)	379	7
Canberra (ACT)	371	4
Adelaide (SA)	103	2
Perth (WA)	52	5
Sunshine Coast (QLD)	29	8
Hobart (TAS)	25	6
Gold Coast (QLD)	14	10
Ipswich (QLD)	10	9

interest, knowledge, and awareness of ACT residents on the smart city concepts and technologies. WA and TAS also have a dispersed interest in technologies, but the lower number of tweets made them insignificant/unreliable. The results displayed that motivation and awareness exist among the local communities of each state in making their cities smarter.

As well as technologies, there were engaging concepts. As given in Table 4.3, eight popular concepts were identified from tweets scrutinised through a word frequency analysis.

Innovation (213), start-ups (145), sustainability (140), and governance (e-governance) (125) were the most popular concepts in NSW. However, compared to the number of tweets, sustainability is much more popular in VIC (207 tweets) as a concept than in NSW. QLD and ACT were interested in smart city agendas to encourage sustainability in their cities through novel innovations and e-governance practices. Accordingly, Twitter users seem to be extensively interested in making their cities smart in transport, governance, innovative economy (e.g., start-ups), and waste management areas.

Table 4.4 demonstrates that Twitter users from the capital cities of Australian states were highly active in using social media to discuss concepts and technologies—i.e.,

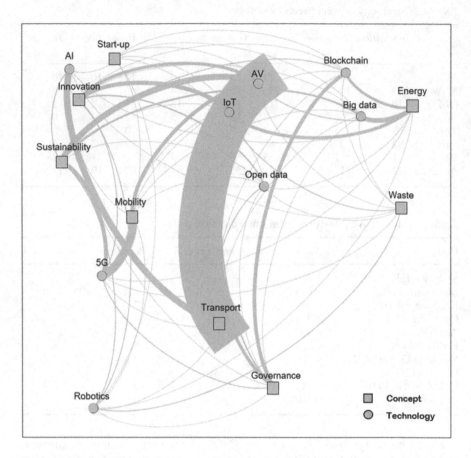

Figure 4.4 Relationships between popular concepts and technologies.

Sydney, Melbourne, Brisbane, Canberra, Adelaide, Perth, Hobart. Top-10 Twitter active cities on smart city discussions also include some locations outside the capital cities—i.e., Sunshine Coast, Gold Cost, Ipswich from QLD. Table 4.4 provides a population-weighted rank of the most active locations in terms of smart city discussion. While the top-10 locations do not change, their order do.

Although Tables 4.1 and 4.2 reflect the trending concepts and technologies, they did not reflect the relationships among popular concepts and technologies. Neither did they reflect the popularity of each concept and technology (when all concepts and technologies are considered). Hence, we conducted a network analysis.

Figure 4.4 presents the layout of network topology, which disclosed the relationships between popular concepts and technologies. Square nodes depict concepts, and circular nodes depict technologies. The widths of the edges show the strength of the relationship existing between nodes. The strength of the relationships among nodes were calculated through the co-occurrence of concepts and technologies in the tweets and retweets analysed.

Then, the study calculated the centrality (popularity) level of each node. We used weighted degree centrality—a measure to identify the nodes' connectedness with the other nodes in the network—to quantify the perceived levels/degrees of the aforesaid concepts and technologies. For instance, a node with five links has a higher degree centrality than a node with two links. The number of co-occurrences was used to create/weight the links among the nodes.

As per Table 4.5, transport (can be merged with mobility) was by far the most central concept. Sustainability was the second most popular concept. Energy, innovation, and governance concepts followed. Waste and start-ups (can be merged with innovation) were other concepts gaining popularity.

Among the technologies, AV was by far the most popular one (by weight) (Table 4.5), and had a strong relationship first with transport, and then with the other concepts such as sustainability, mobility, energy, and innovation (Figure 4.4). 5G technology was the next most popular technology. IoT, AI, blockchain, and big data were to follow. Robotics and open data were the least popular ones, with the lowest centrality.

Within the top-16 themes ranked by weights (Table 4.5), half of them were concepts, and the other half were technologies. This finding presents a balanced view of concepts and technologies in Australia.

Table 4.5 Degree centrality of concepts and technologies

Themes	Concept/technology	Weighted score
AV	Technology	129
Transport	Concept	116
5G	Technology	35
Sustainability	Concept	34
Mobility	Concept	32
IoT	Technology	30
Energy	Concept	29
Innovation	Concept	26
Governance	Concept	24
AI	Technology	22
Block chain	Technology	21
Big data	Technology	20
Robotics	Technology	11
Open data	Technology	11
Waste	Concept	10
Start-ups	Concept	8

4.4.3 What Are the Official Smart City Policies That Influence Perception and Utilisation of Smart City Concepts and Technologies?

In general, Australian states perceived concepts and technologies differently. This is most likely due to the varying degree of externalities of smart city policies on local communities in each state. The more communities feel the impacts of such policies (positive or negative), the more they will discuss, appreciate, or criticise them. Sound and well-communicated policies receive higher support from the public; the opposite is also true.

Australia is rich in urban policy, with numerous government policies focusing on smart cities. Prominent national-level authorities that have prepared and launched smart city policies, funds, and projects include Smart Cities Council of Australia and New Zealand, Australian Department of Infrastructure, Transport, Cities and Regional Development, and Department of the Prime Minister and Cabinet. NSW, VIC, SA, and QLD also have state-level smart city policies. At the local-level, smart city policies are also gaining prominence. Table 4.6 lists cities with smart city strategy.

Smart city policies are categorised into four themes, transport-, energy-, economy- and governance-related policies. All state capitals except WA and NT have clear policies in these areas. There are also smart city projects in progress across all states. NSW has 13 smart city projects, while VIC, QLD, WA, SA have 10, 9, 7, 6, and 2 projects, respectively, and NT has one project.

Transport-related policies are the most prominent. This might be something to do with transport being a major challenge for Australian populations and cities that rely heavily on private motor vehicles. The key smart city strategies in operation that refer to legislative issues for smart cities include: Future Transport Strategy of NSW; Connected and Automated Vehicle Plan; Greater Sydney Service and Infrastructure Plan; National Smart Cities Plan. Policy discussions focusing on new and forthcoming legislation include: AV trial guidelines; new transport rules and regulations; study lessons learned from the US and Singapore; changing the sign boards; changing property and other infrastructure-related guidelines for compliance with automated vehicles; defining vehicle automation levels, designing trial paths; establishing a standby setting date to end analogue cars; and smart airports. AV projects and policies for smart transport planning under discussion include: automated traffic management of Fraser Coast, QLD; driverless shuttle service of Sydney; semi-automated port operations in port Botany; and Australia posts footpath-based delivery through drones.

Energy-related policies of Australia are concerned with balancing energy supply and energy demand and a reduction through smart energy use (Strengers, 2013). Australian policies on energy have already identified the significance of smart energy usage to cut energy bills and reduce environmental impacts. A number of smart city projects are already in operation. These include: resilient energy and water systems of Fremantle, WA; energy-efficient housing of South East Perth, WA; energy data for smart decision-making in Sydney; and smart grid trials in the Greater Newcastle and Sydney CBD. In addition, government policies on

Table 4.6 Local government areas with smart city strategies

State	City	Title	URL
QLD	Brisbane	Smart, Connected Brisbane	www.brisbane.qld.gov.au/about-council/governance-and-strategy/vision-and-strategy/smart-connected-brisbane
	Sunshine Coast	Smart City Framework	www.sunshinecoast.qld.gov.au/Council/Planning-and-Projects/Major-Regional-Projects/Smart-Cities/Smart-City-Implementation-Program
	Townsville	Smart Townsville	www.townsville.qld.gov.au/about-council/news-and-publications/city-update-online/smart-townsville
NSW	Canada Bay	Smart City Draft Plan	https://collaborate.canadabay.nsw.gov.au/smartcity
	Goulburn Mulwaree	Smart City Strategy	https://yoursay.goulburn.nsw.gov.au/smart-city-action-plan
	Lake Macquarie	Smart Council Digital Economy Strategy	www.lakemac.com.au/city/smart-city-smart-council
	Newcastle	Draft Smart City Strategy	http://newcastle.nsw.gov.au/Community/Get-Involved/Completed-Consultation-Projects/Community-Planning/Smart-City-Strategy-2017–2021
	Paramatta	Smart City Masterplan	www.cityofparramatta.nsw.gov.au/smart-city
	Randwick	Draft Smart City Strategy	www.yoursay.randwick.nsw.gov.au/smartcities
	Western Sydney	Smart Cities Plan	https://citydeals.infrastructure.gov.au/western-sydney
NT	Darwin	Smart City Plan	https://citydeals.infrastructure.gov.au/darwin
SA	Adelaide	Smart Cities Plan	https://citydeals.infrastructure.gov.au/adelaide
	Charles Sturt	Smart City Plan	www.charlessturt.sa.gov.au/SmartCity
TAS	Hobart	Connected Hobart Smart Cities Action Plan	https://yoursay.hobartcity.com.au/smart-city
	Launceston	Smart Cities Plan	www.launceston.tas.gov.au/Launceston-City-Deal/City-Deal-Implementation
VIC	Geelong	Smart Cities Plan	https://citydeals.infrastructure.gov.au/geelong
	Wyndham	Smart City Strategy	https://theloop.wyndham.vic.gov.au/smart-city

increasing infrastructure for electric vehicle users and increasing awareness about the solar and battery storage technologies have also contributed towards the smart energy movement.

Economy-related policies received considerably less attention across Australia, even though the economy has weakened in recent years. Cities are only starting to consider the economic growth dimensions of smart policies. NSW has embraced investors to help Sydney on its mission to achieve 2021 goals. New start-ups, namely Nomad restaurants, Swill house group, Jolly Swagman Backpackers Sydney, Sydney Science Park, and Smart Innovation Centre are some businesses supporting the Smart Green Business Program of Sydney. It was awarded with the NSW Green Globe Award in 2013. Innovation districts are being developed across the eastern coast of Australia—Sydney, Melbourne, Brisbane (Esmaeilpoorarabi et al., 2018; Pancholi et al., 2019). However, most of these are not directly linked with the smart city initiatives of their host cities. The national innovation district policy is also divorced from smart cities policy. The only exception is in Queensland. In QLD innovation districts were originally designed as part of the former Smart State Strategy of QLD (Hortz, 2016). However, to address this Australia-wide limitation, in late 2018, a national policy was released. "Principles for Australian Innovation Precincts" is prepared by the Federal Department of Industry, Innovation and Science and emphasises the connection between innovation district and smart cities.

Governance-related policies are gaining momentum. Australia is a global leader in digitalisation of government services. Today, most government services are delivered virtually across many Australian authorities—e.g., tax, development assessment applications. Extensive online services also attract hackers. On cyber security, the Australian Strategic Policy Institute (ASPI) develops strategies to protect the privacy of data and information. Introducing a digital identity, to recognise receipt of a digital signature, and secure data exchange mechanisms are the foci of the APSI policy.

Our policy analysis reflects the existence of, but limitations in or the inadequacy of, the smart city initiatives at the national level. For instance, in 2017, more than 170 local governments applied for a share in AU$50 million smart cities Federal Government funding. This indicates the limitation of the funds for smart city projects in Australia. Some Australian states, such as TAS and NT, do not have strong smart city policies. Instead, they have certain relevant projects implemented on demand. Although this is useful, having a sound national- and state-level policy for smart cities will help advance smart urbanism practices in Australia.

4.5 Discussion and Conclusion

Smart cities have already become a promising approach to create a sustainable and liveable urban future (Yigitcanlar et al., 2019a). Smart city discussions and awareness are especially high within the Australian professional and business communities. Smart cities are also highly popular in urban policy circles around the globe. Local, regional, and national governments have been working to transform their cities into smart ones through strategies, plans, and projects involving the substantial engagement of technology solutions. Still, expectations from smart cities are highly unrealistic as they are full of speculation (Luque-Ayala & Marvin, 2015; Wiig, 2015). There is limited knowledge and understanding about: trending concepts and technologies; relationships between popular concepts and technologies; and policies that influence the perception and use of concepts and technologies.

To bridge the knowledge gap, this study employed systematic geo-located Twitter analysis to scrutinise discourse and policy in Australia. The research particularly focused on addressing the question of: How are the smart city concepts and technologies perceived and utilised in Australian cities? The study findings provide a clear snapshot of community perceptions, and disclose the following insights that inform smart city policymaking.

First, the results of the analysis showed that innovation, also including start-ups (with 692 of 3,073 tweets—23%), sustainability (413 tweets—13%), and governance (with 255—8%) were the most popular concepts in Twitter discourse across Australia. When the degree of centrality of concepts is considered, the top-three concepts were transport (includes mobility), sustainability, and energy. These were followed by innovation and governance.

The ranking of the top-three concepts (i.e., innovation, sustainability, governance) in NSW and ACT were the same as for Australia overall. In VIC and QLD, sustainability took first place (followed by innovation and governance), whereas in TAS, it moved to third place (following innovation and governance). In SA and WA, governance moved to second place (after innovation and before sustainability). The variations between the states are an indication of local contextual differences in policy and planning priorities and conceptualisations of the smart city notion.

Second, the findings revealed that the IoT (with 392 of 3,073 tweets—13%), AI (231 tweets—8%), and AV (220 tweets—7%) were the most popular technologies based on Twitter trends. When the degree centrality of concepts is considered, the top-three ranking was as follows: AV, 5G, and IoT, respectively (followed by AI). No tweets were found from NSW mentioning blockchain technology. However, throughout Australia, blockchain has been widely discussed in relation to energy and governance-related issues (Figure 4.4). The heightened interest in blockchain in VIC is mainly due to the Blockchain Association of Australia being located in Melbourne, VIC. Similarly, in QLD, University of Queensland has a Blockchain Club, and Brisbane, QLD, hosts the Blockchain Australia National Meetup Roadshows.

The three technologies (i.e., IoT, AI, AV) were in the top three in all states except TAS. Additionally, in some states, big data and open data also shared the top-three positions with AV. This finding indicates a degree of consistency across the states. The ranking of the top-three technologies in NSW and QLD were the same as for Australia overall. In VIC, AV moved one step up (following IoT and followed by AI). In ACT and SA, the first position was shared by IoT and AV (followed by AI). In WA, third place was shared by AV and big data (following IoT and AI). In TAS, second place was shared by AV, big data, and open data (following IoT). Like concepts, technologies also showed minor variations across the states. This is an indication of differences in technology adoption and prioritisation, and local smart city plans and projects.

Third, the study disclosed that Sydney, Melbourne, and Brisbane, as major Australian cities—also their greater city regions as the leading Australian metropolitan areas—have greater interest in concepts and technologies. Nevertheless, different policy interventions and priorities of cities cause the increase/decrease of the popularity of the aforesaid concepts and technologies among the public. For instance, although Brisbane's Smart Connected Brisbane Policy was only released in 2017, Brisbane has been benefiting from the Smart State Strategy legacy of the state government dating back to 1998. Similarly, Melbourne's relatively new smart city strategy is the rebranding of knowledge city policy (Millar & Ju-Choi, 2010; Yigitcanlar, 2014) of the city dating back to the early 2000s. In other words, Sydney, Melbourne, and Brisbane benefit from their path-dependency. Furthermore, these greater city-regions recently received lucrative funds for their smart city endeavours/transformation—as part of the Commonwealth Government's Smart Cities Plan. For instance, Western Sydney City Deal in NSW, Geelong City Deal in VIC, and South East Queensland City Deal in QLD are among them—funding is envisaged to stimulate an increase of the economy by improving the productivity and competitiveness of the region.

Fourth, the network analysis findings pointed out a balanced view on the importance of concepts and technologies to achieve smart urbanism or smart city transformation—perhaps this is the Australian way of realising the smart city dream. This is a critical finding as only with such a balanced view—seeing technology as a means to a goal rather than fully relying on it as the panacea—can we address urban developmental problems (Yigitcanlar, 2008). One of the possible reasons for the balanced concept and technology view on smart cities in Australia is the advancing government policy frameworks. Currently, more than a dozen sound smart city policy frameworks are available (Table 4.6) at the local government level, and this number is expected to exponentially increase soon.

Fifth, the study proved that systematic geo-located Twitter analysis is a useful methodological approach for investigating perceptions and utilisation of concepts and technologies. The social media analytics methodology—the capture-understand-present framework (Fan & Gordon, 2014)—was previously applied to other research areas—e.g., business, and tourism and hospitality (Amadio & Procaccino, 2016). This chapter showcases its application in another field—i.e., smart city concepts and technologies.

Next, this study provides a big picture view on Twitter user perspectives on the smart city concepts and technologies in Australian cities. It also showcases the usefulness of social media analysis as a complementary method to the studies that government agencies, not-for-profit organisations, and consultancy firms have been undertaking to follow the latest developments in the field and understand the perceptions of authorities, experts, and the public at large. The findings are informative and encourage authorities to adopt social media analytics in their routine data collection mechanisms to make more informed decisions (Yigitcanlar et al., 2021).

Acknowledgements

This chapter, with permission from the copyright holder, is a reproduced version of the following journal article: Yigitcanlar, T., Kankanamge, N., & Vella, K. (2021). How are smart city concepts and technologies perceived and utilized? a systematic geo-twitter analysis of smart cities in Australia. *Journal of Urban Technology*, 28(1–2), 135–154.

References

Aina, Y. (2007). Achieving smart sustainable cities with GeoICT support. *Cities*, *71*, 49–58.

Albino, V., Berardi, U., Dangelico, R. (2015). Smart cities. *Journal of Urban Technology*, *22*, 3–21.

Alizadeh, T. (2015). A policy analysis of digital strategies. *International Journal of Knowledge-Based Development*, *6*, 85–103.

Alizadeh, T., Sarkar, S., Burgoyne, S. (2019). Capturing citizen voice online. *Cities*, *95*, 2751–2761.

Amadio, W. Procaccino, J. (2016). Competitive analysis of online reviews using exploratory text mining. *Tourism and Hospitality Management*, *22*, 193–210.

Anthopoulos, L. (2017). Smart utopia vs smart reality. *Cities*, *63*, 128–148.

Arbolino, R., Carlucci, F., Cirà, A., Ioppolo, G., Yigitcanlar, T. (2017). Efficiency of the EU regulation on greenhouse gas emissions in Italy. *Ecological Indicators*, *81*, 115–123.

Arbolino, R., De Simone, L., Carlucci, F., Yigitcanlar, T., Ioppolo, G. (2018). Towards a sustainable industrial ecology. *Journal of Cleaner Production*, *178*, 220–236.

Arthur, R., Boulton, C., Shotton, H., Williams, H. (2018). Social sensing of floods in the UK. *Plos One*, *13*, 1–18.

Bibri, S. (2019). On the sustainability of smart and smarter cities in the era of big data. *Journal of Big Data*, *6*, 25.

Brandt, T., Bendler, J., Neumann, D. (2017). Social media analytics and value creation in urban smart tourism ecosystems. *Information & Management*, *54*, 703–713.

Caragliu, A., Del Bo, C., Nijkamp, P. (2011). Smart cities in Europe' *Journal of Urban Technology*, *18*, 65–82.

Cebeillac, A., Rault, Y.M. (2016). Contribution of geotagged twitter data in the study of a social group's activity space. *Netcom. Réseaux, Communication et Territoires*, *30*, 231–248.

Ciuccarelli, P., Lupi, G., Simeone, L. (2014). *Visualizing the Data City*. Berlin: Springer.

De-Jong, M., S. Joss, D. Schraven, C. Zhan, M. Weijnen. (2015). Sustainable–smart–resilient–low carbon–eco–knowledge cities. *Journal of Cleaner Production*, *109*, 25–38.

Deakin, M., Reid, A. (2018). Smart cities. *Journal of Cleaner Production*, *173*, 39–48.

Dufty, N. (2016). Twitter turns ten. *Australian Journal of Emergency Management*, *31*, 50–54.

Errichiello, L., Marasco, A. (2014). Open service innovation in smart cities. *Advanced Engineering Forum*, *11*, 115–124.

Ersoy, A. (2017). Smart cities as a mechanism towards a broader understanding of infrastructure interdependencies. *Regional Studies, Regional Science*, *4*, 26–31.

Esmaeilpoorarabi, N., Yigitcanlar, T., Guaralda, M., Kamruzzaman, M. (2018). Does place quality matter for innovation districts? *Land Use Policy*, *79*, 734–747.

Faisal, A., Yigitcanlar, T., Kamruzzaman, M., Currie, G. (2019). Understanding autonomous vehicles. *Journal of Transport and Land Use, 12*, 45–72.

Fan, W., Gordon, M. (2014). The power of social media analytics. *Communications of the ACM, 57*, 74–81.

Fernandez-Anez, V., Fernández-Güell, J., Giffinger, R. (2018). Smart City implementation and discourses. *Cities, 78*, 4–16.

Giffinger, R., Pichler-Milanović, N. (2007). *Smart cities.* Vienna: Vienna University of Technology.

Grossi, G., Pianezzi, D. (2017). Smart cities. *Cities, 69*, 79–85.

Guan, X., C. Chen. (2014). Using social media data to understand and assess disasters. *Natural Hazards, 74*, 837–850.

Hortz, T. (2016). The smart state test. *International Journal of Knowledge-Based Development, 7*, 75–101.

Joss, S., Sengers, F., Schraven, D., Caprotti, F., Dayot, Y. (2019). The smart city as global discourse. *Journal of Urban Technology, 26*, 3–34.

Kane, G. (2017). The evolutionary implications of social media for organizational knowledge management. *Information and Organization, 27*, 37–46.

Kankanamge, N., Yigitcanlar, T., Goonetilleke, A., Kamruzzaman, M. (2020). Determining disaster severity through social media analysis. *International Journal of Disaster Risk Reduction, 42*, 101360.

Komninos, N. (2016). Smart environments and smart growth. *International Journal of Knowledge-Based Development, 7*, 240–263.

Komninos, N., C. Kakderi, A. Panori, & P. Tsarchopoulos. (2019). Smart city planning from an evolutionary perspective. *Journal of Urban Technology, 26*, 3–20. Kunzmann, K. (2014). Smart cities. *Crios, 4*, 9–20.

Lin, J., Cromley, R.G. (2015). Evaluating geo-located Twitter data as a control layer for areal interpolation of population. *Applied Geography, 58*, 41–47.

Luque-Ayala, A., Marvin, S. (2015). Developing a critical understanding of smart urbanism? *Urban Studies, 52*, 2105–2116.

Mah, D., Vleuten, J., Hills, P., Tao, J. (2012). Consumer perceptions of smart grid development. *Energy Policy, 49*, 204–216.

Millar, C., Ju-Choi, C. (2010). Development and knowledge resources. *Journal of Knowledge Management, 14*, 759–776.

Mora, L., R. Bolici, M. Deakin. (2017). The first two decades of smart-city research. *Journal of Urban Technology, 24*, 3–27.

Mora, L., Deakin, M., Reid, A. (2019). Strategic principles for smart city development. *Technological Forecasting and Social Change, 142*, 70–97.

Mysterud, A. (2017). *Evolutionary Perspectives on Environmental Problems.* New York: Routledge.

Osorio-Arjona, A., García-Palomares, J. (2019). Social media and urban mobility. *Cities, 89*, 268–280.

Pancholi, S., Yigitcanlar, T., Guaralda, M. (2019). Place making in knowledge and innovation spaces. *Technological Forecasting and Social Change, 146*, 616–625.

Pettit, C., Bakelmun, A., Lieske, S.N., Glackin, S., Thomson, G., Shearer, H., Newman, P. (2018). Planning support systems for smart cities. *City, Culture and Society, 12*, 13–24.

Praharaj, S., Han, H., Hawken, S. (2018). Urban innovation through policy integration. *City, Culture and Society, 12*, 35–43.

Söderström, O., Paasche, T., Klauser, F. (2014). Smart cities as corporate storytelling. *City, 18*, 307–320.

Strengers, Y. (2013). *Smart Energy Technologies in Everyday Life.* Melbourne: Springer.

Townsend, A. (2013). *Smart Cities.* New York: W.W.Norton.

Wiig, A. (2015). IBM's smart city as techno-utopian policy mobility. *City, 19,* 258–273.

Williamson, W., Ruming, K. (2020). Can social media support large scale public participation in urban planning? The case of the# MySydney digital engagement campaign. *International Planning Studies, 25*(4), 355–371.

Winden, W., Buuse, D. (2017). Smart city pilot projects. *Journal of Urban Technology, 24,* 51–72.

Yigitcanlar, T. (2006). Australian local governments' practice and prospects with online planning. *URISA Journal, 18,* 7–17.

Yigitcanlar, T. (2009). Planning for smart urban ecosystems. *Theoretical and Empirical Researches in Urban Management, 4,* 5–21.

Yigitcanlar, T. (2014). Position paper. *Expert Systems with Applications, 41,* 5549–5559.

Yigitcanlar, T. (2018). Smart city policies revisited. *World Technopolis Review, 7,* 97–112.

Yigitcanlar, T., Han, H., Kamruzzaman, M., Ioppolo, G., Sabatini-Marques, J. (2019a). The making of smart cities. *Land Use Policy, 88,* 104187.

Yigitcanlar, T., Fabian, L., Coiacetto, E. (2008). Challenges to urban transport sustainability and smart transport in a tourist city. *The Open Transportation Journal, 2,* 29–46.

Yigitcanlar, T., Foth, M., Kamruzzaman, M. (2019b). Towards post-anthropocentric cities. *Journal of Urban Technology, 26,* 147–152.

Yigitcanlar, T., Kamruzzaman, M. (2018). Does smart city policy lead to sustainability of cities? *Land Use Policy, 73,* 49–58.

Yigitcanlar, T., Kamruzzaman, M. (2019). Smart cities and mobility. *Journal of Urban Technology, 2,* 21–46.

Yigitcanlar, T., Kamruzzaman, M., Buys, L., Ioppolo, G., Sabatini-Marques, J., Costa, E., Yun, J. (2018). Understanding 'smart cities'. *Cities, 81,* 145–160.

Yigitcanlar, T., Kamruzzaman, M., Foth, M., Sabatini-Marques, M., Costa, J.E., Ioppolo, G. (2019c). Can cities become smart without being sustainable? *Sustainable Cities and Society, 45,* 348–365.

Yigitcanlar, T., Wilson, M., Kamruzzaman, M. (2019d). Disruptive impacts of automated driving systems on the built environment and land use. *Journal of Open Innovation, 5,* 24.

Yigitcanlar, T., Kankanamge, N., Vella, K. (2021). How are smart city concepts and technologies perceived and utilized? A systematic geo-twitter analysis of smart cities in Australia. *Journal of Urban Technology, 28*(1–2), 135–154.

Yuan, F., Liu, R. (2018). Feasibility study of using crowdsourcing to identify critical affected areas for rapid damage assessment. *International Journal of Disaster Risk Reduction, 28,* 758–767.

Zhang, Q., Huang, T., Zhu, Y., Qiu, M. (2013). A case study of sensor data collection and analysis in smart city. *International Journal of Distributed Sensor Networks, 9,* 382132.

5   Smarter with Technology

5.1 Introduction

There exists a strong scientific consensus that anthropogenic climate change is the biggest crisis of our time [1,2]. In a rapidly urbanising world, climate change and the misuse and mismanagement of land and resources are triggering natural disasters and increasing their intensity [3,4]. Subsequently, cities are becoming frequently subjected to the direct or indirect impacts of natural disasters—for example, the 2019 Amazon Rainforest Fires [5], and the 2020 Australian Bushfires [6]. There have been numerous top-down (e.g., the Paris Agreement, Intergovernmental Panel on Climate Change, UN's Sustainable Development Goals, UN Climate Change Conferences), and bottom-up (e.g., school strikes, extinction rebellion protests, climate emergency declarations) attempts to raise awareness and develop policy actions to address the climate emergency [7,8].

These efforts provided some hope, despite the political and policy quagmires in many countries. Nevertheless, there has been no significant climate action undertaken to address the crisis. Instead, in recent years, with the advancement of the current digital revolution, a large portion of policymakers, practitioners, and scholars have increased their faith in smart urban technologies to mark a major turning point in the history of humankind [9]. This technocentric view—in solving urban and environmental problems with the aid of technology—has increased the popularity of the "smart cities" notion [10]. These cities—also referred to as "geographies of disruption" [11]—harness digital technologies to offer new business opportunities, shape the urban fabric, improve the quality and performance, and overcome many of the challenges confronted by urban areas [12].

The prospects of smart urban technologies range from expanding infrastructure capacity to generating new services, from reducing emissions to engaging the public, from minimising human errors to improved decision-making, and from supporting sustainable development to improving performances of commercial enterprises and cities [13,14]. The most popular technologies in the context of smart cities include but are not limited to the Internet of Things (IoT), autonomous vehicles (AV), big data, 5G, robotics, blockchain, cloud computing, 3D printing, virtual reality (VR), digital twins, and artificial intelligence (AI) [15–17]. While all these technologies are critical in transforming our cities into smarter ones, AI

DOI: 10.1201/9781003403630-7

combined with these technologies has significant potential to address the urbanisation challenges of our time [18]. Furthermore, AI is certainly seen as the most disruptive technology among them [19,20].

The prospective benefits of AI for cities continue to be discussed in the literature in the context of smart cities—that are enabled by community, technology, and policy to deliver productivity, innovation, liveability, wellbeing, sustainability, accessibility, good governance, and planning [15,21,22]. Despite the growing numbers of articles on the topic, there is no scholarly work that provides a comprehensive review of the growing literature. This chapter organises the literature to examine "how AI can contribute to the development of smarter cities". As the methodologic approach, the study adopts a systematic review of the literature on the "AI and the smart city" topic.

5.2 Literature Background

In broad terms, AI is defined as "machines or computers that mimic cognitive functions that humans associate with the human mind, such as learning and problem solving" [23]. In other words, AI, where machines mimic human cognitive functions, can make decisions, think, learn, and improve itself. It was first introduced in 1956 at Dartmouth College, but development was slow until recently due to immature computational technologies. In recent times, advances in hardware, software, and networking technologies have enabled us to design, develop, and deploy AI systems at scale. The application areas of AI range from banking and finance to marketing and gaming, and from agriculture and healthcare to AVs and space exploration—and many more areas [24].

AI-driven computational techniques are diverse and range from rule-based systems to deep learning systems. A popular AI knowledge map was created by Corea [25]. His conceptualisation brings together the AI paradigms and the AI problem domains (Figure 5.1). The x-axis categorises various computational paradigms and the y-axis outlines problem domains. Various technologies are then mapped to illustrate their potential value. For example, rule-based systems (e.g., expert systems, robotic process automation) that are logic-driven knowledge engines, which are common in urban systems are often used to capture and automate structured workflows.

AI applications, today, are being deployed in all facets of cities [26,27]. We can classify these applications based on their underlying AI technologies along with other relevant smart technologies, as shown in Figure 5.1.

AI applications are used to improve and innovate the delivery of public services [28]. Various cities have begun "robotic process automation" (RPA) projects. These projects are focused on automating tasks that are currently conducted by public workers that are mundane, repetitive, and costly. Thus, freeing up valuable resources to be better deployed. Cities are using RPA to process online applications for items such as permits. RPA follows structured rules to reach an outcome [29].

The interest in autonomous vehicles (AV) is palpable. AVs open opportunities for cities to modernise their public transport infrastructure [30]. The UK's

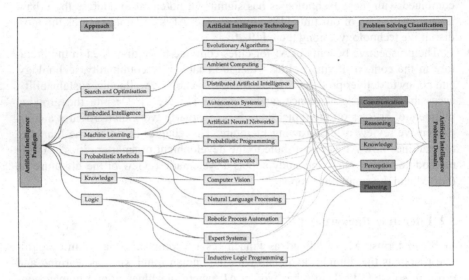

Figure 5.1 AI knowledge map, derived from [25].

first full-sized autonomous buses started operating for passengers in Edinburgh in 2023. All Nippon Airways (ANA) has commenced trials of autonomous buses with minimal human oversight at Haneda International Airport [31]. In recent times, we have also seen AVs complete successful tests in more complex urban environments, including London and Paris [32].

The interest in autonomous systems is not limited to RPA or AVs. Smart cities are exploring how to take advantage of advances in robotics [33]. The City of Houston will be beginning trials of robot police shortly at various transit centres to curb petty crime and free up law enforcement resources [34]. Robots are also being tested to augment law enforcement personnel and lower incidents of conflict between them and the public. In the US, where in recent times, several routine traffic stops have led to confrontations, robots are being tested in mediating encounters between police officers and drivers [35].

Engagement platforms between public agencies and various stakeholders of the city are also being transformed through a range of AI applications. Chatbots are the most popular set of AI applications in this regard. Rammas, a chatbot, was deployed by the Dubai Electricity and Water Authority (DEWA) in January 2017 [36]. DEWA can respond to queries from residents in Arabic and English, and promotes greater knowledge awareness on utility matters. In its first year of operations, Rammas responded to roughly 700,000 queries, which led to an 80% drop in in-person visits.

AI systems ingest vast amounts of data, apply learning algorithms, and learn patterns from the data to enable predicting outcomes [37]. Today, cities are deploying machine learning systems to exploit data across their ecosystem from sensors on public infrastructure, to machine-readable cards that provide access to city services (e.g., public transport), to images and videos that capture movements around the city, and even devices that capture auditory, olfactory, and tactile data [38,39]. Urban infrastructures, such as traffic lights, are becoming connected. Traffic lights are connected to road sensors to reduce wait time at signals based on the traffic flow. Scotland's Glasgow city has installed networks of sensors that connect to streetlights and traffic lights to help monitor traffic flow and increase connectivity, aggregately reducing travel time for drivers. Further, the traffic data also feed into maps in real time to help drivers, cyclists, and pedestrians make decisions to plan their commutes [40].

The Las Vegas Health Department, in partnership with the University of Rochester trialled the nEmesis app which utilised machine learning to collect and examine tweets, the purpose of which was to select restaurants which were suitable for inspection [41]. Following controlled experiments, the nEmesis app was found to be 64% better at identifying restaurants with food safety issues than established processes involving random inspections. It also had success at identifying restaurants that were unlicensed and had infectious staff. Overall, the app was very effective at helping the Las Vegas Health Department address issues with their restaurant inspection process without the need for additional resources [41]. The Harm Assessment Risk Tool (HART) was developed by UK's Durham Constabulary to detect patterns of recidivism among criminals [42]. The tool was trained on crime data from 2008–2012, including information about suspects' gender and zip code. The tool was used to predict the recidivism rate in 2013. It successfully predicted 98% of low-risk offenders and 88% of high-risk offenders.

In 2017, the Seattle Police Department launched a data analytics platform to transition towards improved oversight, data-driven decisions, and community engagement [43]. This platform helps the department to manage, govern, and support insightful policing. The system is designed to help the department's leadership team to track trends related to operations. It integrates 17 internally tracked metrics and develops visualisations for department heads. The system tracks several measures such as use-of-force incidents, number of arrests, self-initiated trips, response to calls, number of stops, and civilian complaints. The department can use this detailed information on each police officer to take appropriate measures (e.g., counselling). Since 2012, the police department in San Diego has collected over 65,000 face scans, to match them to a directory of over 1 million images collected as part of the San Diego County Sheriff's Tactical Identification System (TACIDS) [44]. More recently, London Metropolitan Police has announced plans to use facial recognition technology to aid police in identifying suspects.

While the housing and urban development space today is data rich, much of the data are often left unanalysed, thereby resulting in an inability to keep policies and enforcement standards current. Researchers from Georgia Institute of Technology, Emory University, and University of California, Irvine, collaborated with the Atlanta Fire Rescue Department (AFRD) to develop an algorithm which was able to predict fire risk in buildings [45]. Using data from 2010–2014, the algorithm included over 50 variables—including property location, building size, structure, age, and history of fire incidents—to predict fire risk. The algorithm classified fire risk ratings for 5,000 buildings and found another 19,397 buildings requiring inspection. Furthermore, the algorithm was able to predict 73% of fire incidents which occurred within the study area [45].

AI-enabled computational tools also help in protecting cyber-infrastructure that is the core fabric of smart cities [46]. Four US cities—i.e., Pensacola, New Orleans, Galt, St Lucie—were all victims of different cyberattacks throughout December that rendered telephone and email systems, law enforcement systems, and waste, energy, and payment systems inoperable. Often these attacks demand a ransom, and councils find themselves either paying the attackers or employing external cybersecurity and consulting firms to mitigate and repair the situation. In Lake City, Florida, council reluctantly paid $460,000 "ransom" to attackers after their entire council systems were shut down [47]. Researchers from MIT developed an AI platform called AI2 that outperforms existing systems in predicting cyber-attacks [48]. AI2 detects 85% of cyberattacks, performing about 300% better than previous systems. The system is also able to reduce the instance of false-positive readings to one-fifth of previous outcomes. This high detection rate is enabled through supervised and unsupervised machine learning.

While we have treated each AI application in isolation, it is common to have them bundled and integrated. Researchers from Carnegie Mellon University collaborated with the City of Pittsburgh to develop a Scalable Urban Traffic Control (SURTRAC), which was able to simultaneously monitor and control the flow of traffic [49]. The system has been deployed in the East Liberty neighbourhood since 2012 and covers nine intersections. On average, 29,940 vehicles pass through this area daily. SURTRAC is a schedule-driven system designed to manage multiple competing traffic flow shifts. SUTRAC is a multi-agent decentralised system, where an agent system runs each intersection. Each agent system controls traffic signals for their intersection and monitors traffic flow by dynamically coordinating with other agents in real time. The deployment of SURTRAC resulted in a 34% increase in vehicle speed, and a reduction of 25% in travel time, 40% in waiting time, 31% in traffic stops, and 21% in emissions.

While AI systems have significant potential, their deployments are never straight-forward. In Detroit, a $9 million initiative "Neighborhood Real-Time Intelligence Program" implemented facial recognition software and video surveillance cameras at 500 different Detroit intersections. This initiative built on the previous "Project Green Light" Initiative, which installed 500 cameras outside of businesses cap-able of recording and reporting real-time video footage to the police. The software boasts an ability to match faces with 50 million driver's license photographs in the Michigan police database. Nevertheless, recent research has shown that current facial recognition software more often misidentifies black faces than white faces [50]. Whilst intended to increase public safety, there is widespread public criticism towards this technology, as residents feel their privacy is compromised and know-ledge of the racial biases continue to increase.

Fake news in their purest form are completely made up information, none-theless, they are often hard to identify as they resemble credible journalism and attract maximum attention as they spread like wildfire through various social media channels [51]. A man was caught after he carried an assault rifle and fired shots at a pizza parlour in Northwest Washington Upon arrest, the man informed the police that he was investigating a conspiracy theory which claimed that the pizza parlour—Comet Ping Pong—was the headquarters of a paedophilia ring [52]. This incident caused panic among people in the neighbourhood, resulting in lockdown of several businesses.

In Arizona, the hotbed for testing of AVs by major technology providers, we have seen incidents of residents throwing rocks at these vehicles [53]. There AVs are seen as a threat to jobs and livelihood, and are a source of frustration. As noted by Selby and Desouza [54],

If theory and practice advance over the next few years without paying attention to fragility, then cities will continue to be vulnerable to manageable threats. As the trends of urbanisation continue, it is even more imperative to attend to fractures of social compacts. Cities will continue to grow, and their complexity will only increase. This complexity will continue to mask fragility in the city and could result in the breakdown in one of our society's most valuable artifacts, developed cities, representing a potential loss of life and economic prosperity.

AI technologies, for all their good, do make cities more fragile [55] as they put pressures on local governments to maintain existing, and strengthen, social compacts in the face of job losses, automation, shifts in public finances, and so on.

In May 2016, a Tesla Model S car collided with a tractor-trailer in Williston, Florida. The accident occurred on the highway when the car, on autopilot mode, collided with the truck while crossing an uncontrolled intersection. The Tesla driver sustained fatal injuries, raising several questions about the autopilot functionality. However, the National Highway Traffic Safety Administration's (NHTSA) final investigation report concluded that the accident was caused by the driver's inattention [56]. Since the accident, Tesla has implemented several features to keep drivers engaged while their car is in autopilot mode.

Chrysler recalled about 1.4 million cars and trucks, because these vehicles could be hacked remotely over the Internet [57]. These vehicles used UConnect features to connect with Sprint networks for navigation. Hackers could access these cars' navigation systems to control air conditioners, cut off brakes, shut down engines, and so on. Software installed in vehicles needs to be constantly upgraded to protect against hacks and security breaches [58].

Economically, local governments may lose revenue streams because of AVs due to a decrease in speeding tickets, towing fees, and driving under influence charges [59]. Cities in Arizona such as Phoenix and Mesa collected about $10.8 million and $4.2 million from drivers for traffic violations [60]. On an average, cities in California generated $40 million in towing violations annually [15].

The conceptual and application background of AI as presented above underlines the importance of further investigations into how we can best integrate AI systems in addressing critical urban issues. Particularly, the challenges we face—e.g., climate emergency—call for smarter systems in place. This is also highly critical to increase the smartness of our cities. A recent study that evaluated the smartness levels of 180 Australian local government areas argues the importance of better integration of urban technologies, including AI, into local service delivery and governance [14].

5.3 Methodology

We undertook a systematic review of the literature to answer the following research question: How can AI contribute to the development of smarter cities? We adopted a three-phase methodologic approach (Figure 5.2) following the study steps of Yigitcanlar et al. [61].

The first phase is planning, which involves developing the research aim, research question, a list of keywords, and the criteria for inclusion and exclusion of articles. The research aim was framed to generate insights into forming a greater understanding on how AI can contribute to the development of smarter cities. The inclusion criteria were intended to be peer-reviewed journal articles, that were available online, in English, and had relevance with respect to the research aim. A university's library search engine, which gives access to 393 different databases including Directory of Open Access Journals, Science Direct, Scopus, TRID, Web of Science, and Wiley Online Library, was used to complete an online search. The

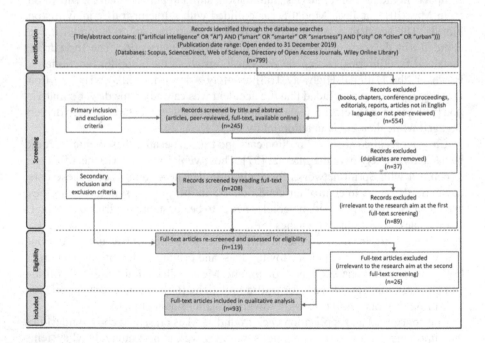

Figure 5.2 Literature selection procedure.

Table 5.1 Selection criteria for formulating categories

Selection criteria
1. Determine literature relevant to the research aim by using the eye-balling technique
2. Identify suitable literature pieces focusing on AI and smart cities after reading the full text
3. Group AI technology, algorithm, and application areas with similarities into categories
4. Narrow down the selected categories and review the reliability of these against other literature
5. Review the selected literature again and update the shortlisted categories if necessary
6. Confirm and finalise the categories selected for the classification of literature
7. Catalogue the literature selected for the review under the selected categories

search was carried out towards the end of December 2019 using the query string of [("artificial intelligence" OR "AI") AND ("smart" OR "smarter" OR "smartness") AND ("city" OR "cities" OR "urban")] to search the titles and abstracts of available articles. The publication date was left open. From this search it was determined that one of the earliest studies on AI and the city was from Schalkoff [23]. The abstracts were then read and if the article was considered to be relevant to the research aim the full text was reviewed to decide whether it was suitable to include in final analysis.

The second phase involved carrying out the review of relevant articles. The initial search resulted in a total of 799 records. These records were then screened and reduced to 245 by applying the inclusion criteria—i.e., journal articles that were peer-reviewed, and available online. The articles were then "eye-balled" to ensure they were consistent with the keyword search, the abstracts assessed against the research aim, and duplicates removed. The total number of articles was reduced to 208. The full texts of the selected articles were read to determine the relevance with respect to the aim of the study and the results were narrowed down to 119 articles. After another round of full-text screening, the number of articles was reduced to 93. Finally, these 93 articles were reviewed, categorised, and analysed. The criteria for formation of the themes are presented in Table 5.1. For the categorisation, the main smart city development dimensions—i.e., economy, society, environment, and governance—were selected. Figure 5.3 presents these dimensions in the context of smart cities.

The third and final phase is reporting and dissemination. This phase involved critically documenting and presenting the results from the 93 articles analysed. A discussion of the perceived benefits and concerns associated with AI implementation were outlined.

5.4 Results

5.4.1 General Observations

The first step in the analysis of the selected 93 articles was to classify them by date of publication. This process revealed interest in AI technology had grown

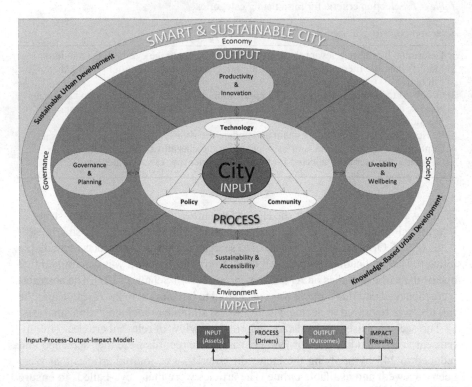

Figure 5.3 Smart city conceptual framework highlighting key domains, derived from [62].

exponentially in recent times. Almost half of the reviewed articles were published in 2019 (n=46; 49%), one-fifth in 2018 (n=18; 20%), and nearly one-tenth in 2017 (n=8; 9%). Slightly less than a quarter of all articles were published before 2016 (n=21; 23%). The earliest article included in the literature review was published in 1999—despite articles on AI and the city dated back to 1990, the earliest one that meet our selection criteria was [63]. These figures reflect the results of other review studies and are representative of the increased interest in how AI systems interact and impact the development of smart cities [64].

Leading authors are affiliated with institutions in Europe (n=28), East Asia (n=24), and North America (n=21). Nonetheless, the Oceania context, particularly in Australia, is often referenced among the best applications of AI in practice [65,66]. Regarding the academic journals the articles were published in, *IEEE Access* appears most often (n=8), followed by *Sensors* (n=5), and then three articles in both *Artificial Intelligence in Medicine* (n=3) and *Procedia Computer Science* (n=3).

Articles were categorised under four groups. These groups were based on the main smart city domains of: (a) Economy; (b) Society; (c) Environment; and (d) Government. More than one-sixth of them (n=17) were in the economy domain,

Table 5.2 The common AI paradigms and applications identified in the literature

Category	Element	Literature
AI paradigms	Machine learning	[26,63,67,70–135]
	Probabilistic methods	[70,73–75,77,80–82,87,90,93–94,96–101,112–114,134,136–138]
	Knowledge-based	[26,63,67–71,73,77,78,82,92,98,100,112,136,139–143]
	Search and optimisation	[26,67–69,77,79, 80,82,86,92,98,101,106,112,116,128,130,134,144–146]
	Logic-based	[63,67–69,71,73,77,78,82,92,98,100,112,136,140–143]
	Embodied intelligence	[26,70,73,75,76,80,82,98,104,116,128,134,137,147]
AI applications	Neural networks	[26,63,67–70,71,73,75,77–85,87,89,90,92,95,97–103,105–107,109–112,116–126,128–134]
	Evolutionary algorithms	[26,67–69,77,79,80,82,86,92,98,101,106,112,116,128,130,134,144–146]
	Expert systems	[26,63,67–70,71,73,77,78,82,92,98,100,112,136,140–143]
	Distributed artificial intelligence	[26,70,73,75,76,80,82,92,98,116,128,134,137,147,148]
	Computer vision	[73–75,87,93,94,96,99,101,113,114,118,138]
	Decision networks	[70,77,80,82,90,98,112,134,136]

slightly more than a quarter (n=24) in the society domain, over one-third (n= 33) in the environment domain, and slightly less than quarter of them (n=19) were in the governance domain.

With reference to the "AI Knowledge Map" (Figure 5.1), most articles discuss AI applications or techniques that fit within the machine learning paradigm (n=71), followed by probabilistic methods (n=25), knowledge-based (n=21), search and optimisation (n=21), logic-based (n=18), and embodied intelligence (n=15). Regarding AI applications, the most common mentioned in the selected literature are neural networks (n=55), evolutionary algorithms (n=21), distributed artificial intelligence (n=15), computer vision (n=13), and decision networks (n=9). The most common AI paradigms and applications identified in the literature are outlined in Table 5.2. A complete list of all articles and the identified AI paradigms, applications, techniques, and supporting technology are shown in Appendix 5.A. Please note, there is some crossover with the number of AI paradigms and applications identified in the literature as many articles discuss multiple, or hybrid, AI systems.

We acknowledge that there is a potential risk in bias resulting from our strategy for selecting literature to be included in the review. Our review focused on journals only, whereas cutting-edge works in engineering, design, and technology field are often published in conference papers. Nonetheless, to complement the reviewed 93 journal articles, the chapter also cited or quoted 112 relevant literature pieces on the "AI and smart cities" topic.

5.4.2 AI in the Economy Dimension of Smart Cities

Papers categorised under the economy dimensions of smart cities are those that provide insights into "how AI can contribute to and enhance the productivity and innovation of smart cities" [33]. Research in this area focused predominately on the technological innovation, economy, and management areas, and the contribution of AI can be summarised as: (a) enhancing productivity and innovation by automating data management and analysis; (b) reducing costs and increasing resources through pattern recognition; (c) supporting decision-making by analysing large volumes of data from multiple sources; and (d) drawing conclusions based on logic, reason, and intuition. Appendix 5.A lists the analysis highlights of the reviewed literature.

AI is a useful tool to manage and analyse large volumes of data to support business decisions [103,112] quickly and accurately. This is particularly relevant in combination with the IoT—a system enabled by the internet, which allows communication between a large network of devices without the need for human intervention [77,106,110]. Together with technologies such as blockchain, cloud storage, and fog computing—which help facilitate the recording, distribution, storage, and decentralised processing of data [128,149]—AI could improve productivity by automating the data management process and removing the need for intermediaries, and hence increasing profitability [126]. Furthermore, AI can improve the stability and effectiveness of the IoT contributing to improved network communication; this in return would help to improve knowledge sharing, and foster innovation and entrepreneurship [106,127,128].

AI can be used to recognise patterns in datasets, helping to optimise the data management process, improve the overall productivity of the data management system [111,149], and identify cyber-attacks [107], coding errors, and other inefficiencies [103]. Deep learning has already had success recognising patterns from a wide range of data sources including images, audio, video, and other sensors [104]. The application of AI has the potential to remove the need for humans to complete many repetitive business tasks—particularly those relying on observation— potentially reducing costs and freeing up resources for more productive or innovative fields [112,130].

In analysing the large amounts of data collected by the sensors, devices, and other sources in a smart city, AI has the potential to accelerate the decision-making process by automating complex statistical analyses [111,130,150]. This is particularly relevant with regards to the application of deep learning technology to the process of data fusion—i.e. the processes of taking data from a variety of sources, combining it, and improving its quality and usefulness by producing sophisticated statistical models [126]. AI has the capability to automate this process and conduct statistical analyses that are much larger and more complex than could be completed with human intervention. This information can then be used to reduce economic uncertainty and assist business decisions [77,103,107], and/or create marketplaces that are more responsive to user needs and desires [130].

The ability of AI to complete complex statistical analysis can also be used to automate decision-making [128,130,150]. The ability to learn can ensure that AI systems are responsive to uncertainty, particularly when working with and around humans [94,119]. This could reduce the possibilities of accidents, errors, and improve the operational efficiency of business and industries [119]. Smart control systems can monitor traffic, collect and analyse data, and, in combination with connected Avs, there is potential to make real-time decisions which enhance the efficiency of transport operations—including freight and supply chain logistics [104,130]. AI systems can be developed with human-like abilities such as creativity, design, intuition, inventiveness, trust, ethics, and values to perceive, understand, and make informed reason-based decisions that would benefit companies [76,94].

5.4.3 AI in the Society Dimension of Smart Cities

Papers in this category provide insights into "how AI can contribute to and improve the livability and wellbeing of citizens in smart cities" [33]. Research in this area focused predominately on the health and education sectors, and the contributions of AI can be summarised as: (a) improving health monitoring; (b) enhancing health diagnosis outcomes; and (c) providing autonomous tutoring systems that are highly individualised and adaptive to needs and external changes. Appendix 5.A lists the analysis highlights of the reviewed literature.

AI systems, in combination with sensors, cameras, and other data collection devices, have been developed to monitor the health and wellbeing of individuals [70,87]. Machine learning techniques can be used to improve the cost and efficiency of fall detection devices [99], and detect changes in sleep, mood, heartbeat, respiration, and other vital signs [118,129]. Wearable devices, or "smart textiles", enabled by AI, can detect changes in the human body and report findings to healthcare providers [129]. In intensive care settings, monitoring devices equipped with AI can be used to adjust the settings on bedside devices, reducing total healthcare costs and improving patient outcomes [67]. In rural settings, the ability to monitor patients remotely could contribute to reduced inequities and improve access to healthcare [89]. This is a particularly critical issue in countries like Australia, where in some remote areas the nearest health service provider or hospital could be located 1,000 km or further away [151]. Additionally, smart tracking of health symptoms could improve communication between patients and healthcare professionals [142].

In addition to health monitoring, AI systems can greatly improve health diagnosis by providing an effective repository of medical knowledge and the ability to access, analyse, and apply complex medical data more efficiently [68,139]. Assisting healthcare workers with tasks involving the collection and recording of data and knowledge could increase the number of resources available for patient care [68,139], improve the quality of life for patients [120], and expand the professional learning capabilities of professionals [122]. Similarly, the improved analytics and reasoning capabilities of AI would provide a decision-support mechanism with the potential to reduce the chances of misdiagnosis [137], facilitate greater communication and collaboration between healthcare professionals [70], and assist with the development of more personalised medical treatments [137,91].

With regards to the education sector, intelligent tutoring systems that mimic the one-on-one interaction between tutor and student can provide highly individualised teaching programs for students [140]. Furthermore, these systems can develop multiple paths to answer any given question and provide highly detailed feedback [140]. Advances in AI technology can increase the effectiveness of these, and similar systems, by automatically collecting information from the web, ensuring the most up-to-date content, and using machine learning to increase the adaptability to individualised learner requirements [81,146]. There is potential to create systems that are far more effective than one-on-one tutoring [143], with improved communication between student and teacher, and superior assessment methods [85]. This is especially promising with regards to identifying and adapting syllabuses to the individual strengths and needs of students with learning disabilities or other special learning requirements [71].

Increased adaptability is important as rapid technological changes are likely to result in an unstable job market [135,143]. AI could potentially bring new skill requirements across multiple sectors and the education sector needs to be at the cutting edge of these changes to ensure students are prepared for future job markets [152]. For example, even in the education sector itself, AI will replace many of the time-consuming tasks, changing teacher roles to one based on student support and the management of AI systems [88,135,153]. Managing the education needs of residents is therefore important to ensure they are able to take advantage of the potential benefits of AI including improved working conditions, better work–life balance, and improved quality of life [135].

Lastly, AI has been used for the modelling of the spread of the recent COVID-19 epidemic. The predictions seem to be showing reliable results as the modelling predicts COVID-19 infections with an accuracy of 96%, and deaths with an accuracy of 99%, up to one week into the future. This information would help governments implement effective contingency plans, and prevent the virus's spread and turn into a global pandemic [154]. Similarly, Lin et al. [155] utilise blockchain with AI to efficiently manage water use under the changing climate conditions, and contribute to climate change adaptation efforts.

5.4.4 AI in the Environment Dimension of Smart Cities

These papers provide insights into "how AI could contribute to sustainable urban development and improved accessibility in smart cities" [33]. Research in this area focused predominately on the transport, energy, land use, and environment sectors/ areas, and the contribution of AI can be summarised as: (a) monitoring changes in the environment; (b) using smart energy systems to optimise energy consumption and production; (c) planning, development, and use of households to reduce energy consumption; and (d) operationalising smart transport systems. Appendix 5.A lists the analysis highlights of the reviewed literature.

When faced with complex environmental issues and large quantities of data, AI systems have the potential to make knowledge-based decisions that balance the environmental outcomes of the city against the social and economic wellbeing of its residents [63,136]. AI systems can be used to monitor changes in the environment including noise, temperature, humidity, emissions [90], water pollutants [133], fish stock, and other environmental indicators [136]. AI systems can respond to these changes, and quickly implement solutions for dealing with any issues [156]. Furthermore, improved data quality from AI systems can contribute to more robust and accurate environmental modelling systems [69,124].

AI has also been identified as a means of creating more energy-efficient cities [156]. Smart grid systems, integrated with AI technology, can be used to control power systems and optimise energy consumption [78,79], including the planning and management of electric vehicle charging [145], public lighting [75], and data [121]. AI can also assist with the distribution of renewable electricity generated from multiple, often non-traditional sources—including body heat [125]—the identification of inefficiencies, and future forecasting [134,157]. By optimising the management of resources, monitoring energy consumption, and better planning for future requirements, cities will be able to use resources more efficiently and better achieve renewable energy goals [80,86].

Smarter homes can be developed with AI systems that monitor changes in the environment, adapt to user requirements, and improve energy efficiency [73,92,116]. AI systems could be used to predict future household energy requirements which can help identify inefficiencies, faults, and control future energy use [81]. In addition, AI can contribute to reduced energy consumption in the construction process [102], and improved environmental outcomes in the design [146] and planning process [26].

With regards to sustainable transportation, the goal of AI in the context of smart cities is to calculate the most efficient means of moving people and goods between places, reducing the number of vehicle kilometres travelled (VKT). This, in turn, leads to a reduction in energy consumption, which in turn leads to lower air and noise pollution, congestion, and other externalities such as the requirements for transportation and parking infrastructure [98,156]. AI can be used for transport optimisation by analysing real-time measurements—such as traffic signal control—to adjust routes [97,74], balance user demands [96], and make parking more efficient [113,104]. Particularly in Avs, these changes can result in substantial reductions in travel time and energy savings [108]. From a transport planning perspective, AI can also be used to differentiate spatial structures in aerial images [113] and collect masses of data for the development of more accurate and responsive models which can be used to develop a more environmentally efficient transportation system [117].

Despite no studies in the reviewed literature directly focusing on how AI can tackle climate change, we are aware of some relevant research. For instance, in their paper entitled "Tackling climate change with machine learning", Rolnick et al. [158] offer areas where machine learning can be deployed. These areas include better climate predictions and modelling, energy production, CO_2 removal, education, solar geoengineering, and finance. Within these areas, the possibilities include more energy-efficient buildings, creating new low-carbon materials, better monitoring of deforestation, and greener transportation. They state that "although AI is not a silver bullet, it brings new insights into the problem". Another study, by O'Gorman and Dwyer [159], demonstrates the use of machine learning to parameterise moist convection and climate change, and extreme event modelling. Likewise, Dayal et al. [160] model Queensland (Australia) droughts based on AI and neural network algorithms for decision-makers and local inhabitants to take precautions.

5.4.5 AI in the Governance Dimension of Smart Cities

How AI can contribute to establishing good governance and planning in smart cities is the focus of this set of papers [33]. Research in this area focused predominately on the security, governance, and decision-making areas, and the contributions of AI can be summarised as: (a) enhancing the operability of surveillance systems; (b) improving cyber security; (c) aiding disaster management planning and operations; and (d) assisting citizens with new technology to support citizen scientists and contribute to the urban decision-making process. Appendix 5.A lists the analysis highlights of the reviewed literature.

Advanced AI surveillance technologies, enabled by motion detection, predictive analytics, drones, and other autonomous devices, can be used to monitor urban areas, and recognise threats, such as crime [72,93,100,148], fraud [109], accidents, and fire [101,123,160]. On a broader scale AI can be used to monitor communication networks and recognise potential terrorist threats, trafficking, crime syndicates, and other illegal behaviours [100]. Once targets are identified, intelligent surveillance systems can evaluate and track targets [93], and collect forensic evidence—such as video recording [138]. AI can also be used to better predict future crime incidents and ensure the optimal allocation of crime law enforcement [144].

Cyber threats also pose significant risks to smart cities, both in terms of data privacy and the protection of connected infrastructure [83,161]. AI can be used to identify irregular behaviour, determine what is a threat, and implement mitigation measures at speeds beyond that of human ability [83,100]. This, together with encryption technologies such as blockchain [100] and a focus on data security at all levels of design [131], can alleviate individual concerns regarding data security and contribute to increased transparency and trust regarding online systems [83,141]. This would allow increased avenues for citizen engagement in policy decisions and citizen scientist engagement with policy development via crowdsourcing [163], along with other online services such as electronic voting [141] and smart contracts [115].

Given the ability for AI to analyse large amounts of data, scenarios to deal with potential threats could be constructed simultaneous to the detection of threats

[161]. This would give decision-makers and other authorities more time to respond to threats such as natural disasters [132], house fires [123], or other incidents. Furthermore, AI can be used to assess the extent of damage caused by these events, helping authorities better respond to and mitigate any damage caused [101,132].

Finally, AI systems can be used to both assist and analyse the acceptance of new systems—particularly those associated with new technologies [109,163]. Online "chatbots" can help residents navigate new websites and online platforms [109], with training and tips customised based on individualised needs and interests [164]. Furthermore, AI uses reasoning and intuition to assist decision-makers understand the reasons behind citizen acceptance, or non-acceptance, of new technology [165]. Where new approaches are required, AI can develop innovative solutions [95], and address future challenges [84].

5.5 Discussion

This review study investigated the impact of the two very powerful and highly popular phenomena of our time—i.e., AI and smart cities. On the one hand, the smart city notion is seen as a potential blueprint for the development of future cities to provide improved productivity, innovation, liveability, wellbeing, sustainability, accessibility, governance, and planning [166,167]. Nevertheless, we still do not have the technical capabilities to develop these technologically advanced futuristic cities [168]. On the other hand, AI provides a hope for overcoming the limits of human capabilities, in the computational sense [169]. Hence, in theory, a happy marriage of AI and the smart cities concepts would bring us closer to producing smarter cities [22].

In this chapter, we attempted to generate insights into forming a better understanding on how AI can contribute to the development of smarter cities by undertaking a systematic review of the literature. Appendix 5.A lists the analysis highlights of the reviewed literature. The results of the review disclosed the following main points, and some of the critical issues are discussed further:

- AI has evident potential to provide a positive change in our cities, societies, and businesses by promoting a more efficient, effective, and sustainable transition/ transformation;
- AI, with its technology, algorithms, and learning capabilities, can be a useful vehicle in automating the problem-solving and decision-making processes; that in return could reform urban landscapes, and support the development of smarter cities;
- AI in the context of smart cities is an emerging field of research and practice; hence, further research is needed to consolidate the knowledge in the field;
- The central focus of the literature is on AI technologies, algorithms, and their current and prospective applications;
- AI applications in the context of smart cities mainly concentrate on business efficiency, data analytics, education, energy, environmental sustainability, health, land use, security, transport, and urban management areas;

- Upcoming disruptions of AI on cities and societies have not been adequately investigated in the literature; thus, further investigations are needed on that issue.

The results of the review revealed that AI-inspired computational systems are bound to make a profound impact on our cities. The impact will not only be on the physical setup of our cities but also in how our cities operate and achieve system-level objectives (e.g., liveability, resilience, and so on). In order to ensure that cities advance in keeping with the values and aspirations of their key stakeholders (i.e., residents, businesses, and so on), it will be vital for us to ensure that AI systems are designed to take on a value-sensitive design approach [170]. AI systems will need to account for the multiple aspects of diversity that are omnipresent in our cities. In addition, these systems will need to possess a degree of transparency, adaptability (to respond to varying environmental conditions), and accountability (for levels of performance). Doing so is non-trivial but is paramount to achieving responsible innovation in the context of AI and cities.

While advances in computational science and technologies will continue to progress at an astounding rate, the level of impact they will have on our future cities comes down to the level of trust individuals and organisations place in these systems. As we continue to live through times where levels of trust in government is at an all-time low [171], planners and public managers needs to consider how social license [172] impacts their ability to deploy emerging technologies. Engaging stakeholders in the design processes when it comes to AI systems will be critical. Stakeholders should be allowed to shape the elements of these systems and their expected deployment trajectories. Engaging stakeholders will also enable a city to increase the overall knowledge of the community when it comes to the innovative potential of these technologies. To date, we have limited frameworks on how to engage many diverse stakeholders, who have varying knowledge of the intricacies of AI systems, into design processes for urban innovation [173].

We need to enable multiple stakeholders to contribute their technology solutions. Cities need to build platforms that promote the co-creation and sharing of technology solutions [174,175]. While cities have embraced the notion of open data [176] and have created periodic programs to source innovation from external stakeholders (e.g., Hackathons) [177], much more is needed when it comes to designing platforms for co-creation in the context of AI technologies. Stakeholders can be engaged in the auditing of algorithms that underlie AI applications. In addition, they can provide feedback on the performances of these systems, and identify critical choke points. As an example, consider the following innovation by a resident in Berlin, who was able to create traffic jam alerts on Google Maps by slowly moving 99 phones with location services turned on around the city [178]. Residents, such as this individual, enable us to see the limits of AI technologies and their failure points. Such perspectives are critically important as we infuse and design next-generation smart urban technologies.

AI systems will impact cities at multiple levels, from the individual to the local community (the residents), the neighbourhood to the organisational (the city), and even the ecosystem (the city is connected to other cities) level. Impacts at the local level will have effects up and down the hierarchy. Consider the case of algorithms used to promote sharing economy platforms (e.g., Uber, Lyft, AirBnB, and so on). These algorithms not only provide opportunities to individuals to earn rents on their assets and fees for their services, but they also impact zoning rules, they impact the use of established public transport networks, they in turn impact the creation of new service opportunities for existing businesses, and even shape the nature of public finances of a city. More effort is needed to understand the cascading effects of AI innovations across the various levels of a city's functions. In addition, the interdependencies between functions and the implications for overall objectives (i.e., ensuring that local optimisation does not compromise global performance) is also critical.

From a design perspective, research on how to design AI technologies in a more agile [179] and frugal [180,181] manner is of critical importance. The public sector has a notorious record of accomplishment when it comes to managing, and delivering on, information systems projects [182]. Cities around the world have had to contend with failed deployments of information system projects that have wasted significant public resources. The study by Desouza et al. [183] provides examples of both success and failure factors of technology-driven smart city attempts—including AI.

Given the significance of technology investments in our cities, we need to see vast improvements in the management of projects to deliver on their intended value. In this regard, two considerations are critical. First, is that we build technologies that are agile, i.e., they could adopt, adjust, and have the capacity for transformation under changing environmental conditions. Second, is that we build technologies in a manner that is in keeping with frugal engineering. Doing so will require us to move away from mega-scale smart cities projects and reconsider the issue of scale. Today, a dominant design paradigm is to build AI technologies that can scale and promote re-use of components. This thinking is outdated; today it is possible to build technologies that work for specific contexts, in an agile and frugal manner, to promote personalisation to a specific context and purpose [184].

The security of our next-generation urban technologies is of paramount importance. AI technologies, like most technologies, should be secured, and this normally takes the form of traditional information security. Technologies that traverse our urban environments are already targets of hackers and have vulnerabilities. For instance, Greenberg [185] highlights a deep flaw in cars that lets hackers shut down safety features. But, even beyond what one thinks of when it comes to traditional security, today, AI-driven systems can cause harm even if they are not hacked. For example, as stressed by BBC [186], China coronavirus misinformation spreads online about its origin and scale; this is to say, AI inspired platforms that are used for different urban functions can also be manipulated to spread fake news. Cities need to be aware of this as they use these platforms to share information on urban functions, such as the use of social media to engage with citizens. For instance, as reported by Martinez [187], "Rumors of child abductors spread through WhatsApp in a small town in Mexico.... . The rumors were fake, but a mob burned two men to death before anyone checked." Likewise, as we have discussed earlier, cities have had their information systems held for ransom. These incidents will only increase as cities infuse more technologies into their environments. Hence, there is a need for research to examine the security and risk implications of AI-enabled system deployments.

The success of AI deployment to make our cities smarter will depend on the knowledge and care with which such technologies are deployed responsibly and in keeping with our public values. If done well, AI can help us tackle some of our most complex urban challenges. However, it can also make our cities more fragile [54]. As stated by Stephen Hawking on the BBC,

> The development of full artificial intelligence could spell the end of humans.... It would take off on its own, and re-design itself at an ever-increasing rate. Humans, who are limited by slow biological evolution, couldn't compete, and would be superseded.

On that very point, Gherhes and Obrad [188] report the findings of their study on technical and humanities student perspectives on the development and sustainability of AI. The study discloses that out of 928 participants 58.3% considers that AI will have a positive influence on society. On the other hand, the percentage of those confessing to being confused or concerned is also quite significant (41.7%). The probability that AI might destroy humankind and might replace people in certain activities and jobs are among the greatest fears [188].

As AI applications are becoming more common, the scepticism on the misuse of the technology grows. For example, most recently the Clearview AI facial recognition system has generated major concerns on privacy issues. Australian police have been using this unaccountable facial recognition service that combines machine learning and wide-ranging data-gathering practices to identify members of the public from online photographs. Stated by Golenfein [189] "Beyond the ethical arguments around facial recognition, Clearview AI reveals Australian law enforcement agencies have such limited technical and organisational accountability that we should be questioning their competency even to evaluate, let alone use, this kind of technology". Similarly, the New South Wales state government of Australia is using AI to spot drivers with mobile phones (often mixed phones with other rectangular items), and the Australian government welfare agency Centrelink is using AI (often incorrectly) to issue debt notices to welfare recipients [190].

Furthermore, scholars warn us of the possible risks of advanced AI. For instance, these risks range from unsafe recommendations for treating illnesses [191] to fatal autonomous car accidents [192], and from racist chatbots [193] to social manipulation [194]. While various dystopian futures have been advanced, including those in which humans eventually become obsolete, with the subsequent extinction of the human race, Ref. [195] put forward the following scenarios to think about the ways to protect ourselves from the risks of advanced AI: (a) an AI system tasked with preventing HIV decides to eradicate the problem by killing everybody who carries the disease, or one tasked with curing cancer decides to kill everybody who has any genetic predisposition for it; (b) an autonomous AI military drone decides the only way to guarantee an enemy target is destroyed is to wipe out an entire community; and (c) an environmentally protective AI decides the only way to slow or reverse climate change is to remove technologies and humans that induce it.

Lastly, the abovementioned challenges also relate to the specific characteristics of AI technologies that include opacity ("black box effect"), complexity, unpredictability, and partially autonomous behaviour, may make it hard to verify compliance with and may hamper the effective enforcement of rules of existing laws meant to protect fundamental rights [196]. In order to address this issue, the white paper entitled "Artificial intelligence: a European approach to excellence and trust" [197] underlined the following seven key requirements for successful AI utilisation: (a) human agency and oversight; (b) technical robustness and safety; (c) privacy and data governance; (d) transparency; (e) diversity, non-discrimination, and fairness; (f) societal and environmental well-being; and (g) accountability. On that very point, Salmon et al. [195] propose the immediate application of the following three sets of controls for AI development and testing: (a) the controls required to ensure AI system designers and developers create safe AI systems; (b) the controls that need to be built into the AIs themselves, such as "common sense", morals, operating procedures, decision-rules, and so on; and (c) the controls that need to be added to the broader systems in which AI will operate, such as regulation, codes of practice, standard operating procedures, monitoring systems, and infrastructure. As Elon Musk stated, "we need to regulate AI to combat 'existential threat' before it's too late" [198]. Fortunately, we are not short of ideas and plans to tackle these issues, and now is the time to implement them before it is too late [199].

5.6 Conclusion

The study reported in this paper offers a novel contribution to the literature by mapping out the scientific landscape of the understudied "AI and the smart city" area. This study helps not only in identifying the current and potential contributions of AI to the development of smarter cities—to aid urban policymakers, planners, and researchers—but also in determining the gaps in the literature to bridge them in prospective studies. The study also gives a heads up for urban policymakers, planners, and scholars for them to prepare for the disruptions that AI will cause in our cites, societies, and businesses [200].

The broad findings of our systematic literature review findings reveal that: (a) AI has an evident potential—but only if utilised responsibly [201]—to provide a positive change in our cities, societies, and businesses by promoting a more efficient, effective, and sustainable transition/transformation [202,203]; and (b) particularly, AI, with its technology, algorithms, and learning capabilities, can be a useful vehicle in automating problem-solving and decision-making processes, which in return could reform urban landscapes, and support the development of smarter cities [62].

The specific findings of our systematic literature review disclose that: (a) AI in the context of smart cities is an emerging field of research and practice; (b) the central focus of the literature is on AI technologies, algorithms, and their current and prospective applications; (c) AI applications in the context of smart cities mainly concentrate on business efficiency, data analytics, education, energy, environmental sustainability, health, land use, security, transport, and urban management areas; (d) there is limited scholarly research investigating the risks of wider AI utilisation; and (e) upcoming disruptions of AI on cities and societies have not been adequately investigated in the literature.

AI provides a new hope for addressing some of the urbanisation problems we have failed to solve due to the complexities involved. Nevertheless, AI is not a silver bullet. While we are currently far away from such advanced application of AI, there are numerous contributions of this rapidly developing technology for our cities and societies. Some of these contributions are presented in the chapter and some warnings have been made for the good use of the technology. While there is a promise of emerging advanced technologies, such as AI, our rapid urbanisation, industrialisation, and globalisation practices are perhaps making even technology struggle with coming up with a solution. The recent anthropogenic climate change triggered environmental catastrophes and disasters—such as the 2020 Australian Bushfires—and urbanisation and globalisation triggered epidemics—such as COVID-19—require more than technology for them not to be repeated.

The chapter opened with a viewpoint on technocentric solutions being widely seen as remedies for global issues—including climate change and urbanisation problems. Indeed, AI and other technologies will equip us with better data analytics and prediction models in more efficient and effective ways. To date, there are two different approaches to AI: rules-based (coded algorithms of if-then statements that are basically meant to solve simple problems) and learning-based (diagnoses problems by interacting with the problem), where both AI approaches have valid use cases when it comes to studying the environment and solving climate change. In other words, when it comes to helping solve climate change, a learning-based AI could essentially do more than just crunch CO_2 emission numbers, where a learning-based AI could record those numbers, study causes and solutions, and then recommend the best solution [204]—"in theory". We say, "in theory", because "fully functioning AI systems do not yet exist, and it has been estimated that they will be with us anywhere between 2029 and the end of the century" [195].

While we do not disagree with the positive contributions of technological prescriptions—such as AI and other urban technologies—[205], we close the chapter with the following quote by Andrew Ng, co-founder and lead of Google Brain [206].

Much has been written about AI's potential to reflect both the best and the worst of humanity. For example, we have seen AI providing conversation and comfort to the lonely; we have also seen AI engaging in racial discrimination. Yet the biggest harm that AI is likely to do to individuals in the short term is job displacement, as the amount of work we can automate with AI is vastly bigger than before. As leaders, it is incumbent on all of us to make sure we are building a world in which every individual has an opportunity to thrive.

Acknowledgements

This chapter, with permission from the copyright holder, is a reproduced version of the following journal article: Yigitcanlar, T., Desouza, K., Butler, L., & Roozkhosh, F. (2020). Contributions and risks of artificial intelligence (AI) in building smarter cities: Insights from a systematic review of the literature. *Energies*, 13(6), 1473.

Appendix 5.A Analysis highlights of the reviewed literature

Literature	Domain	Paradigm	Application	Method	Technology
Abduljabbar et al. [98]	Environment	LB KB PM ML EI SO	ES DN NN DAI EA	FS DL SI GA	Smart Transport
Ajerla et al. [99]	Society	PM ML	NN CV	AR	IoT Smart Health
Alam et al. [77]	Economy	LB KB PM ML SO	ES DN NN EA	FS BN DL GA	IoT
Allama & Dhunny [100]	Governance	LB KB PM ML	ES NN	FS	IoT
Alsamhi et al. [101]	Governance	PM ML SO	NN CV EA	AR IR MV GA	IoT Drones
Altulyan et al. [149]	Economy	n/a	n/a	n/a	IoT
Alzoubi et al. [102]	Environment	ML	NN	n/a	n/a
Bajaj & Sharma [82]	Society	LB KB PM ML EI SO	ES DN PP NN DAI EA	FS BN BPS MAS SI GA	Smart Education
Bennett & Hauser [137]	Society	PM EI	DAI	MAS	Smart Health
Bose [78]	Environment	LB KB ML	ES NN AS	FS DL	Smart Energy
Brady [103]	Economy	ML	NN	n/a	n/a
Braun et al. [83]	Governance	ML	NN	n/a	Smart Surveillance
Bui & Jung [104]	Economy	ML EI	AS	n/a	IoT
Cai et al. [105]	Environment	ML	NN	DL	IoT Smart Parking
Casares [84]	Governance	ML	NN	DL	n/a

(*Continued*)

Appendix 5.A (Continued)

Literature	Domain	Paradigm	Application	Method	Technology
Castelli et al. [144]	Governance	SO	EA	GA	n/a
Chassignol et al. [85]	Society	ML	NN	n/a	Smart Education Augment. Reality Virtual Reality
Chatterjee et al. [164]	Governance	n/a	n/a	n/a	IoT ICT
Chau [69]	Environment	LB KB ML SO	ILP ES NN EA	FS DL GA	Smart Environment
Chen et al. [107]	Economy	ML SO	NN EA	DL GA	IoT Smart Energy
Chen et al. [106]	Economy	ML	NN	DL	IoT
Chmiel [74]	Environment	PM ML	CV	IR MV	Smart Transport
Chui et al. [86]	Environment	ML SO	EA	GA	IoT Smart Energy
Cortes et al. [136]	Environment	LB KB PM	Expert System DN	n/a	Smart Environment
Cui et al. [108]	Environment	ML	n/a	n/a	IoT Smart Transport
De Paz et al. [75]	Environment	PM ML EI	CV NN DAI	IR MV MAS	Smart Energy
Desouza et al. [109]	Governance	ML	NN	DL	n/a
Devedzic [147]	Society	EI	DAI	ABM	Smart Education
Din et al. [110]	Economy	ML	NN	DL	IoT
Dobrescu & Dobrescu [87]	Society	PM ML	NLP CV NN	DL IR NLU NLG	n/a
Dong et al. [111]	Economy	ML	n/a	n/a	IoT
Drigas & Ioannidou [71]	Society	LB KB ML	ES NN	FS	Smart Education
Edwards et al. [88]	Society	ML	NLP	NLG	Social Robots Smart Education
Eldrandaly et al. [148]	Governance	EI	DAI	SI	IoT Smart Surveillance
Falco et al. [162]	Governance	n/a	n/a	n/a	IoT

Appendix 5.A (Continued)

Literature	Domain	Paradigm	Application	Method	Technology
Feng & Xu [63]	Environment	LB KB ML	ES NN	FS DL	n/a
Fernández et al. [138]	Governance	PM	CV	IR	Smart Surveillance
Garlík [79]	Environment	ML SO	NN EA	GA	Smart Energy
Guilherme [153]	Society	n/a	n/a	n/a	Smart Education
Guo & Li [89]	Society	ML	NN	n/a	Smart Health
Guo et al. [90]	Environment	PM ML	DN NN	BN DL	IoT
Håkansson [91]	Society	ML	n/a	n/a	IoT ICT Cyber-Physical Smart Infrastructure
Hanson & Marshall [67]	Society	LB KB ML SO	ES NN EA	FS DL GA	Smart Health
Hariri et al. [112]	Economy	LB KB PM ML SO	ES DN EA	FS BN	IoT
Ibrahim et al. [113]	Environment	PM ML	CV NN	IR DL	n/a
Inclezan & Prádanos [156]	Environment	n/a	n/a	n/a	n/a
Iqbal et al. [114]	Environment	PM ML	CV NN	AR IR MV DL	IoT Smart Parking
Jha et al. [80]	Environment	PM ML EI SO	DN PP NN DAI EA	BN BPS GA MAS SI	Smart Energy
Khalifa [161]	Governance	n/a	n/a	n/a	n/a
Kopytko et al. [92]	Environment	LB KB ML SO	ES NN DAI EA	FS DL MAS GA	IoT Smart Homes
Kundu [115]	Governance	ML	n/a	n/a	IoT Blockchain

(*Continued*)

Appendix 5.A (Continued)

Literature	Domain	Paradigm	Application	Method	Technology
Le et al. [116]	Environment	ML EI SO	NN DAI EA	DL SI GA	Smart Energy
Leung et al. [117]	Environment	ML	NN	DL	IoT GNS GPS GIS
Li et al. [118]	Society	ML	NN CV	DL MV	IoT Smart Surveillance
Liu et al. [93]	Governance	PM ML	CV	AR IR MV	Smart Surveillance
Liu et al. [119]	Economy	ML	NN	DL	Robotics
Lukowicz & Slusalle [94]	Economy	PM ML	CV NLP	IR NLU	n/a
Lytras et al. [120]	Society	ML	NN	DL	IoT Smart Health
Martins [95]	Governance	ML	NN	DL	n/a
McArthur et al [140]	Society	LB KB	ES	n/a	Smart Education
Meena et al. [145]	Environment	SO	EA	GA	IoT
Muhammad et al. [121]	Environment	ML	NN	DL	IoT
Nápoles et al. [96]	Environment	PM ML	CV	AR IR MV	Smart Transport
Neuhauser et al. [142]	Society	LB KB	ES	n/a	Smart Health
Noorbakhsh-Sabet [122]	Society	ML	NN	DL	Smart Health
Park et al. [123]	Governance	ML	NN	DL	IoT Smart Fire Detection
Patel et al. [70]	Society	KB PM ML EI	ES DN NN DAI	BN ABM	Smart Health
Pence [152]	Society	n/a	n/a	n/a	n/a
Pieters [141]	Governance	LB KB	ES	n/a	n/a

Ponce & Gutiérrez
  [124]
	Environment	ML	NN	n/a	IoT
					Artificial
					  Hydrocarbon
					  Networks

Appendix 5.A (Continued)

Literature	Domain	Paradigm	Application	Method	Technology
Puri et al. [125]	Environment	ML	NN	n/a	IoT Smart Energy
Quan et al. [146]	Environment	SO	EA	GA	Smart Design
Rahman et al. [126]	Economy	ML	NN	DL	IoT Blockchain
Ramesh et al. [68]	Society	LB KB ML SO	ES NN EA	FS DL GA	Smart Health
Reaz [73]	Environment	LB KB PM ML EI	ES CV NN AS DAI	FS AR MAS	Smart Home
Rho et al. [72]	Governance	ML	n/a	n/a	Smart Surveillance Smart Homes
Roll & Wylie [143]	Society	LB KB	ES	n/a	Smart Education
Ruohomaa et al. [127]	Economy	ML	n/a	n/a	IoT
Sgantzos & Grigg [128]	Economy	ML EI SO	NN DAI EA	MAS GA	IoT Blockchain
Shi et al. [129]	Society	ML	NN	n/a	Smart Textiles
Soomro et al. [130]	Economy	ML SO	NN EA	GA	n/a
Stefanelli [139]	Society	KB	n/a	n/a	Smart Health
Streitz [131]	Governance	ML	NN	DL	IoT
Syifa et al. [132]	Governance	ML	NN	n/a	n/a
Wan & Hwang [97]	Environment	PM ML	PP NN	DL	Smart Transport
Wang & Srinivasan [81]	Environment	PM ML	PP NN	n/a	n/a
Wang et al. [133]	Environment	ML	NN	DL	Smart Environment
Wei et al. [134]	Environment	PM ML EI SO	DN NN DAI EA	BN DL SI GA	Smart Energy
Wogu et al. [135]	Society	ML	n/a	n/a	Smart Education
Wu & Silva [26]	Environment	KB ML EI SO	ES NN DAI EA	FS ABM SI GA	n/a

(Continued)

Appendix 5.A (Continued)

Literature	Domain	Paradigm	Application	Method	Technology
Yu et al. [150]	Economy	n/a	n/a	n/a	Blockchain
Yun et al. [76]	Economy	ML EI	AS DAI	SI	n/a
Zou et al. [157]	Environment	n/a	n/a	n/a	n/a

Notes: n/a= not available as not identified in the article.

AI Paradigms: Logic-based (LB), Knowledge-based (KB), Probabilistic Methods (PM), Machine Learning (ML), Embodied Intelligence (EI), and Search and Optimisation (SO).

AI Applications: Autonomous Systems (AS), Computer Vision (CV), Distributed Artificial Intelligence (DAI), Decision Networks (DN), Evolutionary Algorithms (EA), Expert Systems (ES), Inductive Logic Programming (ILP), Natural Language Processing (NLP), Neural Networks (NN), and Probabilistic Programming (PP).

AI Methods: Agent-Based Modelling (ABM), Activities Recognition (AR), Bayesian Networks (BN), Bayesian Program Synthesis (BPS), Deep Learning (DL), Fuzzy Systems (FS), Genetic Algorithms (GA), Image Recognition (IR), Multi-Agent Systems (MAS)., Machine Vision (MV), Natural Language Generation (NLG), Natural Language Understanding (NLU), and Swarm Intelligence (SI).

References

1. Oreskes, N. The scientific consensus on climate change. *Science* 2004, 306, 1686–1686.
2. Cook, J.; Nuccitelli, D.; Green, S.; Richardson, M.; Winkler, B.; Painting, R.; Skuce, A. Quantifying the consensus on anthropogenic global warming in the scientific literature. *Environmental Research Letters* 2013, 8, 024024.
3. Yigitcanlar, T.; Foth, M.; Kamruzzaman, M. Towards post-anthropocentric cities. *Journal of Urban Technology* 2019, 26, 147–152.
4. Kankanamge, N.; Yigitcanlar, T.; Goonetilleke, A.; Kamruzzaman, M. Determining disaster severity through social media analysis. *International Journal of Disaster Risk Reduction* 2020, 42, 101360.
5. Sotto, D.; Philippi, A.; Yigitcanlar, T.; Kamruzzaman, M. Aligning urban policy with climate action in the global South. *Energies* 2019, 12, 3418.
6. Yu, P.; Xu, R.; Abramson, M.; Li, S.; Guo, Y. Bushfires in Australia. *The Lancet Planetary Health* 2020, 4, 7–8.
7. Zhenmin, L.; Espinosa, P. Tackling climate change to accelerate sustainable development. *Nature Climate Change* 2019, 9, 494–496.
8. Kinniburgh, C. Can extinction rebellion survive? *Dissent* 2020, 67, 125–133.
9. Tomitsch, M.; Haeusler, M. Infostructures. *Journal of Urban Technology* 2015, 22, 37–53.
10. Yigitcanlar, T.; Kamruzzaman, M. Does smart city policy lead to sustainability of cities? *Land Use Policy* 2018, 73, 49–58.
11. Yigitcanlar, T.; Inkinen, T. *Geographies of Disruption*. Springer International Publishing, 2019.
12. Yigitcanlar, T.; Kamruzzaman, M. Smart cities and mobility. *Journal of Urban Technology* 2019, 26, 21–46.

13. Arbolino, R.; De Simone, L.; Carlucci, F.; Yigitcanlar, T.; Ioppolo, G. Towards a sustainable industrial ecology. *Journal of Cleaner Production* 2018, 178, 220–236.
14. Yigitcanlar, T.; Kamruzzaman, MD.; Buys, L.; Perveen, S. Available online: https://epri nts.qut.edu.au/118349/ (accessed on 10 Feb 2020).
15. Desouza, K.; Swindell, D.; Smith, K.; Sutherland, A.; Fedorschak, K.; Coronel, C. Local government 2035. *Issues in Technology Innovation* 2015, 27, 1–27.
16. Kyriazopoulou, C. Smart city technologies and architectures. In: *2015 International Conference on Smart Cities and Green ICT Systems*. IEEE 2015, 1–12.
17. Ab-Rahman, A.; Hamid, U.; Chin, T. Emerging technologies with disruptive effects. *Perintis e-Journal* 2017, 7, 111–128.
18. Gatzweiler, F. Advancing urban health and wellbeing through collective and artificial intelligence. In: *Urban Health and Wellbeing Programme*. Springer 2020, pp. 33–38
19. King, B.; Hammond, T.; Harrington, J. Disruptive technology. *Journal of Strategic Innovation and Sustainability* 2017, 12, 53–67.
20. Tegmark, M. *Life 3.0*. Knopf, 2017.
21. Yigitcanlar, T. *Technology and the City*. Routledge, 2016.
22. Batty, M. Artificial intelligence and smart cities. *Environment and Planning B: Urban Analytics and City Science* 2018, 45, 3–6.
23. Schalkoff, R.J. *Artificial Intelligence*. McGraw-Hill: New York, United States, 1990.
24. Pannu, A. Artificial intelligence and its application in different areas. Artificial Intelligence 2015, 4, 79–84.
25. Corea, F. Available online: www.forbes.com/sites/cognitiveworld/2018/08/22/ai-knowledge-map-how-to-classify-ai-technologies/#5e99db627773 (accessed on 18 Jan 2020).
26. Wu, N.; Silva, E. Artificial intelligence solutions for urban land dynamics. *Journal of Planning Literature* 2010, 24, 246–265.
27. Jiafeng, Z.; Tian, L.; Lin, Z. Artificial intelligence approach to creative data manipulation for optimisation of livelihood oriented urban planning and management. *International Journal of Performability Engineering* 2019, 15, 602–610.
28. Wirtz, B.; Weyerer, J.; Geyer, C. Artificial intelligence and the public sector. *International Journal of Public Administration* 2019, 42, 596–615.
29. Mendling, J.; Decker, G.; Hull, R.; Reijers, H.; Weber, I. How do machine learning, robotic process automation, and blockchains affect the human factor in business process management? *Communications of the Association for Information Systems* 2018, 43, 19.
30. Faisal, A.; Yigitcanlar, T.; Kamruzzaman, M.; Currie, G. Understanding autonomous vehicles. *Journal of Transport and Land Use* 2019, 12, 45–72.
31. Japan Times. Available online: www.japantimes.co.jp/news/2020/01/22/national/ana-starts-testing-autonomous-bus-operation-haneda-airport/#.XjN_rGgzZnI (accessed on 31 Jan 2020).
32. Yigitcanlar, T.; Wilson, M.; Kamruzzaman, M. Disruptive impacts of automated driving systems on the built environment and land use. *Journal of Open Innovation: Technology, Market, and Complexity* 2019, 5, 24.
33. Yigitcanlar, T.; Kamruzzaman, M.; Foth, M.; Sabatini-Marques, J.; da Costa, E.; Ioppolo, G. Can cities become smart without being sustainable? *Sustainable Cities and Society* 2019, 45, 348–365.
34. Houston Chronicle. Available online: www.houstonchronicle.com/news/transportat ion/article/Robot-police-coming-to-Houston-transit-center-14999004.php (accessed on 23 Jan 2020).

35. Washington Post. Available online: www.washingtonpost.com/technology/2019/05/14/one-solution-keeping-traffic-stops-turning-violent-robot-that-separates-police-officers-drivers/ (accessed on 25 Jan 2020).

36. Swindell, D.; Desouza, K.; Hudgens, R. Dubai offers lessons for using artificial intelligence in local government. *Brookings* 2018.

37. Chang, C.; Lee, H.; Liu, C. A review of artificial intelligence algorithms used for smart machine tools. *Inventions* 2018, 3, 41.

38. Desouza, K.; Smith, K. *Big Data and Planning*. American Planning Association 2016, 585, 2–102.

39. Desouza, K. *Delivering Artificial Intelligence in Government*. IBM Center for the Business of Government, 2018.

40. Thakuriah, P.; Tilahun, N.; Zellner, M. *Seeing Cities through Big Data*. Springer 2017. 1–9.

41. Sadilek, A.; Kautz, H.; DiPrete, L.; Labus, B.; Portman, E.; Teitel, J.; Silenzio, V. Deploying nEmesis: preventing foodborne illness by data mining social media. *Proceedings of the 13th IAAI Conference on AI, 2016*. 3982–3989.

42. BBC. Available online: www.bbc.com/news/technology-39857645 (accessed on 31 Jan 2020).

43. Accenture. Available online: https://newsroom.accenture.com/news/accenture-helps-seattle-police-department-implement-data-analytics-platform.htm (accessed on 1 Feb 2020)

44. Fastcompany. Available onlinewww.fastcompany.com/90440198/san-diegos-massive-7-year-experiment-with-facial-recognition-technology-appears-to-be-a-flop (accessed on 17 Feb 2020).

45. Madaio, M.; Haimson, O.; Zhang, W.; Cheng, X.; Hinds-Aldrich, M.; Dilkina, B.; Chau, D. *Identifying and Prioritizing Fire Inspections*. Bloomberg Data for Good Exchange 2015.

46. Yigitcanlar, T.; Han, H.; Kamruzzaman, M. Approaches, advances, and applications in the sustainable development of smart cities. *Energies* 2019, 12, 4554.

47. New York Times. Available online: www.nytimes.com/2019/06/27/us/lake-city-florida-ransom-cyberattack.html (accessed on 1 Feb 2020).

48. MIT News. Available online: http://news.mit.edu/2016/ai-system-predicts-85-percent-cyber-attacks-using-input-human-experts-0418 (accessed on 30 Jan 2020).

49. Smith, S.; Barlow, G.; Xie, X.; Rubinstein, Z. *Smart urban signal networks*. Proceedings of the 23rd International Conference on Automated Planning and Scheduling. Association for the Advancement of Artificial Intelligence, 2013, 434–442.

50. Curbed. Available online: https://detroit.curbed.com/2019/7/8/20687045/project-green-light-detroit-facial-recognition-technology (accessed on 1 Feb 2020).

51. Guardian. Available online: www.theguardian.com/media/2016/dec/18/what-is-fake-news-pizzagate (accessed on 1 Feb 2020).

52. Washington Post. Available online: www.washingtonpost.com/news/local/wp/2016/12/04/d-c-police-respond-to-report-of-a-man-with-a-gun-at-comet-ping-pong-restaurant/ (accessed on 1 Feb 2020).

53. Azcentral. Available online: www.azcentral.com/story/money/business/tech/2018/12/11/waymo-self-driving-vehicles-face-harassment-road-rage-phoenix-area/2198220002/ (accessed on 1 Feb 2020).

54. Selby, J.; Desouza, K. Fragile cities in the developed world: a conceptual framework. *Cities* 2019, 91, 180–192.

55. Desouza, K.; Selby, J. *How Technological Progress can Cause Urban Fragility*. Brookings Institute 2019.
56. NHTSA. Available online: https://static.nhtsa.gov/odi/inv/2016/INCLA-PE16007–7876.pdf (accessed on 1 Feb 2020).
57. CNN. Available online: http://money.cnn.com/2015/07/24/technology/chrysler-hack-recall/index.html (accessed on 1 Feb 2020).
58. CNN. Available online: http://money.cnn.com/2015/07/21/technology/chrysler-hack/index.html (accessed on 1 Feb 2020).
59. Slate. Available online: www.slate.com/blogs/future_tense/2015/06/16/autonomous_vehicles_will_cost_local_governments_big_bucks.html (accessed on 1 Feb 2020).
60. Az Central. Available online: www.azcentral.com/story/news/arizona/politics/2015/07/01/self-driving-cars-city revenue/29598929/ (accessed on 1 Feb 2020).
61. Yigitcanlar, T.; Kamruzzaman, M.; Buys, L.; Ioppolo, G.; Sabatini-Marques, J.; da Costa, E.; Yun, J. Understanding 'smart cities'. *Cities* 2018, 81, 145–160.
62. Yigitcanlar, T.; Han, H.; Kamruzzaman, M.; Ioppolo, G.; Sabatini-Marques, J. The making of smart cities. *Land Use Policy* 2019, 88, 104187.
63. Feng, S.; Xu, L. An intelligent decision supoport system for fuzzy comprehensive evaluation of urban development. *Expert Systems with Applications* 1999, 16, 21–32.
64. Shrivastava, R.; Mahajan, P. Artificial intelligence research in India. *Science & Technology Libraries* 2016, 35, 136–151.
65. Makarynskyy, O.; Makarynska, D.; Kuhn, M.; Featherstone, W. Predicting sea level variations with artificial neural networks at Hillarys Boat Harbour, Western Australia. *Estuarine, Coastal and Shelf Science* 2004, 61, 351–360.
66. Aziz, K.; Haque, M.; Rahman, A.; Shamseldin, A.; Shoaib, M. Flood estimation in ungauged catchments. *Stochastic Environmental Research and Risk Assessment* 2017, 31, 1499–1514.
67. Hanson, C.; Marshall, B. Artificial intelligence applications in the intensive care unit. *Critical Care Medicine* 2001, 29, 427–435.
68. Ramesh, A.; Kambhampati, C.; Monson, J.; Drew, P. Artificial intelligence in medicine. *Annals of The Royal College of Surgeons of England* 2004, 86, 334.
69. Chau, K. A review on integration of artificial intelligence into water quality modelling. *Marine Pollution Bulletin* 2006, 52, 726–733.
70. Patel, V.; Shortliffe, E.; Stefanelli, M.; Szolovits, P.; Berthold, M.; Bellazzi, R.; Abu-Hanna, A. The coming of age of artificial intelligence in medicine. *Artificial Intelligence in Medicine* 2009, 46, 5–17.
71. Drigas, A.; Ioannidou, R. Artificial intelligence in special education. *International Journal of Engineering Education* 2012, 28, 1366.
72. Rho, S.; Min, G.; Chen, W. Advanced issues in artificial intelligence and pattern recognition for intelligent surveillance system in smart home cnvironment. *Engineering Applications of Artificial Intelligence* 2012, 25, 1299–1300.
73. Reaz, M. Artificial intelligence techniques for advanced smart home implementation. *Acta Technica Corvininesis-Bulletin of Engineering* 2013, 6, 51–57.
74. Chmiel, W.; Dańda, J.; Dziech, A.; Ernst, S.; Kadłuczka, P.; Mikrut, Z.; Pawlik, P.; Szwed, P.; Wojnicki, I. INSIGMA. *Multimedia Tools and Applications* 2016, 75, 10529–10560.
75. De Paz, J.; Bajo, J.; Rodríguez, S.; Villarrubia, G.; Corchado, J. Intelligent system for lighting control in smart cities. *Information Sciences* 2016, 372, 241–255.

76. Yun, J.; Lee, D.; Ahn, H.; Park, K.; Yigitcanlar, T. Not deep learning but autonomous learning of open innovation for sustainable artificial intelligence. *Sustainability* 2016, 8, 797

77. Alam, F.; Mehmood, R.; Katib, I.; Albogami, N.; Albeshri, A. Data fusion and IoT for smart ubiquitous environments. *IEEE Access* 2017, 5, 9533–9554.

78. Bose, B. Artificial intelligence techniques in smart grid and renewable energy systems. *Proceedings of the IEEE* 2017, 105, 2262–2273.

79. Garlík, B. The application of artificial intelligence in the process of optimizing energy consumption in intelligent areas. *Neural Network World* 2017, 27, 415.

80. Jha, S.; Bilalovic, J.; Jha, A.; Patel, N.; Zhang, H. Renewable energy. *Renewable and Sustainable Energy Reviews* 2017, 77, 297–317.

81. Wang, Z.; Srinivasan, R. A review of artificial intelligence-based building energy use prediction. *Renewable and Sustainable Energy Reviews* 2017, 75, 796–808.

82. Bajaj, R.; Sharma, V. Smart education with artificial intelligence-based determination of learning styles. *Procedia Computer Science* 2018, 132, 834–842.

83. Braun, T.; Fung, B.; Iqbal, F.; Shah, B. Security and privacy challenges in smart cities. *Sustainable Cities and Society* 2018, 39, 499–507.

84. Casares, A. The brain of the future and the viability of democratic governance. *Futures* 2018, 103, 5–16.

85. Chassignol, M.; Khoroshavin, A.; Klimova, A.; Bilyatdinova, A. Artificial intelligence trends in education. *Procedia Computer Science* 2018, 136, 16–24.

86. Chui, K.; Lytras, M.; Visvizi, A. Energy sustainability in smart cities. *Energies* 2018, 11, 2869.

87. Dobrescu, E.; Dobrescu, E. Artificial intelligence (AI)-the technology that shapes the world. *Global Economic Observer* 2018, 6, 71–81.

88. Edwards, C.; Edwards, A.; Spence, P.; Lin, X. I, teacher. *Communication Education* 2018, 67, 473–480.

89. Guo, J.; Li, B. The application of medical artificial intelligence technology in rural areas of developing countries. *Health Equity* 2018, 2, 174–181.

90. Guo, K.; Lu, Y.; Gao, H.; Cao, R. Artificial intelligence-based semantic internet of things in a user-centric smart city. *Sensors* 2018, 18, 1341.

91. Håkansson, A. Ipsum. *Procedia Computer Science* 2018, 126, 2107–2116.

92. Kopytko, V.; Shevchuk, L.; Yankovska, L.; Semchuk, Z.; Strilchuk, R. Smart home and artificial intelligence as environment for the implementation of new technologies. *Traektoriâ Nauki (Path of Science)* 2018, 4, 2007–2012.

93. Liu, G.; Liu, S.; Muhammad, K.; Sangaiah, A.; Doctor, F. Object tracking in vary lighting conditions for fog based intelligent surveillance of public spaces. *IEEE Access* 2018, 6, 29283–29296.

94. Lukowicz, P.; Slusallek, P. How to avoid an AI interaction singularity. *Interactions* 2018, 25, 72–78.

95. Martins, J. Towards smart city innovation under the perspective of software-defined networking, artificial intelligence and big data. *Revista de Tecnologia da Informacao e Comunicacao* 2018, 8, 1–8.

96. Nápoles, V.; Rodríguez, M.; Páez, D.; Penelas, J.; García-Ochoa, A.; Pérez, A. MUSA–I. *Multidisciplinary Digital Publishing Institute Proceedings* 2018, 2, 1215.

97. Wan, C.; Hwang, M. Value-based deep reinforcement learning for adaptive isolated intersection signal control. *IET Intelligent Transport Systems* 2018, 12, 1005–1010.

98. Abduljabbar, R.; Dia, H.; Liyanage, S.; Bagloee, S. Applications of artificial intelligence in transport. *Sustainability* 2019, 11, 189.

99. Ajerla, D.; Mahfuz, S.; Zulkernine, F. A real-time patient monitoring framework for fall detection. *Wireless Communications and Mobile Computing* 2019, 9507938.
100. Allam, Z.; Dhunny, Z. On big data, artificial intelligence and smart cities. *Cities* 2019, 89, 80–91.
101. Alsamhi, S.; Ma, O.; Ansari, M.; Almalki, F. Survey on collaborative smart drones and internet of things for improving smartness of smart cities. *IEEE Access* 2019, 7, 128125–128152.
102. Alzoubi, I.; Delavar, M.; Mirzaei, F.; Arrabi, B. Prediction of environmental indicators in land leveling using artificial intelligence techniques. *Journal of Environmental Health Science and Engineering* 2019, 16, 65–80.
103. Brady, H. The challenge of big data and data science. *Annual Review of Political Science* 2019, 22, 297–323.
104. Bui, K.; Jung, J. Computational negotiation-based edge analytics for smart objects. *Information Sciences* 2019, 480, 222–236.
105. Cai, B.; Alvarez, R.; Sit, M.; Duarte, F.; Ratti, C. Deep learning-based video system for accurate and real-time parking measurement. *IEEE Internet of Things Journal* 2019, 6, 7693–7701.
106. Chen, M.; Miao, Y.; Jian, X.; Wang, X.; Humar, I. Cognitive-LPWAN. *IEEE Transactions on Green Communications and Networking* 2019, 3, 409–417.
107. Chen, N.; Qiu, T.; Zhou, X.; Li, K.; Atiquzzaman, M. An intelligent robust networking mechanism for the internet of things. *IEEE Communications Magazine* 2019, 57, 91–95.
108. Cui, Q.; Wang, Y.; Chen, K.; Ni, W.; Lin, I.; Tao, X.; Zhang, P. Big data analytics and network calculus enabling intelligent management of autonomous vehicles in a smart city. *IEEE Internet of Things Journal* 2018, 6, 2021–2034.
109. Desouza, K.; Dawson, G.; Chenok, D. Designing, developing, and deploying artificial intelligence systems. *Business Horizons* 2019, 63, 205–213.
110. Din, I.; Guizani, M.; Rodrigues, J.; Hassan, S.; Korotaev, V. Machine learning in the internet of things. *Future Generation Computer Systems* 2019, 100, 826–843.
111. Dong, Y.; Guo, S.; Liu, J.; Yang, Y. Energy-efficient fair cooperation fog computing in mobile edge networks for smart city. *IEEE Internet of Things Journal* 2019, 6, 7543–7554.
112. Hariri, R.; Fredericks, E.; Bowers, K. Uncertainty in big data analytics: survey, opportunities, and challenges. *Journal of Big Data* 2019, 6, 44.
113. Ibrahim, M.; Haworth, J.; Cheng, T. Urban-i. *Environment and Planning B: Urban Analytics and City Science* 2019, 2399808319846517.
114. Iqbal, R.; Maniak, T.; Karyotis, C. Intelligent remote monitoring of parking spaces using licensed and unlicensed wireless technologies. IEEE Network 2019, 33, 23–29.
115. Kundu, D. Blockchain and trust in a smart city. *Environment and Urbanization Asia* 2019, 10, 31–43.
116. Le, L.; Nguyen, H.; Dou, J.; Zhou, J. A comparative study of PSO-ANN, GA-ANN, ICA-ANN, and ABC-ANN in estimating the heating load of buildings' energy efficiency for smart city planning. *Applied Sciences* 2019, 9, 2630.
117. Leung, C.; Braun, P.; Cuzzocrea, A. AI-based sensor information fusion for supporting deep supervised learning. *Sensors* 2019, 19, 1345.
118. Li, L.; Shuang, Y.; Ma, Q.; Li, H.; Zhao, H.; Wei, M.; Liu, C.; Hao, C.; Qiu, C.; Cui, T. Intelligent metasurface imager and recognizer. *Light: Science & Applications* 2019, 8, 1–9.

119. Liu, N.; Li, L.; Hao, B.; Yang, L.; Hu, T.; Xue, T.; Wang, S. Modeling and simulation of robot inverse dynamics using LSTM-based deep learning algorithm for smart cities and factories. *IEEE Access* 2019, 7, 173989–173998.

120. Lytras, M.; Chui, K.; Visvizi, A. Data analytics in smart healthcare. *Applied Sciences* 2019, 9, 2812.

121. Muhammad, K.; Lloret, J.; Baik, S. Intelligent and energy-efficient data prioritization in green smart cities. *IEEE Communications Magazine* 2019, 57, 60–65.

122. Noorbakhsh-Sabet, N.; Zand, R.; Zhang, Y.; Abedi, V. Artificial intelligence transforms the future of healthcare. *American Journal of Medicine* 2019, 132, 795–801.

123. Park, J.; Lee, S.; Yun, S.; Kim, H.; Kim, W. Dependable fire detection system with multifunctional artificial intelligence framework. *Sensors* 2019, 19, 2025.

124. Ponce, H.; Gutiérrez, S. An indoor predicting climate conditions approach using Internet-of-Things and artificial hydrocarbon networks. *Measurement* 2019, 135, 170–179.

125. Puri, V.; Jha, S.; Kumar, R.; Priyadarshini, I.; Abdel-Basset, M.; Elhoseny, M.; Long, H. A hybrid artificial intelligence and internet of things model for generation of renewable resource of energy. *IEEE Access* 2019, 7, 111181–111191.

126. Rahman, M.; Rashid, M.; Hossain, M.; Hassanain, E.; Alhamid, M.; Guizani, M. Blockchain and IoT-based cognitive edge framework for sharing economy services in a smart city. *IEEE Access* 2019, 7, 18611–18621.

127. Ruohomaa, H.; Salminen, V.; Kunttu, I. Towards a smart city concept in small cities. Technology Innovation Management Review 2019, 9, 5–14.

128. Sgantzos, K.; Grigg, I. Artificial intelligence implementations on the blockchain. *Future Internet* 2019, 11, 170.

129. Shi, J.; Liu, S.; Zhang, L.; Yang, B.; Shu, L.; Yang, Y.; Chai, Y. Smart textile-integrated microelectronic systems for wearable applications. *Advanced Materials* 2019, 32, 1901958.

130. Soomro, K.; Bhutta, M.; Khan, Z.; Tahir, M. Smart city big data analytics. *Wiley Interdisciplinary Reviews: Data Mining and Knowledge Discovery* 2019, 9, e1319.

131. Streitz, N. Beyond 'smart-only' cities. *Journal of Ambient Intelligence and Humanized Computing* 2019, 10, 791–812.

132. Syifa, M.; Kadavi, P.; Lee, C. An artificial intelligence application for post-earthquake damage mapping in Palu, Central Sulawesi, Indonesia. *Sensors* 2019, 19, 542.

133. Wang, P.; Yao, J.; Wang, G.; Hao, F.; Shrestha, S.; Xue, B.; Peng, Y. Exploring the application of artificial intelligence technology for identification of water pollution characteristics and tracing the source of water quality pollutants. *Science of The Total Environment* 2019, 693, 133440.

134. Wei, N.; Li, C.; Peng, X.; Zeng, F.; Lu, X. Conventional models and artificial intelligence-based models for energy consumption forecasting: a review. *Journal of Petroleum Science and Engineering* 2019, 181, 106187.

135. Wogu, I.; Misra, S.; Assibong, P.; Apeh, H.; Olu-Owolabi, F.; Awogu-Maduagwu, E. Artificial intelligence, smart classrooms and online education in the 21st century. *Journal of Cases on Information Technology* 2018, 21, 66–79.

136. Cortès, U.; Sànchez-Marrè, M.; Ceccaroni, L.; R-Roda, I.; Poch, M. Artificial intelligence and environmental decision support systems. *Applied Intelligence* 2000, 13, 77–91.

137. Bennett, C.; Hauser, K. Artificial intelligence framework for simulating clinical decision-making. *Artificial Intelligence in Medicine* 2013, 57, 9–19.

138. Fernández, J.; Calavia, L.; Baladrón, C.; Aguiar, J.; Carro, B.; Sánchez-Esguevillas, A.; Alonso-López, J.; Smilansky, Z. An intelligent surveillance platform for large metropolitan areas with dense sensor deployment. *Sensors* 2013, 13, 7414–7442.
139. Stefanelli, M. The socio-organizational age of artificial intelligence in medicine. *Artificial Intelligence in Medicine* 2001, 23, 25–47.
140. McArthur, D.; Lewis, M.; Bishary, M. The roles of artificial intelligence in education. *Journal of Educational Technology* 2005, 1, 42–80.
141. Pieters, W. Explanation and trust. *Ethics and Information Technology* 2011, 13, 53–64.
142. Neuhauser, L.; Kreps, G.; Morrison, K.; Athanasoulis, M.; Kirienko, N.; Van Brunt, D. Using design science and artificial intelligence to improve health communication. *Patient Education and Counseling* 2013, 92, 211–217.
143. Roll, I.; Wylie, R. Evolution and revolution in artificial intelligence in education. *International Journal of Artificial Intelligence in Education* 2016, 26, 582–599.
144. Castelli, M.; Sormani, R.; Trujillo, L.; Popovič, A. Predicting per capita violent crimes in urban areas. *Journal of Ambient Intelligence and Humanized Computing* 2017, 8, 29–36.
145. Meena, N.; Parashar, S.; Swarnkar, A.; Gupta, N.; Niazi, K.; Bansal, R. Mobile power infrastructure planning and operational management for smart city applications. *Energy Procedia* 2017, 142, 2202–2207.
146. Quan, S.; Park, J.; Economou, A.; Lee, S. Artificial intelligence-aided design. *Environment and Planning B: Urban Analytics and City Science* 2019, 46, 1581–1599.
147. Devedzic, V. Web Intelligence and artificial intelligence in education. *Educational Technology & Society* 2004, 7, 29–39.
148. Eldrandaly, K.; Abdel-Basset, M.; Abdel-Fatah, L. PTZ-surveillance coverage based on artificial intelligence for smart cities. *International Journal of Information Management* 2019, 49, 520–532.
149. Altulyan, M.; Yao, L.; Kanhere, S.; Wang, X.; Huang, C. A unified framework for data integrity protection in people-centric smart cities. *Multimedia Tools and Applications* 2019, 79, 4989–5002.
150. Yu, H.; Yang, Z.; Sinnott, R. Decentralized big data auditing for smart city environments leveraging blockchain technology. *IEEE Access* 2019, 7, 6288–6296.
151. Bowman, S.; Easpaig, G.; Nic, B.; Fox, R. Virtually caring. *Rural & Remote Health* 2020, 20, 31–38.
152. Pence, H. Artificial intelligence in higher education. *Journal of Educational Technology Systems* 2019, 48, 5–13.
153. Guilherme, A. AI and education. *AI & Society* 2019, 34, 47–54.
154. Conversation. Available online: https://theconversation.com/covid-19-death-toll-estimated-to-reach-3-900-by-next-friday-according-to-ai-modelling-133052 (accessed on 11 Mar 2020).
155. Lin, Y.; Petway, J.; Lien, W.; Settele, J. Blockchain with artificial intelligence to efficiently manage water use under climate change. *Environments* 2018, 5, 34.
156. Inclezan, D.; Prádanos, L. A critical view on smart cities and AI. *Journal of Artificial Intelligence Research* 2017, 60, 681–686.
157. Zou, Y.; Zhang, S.; Min, Y. Exploring urban population forecasting and spatial distribution modelling with artificial intelligence technology. *Computer Modeling in Engineering & Sciences* 2019, 119, 295–310.
158. Rolnick, D., Donti, P. L., Kaack, L. H., Kochanski, K., Lacoste, A., Sankaran, K., ... Bengio, Y. (2022). Tackling climate change with machine learning. *ACM Computing Surveys (CSUR)*, 55(2), 1–96.

159. O'Gorman, P.; Dwyer, J. Using machine learning to parameterize moist convection. *Journal of Advances in Modeling Earth Systems* 2018, 10, 2548–2563.

160. Dayal, K.; Deo, R.; Apan, A. Drought modelling based on artificial intelligence and neural network algorithms. In: *Climate Change Adaptation in Pacific Countries.* Springer 2017, 177–198.

161. Khalifa, E. Smart cities. *Journal of Strategic Innovation and Sustainability* 2019, 14, 79–88.

162. Falco, G.; Viswanathan, A.; Caldera, C.; Shrobe, H. A master attack methodology for an AI-based automated attack planner for smart cities. *IEEE Access* 2018, 6, 48360–48373.

163. Kankanamge, N.; Yigitcanlar, T.; Goonetilleke, A.; Kamruzzaman, M. Can volunteer crowdsourcing reduce disaster risk? *International Journal of Disaster Risk Reduction* 2019, 35, 101097.

164. Chatterjee, S.; Kar, A.K.; Gupta, M. Success of IoT in smart cities of India. *Government Information Quarterly* 2018, 35, 349–361.

165. Luo, X.; Tong, S.; Fang, Z.; Qu, Z. Frontiers: machines vs. humans. *Marketing Science* 2019, 38, 937–947.

166. Yigitcanlar, T. Smart cities: an effective urban development and management model? *Australian Planner* 2015, 52, 27–34.

167. Rotta, M.; Sell, D.; Pacheco, R.; Yigitcanlar, T. Digital commons and citizen coproduction in smart cities. *Energies* 2019, 12, 2813.

168. Yigitcanlar, T. Smart city policies revisited. *World Technopolis Review* 2018, 7, 97–112.

169. Rjab, A.; Mellouli, S. Smart cities in the era of artificial intelligence and internet of things. *Proceedings of the 19th Annual International Conference on Digital Government Research*, 2018. 1–10.

170. Friedman, B.; Hendry, D. *Value Sensitive Design: Shaping Technology with Moral Imagination.* MIT Press, 2019.

171. LSE. Available online: https://blogs.lse.ac.uk/usappblog/2019/12/23/why-low-trust-in-government-may-mean-americans-dont-want-anything-done-about-inequality/ (accessed on 20 Feb 2020).

172. Morishita, L.; van Zyl, D. Exploring the significance of earning a social license to operate in an urban setting. *Geo-Resources Environment and Engineering* 2017, 2, 265–270.

173. Yuttapongsontorn, N.; Desouza, K.; Braganza, A. Complexities of large-scale technology project failure. *Public Performance & Management Review* 2008, 31, 443–478.

174. Mergel, I.; Desouza, K. Implementing open innovation in the public sector. *Public Administration Review* 2013, 73, 882–890.

175. Desouza, K.; Bhagwatwar, A. Technology-enabled participatory platforms for civic engagement. *Journal of Urban Technology* 2014, 21, 25–50.

176. Liu, Y. Research on the evaluation of urban open data. *World Journal of Engineering and Technology* 2017, 5, 122.

177. Perng, S.; Kitchin, R.; MacDonncha, D. Hackathons, entrepreneurial life and the making of smart cities. *Geoforum* 2018, 97, 189–197.

178. CNN. Available online: https://us.cnn.com/style/article/artist-google-traffic-jam-alert-trick-scli-intl/index.html (accessed on 20 Feb 2020).

179. Desouza, K. *Agile Information Systems.* Routledge, 2006.

180. Watson, R.; Kunene, K.; Islam, M. Frugal information systems. *Information Technology for Development* 2013, 19, 176–187.

181. Planetizen. Available online: www.planetizen.com/node/67338 (accessed on 19 Feb 2020).
182. Purao, S.; Desouza, K.; Becker, J. Investigating failures in large-scale public sector projects with sentiment analysis. *e-Service Journal* 2012, 8, 84–105.
183. Desouza, K.; Hunter, M.; Yigitcanlar, T. Under the hood. *Public Management* 2019, 12, 30–35.
184. Krishnamurthy, R.; Smith, K.; Desouza, K. Urban informatics. In: *Seeing Cities through Big Data*. Springer 2017, 163–188.
185. Wired. Available online: www.wired.com/story/car-hack-shut-down-safety-features/ (accessed on 14 Feb 2020).
186. BBC. Available online: www.bbc.com/news/blogs-trending-51271037 (accessed on 20 Feb 2020).
187. BBC. Available online: www.bbc.com/news/world-latin-america-46145986 (accessed on 30 Dec 2019).
188. Gherhes, V.; Obrad, C. Technical and humanities students' perspectives on the development and sustainability of artificial intelligence. *Sustainability* 2018, 10, 3066.
189. Conversation. Available online: https://theconversation.com/australian-police-are-using-the-clearview-ai-facial-recognition-system-with-no-accountability-132667 (accessed on 11 Mar 2020).
190. Conversation. Available online: https://theconversation.com/airlines-take-no-chances-with-our-safety-and-neither-should-artificial-intelligence-132580 (accessed on 11 Mar 2020).
191. Verge. Available online: www.theverge.com/2018/7/26/17619382/ibms-watson-cancer-ai-healthcare-science (accessed on 12 Mar 2020).
192. NTSB. Available online: www.ntsb.gov/news/press-releases/Pages/NR20180524.aspx (accessed on 13 Mar 2020).
193. Conversation. Available online: https://theconversation.com/microsofts-racist-chatbot-tay-highlights-how-far-ai-is-from-being-truly-intelligent-56881 (accessed on 13 Mar 2020).
194. Forbes. Available online: www.forbes.com/sites/bernardmarr/2018/11/19/is-artificial-intelligence-dangerous-6-ai-risks-everyone-should-know-about/#65ee8ba22404 (accessed on 13 Mar 2020).
195. Conversation. Available online: https://theconversation.com/to-protect-us-from-the-risks-of-advanced-artificial-intelligence-we-need-to-act-now-107615 (accessed on 13 Mar 2020).
196. Medium. Available online: https://medium.com/@tibastar/summary-of-eu-white-paper-on-artificial-intelligence-a-european-approach-to-excellence-and-trust-e04a1a018b5 (accessed on 11 Mar 2020).
197. EU. Available online: https://ec.europa.eu/info/sites/info/files/commission-white-paper-artificial-intelligence-feb2020_en.pdf (accessed on 11 Mar 2020).
198. Guardian. Available online: www.theguardian.com/technology/2017/jul/17/elon-musk-regulation-ai-combat-existential-threat-tesla-spacex-ceo (accessed on 13 Mar 2020).
199. Schleiger, E.; Hajkowicz, S. Available online: www.themandarin.com.au/107060-artificial-intelligence-in-australia-needs-to-get-ethical-so-we-have-a-plan (accessed on 15 Mar 2020).
200. Nica, E.; Manole, C.; Stan, C. A laborless society? *Journal of Self-Governance & Management Economics* 2018, 6, 25–30.
201. Gunkel, D. *The Machine Question*. MIT Press, 2012.

202. Makridakis, S. The forthcoming artificial intelligence (AI) revolution. *Futures* 2017, 90, 46–60.
203. Sheikhnejad, Y.; Yigitcanlar, T. Scientific landscape of sustainable urban and rural areas research. *Sustainability* 2020, 12, 1293.
204. Smashing. Available online: www.smashingmagazine.com/2019/09/ai-climate-change (accessed on 11 Mar 2020).
205. Yigitcanlar, T.; Vella, K.; Desouza, K.; Butler, L.; Kankanamge, N. Available online. https://eprints.qut.edu.au/137164 (accessed on 15 Mar 2020).
206. Yigitcanlar, T.; Desouza, K.; Butler, L.; Roozkhosh, F. Contributions and risks of artificial intelligence (AI) in building smarter cities: Insights from a systematic review of the literature. *Energies* 2020, 13(6), 1473.

6 Urban Artificial Intelligences

6.1 Introduction

Artificial intelligence (AI) is one of the most disruptive technologies of our time [1]. In simple terms, AI can be defined as machines or computers that mimic cognitive functions that humans associate with the human mind, such as learning and problem solving [2]. The field of AI is vast and constantly expanding, and such characterisation concerns AI beyond its current capabilities, namely artificial narrow intelligence, thereby comprehending two potential future types of AI: artificial general intelligence and artificial super intelligence [3–5].

AI is already here. AI applications are being used in areas ranging from marketing to banking and finance, from agriculture to healthcare and security, from space exploration to robotics and transport, and from chatbots to artificial creativity and manufacturing [6,7]. In recent years, AI applications have been also started to become an integral part of the city. AIs manage the transport systems of cities in the shape of autonomous cars [8–10]. Robots run restaurants and shops where core aspects of urban life are every day played out, and repair urban infrastructure [11,12]. Invisible intelligent platforms govern multiple urban domains ranging from traffic to safety, and from garbage collection to air quality monitoring [13,14]. We refer to this strand of AI as *urban artificial intelligences*—where AIs are embodied in urban spaces, urban infrastructures, and urban technologies, which together are turning cities into autonomous entities operating in an unsupervised manner [15].

Focusing mostly on artificial narrow intelligence and present AI technology, this chapter elaborates the rise of AI in cities and discusses the *sustainability of urban artificial intelligence* from the lens of *smart and sustainable cities* [16–19]—where such cities utilise digital technologies to make infrastructure services more efficient and reactive to reduce resource consumption, increase environmental quality, and cut down on carbon emissions [20]. In other words, this chapter investigates how AI is being utilised in urban domains, unpacking the sustainability potential and risks that AI technology poses for our cities and their citizens.

DOI: 10.1201/9781003403630-8

6.2 Planetary Sustainability Challenges

We live in "interesting times", where such a period refers to—as in the legendary Chinese curse—a time of danger, uncertainty, and complexity [21]. Unless the underlining drivers behind such dangers, uncertainties, and complexities are not eliminated or brought to a manageable level, these interesting times might coincide with the end of human civilisation [22]. The primary underlining reasons—which are the key challenges of humanity today—include: (a) rapidly increasing global population; (b) rapidly depleting natural resources and climate change; (c) technological inequality and disruption; (d) misuse of data and information; (d) ruthless neoliberal economies; (e) global, regional, local conflicts; and (f) corrupt or ineffective governance. These challenges are illustrated in Figure 6.1, and further elaborated below.

Rapidly increasing global population: With the appearance of *Homo sapiens*, the origin of humankind goes back to about 300,000 years ago. However, it is only during the last 10,000 years that we have managed to establish safer living conditions thanks to progress in the spheres of technology, knowledge, and wisdom. Subsequently, in the year 1800, the world's population reached the one billion mark. During the same year, London was the only city in the world hosting a million people. Today over 220 years later, our population is over 7.8 billion, and London is home to 9.3. million people. However, London is no longer the largest city in the world. The metropolitan region of Tokyo is approaching 40 million people, and there are over 30 other megacities around the world with over 10 million people. Population projections suggest that by the end of the century the global population will range between 9 and 12 billion. Along with megacity developments, all major

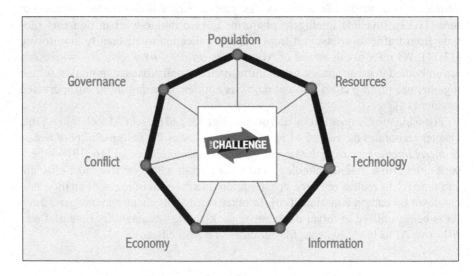

Figure 6.1 Key global sustainability challenges.

metropolitan regions are also experiencing rapid peri-urban expansion [23]. This dual human–urban growth is causing alarming water, food, and energy insecurity [24–26].

Rapidly depleting natural resources and climate change: Ever-increasing populations, coupled with unsustainable development practices, are pushing the limits of the world's carrying capacity [27–30]. Heavy fossil fuel dependency and limited clean-energy options—only about 25% of all the world's energy comes from renewable resources—together with various other contributing factors, are triggering biodiversity loss and anthropogenic climate change, and increasing the frequency and severity of natural disasters dramatically [31–33].

Technological (or digital) inequality and disruption: Whilst there have been many positive technological inventions and developments, technology also creates disruption in our societies—particularly for those who cannot afford, access, or adopt new technologies [34,35]. For instance, despite the fact that there are four billion smartphone users in the world, not everyone has access to the internet and mobile services at the same speed and bandwidth [36]. Particularly from an urban perspective, expensive urban technologies are often unevenly distributed across cities, thus contributing to the fracturing of urban societies and to the formation of high-tech *premium ecological enclaves* where only rich minorities can shield themselves from the burdens of climate change and environmental degradation [37–39].

Misuse of data and information: During the last two decades, with the rise of the second digital revolution and mass digitisation, data and information have become more widely and easily accessible. Especially, social media platforms and shared user-generated contents have provided large volumes of data. Nonetheless, this has also led to fake news and data integrity issues [40]. Furthermore, targeted Facebook and WhatsApp campaigns changed the results of the 2016 USA and 2018 Brazil presidential elections, and the 2016 Brexit referendum [41–43], thereby showing how data are being used not to inform, but rather to misinform and to protect the interests of certain political elites/groups.

Ruthless neoliberal economies: Today, the world is facing harsh economic challenges. Globally, we are moving towards another recession, if we are not already in one. While some might blame the recent COVID-19 pandemic, the origin of the issue is neoliberal capitalism and the consumeristic and materialistic practices that it reproduces [44,45]. Only eight people, the richest in the world, have a net worth equivalent to that of the lower half of the world's population (about 3.8 billion people); this is the product of ruthless neoliberal economies [46]. Socioeconomic inequality is rapidly widening, and poverty and recession are making life harder for most people across the globe. Particularly with the existing COVID-19 pandemic, the situation is much more dramatic and unsustainable in developing countries, and for disadvantaged communities and individuals [47].

Global, regional and local conflicts: Human civilisation has always experienced conflicts and wars over resources, land, or power. However, contemporary wars are not only taking place as trade, diplomatic, and armed conflicts, but also as cyber warfare [48]. These multiple conflicts, together with climate change, are displacing many people, thus substantially increasing the number of refugees in the world [49,50].

Corrupt or ineffective governance: Governments should have supposedly addressed the aforementioned challenges. Instead, short termism in political circles, corporate influence, and various degrees of corruption make governments unable to be part of the solution [51]. An example is the Paris Agreement on Climate Change, which, although signed by 197 countries (and ratified by 189), has led to little or no tangible outcome due to government inaction [52].

6.3 Smart and Sustainable Cities

The aforementioned issues are extremely challenging to tackle, but they are not discouraging many scholars and thinkers from searching for solutions to realise more sustainable futures [53–55]. Today, approximately 55% of the global population lives in cities whose fabric is rapidly expanding across the planet [56]. The figure is over 85% in many countries—such as Australia, the UK, and the Netherlands [57]. This makes urban areas the prime focus of sustainability policy, not only because they house the majority of the world's population, but also because they contain the core of global socioeconomic activities [58,59]. The changing focus from *nation* to *city* has created new and alternative ideas for building sustainable futures by placing cities at the centre of policy actions [60].

In recent years, one of the most prominent ideas in urban policy circles has been the imperative to employ information and communication technology (ICT), in order to address major urban and societal challenges [61]. This trend gave birth to the notion of a "smart city". While the origin of the concept of smart city dates back centuries, the practice of smart urbanism was made popular only in the 2000s with urban projects led by private companies like IBM and Cisco [62–64]. Since then, many major technology, construction, and consultancy companies, together with policymakers and city planners, have jumped onto the smart city bandwagon [65,66]. This has resulted in a myriad of smart-city initiatives that are reshaping existing cities and building new ones all over the world [67,68]. In a nutshell, a smart city is, in theory, a locality that uses digital data and technology to improve efficiency in different interconnected urban domains (such as energy, transport, and safety), eventually resulting in economic development, better quality of life, and sustainability [69].

Nevertheless, in practice, this is not always the case. Numerous studies have shown that, actually, existing smart cities are often disproportionately driven by economic objectives and incapable of addressing social and environmental concerns [70–75]. This is why, in recent years, the focus of smart-city research has shifted towards the "smart and sustainable city", in the attempt to rebalance the economic, social, and environmental dimensions of smart urbanism [76–78]. A conceptual framework is provided in Figure 6.2. A smart and sustainable city is defined as an urban locality functioning as a robust system of systems with sustainable practices, supported by community, technology, and policy, to generate desired outcomes and futures for all humans and non-humans [79].

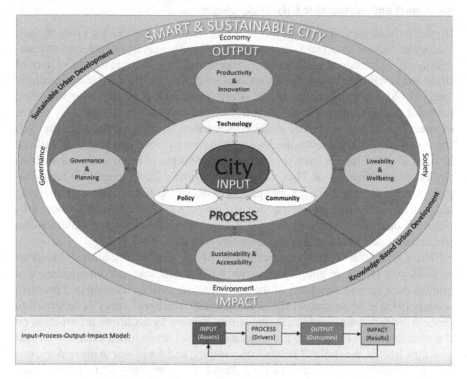

Figure 6.2 A conceptual framework of smart and sustainable cities, derived from [79].

This conceptualisation utilises the input–process–output–impact approach [80]. As the key "input", we have the city and its indigenous assets. By using this asset base, three "processes"—i.e., technology, policy, and community—generate strategies, actions, and initiatives. These result in "outputs" in the economy, society, environment, and governance domains. When these outputs are aligned with knowledge-based and sustainable urban development goals, principles, and practices, they produce the desired "impact" for a smart and sustainable city [79].

The framework underlines that, despite the prevalent technocentric perspective in the making of smart cities, in order to create cities that are smart *and* sustainable, we actually need a balanced view on the community, technology, and policy trio as the driver of transformation. It also highlights that cities should not be understood and treated as mere technological artefacts, but rather as social processes, and that sustainability should not be approached in a one-dimensional way, but rather holistically as the equilibrium among diverse social, environmental, and economic spheres [81–83]. In other words, technology will only lead to sustainability if its adequateness is thoroughly scrutinised via community engagement, and its implementation is carried out via a sound policy and government monitoring [79].

6.4 Smart and Sustainable City Technologies

Digital technologies are increasingly offering new opportunities for cities in their journey to become smart and sustainable—especially in relation to issues of community engagement and participatory governance [84]. There is a large variety of smart and sustainable city technologies available today and their list is exhaustingly long [85,86]. For instance, in a recent study, Yigitcanlar et al. [87] have identified the most popular smart and sustainable city technologies in Australia by means of social media analytics. The study concentrated on determining what the key smart city concepts and technologies are, and how they are perceived and utilised in Australia. The results have shown that the concepts of innovation and sustainability, and the Internet of Things (IoT) and artificial intelligence (AI) technologies, are the dominant ones. Unsurprisingly, these top technologies are merging today to form the Artificial Intelligence of Things (AIoT) [88] to achieve more efficient IoT operations, improve decision-making and human–machine interactions, and enhance data management and analytics [89].

There is neither a universal definition of AI, nor an established blueprint to build one [4,90]. In simple terms, an AI is a nonbiological intelligence that mimics the cognitive functions of the human mind, such as learning and problem solving [91,92]. More specifically, an artificially intelligent entity is supposed to possess the following capabilities: the ability to learn by acquiring information on the surrounding environment, the capacity to make sense of the data and extract concepts from it, the skill of handling uncertainty, and the power to make decisions and act without being supervised [15]. There are several types of machines and algorithms, which possess the above capabilities at different levels of development, meaning that there are various levels of AI [93]. These levels are illustrated in Figure 6.3 and described below.

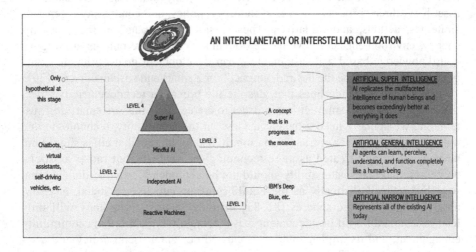

Figure 6.3 Levels of artificial intelligence.

In 1997, IBM's Deep Blue defeated the then World Chess Champion Garry Kasparov—that was a remarkable twist in the story of AI and intelligent machines. However, it is more appropriate to classify Deep Blue as a "reactive machine" (Level 1), since this AI is programmed to undertake one single task, and it does not have the capacity to learn and improve itself [94]. Above all, this type of AI does not take the initiative. It mostly *reacts* to human inputs, rather than planning and pursuing its own original agenda. Its actions and ideas are derivative and are triggered in response to external stimuli.

The next level (Level 2) is the "independent AI". In 2016, Google's AlphaGo beat the international Go champion Lee Sedol. Go is arguably the most complex board game ever invented by mankind, and AlphaGo won thanks to its learning ability and capacity to take original actions that its human opponent could not foresee. This victory was an extraordinary outcome and boosted AI research world-wide. A similar, although less spectacular example, is now common AI chatbots which today many companies are using to interact with their customers on their websites. Other examples range from apps that regulate our phones and homes, to autonomous vehicles that are capable of determining and executing complex routes in chaotic urban environments [95–97]. What these AIs have in common is that they all operate independently. Human actions do not dictate their actions. Independent AIs proactively come up with their own agenda and implement it without humans leading the way.

The above categories constitute what is commonly referred to as "artificial narrow intelligence". This is the AI level that we have reached to date in practice, and that is becoming a common sight in contemporary cities and societies. However, R&D efforts are constantly leading to bolder and more innovative theories such as the "theory of mind AI", which pictures an AI system that has beliefs, desires, and emotions [98]. A "self-aware AI" is likely to be the next level of AI, thereby producing machines which actually function like us [99]. We call this level "mindful AI" (Level 3) to denote artificial intelligences which not only have a mind and are capable of thinking. They are also conscious of their own mind and thoughts which they apply to multiple domains of knowledge. This is the level of "artificial general intelligence" at which machine behaviour is almost indistinguishable from human behaviour.

Mindful AIs, and artificial general intelligence more generally, are hypothetical stages of development, which could become the steppingstones to further technological progress in the field of AI. The ultimate level of AI that has so far been imagined is the "artificial super intelligence". Here at the "Super AI" level (Level 4), the AI does everything and anything better than us humans. The opinions of scholars on superintelligence are mixed. While some believe that this could be mankind's last invention leading to the end of human civilisation, others posit that this technology could be the beginning of a new era as our only chance of leaving this planet and establishing an interplanetary or interstellar civilisation [100–102].

As urbanists interested in the present and near future of urban development, we deal with those existing technologies that are already in the process of altering the sustainability of cities. The rest of this chapter will, therefore, focus on artificial narrow intelligence. This vast field of AI includes technologies with at least one of the following capabilities: (a) *perception* including audio/visual/textual/tactile (e.g., face recognition); (b) *decision-making* (e.g., medical diagnosis systems); (c) *prediction* (e.g., weather forecasting); (d) *automatic knowledge extraction and pattern recognition* (e.g., discovery of fake news); (e) *interactive communication* (e.g., social robots or chat bots); and (f) *logical reasoning and concept extraction* (e.g., theory development from premises) [103]. Mapping out the state of the art in AI is highly useful to better understand the capacities and impact of artificial narrow intelligence. Figure 6.4 illustrates the key AI problem domains and paradigms.

Artificial narrow intelligence is increasingly becoming part of our lives, and an integral element of our cities. For instance, in many parts of the world, states are trialling AI-driven cars to prepare their cities and citizens for the disruptions that autonomous driving will generate [97,104–107]. Robotic dogs are employed in places like Singapore for monitoring social distancing in the era of COVID-19 [108]. A couple of years ago, Dubai started robot police services meant to stop petty crime [109]. Hospitals in a number of countries, such as Japan, are employing robot doctors [110]. Many homes are getting safer and more energy efficient due to smart home technology and services, and home automation, or *domotics*, is becoming a big part of the construction industry [111]. Websites of both major corporations and ordinary companies now have chatbots to respond to clients' inquiries [112]. In China and Malaysia, large-scale urban artificial intelligences called *city brains* are managing the transport, energy, and safety systems of several cities [15].

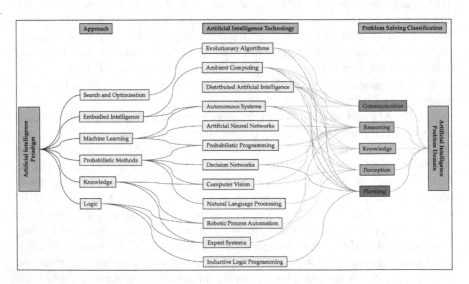

Figure 6.4 Artificial intelligence knowledge map, derived from [104].

Additionally, AI is an integral part of environmental research in a number of countries such as Australia, where autonomous drones are detecting via machine learning environmental hazards and animals in danger of extinction [113,114]. Today, most smart phones offer an AI as a personal assistant [115]. Overall, these examples are only the tip of the AI iceberg, as the largest application of AI technology is in analytics. Many of the decisions impacting our life are being made as a result of descriptive, predictive, and prescriptive analyses of data collected and processed by AI [116,117]. In other words, AI-aided urban data science is being extensively used today in cities across the globe, to address the uncertainties and complexities of urbanity [118,119].

6.5 The Symbiosis

AI is one of the most powerful and disruptive technologies of our time, and its influence on urban settlements and activities is growing rapidly, ultimately affecting everyday life [120,121]. Given that cities are the main hubs and drivers of most socioeconomic activities, political actions, and environmental transformations, it is important to understand how the development of AI and the development of the city are intertwining [122]. This brings up the question of whether there is or could be a symbiotic relationship between them, and if this revolutionary technology could offer novel sustainability solutions feeding into new urban models. After all, AI has already entered our cities, and it is therefore essential to critically examine and question its urban sustainability potential [15].

A study by Yigitcanlar et al. [123] investigated these questions through a thorough systematic literature review—99 peer-reviewed research articles concentrating on both smart cities and AI. The study arranged the findings under four smart city domains, as shown in Figure 6.2—i.e., economy, society, environment, governance.

In terms of the "economy" domain of smart cities, the AI focus is predominately on technological innovation, and business productivity, profitability, and management. Some of the most typical contributions of AI to this domain include [123]:

- Enhancing firm productivity and innovation by automating data management and analysis processes;
- Increasing the efficiency and effectiveness of existing resources, and reducing additional costs through pattern recognition;
- Supporting decision-making by analysing large volumes of data—e.g., big data analytics—from multiple sources;
- Drawing conclusions to facilitate informed decisions based on logic, reason, and intuition via deep learning.

In terms of the "society" domain of smart cities, the AI focus is predominately on the public health, wellbeing, and education areas. The COVID-19 pandemic is particularly accelerating the use of AI in these areas. The main contributions of AI to this domain include [123]:

- Improving community health monitoring via smart sensors and analytics tools embedded in homes and/or workplaces;
- Enhancing public health diagnoses through medical imaging analytics, particularly in radiology and healthcare services;
- Providing autonomous tutoring systems to teach algebra, grammar, and other subjects to pupils and adults;
- Offering personalised learning options to facilitate students' progress and expand their curriculum.

In terms of the "environment" domain of smart cities, the AI focus is predominately on the transport, energy, land use, and climate areas. Some of the key contributions of AI to this domain include [123]:

- Operationalising smart urban transport systems via mobility-as-a-service (MaaS)—integration of various transport services into a single on-demand mobility service;
- Optimising energy production and consumption via domotics—home technologies with a focus on environmental issues, energy saving, and lifestyle improvement;
- Monitoring changes in the natural and the built environments via remote sensing with autonomous drones—used for multiple-object detection and tracking in aerial videos;
- Predicting the risks of climate change via machine learning algorithms combined with climate models—employed to foresee potential disastrous events in specific geographical areas and act in advance.

Moreover, beyond urban environmental issues, AI is also being used for addressing planetary environmental challenges. Overall, as Vinuesa et al. [103] have argued, AI applications can potentially contribute to achieving 17 Sustainable Development Goals (SDGs). Below, we provide a summary of the application areas touched by AI technologies, specifically in relation to environmental sustainability.

- AI application areas for *climate change/crisis mitigation* include: research, urban, and regional planning, land use, home, mobility, energy production and consumption [124–126];
- AI application areas for *ocean health* include: sustainable fishery, pollution monitoring, reduction, and prevention, habitat and species protection, and acidification reduction [127–129];
- AI application areas for *clean air* include: pollutant filtering and capture, pollution monitoring, reduction, and prevention, early pollution and hazard warning, clean energy, and real-time, integrated, adaptive urban management [130–132];
- AI application areas for *biodiversity and conservation* include: habitat protection and restoration, sustainable trade, pollution monitoring, reduction, and

prevention, invasive species and disease control, and natural capital enhancement and protection [133–135];
- AI application areas for *clean water security* include: water supply quantity, quality, and efficiency management, water catchment control, sanitation, and drought planning [136–138];
- AI application areas for *weather and disaster resilience* include: prediction and forecasting, early warning systems, resilient infrastructure and planning, and financial instruments [139–141].

In terms of the "governance" domain of smart cities, the AI focus is predominately on national and public security, urban governance, and decision-making in government. Some of the principal contributions of AI to this domain include [123]:

- Deploying smart poles as digital sensors, and providing technological tools for citizen scientists to act like human sensors, for making informed decisions— smart poles and volunteer citizens equipped with smart tech generate big data that is processed by AI;
- Aiding management, planning, and operations related to disasters, pandemics, and other emergencies via predictive analytics—using AI to make predictions about future events;
- Enhancing the operability of surveillance systems via smart poles with the AIoT (although due to cyber-attacks and privacy issues, benefits exist together with major concerns);
- Improving cybersecurity by analysing data and records on cyber incidents, identifying potential threats, and providing patches and options to improve cyber security.

Nonetheless, the above list of benefits should not obscure that of the many problems that AI is bringing. AI is a double-edged sword. This sentient sword can be used to fight against global sustainability issues, but it can also cause much collateral damage as well as harm those who wield it. The drawbacks of AI are equal to its potentials [142]. Below, we provide a summary of prospects and constraints of AI according to different smart city domains [143]. As pointed out earlier, we need more than *technology* to achieve urban sustainability. Particularly *policy* and *community*, which are the other two drivers of smart and sustainable cities (see Figure 6.2), should be refined and operationalised to neutralise the technological shortcomings of AI.

- On the one hand, the *prospects* of AI in the *economy* domain include: enhancing productivity and innovation, reducing costs and increasing resources, supporting the decision-making process, and automating decision-making [144–146]. On the other hand, the *constraints* of AI include: making biased decisions, having an unstable job market, losing revenue streams and employment, and generating economic inequality [147–149].

- On the one hand, the *prospects* of AI in the *society* domain include: improving healthcare monitoring, enhancing medical diagnoses, increasing the adaptability of education systems, personalising teaching and learning, and optimising tasks [150–152]. On the other hand, the *constraints* of AI involve: making biased decisions, making misdiagnoses, having an unstable job market, losing employment, and undermining data privacy and security [153–155].
- On the one hand, the *prospects* of AI in the *environment* domain include: assisting environmental monitoring, optimising energy consumption and production, optimising transport systems, and assisting the development of more environmentally efficient transport and logistic systems [156–158]. On the other hand, the *constraints* of AI involve: making biased decisions, increasing urban sprawl, leading to more motor vehicle kilometres travelled, destabilising property values, establishing heavy energy dependency due to intensive use of technology, and increasing carbon footprints [159–161].
- On the one hand, the *prospects* of AI in the *governance* domain include: enhancing surveillance system capacity, improving cyber safety, aiding disaster management planning and operations, and assisting citizen scientists with new technologies in producing crowdsourced data/information [162–164]. On the other hand, the *constraints* of AI involve: making biased decisions including racial bias and discrimination, suppressing public voice/protests/rights, violating civil liberties, causing privacy concerns, using technology unethically, risking the spread of misinformation, and creating cybersecurity concerns [165–167].

The above prospects and constraints should be evaluated in relation to the five different levels of autonomy that characterise the decision-making power of AI [15,168]. Level 0 corresponds to no autonomy—meaning full human control on every decision. Levels 1 and 2 correspond to assisted decision-making, where in Level 2 AI offers moderate assistance or recommendation. In Level 3, decisions require human approval, whilst in Level 4 only human monitoring or human oversight is needed, to step in in case of a problem. Level 5 is equal to complete autonomy, meaning that decisions are taken by an AI in an unsupervised manner. As we progress to Level 5, both the magnitude of disruption and opportunity will become greater. With this greater power, AI will have to assume greater responsibility, and it will thus be crucial to develop "responsible and ethical AI" before we get to Level 5 [169–171]. From an urban point of view, AI technology is progressing fast, thereby gaining more and more autonomy in cities. Especially in experimental cities, where the pace of technological innovation is usually rapid, we can already see parts of the built environment that are not *automated* but rather *autonomous*.

The key difference between *automation* and *autonomy* is that an automated technology repetitively follows patterns previously established by a human intelligence, while an autonomous technology establishes its own patterns, seldom repeating the exact same action [15]. Simply put, this is the difference between an elevator always going up or down stopping at invariable floors, and an autonomous car which can traverse entire cities and never follow the same route twice. The difference is critical because autonomous AIs operate in real-life environments where the lives of real people are at risk. Not in a confined elevator shaft but in, for example, an urban road shared by hundreds of individuals. Here unsupervised, AIs have to make important decisions and take actions that could actually kill. This is the case of the first pedestrian fatality caused by an autonomous car in Tempe (Arizona) in March 2018. An autonomous Uber was incapable of dealing with the uncertainty that is typical of unconfined urban spaces, and its incapacity killed a woman that was crossing a road outside the designated crossing lane [172]. The greater the autonomy of AI is, the greater its constraints are, given that, to date, we now have urban artificial intelligences that can fully understand what is right or wrong (the issue of ethics) and then answer for their behaviour (the issue of responsibility).

Furthermore, it is important to recognise that both the fields of smart and sustainable cities and AI are in constant evolution. As Sections 3 and 4 have illustrated, numerous smart-city projects have been implemented and an even larger number are under development, while the evolution of AI has reached only two levels out of four. This means that we have seen only a small part of what smart urbanism and AI can potentially offer. Whether the best or the worst is yet to come, is an open question. For sure, at the moment there is neither an ideal AI system, nor an ideal smart and sustainable city that can serve as a universal model of development and, given the many geographical differences that exist in the world, the very idea of having a global paradigm is questionable in the first place [68,173,174]. This is to say that we need to continue researching both conceptualisations and practical applications of AI and smart and sustainable cities, across geographical spaces and scales [175]. Only then will we be able to analyse and fully evaluate the symbiosis between AI and the city and understand whether this can give birth in particular places to "artificially intelligent cities" [143].

Lastly, there is the critical issue of how we define and construct artificially intelligent cities. In its current conceptualisation, an *artificially intelligent city*

is a city where algorithms are the dominant decision-makers and arbitrators of governance protocols—the rules and frameworks that enable humans and organisations to interact, from traffic lights to tax structures—and where humans might have limited say in the choices presented to them for any given interaction.

[176]

For such a type of cities to achieve a condition of sustainability, the issues of transparency, fairness, ethics, and the preservation of human values need to be carefully considered. These unresolved issues are intrinsic to AI and thus hinder its sustainability. In other words, in order to improve the chances that a city of artificial intelligence becomes a sustainable city, we need better AI, and this will be the topic of the next section.

6.6 Discussion

Makridakis [177] asks the question of whether the AI revolution creates a utopian or dystopian future, or somewhere in between. The answer to this question fully depends on how we are going to tackle the drawbacks of AI, and how we are going to utilise AI in our cities, businesses and, more generally, in our lives. As Batty [178] remarks, it is difficult to predict the exact future of cities, while it is possible to build future cities, meaning that we can actively work in the present to improve contemporary cities and our results will ultimately be the cities of the future. Following this line of thought, if we focus on the pitfalls of AI, we can then search for ways to actually make AI better. *Better* in the sense of more useful in making our cities and societies more sustainable. The key areas of improvement to reach AIs that are conducive to sustainability are illustrated in Figure 6.5 and further elaborated below.

The first issue to consolidate a sustainability-oriented AI is *stakeholder engagement*. In general, AI technologies are created exclusively by technology companies without any or much consultation with wider interest groups or stakeholders. Active collaboration among a wide and inclusive range of stakeholders—ideally in the form of quadruple helix model participation of public, private, academia, and community—in the development and deployment stages, in particular, will improve the calibre of the sustainability potential of AI [179,180]. This is, in essence, a matter of inclusion and democracy. Given that the ethos of sustainability is about achieving a *common future*, we argue that no common future can be envisioned and realised unless proper forms of democratic governance are in place. Specifically, in relation to AI, this means that each AI technology affecting

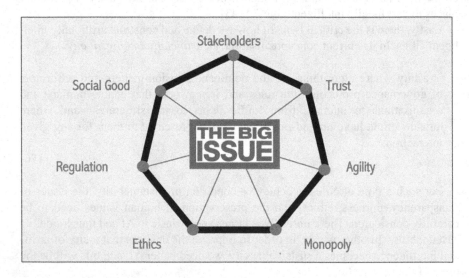

Figure 6.5 Areas of improvement for artificial intelligence.

cities should be discussed by all urban stakeholders, instead of being imposed in a top-down manner by influential tech companies.

The second issue is the *trust* problem. The blackbox nature of the decisions taken by AIs without much transparency (which, at times, are wrong), the possibility of AI failing in a life-or-death context, and cybersecurity vulnerabilities all limit public trust. AI technology needs to earn the trust not only of the public and the way people perceive it, but also in the minds of companies and government agencies that will be investing in AI [181–183]. This is a challenging problem because, as Greenfield [120] notes, AI is an arcane technology meaning that, although it is already part of the everyday of many people, its mechanics and actual functioning are understood by only a few.

The next area of improvement concerns the *agility* issue. AI systems should be competent enough to deal with complexity and uncertainty, which are extremely common features of contemporary cities [184]. Besides, AI systems should focus on the problem to be solved, rather than just on the data whose collection is arguably meaningless from a sustainability point of view, unless it serves the purpose of addressing a previously identified SDG. In addition, AI technology needs to be as frugal and affordable as possible. This is critical for a wider uptake of AI across cities through public sector funds [185,186]. Expensive AIs are ultimately elitist AIs, which only a rich minority can afford. Elitist AIs can only be unevenly distributed, thus creating a divide among richer and poorer cities, as well as internal fractures within individual cities where small premium enclaves coexist next to disadvantaged districts.

The fourth issue is the *monopoly*. A monopolistic structure behind technology development and deployment is problematic as a lack of competition limits technological variation. Avoiding AI monopolies can make AI technologies more affordable and support current efforts in "open AI" development. This, in turn, would also promote the democratisation of AI research and practice, as well as decrease the risk of the formation of a *singleton* [187,188]. According to Bostrom [4], a singleton is a world order in which one super-intelligent agent is in charge. This is an unlikely situation when it comes to Level 1 and 2 AIs, but it might not be a remote possibility if only one tech company in the world has the capacity to build an artificial super intelligence.

Another critical issue is *ethics*. We need to develop AI in a way that it respects human rights, diversity, and the autonomy of individuals. The European Commission's recent ethical guidelines for AI development offer a good starting point [189]. However, as stated by Mittelstadt [190], principles alone cannot guarantee the development of an ethical AI. Hence, we need to develop globally an AI ethics—a multicultural system of moral principles that takes the risks of AI seriously—together with a mechanism to monitor ethics violations. Ethics should ensure the design of AI technologies for human flourishing around the world [191,192], but this is a very complex matter given that, as the work of Awad et al. [193,194] clearly demonstrates, universally valid and accepted ethical principles do not exist.

The sixth issue relates to *regulation* and regulatory challenges. AI cannot achieve sustainability and the common good if it is not regulated. In a situation in which different AI users (or potentially different mindful and super-intelligent AIs) can do whatever they want, it is extremely unlikely that the common good will be achieved. Different actors will follow diverse trajectories and reach heterogeneous (and not necessarily mutually beneficial) outcomes. This poses a big risk for society—particularly for disadvantaged groups, historically marginalised groups, and low-income countries. Thus, we need well-regulated and responsible AIs with disruption mitigation mechanisms in place. Such regulation should also protect public values [195,196], and extend to the built environment. It is well documented in urban studies that, when urban development is unregulated, key sustainability themes (such as justice and environmental preservation) get neglected and overshadowed by economic interests [197,198]. Therefore, the regulation of AI and the regulation of the built environment should go hand in hand as a dual policy priority.

The last issue concerns the development of AI for *social good*, and for the benefit of every member of society [199]. AI and data need to be a shared resource employed for the good of society, rather than for serving the economic agenda of corporations and the interests of political elites. An *AI for all* would require establishing AI commons [200] and a similar attempt has been previously made to establish digital commons [201]. AI commons are supposed to allow anyone, anywhere, to enjoy the multiple benefits that AI can provide [202]. AI commons should be studied and pursued to enable AI adopters to connect with AI specialists and AI developers, with the overall aim of aligning every AI towards a shared common goal [203]. From an urbanistic perspective, this is arguably the biggest challenge, because opening up AI as a common good requires also opening up urban spaces, thinking about the city as a truly public resource rather than a territory balkanised by neoliberal ambitions.

6.7 Conclusion

This chapter has explored the prospects and constraints of developing and deploying AI technology to make present and future cities more sustainable. The analysis has shown that, while AI technology is evolving and becoming an integral part of urban services, spaces, and operations, we still need to find ways to integrate AI in our cities in a sustainable manner, and also to minimise the negative social, environmental, economic, and political externalities that the increasingly global adoption of AI is triggering. In essence, a city of AI is not a sustainable city. Both the development of AI and the development of cities need to be refined and better aligned towards sustainability as the overarching goal. With this in mind, this chapter has generated the following insights, in the attempt to improve the sustainability of AI and that of those cities that are adopting it.

First of all, AI as part of urban informatics significantly advances our knowledge of computational urban science [204]. In the age of uncertainty and complexity, urban problems are being diagnosed and addressed by numerous AI technologies. However, from a sustainability perspective, the quality of our decisions about the future of cities heavily depends on this computational power (technology), *and* on the inclusivity of decision-making and policy processes. The greater computational power offered by AI, therefore, is not enough to achieve sustainability, unless it is coupled with systems of democratic governance and participatory planning.

Second, AI is being exponentially used to improve the efficiency of several urban domains such as business, data analytics, health, education, energy, environmental monitoring, land use, transport, governance, and security. This has a direct implication for our cities' planning, design, development, and management [205]. Yet, the different uses of AI tend to be fragmented, in the sense that heterogeneous AIs are targeting heterogeneous issues and goals without a holistic approach. Coordinating the many AIs present in our cities is thus necessary for a sustainable urbanism, given that sustainability is about thinking and acting in terms of *the whole* rather than single parts. On these terms, artificial narrow intelligences working on narrow tasks are missing the broad spectrum of social, environmental, and political issues, which is essential to achieve sustainability. We cannot and should not expect a hypothetical future artificial general intelligence to fill this lacuna [206]. Human initiative and coordination are needed now.

Third, the autonomous problem-solving capacity of AI can be useful in some urban decision-making processes. Still, the utmost care is needed to check and monitor the accuracy of any autonomous decisions made by an AI—human inputs and oversight are now critical in relation to artificial narrow intelligence, and they would be even more important should innovation reach the stage of artificial general intelligence [207]. AI can help us optimise various urban processes and can actually make cities smarter. We can move faster towards the goal of smart urbanism, but if we want to create smart *and* sustainable cities, then human intelligence must not be overshadowed by AI.

Fourth, AI can drive positive changes in cities and societies, and contribute to several SDGs [103,208]. Nonetheless, despite these positive prospects, we still need to be cautious about selecting the right AI technology for the right place and ensuring its affordability and alignment with sustainability policies, while also considering issues of community acceptance [209]. AI should not be imposed on society and cities, but rather discussed locally at the community level, taking into account geographical, cultural, demographic, and economic differences. Sustainability can only be achieved with a healthy combination of technology, community, and policy drivers, hence the urgent need to develop not only technologically, but also socially and politically.

Fifth, we need to be prepared for the upcoming and inevitable disruptions that AI will create in our cities and societies. The diffusion of AI will not be a black-and-white phenomenon. Many shades of grey will characterise the deployment of heterogeneous AIs in different parts of the world. Even in an optimistic scenario in which a "benign AI" is promoting sustainability, somewhere someone/something will still be suffering. It is thus imperative to develop appropriate policies and regulations, and to allocate adequate funds, in order to mitigate the disruption that AI will cause to the most disadvantaged cities and social groups, and nature [210]. As we mentioned earlier, sustainability is not about single parts, but rather about the whole. Any form of development that fractures cities, societies, and the natural environment, producing winners and losers, is not sustainable. Like a hurricane, AI is likely to shake everything that we see, know, and care about. It should not be forgotten that we are only as strong as the weakest member of the society.

Sixth, a symbiotic relationship between AI and cities might become a concrete possibility in the future. Combined with progress in public policy and community engagement, progress in AI technology could mitigate the global sustainability challenges discussed in Section 2 [211]. In so doing, while the city might benefit from AI technologies and applications, AI might also benefit from the city to advance itself. This is a key aspect of the intersection between the development of AI and the development of the city. As we explained in Section 4, a key AI skill is learning. AIs learn by sensing the surrounding environment, thereby gaining and accumulating knowledge [15]. Learning is also how AIs improve themselves. AI is a technology that learns from the collected data, from its errors as well as from the mistakes made by other AIs and human intelligences. On these terms, the city represents the ideal learning environment for AI. Cities are the places where knowledge concentrates the most, where a wide range of events occur, where numerous actors meet, and where the biggest mistakes and greatest discoveries of mankind have been made. It this in this cauldron of ideas and experiences that we call *city* that contemporary artificial narrow intelligences can learn the most, potentially evolving into artificial general intelligences.

Seventh, we need to further decentralise political power and economic resources to make our local governments ready for the AI era that is upon us. While planning for a sustainable AI uptake in our cities is crucial, presently, almost all local governments in the globe are not ready—in terms of technical personnel, budget, and gear—to thoroughly plan and implement AI projects city-wide [212,213]. Most AI technologies are expensive and it is therefore important to make them affordable, in order to avoid an uneven distribution and ultimately injustice. If AI is to become part of the city, then we need to think of AI not as an elitist technology, but rather as a common good on which everybody has a say. This is, in turn, a question of urban politics and a matter of politicising AI so that its deployment in cities is discussed and agreed as inclusively and as democratically as possible, instead of being dictated by a handful of influential tech companies. Sustainability will not be achieved in a technocracy.

Eighth, some of the changes triggered by AI might be invisible and silent and, yet, their repercussions are likely to be tangible and loud from an urban perspective. For example, AI is clearly impacting on the economies of cities [214]. This impact will get deeper and wider as innovation keeps improving and expanding the capabilities of artificial narrow intelligences. *What is the role of humans in an economy in which artificial narrow intelligences, artificial general intelligences, and artificial super intelligences can cheaply perform human tasks faster and better?* This is a recurring question in AI studies, to which we add a complementary urban question: *What is the role of cities as economic hubs in the era of AI?* A key reason why cities exist is that they provide the spaces that are necessary to perform and accommodate human labour and to train humans in many work-related fields. However, AI is undermining this *raison d'etre*. If human labour decreases or, worse, ceases to exist in cities, then cities are likely to decline and cease to exist too [1]. Now more than ever it is therefore vital to reimagine, replan, and redesign cities in a way that their function and shape are not dictated by and dependent on human economies. This is both a matter of rethinking the economic dimension of cities and galvanising the social, cultural, psychological, political, and environmental dimensions of urban spaces.

Finally, in the context of smart and sustainable cities, AI is an emerging area of research. Further investigations, both theoretical and empirical, from various angles of the phenomenon and across disciplines, are required to build the knowledge base that is necessary for urban policymakers, managers, planners, and citizens to make informed decisions about the uptake of AI in cities and mitigate the inevitable disruptions that will follow. This will not be an easy task because AI is a technology while the city is not. Cities are primarily made of humans and are the product of human intelligence. The *merging of artificial and human intelligences in cities* is the world's *next big sustainability challenge* [215].

Acknowledgements

This chapter, with permission from the copyright holder, is a reproduced version of the following journal article: Yigitcanlar, T., & Cugurullo, F. (2020). The sustainability of artificial intelligence: An urbanistic viewpoint from the lens of smart and sustainable cities. *Sustainability*, 12(20), 8548.

References

1. Kassens-Noor, E., Hintze, A. (2020) Cities of the future. *Artificial Intelligence* 1, 192–197.
2. Schalkoff, R.J. (1990) *Artificial Intelligence,*. McGraw-Hill: New York, NY, USA.
3. Yampolskiy, R.V. (2015) *Artificial Superintelligence.*, CRS Press: New York, NY, USA.
4. Bostrom, N. (2017) *Superintelligence.*, Oxford University Press: Oxford, UK, 2017.
5. Kak, S.C. (1996) Can we define levels of artificial intelligence? *Journal of Intelligent Systems* 6, 133–144.
6. Yun, J., Lee, D., Ahn, H., Park, K., Lee, S., Yigitcanlar, T. (2016) Not deep learning but autonomous learning of open innovation for sustainable artificial intelligence. *Sustainability* 8, 797.
7. Faisal, A., Yigitcanlar, T., Kamruzzaman, M., Paz, A. (2021) Mapping two decades of autonomous vehicle research: A systematic scientometric analysis. *Journal of Urban Technology*, 28(3–4), 45–74.
8. Acheampong, R.A., Cugurullo, F. (2019) Capturing the behavioural determinants behind the adoption of autonomous vehicles. *Transportation Research Part F* 62, 349–375.
9. Milakis, D., Van Arem, B., Van Wee, B. (2017) Policy and society related implications of automated driving. *Journal of Intelligent Transportation Systems* 21, 324–348.
10. Nikitas, A., Michalakopoulou, K., Njoya, E.T., Karampatzakis, D. (2020) Artificial intelligence, transport and the smart city. *Sustainability* 12, 2789.
11. Macrorie, R., Marvin, S., While, A. (2021) Robotics and automation in the city: a research agenda. *Urban Geography*, 42(2), 197–217.

12. Mende, M., Scott, M.L., van Doorn, J., Grewal, D., Shanks, I. (2019) Service robots rising. *Journal of Marketing Research* 56, 535–556.
13. Caprotti, F., Liu, D. (2020) Emerging platform urbanism in China. *Technological Forecasting Social Change* 151, 119690.
14. Barns, S. (2019) *Platform Urbanism.*, Palgrave Macmillan: Singapore.
15. Cugurullo, F. (2020) Urban artificial intelligence. *Frontiers in Sustainable Cities* 2, 38.
16. Yigitcanlar, T., Kamruzzaman, M. (2015) Planning, development and management of sustainable cities. *Sustainability* 7, 14677–14688.
17. Voda, A.I., Radu, L.D. (2018) Artificial intelligence and the future of smart cities. *Broad Research in Artificial Intelligence Neuroscience* 9, 110–127.
18. Walshe, R., Casey, K., Kernan, J., Fitzpatrick, D. (2020) AI and big data standardization. *Journal of ICT Standardization* 8, 77–106.
19. Yigitcanlar, T. (2010) *Sustainable Urban and Regional Infrastructure Development,*. IGI Global: Hersey, PA, USA.
20. Evans, J., Karvonen, A., Luque-Ayala, A., Martin, C., McCormick, K., Raven, R., Palgan, Y. (2019) Smart and sustainable cities? *Local Environment* 24, 557–564.
21. Coaffee, J., Therrien, M., Chelleri, L., Henstra, D., Aldrich, D., Mitchell, C. (2018) Urban resilience implementation. *Journal of Contingencies and Crisis Management* 26, 403–410.
22. Yigitcanlar, T., Foth, M., Kamruzzaman, M. (2019) Towards post-anthropocentric cities. *Journal of Urban Technology* 26, 147–152.
23. Mortoja, M., Yigitcanlar, T., Mayere, S. (2020) What is the most suitable methodological approach to demarcate peri-urban areas? *Land Use Policy* 95, 104601.
24. Tscharntke, T., Clough, Y., Wanger, T., Jackson, L., Motzke, I., Perfecto, I., Whitbread, A. (2012) Global food security, biodiversity conservation and the future of agricultural intensification. *Biological Conservation* 151, 53–59.
25. Rasul, G. (2014) Food, water, and energy security in South Asia. *Environ. Sci. Policy* 39, 35–48.
26. Cohen, J. (2003) Human population. *Science* 302, 1172–1175.
27. Arbolino, R., De Simone, L., Carlucci, F., Yigitcanlar, T., Ioppolo, G. (2018) Towards a sustainable industrial ecology. *Journal of Cleaner Production* 178, 220–236.
28. Berck, P., Levy, A., Chowdhury, K. (2012) An analysis of the world's environment and population dynamics with varying carrying capacity, concerns and skepticism. *Ecological Economics* 73, 103–112.
29. Mortoja, M., Yigitcanlar, T. (2020) Local drivers of anthropogenic climate change. *Remote Sensing* 12, 2270.
30. Mahbub, P., Goonetilleke, A., Ayoko, G., Egodawatta, P., Yigitcanlar, T. (2011) Analysis of build-up of heavy metals and volatile organics on urban roads in Gold Coast, Australia. *Water Science & Technology* 63, 2077–2085.
31. Konikow, L., Kendy, E. (2005) Groundwater depletion. *Hydrogeology Journal* 13, 317–320.
32. Sotto, D., Philippi, A., Yigitcanlar, T., Kamruzzaman, M. (2019) Aligning urban policy with climate action in the global south. *Energies* 12, 3418.
33. Prior, T., Giurco, D., Mudd, G., Mason, L., Behrisch, J. (2012) Resource depletion, peak minerals and the implications for sustainable resource management. *Global Environmental Change* 22, 577–587.
34. Robinson, L., Cotten, S., Ono, H., Quan-Haase, A., Mesch, G., Chen, W., Stern, M. (2015) Digital inequalities and why they matter. *Information Communication and Society* 18, 569–582.

35. Ragnedda, M. (2017) *The Third Digital Divide,*. Taylor & Francis: New York, NY, USA.
36. Riddlesden, D., Singleton, A. (2014) Broadband speed equity. *Appl. Geogr.* 52, 25–33.
37. Anguelovski, I., Irazábal-Zurita, C., Connolly, J. (2019) Grabbed urban landscapes. *Int. J. Urban. Reg. Res.* 43, 133–156.
38. Cugurullo, F. (2013) How to build a sandcastle. *Journal of Urban Technology* 20, 23–37.
39. Hodson, M., Marvin, S. (2010) Urbanism in the Anthropocene. *City* 14, 298–313.
40. Guess, A., Nagler, J., Tucker, J. (2019) Less than you think. *Science Advances* 5, eaau4586.
41. Bastos, M., Mercea, D. (2018) The public accountability of social platforms. *Philosophical Transactions of the Royal Society A* 376, 20180003.
42. Isaak, J., Hanna, M. (2018) User data privacy. *Computer* 51, 56–59.
43. Evangelista, R., Bruno, F. (2019) WhatsApp and political instability in Brazil. *Internet Policy Review* 8, 1–23.
44. Rapley, J. (2004) *Globalization and Inequality,*. Lynne Rienner Publishers: London, UK.
45. Regilme, S. (2019) The decline of American power and Donald Trump. *Geoforum* 102, 157–166.
46. Gould-Wartofsky, M. (2015) *The Occupiers,*. Oxford University Press: London, UK.
47. Grigoryev, L. (2020) Global social drama of pandemic and recession. *Journal of Population Economics* 4, 18–25.
48. Taplin, R. (2020) *Cyber Risk, Intellectual Property Theft and Cyberwarfare,*. Routledge: London, UK.
49. Atapattu, S. (2020) Climate change and displacement. *Journal of Human Rights and the Environment* 11, 86–113.
50. Berchin, I., Valduga, I., Garcia, J., de Andrade, J. (2020) Climate change and forced migrations. *Geoforum* 84, 147–150.
51. Rothstein, B. (2013) Corruption and social trust. *Social Science Research* 80, 1009–1032.
52. Accord, C. (2017) Trump decision on climate change 'major disappointment'. *Waste Water Management Australia* 44, 35.
53. Jury, W., Vaux, H. (2005) The role of science in solving the world's emerging water problems. *Proceedings of the. National Academy of Science USA* 102, 15715–15720.
54. Yigitcanlar, T. (2010) *Rethinking Sustainable Development,*. IGI Global: Hersey, PA, USA.
55. Wheeler, S. (2013) *Planning for Sustainability,*. Routledge: New York, NY, USA.
56. Chen, G., Li, X., Liu, X., Chen, Y., Liang, X., Leng, J., Huang, K. (2020) Global projections of future urban land expansion under shared socioeconomic pathways. *Nature Communications* 11, 1–12.
57. Metaxiotis, K., Carrillo, J., Yigitcanlar, T. (2010) *Knowledge-Based Development for Cities and Societies,*. IGI Global: Hersey, PA, USA.
58. Praharaj, S., Han, J., Hawken, S. (2018) Urban innovation through policy integration. *City, Culture, and Society* 12, 35–43.
59. Yigitcanlar, T., Dur, F. (2013) Making space and place for knowledge communities. *Australian Journal Regional Studies* 19, 36–63.
60. Chu, E. (2016) The governance of climate change adaptation through urban policy experiments. *Environmental Policy and Governance* 26, 439–451.
61. Trencher, G. (2019) Towards the smart city 2.0. *Technological Forecasting of Social Change* 142, 117–128.
62. Angelidou, M. (2015) Smart cities. *Cities* 47, 95–106.

63. Cugurullo, F. (2018) The origin of the smart city imaginary. In: *The Routledge Companion to Urban Imaginaries*,. Routledge: London, UK, pp. 113–124.

64. Desouza, K. C., Hunter, M., Jacob, B., Yigitcanlar, T. (2020) Pathways to the making of prosperous smart cities: An exploratory study on the best practice. *Journal of Urban Technology*, 27(3), 3–32.

65. Yigitcanlar, T. (2016) *Technology and the City*,. Routledge: New York, NY, USA.

66. Yigitcanlar, T., Inkinen, T. (2019) *Geographies of Disruption*,. Springer: Cham, Switzerland.

67. Coletta, C., Evans, L., Heaphy, L., Kitchin, R. (2019) *Creating Smart Cities*,. Routledge: London, UK.

68. Karvonen, A., Cugurullo, F., Caprotti, F. (2018) *Inside Smart Cities*,. Routledge: London, UK.

69. Allam, Z., Newman, P. (2018) Redefining the smart city. *Smart Cities* 1, 4–25.

70. Cugurullo, F. (2016) Urban eco-modernisation and the policy context of new eco-city projects. *Urban Studies* 53, 2417–2433.

71. Cugurullo, F. (2018) Exposing smart cities and eco-cities. *Environment and Planning A* 50, 73–92.

72. Kaika, M. (2017) Don't call me resilient again! *Environment and Urbanization* 29, 89–102.

73. Perng, S., Kitchin, R., MacDonncha, D. (2018) Hackathons, entrepreneurial life and the making of smart cities. *Geoforum* 97, 189–197.

74. Vanolo, A. (2016) Is there anybody out there? *Futures* 82, 26–36.

75. Shelton, T., Zook, M., Wiig, A. (2015) The 'actually existing smart city'. *Cambridge Journal of Regions, Economy and Society* 8, 13–25.

76. Haarstad, H., Wathne, M. (2019) Are smart city projects catalyzing urban energy sustainability? *Energy Policy* 129, 918–925.

77. Machado, J., Ribeiro, D., da Silva, P., Bazanini, R. (2018) Do Brazilian cities want to become smart or sustainable? *Journal of Cleaner Production* 199, 214–221.

78. Martin, C., Evans, J., Karvonen, A. (2018) Smart and sustainable? *Technological Forecasting of Social Change* 133, 269–278.

79. Yigitcanlar, T., Hoon, M., Kamruzzaman, M., Ioppolo, G., Sabatini-Marques, J. (2019) The making of smart cities. *Land Use Policy* 88, 104187.

80. Noori, N., de Jong, M., Janssen, M., Schraven, D., Hoppe, T. (2021) Input-output modeling for smart city development. *Journal of Urban Technology*, 28(1–2), 71–92.

81. James, P. (2014) *Urban Sustainability in Theory and Practice*,. Routledge: London, UK.

82. Elmqvist, T., Andersson, E., Frantzeskaki, N., McPhearson, T., Olsson, P., Gaffney, O., Takeuchi, K., Folke, C. (2019) Sustainability and resilience for transformation in the urban century. *Nature Sustainability* 2, 267–273.

83. Robertson, M. (2017) *Sustainability Principles and Practice*,. Routledge: London, UK.

84. Zhuravleva, N., Nica, E., Durana, P. (2019) Sustainable smart cities. *Geopolitics, History, and International Relations* 11, 41–47.

85. Chaurasia, V., Yunus, A., Singh, M. (2020) An overview of smart city. In: *Blockchain Technology for Smart Cities*,. Springer: Singapore, pp. 133–154.

86. Ullah, Z., Al-Turjman, F., Mostarda, L., Gagliardi, R. (2020) Applications of artificial intelligence and machine learning in smart cities. *Computer Communications* 154, 313–323.

87. Yigitcanlar, T., Kankanamge, N., Vella, K. (2021) How are smart city concepts and technologies perceived and utilized? A systematic geo-Twitter analysis of smart cities in Australia. *Journal of Urban Technology*, 28(1–2), 135–154.

88. Adly, A., Adly, A., Adly, M. (2020) Approaches based on artificial intelligence and the internet of intelligent things to prevent the spread of COVID-19. *Journal of Medical Internet Research* 22, e19104.

89. Mohamed, E. (2020) The relation of artificial intelligence with internet of things. *Journal of Cybersecurity and Information Management* 1, 30–34.

90. Clifton, J., Glasmeier, A., Gray, M. (2020) When machines think for us. *Cambridge Journal of Regions, Economy and Society* 13, 3–23.

91. Smith, T. (1984) Artificial intelligence and its applicability to geographical problem solving. *The Professional Geographer* 36, 147–158.

92. Russell, S., Norvig, P. (2016) *Artificial Intelligence.* Pearson Education Limited, Harlow, UK.

93. Bach, J. (2020) When artificial intelligence becomes general enough to understand itself. *Journal of Artificial General Intelligence* 11, 15–18.

94. Girasa, R. (2020) AI as a disruptive technology. In: *Artificial Intelligence as a Disruptive Technology,.* Palgrave Macmillan: Cham, Switzerland, pp. 3–21.

95. Butler, L., Yigitcanlar, T., Paz, A. (2020) How can smart mobility innovations alleviate transportation disadvantage? *Applied Sciences* 10, 6306.

96. Hassani, H., Silva, E., Unger, S., TajMazinani, M., MacFeely, S. (2020) Artificial intelligence (AI) or intelligence augmentation (IA). *Artificial Intelligence* 1, 143–155.

97. Cugurullo, F., Acheampong, R. A., Gueriau, M., Dusparic, I. (2021) The transition to autonomous cars, the redesign of cities and the future of urban sustainability. *Urban Geography,* 42(6), 833–859.

98. Cuzzolin, F., Morelli, A., Cîrstea, B., Sahakian, B. (2020) Knowing me, knowing you. *Psychological Medicine* 50, 1057–1061.

99. Gonzalez-Jimenez, H. (2018) Taking the fiction out of science fiction. *Futures* 98, 49–56.

100. Pueyo, S. (2018) Growth, degrowth, and the challenge of artificial superintelligence. *Journal of Cleaner Production* 197, 1731–1736.

100. Gurzadyan, G. (1996) *Theory of Interplanetary Flights,.* CRC Press: New York, NY, USA.

101. Lovelock, J. (2019) *Novacene,.* Allen Lane: London, UK.

102. Tegmark, M. (2017) *Life 3.0,.* Penguin: London, UK.

103. Vinuesa, R., Azizpour, H., Leite, I., Balaam, M., Dignum, V., Domisch, S., Nerini, F. (2020) The role of artificial intelligence in achieving the sustainable development goals. *Nature Commununications.* 11, 233.

104. Corea, F. (2018) *AI Knowledge Map.* Available online: www.forbes.com/sites/cogniti veworld/2018/08/22/ai-knowledge-map-how-to-classify-aitechnologies/#5e99db627 773 (accessed on 11 May 2020).

105. Faisal, A., Yigitcanlar, T., Kamruzzaman, M., Currie, G. (2019) Understanding autonomous vehicles. *Journal of Transport and Land Use* 12, 45–72.

106. Golbabaei, F., Yigitcanlar, T., Bunker, J. (2021) The role of shared autonomous vehicle systems in delivering smart urban mobility: A systematic review of the literature. *International Journal of Sustainable Transportation,* 15(10), 731–748.

107. Narayanan, S., Chaniotakis, E., Antoniou, C. (2020) Shared autonomous vehicle services. *Transportation Research Part. C* 111, 255–293.

108. Schellin, H., Oberley, T., Patterson, K., Kim, B., Haring, K., Tossell, C., de Visser, E. (2020) Man's new best friend? In: *Proceedings of the 2020 Systems and Information Engineering Design Symposium.* Charlottesville, VA, USA, 24 April 2020, pp. 1–6.

109. Lakshmi, V., Bahli, B. (2020) Understanding the robotization landscape transformation. *Journal of Innovation & Knowledge* 5, 59–67.
110. Suwa, S., Tsujimura, M., Kodate, N., Donnelly, S., Kitinoja, H., Hallila, J., Ishimaru, M. (2020) Exploring perceptions toward home-care robots for older people in Finland, Ireland, and Japan. *Archives of Gerontology and Geriatrice* 91, 104178.
111. Jaihar, J., Lingayat, N., Vijaybhai, P., Venkatesh, G., Upla, K. (2020) Smart home automation using machine learning algorithms. In: *Proceedings of the 2020 International Conference for Emerging Technology*. Belgaum, India, 5–7 June 2020, pp. 1–4.
112. Brandtzaeg, P., Følstad, A. (2018) Chatbots. *Interactions* 25, 38–43.
113. Aziz, K., Haque, M., Rahman, A., Shamseldin, A., Shoaib, M. (2017) Flood estimation in ungauged catchments. *Environmental Research and Risk Assessment* 31, 1499–1514.
114. Wearn, O., Freeman, R., Jacoby, D. (2019) Responsible AI for conservation. *Nature Machine Intelligence* 1, 72–73.
115. Kaplan, A., Haenlein, M. (2019) Siri, Siri, in my hand. *Business Horizons* 62, 15–25.
116. Wu, N., Silva, E. (2010) Artificial intelligence solutions for urban land dynamics. *Journal of Planning Literature* 24, 246–265.
117. El Morr, C., Ali-Hassan, H. (2019) Descriptive, predictive, and prescriptive analytics. In: *Analytics in Healthcare.*, Springer: Cham, Switzerland, pp. 31–55.
118. Allam, Z., Dhunny, Z. (2019) On big data, artificial intelligence and smart cities. *Cities* 89, 80–91.
119. Engin, Z., Treleaven, P. (2019) Algorithmic government. *Computer Journal* 62, 448–460.
120. Greenfield, A. (2018) *Radical Technologies,*. Verso Books: London, UK.
121. Lu, H., Li, Y., Chen, M., Kim, H., Serikawa, S. (2018) Brain intelligence. *Mobile Networks and Applications.* 23, 368–375.
122. Boenig-Liptsin, M. (2017) AI and robotics for the city. *Field Actions Science Report* 17, 16–21.
123. Yigitcanlar, T., Desouza, K., Butler, L., Roozkhosh, F. (2020) Contributions and risks of artificial intelligence (AI) in building smarter cities. *Energies* 13, 1473.
124. Barnes, E., Hurrell, J., Ebert-Uphoff, I., Anderson, C., Anderson, D. (2019) Viewing forced climate patterns through an AI Lens. *Geophysical Research Letters* 46, 13389–13398.
125. Huntingford, C., Jeffers, E., Bonsall, M., Christensen, H., Lees, T., Yang, H. (2019) Machine learning and artificial intelligence to aid climate change research and preparedness. *Environmental Research Letters* 14, 124007.
126. Jha, S., Bilalovic, J., Jha, A., Patel, N., Zhang, H. (2017) Renewable energy. *Renewable and Sustainable Energy Reviews* 77, 297–317.
127. Wang, P., Yao, J., Wang, G., Hao, F., Shrestha, S., Xue, B., Peng, Y. (20190 Exploring the application of artificial intelligence technology for identification of water pollution characteristics and tracing the source of water quality pollutants. *Science of the Total Environment* 693, 133440.
128. Lu, H., Li, H., Liu, T., Fan, Y., Yuan, Y., Xie, M., Qian, X. (2019) Simulating heavy metal concentrations in an aquatic environment using artificial intelligence models and physicochemical indexes. *Science of the Total Environment* 694, 133591.
129. Probst, W. (2020) How emerging data technologies can increase trust and transparency in fisheries. *Journal of Materials Science* 77, 1286–1294.
130. AlOmar, M., Hameed, M., AlSaadi, M. (2020) Multi hours ahead prediction of surface ozone gas concentration. *Atmospheric Pollution Research* 11, 1572–1587.

131. Schürholz, D., Kubler, S., Zaslavsky, A. (2020) Artificial intelligence-enabled context-aware air quality prediction for smart cities. *Journal of Cleaner Production* 271,121941.

132. Sun, W., Bocchini, P., Davison, B. D. (2020) Applications of artificial intelligence for disaster management. *Natural Hazards*, 103(3), 2631–2689.

133. Jahani, A., Rayegani, B. (2020) Forest landscape visual quality evaluation using artificial intelligence techniques as a decision support system. *Stochastic Environmental Research and Risk Assessment*, 34(10), 1473–1486.

134. Granata, F., Gargano, R., de Marinis, G. (2020) Artificial intelligence-based approaches to evaluate actual evapotranspiration in wetlands. *Science of the Total Environment* 703, 135653.

135. Santangeli, A., Chen, Y., Kluen, E., Chirumamilla, R., Tiainen, J., Loehr, J. (2020) Integrating drone-borne thermal imaging with artificial intelligence to locate bird nests on agricultural land. *Scientific Reports* 10, 1–8.

136. Martínez-Santos, P., Renard, P. (2020) Mapping groundwater potential through an ensemble of big data methods. *Groundwater* 58, 583–597.

137. Singh, T. P., Nandimath, P., Kumbhar, V., Das, S., Barne, P. (2021) Drought risk assessment and prediction using artificial intelligence over the southern Maharashtra state of India. *Modeling Earth Systems and Environment*, 7, 2005–2013.

138. Tung, T., Yaseen, Z. (2020) A survey on river water quality modelling using artificial intelligence models. *Journal of Hydrology* 585, 124670.

139. Pham, B., Le, L., Le, T., Bui, K., Le, V., Ly, H., Prakash, I. (2020) Development of advanced artificial intelligence models for daily rainfall prediction. *Atmospheric Research* 237, 104845.

140. Ji, L., Wang, Z., Chen, M., Fan, S., Wang, Y., Shen, Z. (2019) How much can AI techniques improve surface air temperature forecast? *Journal of Meteorological Research* 33, 989–992.

141. Raza, M., Awais, M., Ali, K., Aslam, N., Paranthaman, V., Imran, M., Ali, F. (2020) Establishing effective communications in disaster affected areas and artificial intelligence-based detection using social media platform. *Future Generation Computer Systems* 112, 1057–1069.

142. Turchin, A., Denkenberger, D. (2020) Classification of global catastrophic risks connected with artificial intelligence. *AI & Society* 35, 147–163.

143. Yigitcanlar, T., Butler, L., Windle, E., Desouza, K., Mehmood, R., Corchado, J. (2020) Can building 'artificially intelligent cities' protect humanity from natural disasters, pandemics and other catastrophes? *Sensors* 20, 2988.

144. Agrawal, A., Gans, J., Goldfarb, A. (2018) *Prediction Machines*, Harvard Business Press: Boston, MA, USA.

145. Li, B., Hou, B., Yu, W., Lu, X., Yang, C. (2017) Applications of artificial intelligence in intelligent manufacturing. *Frontiers of Information Technology and Electronic Engineering* 18, 86–96.

146. Jarrahi, M. (2018) Artificial intelligence and the future of work. *Business Horizons* 61, 577–586.

147. Korinek, A., Stiglitz, J. E. (2018) Artificial intelligence and its implications for income distribution and unemployment. In: *The Economics of Artificial Intelligence: An Agenda* (pp. 349–390). University of Chicago Press.,

148. Truby, J., Brown, R., Dahdal, A. (2020) Banking on AI: Mandating a proactive approach to AI regulation in the financial sector. *Law and Financial Markets Review* 14, 110–120.

149. Dauvergne, P. (2022) Is artificial intelligence greening global supply chains? Exposing the political economy of environmental costs. *Review of International Political Economy*, 29(3), 696–718.

150. Chatterjee, S., Bhattacharjee, K. K. (2020) Adoption of artificial intelligence in higher education: A quantitative analysis using structural equation modelling. *Education and Information Technologies*, 25, 3443–3463.

151. Kerasidou, A. (2020) Artificial intelligence and the ongoing need for empathy, compassion and trust in healthcare. *Bulletein of the World Health Organization* 98, 245.

152. Yu, K., Beam, A., Kohane, I. (2018) Artificial intelligence in healthcare. *Nature Biomedical Engineering* 2, 719–731.

153. Hoffmann, A. (2019) Where fairness fails. *Information Communication and Society* 22, 900–915.

154. Noble, S. (2018) *Algorithms of Oppression,*. New York University Press: New York, NY, USA.

155. O'Neil, C. (2016) *Weapons of Math Destruction,*. Penguin: London, UK.

156. Bottarelli, L., Bicego, M., Blum, J., Farinelli, A. (2019) Orienteering-based informative path planning for environmental monitoring. *Enginering Applications of Artificial Intelligence* 77, 46–58.

157. Guériau, M., Cugurullo, F., Acheampong, R. A., Dusparic, I. (2020) Shared autonomous mobility on demand: A learning-based approach and its performance in the presence of traffic congestion. *IEEE Intelligent Transportation Systems Magazine*, 12(4), 208–218.,,,

158. Lu, J., Feng, L., Yang, J., Hassan, M.M., Alelaiwi, A., Humar, I. (2019) Artificial agent. *Future Genereration Computer Systems* 95, 45–51.

159. Brevini, B. (2020) Black boxes, not green. *Big Data Society* 7, 2053951720935141.

160. Hawkins, J., Nurul Habib, K. (2019) Integrated models of land use and transportation for the autonomous vehicle revolution. *Transport Reviews* 39, 66–83.

161. Dauvergne, P. (2021) The globalization of artificial intelligence: consequences for the politics of environmentalism. *Globalizations*, 18(2), 285–299.

162. Zeadally, S., Adi, E., Baig, Z., Khan, I.A. (2020) Harnessing artificial intelligence capabilities to improve cybersecurity. *IEEE Access* 8, 23817–23837.

163. Zhang, J., Hua, X.S., Huang, J., Shen, X., Chen, J., Zhou, Q. (2019) City brain. *IET Smart Cities* 1, 28–37.

164. Shneiderman, B. (2020) Human-centered artificial intelligence. *International Journal of Human–Computer Interaction* 36, 495–504.

165. Dignam, A. (2020) Artificial intelligence, tech corporate governance and the public interest regulatory response. *Cambridge Journal of Regions, Economy and Society.* 13, 37–54.

166. Taddeo, M., McCutcheon, T., Floridi, L. (2019) Trusting artificial intelligence in cybersecurity is a double-edged sword. *Nature Machine Intelligence*, 1(12), 557–560.

167. Taeihagh, A., Lim, H. (2019) Governing autonomous vehicles. *Transport Reviews* 39, 103–128.

168. Teoh, E. (2020) What's in a name? *Journal of Safety Research* 72, 145–151.

169. Arrieta, A., Díaz-Rodríguez, N., Del Ser, J., Bennetot, A., Tabik, S., Barbado, A., Chatila, R. (2020) Explainable artificial intelligence. *Information Fusion* 58, 82–115.

170. Burton, S., Habli, I., Lawton, T., McDermid, J., Morgan, P., Porter, Z. (2020) Mind the gaps. *Artificial Intelligence* 279, 103201.

171. Matthias, A. (2004) The responsibility gap. *Ethics and Information Technology* 6, 175–183.
172. Stilgoe, J. (2019) *Who's Driving Innovation?*, Springer Nature: Berlin, Germany.
173. Yigitcanlar, T. (2018) Smart city policies revisited. *World Technopolis Review* 7, 97–112.
174. Yigitcanlar, T. (2009) Planning for smart urban ecosystems. *Theoretical and Empirical Researches in Urban Management* 4, 5–21.
175. Leitheiser, S., Follmann, A. (2020) The social innovation–(re) politicisation nexus. *Urban Studies* 57, 894–915.
176. Desouza, K. (2017) *Governing in the Age of the Artificially Intelligent City.* Available online: www.governing.com/commentary/col-governing-age-artificially-intelligent-city.html (accessed on 15 September 2020).
177. Makridakis, S. (2017) The forthcoming artificial intelligence (AI) revolution. *Futures* 90, 46–60.
178. Batty, M. (2018) *Inventing Future Cities,.* MIT Press: Cambridge, MA, USA.
179. Erskine, M. (2019) Artificial intelligence, the emerging needs for human factors engineering, risk management and stakeholder engagement. In: *Proceedings of the World Engineers Convention, Engineers Australia.* Melbourne, Australia, 20–22 November 2019, pp. 9–10.
180. Loi, D., Wolf, C., Blomberg, J., Arar, R., Brereton, M. (2019) Co-designing AI futures. In: *Proceedings of the 2019 on Designing Interactive Systems Conference.* San Diego, CA, USA, 23–28 Jun 2019, pp. 381–384.
181. Ahmad, M., Teredesai, A., Eckert, C. (2020) Fairness, accountability, transparency in AI at scale: Lessons from national programs. In: *Proceedings of the 2020 Conference on Fairness, Accountability, and Transparency.* Barcelona, Spain, 27–30 January 2020, pp. 690–699.
182. Chen, S., Kuo, H., Lee, C. (2020) Preparing society for automated vehicles. *Sustainability* 12, 7844.
183. Larsson, S., Heintz, F. (2020) Transparency in artificial intelligence. *Internet Policy Review* 9, 1–12.
184. Kaker, S., Evans, J., Cugurullo, F., Cook, M., Petrova, S. (2020) Expanding cities. In: *The Politics of Uncertainty*, Scoones, I., Stirling, A., Eds., Routledge: London, UK, pp. 85–98.
185. Masanja, N., Mkumbo, H. (2020) The application of open source artificial intelligence as an approach to frugal innovation in Tanzania. *International Journal of Research and Innovation in Applied Sciences* 5, 36–46.
186. Brock, J., Von Wangenheim, F. (2019) Demystifying AI. *Calif. Manag. Rev.* 61, 110–134.
187. Allen, B., Agarwal, S., Kalpathy-Cramer, J., Dreyer, K. (2019) Democratizing AI. *Journal of the American. College of Radiology* 16, 961–963.
188. Moreau, E., Vogel, C., Barry, M. (2019) A paradigm for democratizing artificial intelligence research. In: *Innovations in Big Data Mining and Embedded Knowledge,.* Springer: Cham, Switzerland, pp. 137–166.
189. Floridi, L. (2019) Establishing the rules for building trustworthy AI. *Nature Machine Intelligence* 1, 261–262.
190. Mittelstadt, B. (2019) Principles alone cannot guarantee ethical AI. *Nature Machine Intelligence* 1, 501–507.
191. Jobin, A., Ienca, M., Vayena, E. (2019) The global landscape of AI ethics guidelines. *Nature Machine Intelligence* 1, 389–399.

192. Hagendorff, T. (2020) The ethics of AI ethics: An evaluation of guidelines. *Minds and Machines* 30, 1–22.
193. Awad, E., Dsouza, S., Kim, R., Schulz, J., Henrich, J., Shariff, A., Bonnefon, J., Rahwan, I. (2018) The moral machine experiment. *Nature* 563, 59–64.
194. Awad, E., Dsouza, S., Shariff, A., Rahwan, I., Bonnefon, J. (2020) Universals and variations in moral decisions made in 42 countries by 70,000 participants. *Proceedings of the National. Academy of Sciences USA* 117, 2332–2337.
195. Scherer, M. (2015) Regulating artificial intelligence systems. *Harvard Journal of Law & Technology* 29, 353.
196. Reed, C. (2018) How should we regulate artificial intelligence? *Philosophical Transactions of the Royal Society A* 376, 20170360.
197. Cugurullo, F. (2016) Speed kills. In: *Mega-Urbanization in the Global South*, Datta, A., Shaban, A., Eds., Routledge: London, UK, pp. 78–92.
198. Imrie, R., Street, E. (2009) Regulating design. *Urban Studies* 46, 2507–2518.
199. Floridi, L., Cowls, J., King, T., Taddeo, M. (2020) How to design AI for social good. *Science and Engineering Ethics* 26, 1771–1796.
200. Tzimas, T. (2018) Artificial intelligence as global commons and the "international law supremacy" principle. In: *Proceedings of the 10th International RAIS Conference on Social Sciences and Humanities*. Princeton, NJ, USA, 22–23 August 2018, pp. 83–88.
201. Rottz, M., Sell, D., Pacheco, R., Yigitcanlar, T. (2019) Digital commons and citizen coproduction in smart cities. *Energies* 12, 2813.
202. Cath, C., Wachter, S., Mittelstadt, B., Taddeo, M., Floridi, L. (2018) Artificial intelligence and the 'good society'. *Science and Engineering Ethics* 24, 505–528.
203. ITU News. (2020) *Introducing 'AI Commons'*. Available online: https://news.itu.int/introducing-ai-commons (accessed on 20 September 2020).
204. Kontokosta, C. E. (2021) Urban informatics in the science and practice of planning. *Journal of Planning Education and Research*, 41(4), 382–395.
205. Quan, S., Park, J., Economou, A., Lee, S. (2019) Artificial intelligence-aided design. *Environment and Planning B* 46, 1581–1599.
206. Bundy, A. (2017) Preparing for the future of artificial intelligence. *AI and Society* 32, 285–287.
207. Kirsch, D. (2020) Autopilot and algorithms: accidents, errors, and the current need for human oversight. *Journal of Clinical Sleep Medicine*, 16(10), 1651–1652.
208. Dwivedi, Y. K., Hughes, L., Ismagilova, E., Aarts, G., Coombs, C., Crick, T., ... Williams, M. D. (2021) Artificial Intelligence (AI): Multidisciplinary perspectives on emerging challenges, opportunities, and agenda for research, practice and policy. *International Journal of Information Management*, 57, 101994.
209. Sohn, K., Kwon, O. (2020) Technology acceptance theories and factors influencing artificial intelligence-based intelligent products. *Telematics and Informatics* 47, 101324.
210. Donald, M. (2019) *Leading and Managing Change in the Age of Disruption and Artificial Intelligence*,. Emerald: London, UK.
211. Musikanski, L., Rakova, B., Bradbury, J., Phillips, R., Manson, M. (2020) Artificial intelligence and community well-being. *International Journal of. Community Well-Being* 3, 39–55.

212. Mikhaylov, S., Esteve, M., Campion, A. (2018) Artificial intelligence for the public sector. *Philosophical Transactions of the Royal Society A* 376, 20170357.
213. Sousa, W., de Melo, E., Bermejo, P., Farias, R., Gomes, A. (2019) How and where is artificial intelligence in the public sector going? *Government Information Quarterly* 36, 101392.
214. Furman, J., Seamans, R. (2019) AI and the economy. *Innovation Policy and the Economy* 19, 161–191.
215. Yigitcanlar, T., Cugurullo, F. (2020) The sustainability of artificial intelligence: An urbanistic viewpoint from the lens of smart and sustainable cities. *Sustainability*, 12(20), 8548.

7 Green Artificial Intelligence

7.1 Introduction

The Second Digital and Fourth Industrial Revolutions cultivated an innovation culture for the flourishing of many technological developments and breakthroughs [1,2]. For instance, the field of artificial intelligence (AI)—defined as algorithms that mimic the cognitive functions of the human mind to make decisions without being supervised [3]—has undergone remarkable exponential growth over the last couple of decades [4]. Today, AI is unarguably an in-trend disruptive technology with countless applications, and even more prospects, for all industry sectors and areas of life—ranging from health to agriculture, engineering to finance, gaming to transportation and so on [5]. Besides, AI is one of the fundamental drivers of the global smart city movement [6].

Smart cities are widely seen as locations where digital technology and data are widely applied to generate efficiencies for economic growth, quality of life, and sustainability [7]. Today, in many urban policy circles and debates concerning smart city transformation, AI has become a subject of debate, particularly among urban policymakers and planners who search for technocentric solutions to the alarming urbanisation problems [8]. This popularity is due to the rising recognition of the technocentric solutions as a potential panacea to the complex and complicated urbanisation challenges—ranging from quality of life to climate change, and safety and security to mobility and accessibility [9]. The effective use of big data, and AI-powered smart urban technologies and platforms is believed to produce urban infrastructure and service efficiency to address or at least significantly ease these challenges [10,11].

As stated by Wang and Cao [12], technological advancements have generated an era that large volumes of data—i.e., big data—are collected via smart sensors deployed in cities and are made available via various commercial and public channels. Due to the recent advances in AI techniques and ubiquitous computing, these data now feed into the services that improve the quality of lives, city operation systems, and the environment. In the context of cities, AI has various application areas that aim to create efficiencies in urban infrastructures and services [13]. The following are among the most prevalent AI-powered examples:

DOI: 10.1201/9781003403630-9

- Automated algorithmic urban decision-making (e.g., identification and penalisation of traffic offences and tax evasions through smart sensors and machine learning-based data analytics) [14];
- Automated urban infrastructure assessment (e.g., monitoring urban infrastructure health through automated aerial mapping and deep-learning characterisations) [15–17];
- Autonomous urban post-disaster reconnaissance (e.g., detecting disaster damage and impact through synergistic use of deep learning and 3D point cloud features) [18];
- Autonomous and connected urban mobility (e.g., offering increased urban mobility through shared autonomous vehicles and autonomous shuttle bus fleets) [19,20];
- Urban descriptive, diagnostic, predictive, and prescriptive analytics (e.g., gathering and interpreting urban air pollution data to describe what the pollution level is, why it happened, when it may occur again, and actions to influence future desired outcomes) [21];
- Urban security, safety, rescue, and maintenance robots (e.g., emergency services operating rescue robots in risky and dangerous environments such as natural disaster events, mining accidents, and building collapses and fires) [22];
- Urban service agent chatbots (e.g., offering improved customer experience with reduced waiting times to service access in different languages on taxation, health services, public transport, family services, job opportunities, and so on) [23].

In an attempt to generate required efficiencies and proficiencies, many governments across the globe have started to deploy various AI system initiatives—at the national, state, and local levels [24,25]. The following are among the most common AI-driven applications [26]:

- AI process automation systems;
- AI-based knowledge management software;
- Chatbots/virtual agents;
- Cognitive robotics and autonomous systems;
- Cognitive security analytics and threat intelligence;
- Identity analytics;
- Intelligent digital assistants;
- Predictive analytics and data visualisation;
- Recommendation systems;
- Speech analytics.

Despite the efforts made to adopt and deploy AI in the public sector, almost all of these initiatives have either struggled, failed, or lacked the adequate potential to generate ethical, responsible, and sustainable solutions [27,28]. This is also the case for the smart city domain, where existing purely technocentric or algorithmic AI perspectives could not play a prominent role in the smart city transformation [26]. Toronto Sidewalk, Masdar, and Songdo are among the major smart city initiatives that resulted in project cancellations or disappointment in living up to their smart urban future promises [29].

The fundamental reason behind this failure is that AI system adoption practices are heavily technologically determined and reductionist in nature, and do not envisage and develop long-term, ethical, responsible, and sustainable solutions [30]. Most government AI approaches also overlooked urban, human, and social complexities; subsequently, this has created conditions for new forms of societal control, and boosted inequality and marginalisation among the layers of our societies [31]. Thus, the current practice of AI has generated as many constraints as prospects, where at times the constraints outweigh the prospects [32].

Against this brief backdrop, this chapter highlights the fundamental shortfalls in current AI system conceptualisation and practice, and points to a novel approach— i.e., green AI that also accommodates green sensing—that moves away from short-term efficiency solutions to focus on a long-term ethical, responsible, and sustainable AI practice that will help build sustainable urban futures for all through smart city transformation.

7.2 AI for Smart City Transformation

Utilisation of smart and innovative digital technologies has become a mainstream effort in tackling urban crises—whether they are related to climate, pandemics, natural disasters, or socioeconomic factors [33,34]. In recent years, particularly the advancements at the AI front—as one of the most prominent technologies of our time with significant impacts on our economy, society, environment, and governance—have resulted in invaluable opportunities for cities to increase their infrastructural efficiencies and predictive analytic capabilities, and hence to a degree, improve the quality of life and sustainability in cities—under the smart city brand [35]. According to Ullah et al. [36], today, AI is rapidly becoming a critical smart city element that helps in achieving necessary efficiencies and automation ability to deliver urban infrastructures, services, and amenities.

Especially when coupled with other smart urban technologies, AI applications— e.g., chatbots and virtual agents, cognitive robotics and autonomous systems, cognitive security analytics, expert systems, identity analytics, intelligent digital assistants, knowledge management systems, predictive analytics and data visualisation, process automation systems, recommendation systems, speech analytics, threat intelligence—provide new capabilities and directions for our cities, such as building the next-generation smart cities—i.e., "artificially intelligent cities" of the future [37]. There is a vast literature on the prospects of AI for smart cities [38].

Nonetheless, as much as creating benefits—for instance generating operational infrastructure or service efficiencies— the impacts of AI technology also pose substantial risks and disruptions for cities and citizens through the opaque decision-making processes and the privacy violations it causes—e.g., automating inequality, generating algorithmic bias due to bad or limited data and training, removing or limiting human responsibility, and lacking an adequate level of transparency and accountability [39]. Additionally, in comparison to the other technologies, AI has some unique data-related challenges that include data acquisition, large volume of data and streaming data, heterogeneous data, complex dependencies among the data, noisy and incomplete data, distributed data storage and processing, training data, and data privacy [12].

Some examples of the AI mishaps that impact society—and also diminish public trust in the AI solutions implemented as part of smart city projects—include, but are not limited to, the following:

- AI misdiagnosis of child maltreatment and prescription of wrong solutions in Pittsburgh, PA [40];
- Amazon's AI recruiting tool which took biased decisions towards women [41];
- Bias towards people of colour in the decisions made by AI algorithms used in US hospitals [42];
- Clearview AI's scandalous facial recognition image database developed with images from social media, which got hacked in 2020—leaving the citizens of democratic countries with privacy threats, and the citizens of autocratic regimes with an onslaught of the Orwellian nightmare [43];
- Malfunctioning of the Australian government's automated debt recovery program, called Robodebt, resulting in a scandal as it had unlawfully taken $721M from over 400,000 Australians [44].

One of the main reasons behind the failure of AI systems comes from the development and integration stages of AI in urban and public services. Pasquinelli [45] links the underlining issues around AI, or in broader terms how machines learn, failure to the development of AI systems when operators engage in training data, learning algorithm, and model application stages. In these stages operators could lead to three types of bias, namely:

- Just-world bias (e.g., a cognitive bias that assumes people get what they deserve and, hence, leads to failure in helping or feeling compassion for others or disadvantaged groups—such as poor or homeless people);
- Data bias (e.g., an error caused by certain elements of data being more heavily represented or weighted than other elements, leading to wrong decisions or inequity issues—such as women, people of colour or minorities);
- Algorithmic bias (e.g., a lack of fairness, originating from the output of an algorithmic system, with consequential undesired decisions, actions, or externalities—such as a credit score algorithm may deny a loan).

When an AI system containing such bias is integrated with an urban or public service, the failure of the service, or dissatisfaction from the service, is inevitable [46].

The growing concern over negative AI externalities and service failures, particularly in smart cities, proves the need for the development of more ethical and regulated AI systems [47]. Subsequently, in recent years, the attempts to provide a more holistic perspective for AI resulted in giving birth to a number of new AI conceptualisations [48]. These include "responsible AI", "ethical AI", "explainable

AI", "sustainable AI", "green AI", and the like, where the aim is to ensure the ethical, transparent, and accountable use of AI applications in a manner that is consistent with user expectations, organisational values, environmental conservation, and societal laws and norms [49]. It is also argued that such renewed approaches to AI will help maximise the desired smart city outcomes and positive impacts for all citizens, while minimising the negative consequences [50].

7.3 The Green AI Approach

The effects of human activity—e.g., unsustainable and rapidly growing population, urbanisation, industrialisation, and consumerism—since the Industrial Revolution of the 1850s, and particularly during the last five decades, have had their toll on the environment [51–53]. As presented by Hunter and Hewson [54], the greatest catastrophic threats humanity is facing today are vast and include the followings:

- Chemical pollution of the earth system, including the atmosphere and oceans;
- Collapse of ecosystems and loss of biodiversity;
- Decline of natural resources, particularly water;
- Global warming and human-induced climate change;
- Human population growth beyond Earth's carrying capacity;
- National and global failure to understand and act preventatively on these risks;
- Nuclear weapons and other weapons of mass destruction;
- Pandemics of new and untreatable disease;
- Rising food insecurity and failing nutritional quality;
- The advent of powerful, uncontrolled new technology.

Among those threats, "national and global failure to understand and act preventatively on these risks" is the most important one. That is the incapability of governments [55] and the public [56] to understand and take actions against threats that most likely, or definitely, leads to a catastrophe. This issue is the root cause of the failure of AI solutions—even if they target sustainability [57]— they are mainly used to improve business efficiency and economic productivity in our cities [58] rather than actually tackling the aforementioned global threats that are mostly anthropogenic in origin [59].

The flourishing of humankind over the last 10,000 years, in the Holocene, is a consequence of the planet's thriving conditions—e.g., the perfect climate and ecosystem offering [60]. Hence, investigating the ways in which AI can help establish thriving conditions for humans and the planet in the Anthropocene, has been the subject of recent scholarly work [61].

For example, Vinuesa et al. [62] explored the role of AI in achieving the UN's sustainable development goals (SDGs). Their study found that

AI may act as an enabler on 134 targets (79%) across all SDGs, generally through a technological improvement, which may allow to overcome certain present limitations. However, 59 targets (35%, also across all SDGs) may experience a negative impact from the development of AI.

In another study, Gupta et al. [63] assessed whether AI is an enabler, or an inhibitor, of sustainability measured via SDGs. Their study disclosed that

when SDGs related to Society, Economy, and Environment were analyzed, it was observed that the Environment category has the highest potential, with 93% of the targets being positively affected, whereas Society has the largest negative effect with 38% of the targets exhibiting a negative interaction with AI.

Figure 7.1 shows the 17 SDGs.

Likewise, Goranski and Tan [64] examined the role of AI in accelerating the progress of SDGs. Their investigation revealed that

AI can generate data for more intelligent targeting of intervention, reduce waste and losses in production and consumption, create new applications that will transform entire industries and professions, and provide the necessary improvements in connectivity and cost reductions that brings the benefits of the rapid pace of technological development to many people worldwide.

Figure 7.1 Sustainable Development Goals [74].

While AI poses an opportunity for achieving SDGs, as stated by Dwivedi et al. [65], AI-supported delivery of SDGs will "require significant investment from governments and industry together with collaboration at an international level to effect governance, standards and security".

Additionally, in recent years we have witnessed an increase in academic literature reporting the outcomes of AI technology applications for social good—tackling social and environmental issues [66]. The environmental areas in which AI applications are utilised range from air pollution monitoring [67] to wastewater treatment [68], from endangered species protection [69,70] to climate change detection [71], from natural disaster prediction [27] to ecosystem service assessment [72], and other applications in environmental sciences [73].

While the existing and potential benefits of AI for the environment have been presented in the abovementioned studies, they also underlined the critical importance of addressing the risks involved. For instance, studies emphasised the critical importance of the need for:

- Being supported by the necessary regulatory insight and oversight for AI-based technologies to enable sustainable development, and avoid gaps in transparency, safety and ethical standards [62];
- Going beyond the development of AI in sectorial silos, so as to understand the impacts AI might have across societal, environmental and economic outcomes [63];
- Offering a constructive, rather than optimistic or pessimistic, outlook on AI for promoting desired sustainable outcomes [75].

The most common negative externalities of AI on the environment include increased electricity usage (computation and transmission power consumption) and resulting carbon emissions along with errors in critical decisions due to user and data bias [76–78]. Given that the global technology uptake is growing at an exponential rate, the impact of these externalities is expected to be immense [79]. Just to give an example, cryptocurrency mining in the recent years has led to increased energy consumption globally.

As stated by Cuen [80], the bitcoin electricity consumption index of the University of Cambridge indicates that

> bitcoin miners are expected to consume roughly 130 Terawatt-hours of energy (TWh), which is roughly 0.6% of global electricity consumption. This puts the bitcoin economy on par with the CO_2 emissions of a small developing nation like Sri Lanka or Jordan.

These undesired externalities call for a sustainable approach to AI that involves a green-based technological perspective in the AI industry, including switching to a sustainable AI infrastructure [81–85]. In their study on the climate cost of global computation, Dobbe and Whittaker [86] advocated the following policy recommendations for tech-aware climate policy, and climate-aware tech policy:

- Account for the entire tech ecosystem;
- Address AI's impact on climate refugees;.
- Curb the use of AI to extract fossil fuels;
- Integrate tech and climate policy;
- Make non-energy policy a standard practice;
- Mandate transparency;
- Watch for rebound effects.

Making AI green and sustainable, i.e., the green AI approach, requires a bias-free (besides a reasonable environmental bias or positive discrimination), inclusive, trustworthy, explainable, ethical, and responsible approach to technology that aims to alleviate the developmental challenges of the planet in a sustainable way [30,87]. This approach, using AI to solve sustainability challenges and using AI in a more sustainable way, will also serve as an enabler of smart city transformation [88,89].

7.4 Green Sensing, Communications, and Computing

Now that we have discussed a number of policy and high-level issues related to green AI, we define and discuss issues that relate to the development of digital infrastructure for green AI. Our intention is to discuss these infrastructural issues here, together with the high-level issues, and to provide a holistic overview such that different communities working in policy and infrastructure research can understand the cross-disciplinary issues and collaboratively devise holistic and globally optimum solutions.

Sensing, communications, and computing were never so interdependent as they have become now due to the emergence and convergence of technologies including miniaturisation of sensors, the Internet- f Things (IoT), data-driven methods, AI-driven optimisations, cloud, fog, and edge computing. The whole ecosystem of smart applications and systems is converging due to the need for these applications to be intrinsically collaborative and distributed.

These smart applications and systems require a certain level of smartness that enhances our ability to engage, sense, and act on with our environments, analyse them and make timely, effective, and sustainable decisions [90]. The trend is an increase in the number of IoT devices, expected to reach 25 billion by 2030 [91], which in turn increases the requirements for data pre-processing, storage, communications, and processing. AI provides the brain for smartness, i.e., the analyses and the decision-making processes. AI, while requiring significant computational resources (storage, communications, and processing), has the capability to improve the efficiency of the whole infrastructure ecosystem by holistic analysis and optimisation of the system.

To aid the development of green AI both at the policy and infrastructure levels, we herewith introduce and define the concept of "green sensing" as physical and virtual green sensing to enable triple bottom line (social, environmental, and economic) sustainability. This definition proposes the development of methods and technologies to sense and measure social, environmental, and economic sustainability. Sustainability is affected by challenges such as security, privacy, the safety of people, ethical standards, and compliance, and so on, and therefore these are included in our definition of green sensing. These methods and technologies per se should be green in terms of their efficiency and energy usage.

What are the potential examples of green sensing methods and technologies in the broader sense of the term green sensing as we have defined it above? A physical sensor to measure sustainability of urban infrastructure and environmental pollution can be considered a green sensor [92,93]. A virtual sensor such as using big data or social media data to detect congestion on the road can be considered a green sensor for environmental sustainability in the sense that it detects environmental pollution that may be caused by a high intensity of pollution in the geographical area where congestion is happening [94].

The same can also be considered a green sensor for social sustainability (or social sustainability sensor) because it can detect people's anguish and potential health-related harms to the people living or travelling through that geographical area [95]. AI-based virtual sensors can be developed by analysing various literature, news media, or government regulations to understand their economic impacts and sustainability. The possibilities are almost endless. Sensors can be considered of two broad types: the ones that measure the impact of phenomena directly (e.g., power or gas/petrol consumption of a community, or real-time or future crowd detection in public spaces) [96,97] and the sensors that measure the impact indirectly (e.g., via social media) [98,99].

The concept of green sensing we define here is different and much broader from the earlier usage of this term, green sensing, which refers to the methods used to save energy in the sensing process; the earlier use of the term has mostly appeared in the context of wireless sensor networks (WSNs) [100]. A range of methods and technologies have been developed under the umbrella of wireless sensor networks to reduce the energy usage of sensors. These techniques have been naturally extended to the IoT paradigm. WSNs and the IoT have been used for many applications including those for environmental monitoring and protection such as forest fire detection, ambience monitoring, and so on. The main motivation for developing these techniques has been to save energy for the sensing devices that typically are wirelessly connected, and battery powered.

The techniques to save energy include duty cycling (periodically turn the radio on/off to save energy), wake-up radio (on-demand radio on/off), sensor selection or scheduling (select or schedule a subset of sensors instead of all the sensors), adaptive sampling (adapt the selection of sensors based on the context and application), and more. These green sensing techniques not only can reduce the energy required for sensing, but also reduce the generated data, reducing the energy needed for data storage or pre-processing. Energy-harvesting techniques by all or a selection of sensors using renewable energies or electric signals also have been proposed to make the sensing process green [101].

The data sensed through the IoT and other media are usually transferred to a central location such as a master node or cloud computing centres for their analysis. An astonishingly great deal of energy is required to transfer data across networks.

Naturally, a range of techniques has been developed to reduce data communication energy and improve network efficiency. In addition to reducing data generation through various green sensing techniques mentioned earlier, various data-pruning methods have been developed such as using data compression to reduce communication and bandwidth requirements.

Probably the most important development in this respect is fog and edge computing-based solutions that reduce the data transfer and bandwidth requirements of smart applications by processing data at the edge or fog layers, near the sensors and devices, while offering other benefits such as data security and privacy. Several works have investigated the energy efficiency and other benefits of fog- and edge-based solutions [102].

For instance, Janbi et al. [103] developed a framework for Distributed-AI-as-a-Service (DAIaaS) provisioning in future environments. The framework divides "the actual training and inference computations of AI workflow into smaller computations that are executed in parallel according to the level and capacity of resources available with cloud, fog, and edge layers" [103]. They consider "multiple provisioning scenarios for DAIaaS in three case studies comprising nine applications and AI delivery models and 50 distinct sensor and software modules" and report energy consumption and other benefits of edge- and fog-based AI delivery solutions.

Mohammed et al. [104] proposed the UbiPriSEQ framework that aims to holistically and adaptively optimise energy efficiency, security, privacy, and quality of service (QoS). They report an implementation of the proposed framework UbiPriSEQ using deep reinforcement learning (DRL) that allows devising policies and making decisions related to important parameters such as transmit power, the specific fog nodes to be selected for offloading data and computation, and so on.

A number of key technological developments are shaping the development of high-speed and low-latency networks, currently the fifth-generation networks (5G), offering along with the IoT—a powerful system for ubiquitous environments with advance sensing and processing capabilities [104]. The requirements for the next-generation societies are underpinned by the need to ubiquitously deliver smart services (AI- and data-driven) and the increase in the number of sensors, and these requirements are expected to be met by 6G, the next generation of cellular networks [103–106].

The 6G networks are expected to meet these requirements by higher spectrum and multiple communication technologies [107], ultra-dense heterogeneous networking [106], terrestrial and non-terrestrial communications [108], and the use of AI to optimise service-oriented network operations [109,110]. An important feature of the 6G networks would be to support ubiquitous AI services. More importantly, 6G considers energy efficiency as its critical requirement, expected to be ten to a hundred times better than 5G, to be addressed using novel antenna designs, zero-energy nodes, and others to enable low-rate sensing applications [105,111].

Energy efficiency is a grand challenge in the design of large-scale computing systems such as supercomputers and computational clouds. For example, the currently ranked number one system on the list of top-500 supercomputers, Fugaku, has over seven million cores and requires 28.3MW of power for its operation. While AI algorithms consume large amounts of power, these can be used to reduce the energy requirements of computations while optimising performance [112], allowing by such approaches the concept of green (virtual) sensing and optimisations to be introduced in computing systems.

7.5 Conclusion

This chapter, at large, contributes to the growing AI literature by underlining the fundamental shortfalls in the mainstream AI system conceptualisation and practice, and by advocating the need for a green AI approach to further support smart city transformation and SDGs.

The chapter, particularly, provides a perspective on the green AI concept. It defines and elaborates on the concept and discusses why a consolidated effort is needed on the topic, including the benefits of a strengthened green AI approach. The elaborations are supported by the literature from diverse disciplines including computer, environmental, and social sciences and urban studies. The chapter also discusses issues that relate to the development of digital infrastructure for green AI. The intention is to discuss these infrastructural issues together with the high-level issues and to provide a holistic overview such that different communities working in policy and infrastructure research can understand the cross-disciplinary issues and collaboratively devise holistic and globally optimum solutions.

Moreover, in order to aid the development of green AI, both at the policy and infrastructure levels, the chapter introduces and defines the concept of "green sensing" as physical and virtual green sensing to enable triple bottom line (social, environmental, and economic) sustainability. This chapter also highlights the importance and advocates the need for the development of methods and technologies to (green) sense and measure social, environmental, and economic sustainability.

This chapter is an invaluable contribution to the emerging field of green AI—as there is no scholarly literature that discusses the policy and infrastructural issues on the given topics in an abstracted way. Our approach, here, allows readers to have a holistic understanding of the issues related to green AI with a relatively succinct and to-the-point perspective piece, and presents prospective research and development directions.

We conclude the chapter with the following remarks as it is of utmost importance to have timely, effective, and efficient government policy in place for making AI greener and our cities smarter.

Firstly, we underline that the field of AI is on steroids; technological advancements are exponential, and applications are disruptive [113,114]. In such a situation, without appropriate government intervention, the business-as-usual scenario will create extended negative risks and consequences for our society and the planet [115]. Unfortunately, these risks and consequences have not yet been fully understood by governments, which means they do not act upon them or take preventative measures [116].

Secondly, as evidenced in the literature, there are colossal policy challenges before us to make AI green [117]. Perhaps the most critical one is the need for governments to develop legal and ethical frameworks for AI and its use [118]. Expanding on this issue, Dwivedi et al. [65] list fairness and equity, accountability and legal issues, ethics, misuse protection, transparency and audit, and digital divide and data deficit as the fundamental public and environmental policy challenges of AI. Another study, by Jobin et al. [119], discloses "the primary AI ethical principles as follows: transparency, justice and fairness, non-maleficence, responsibility, privacy, beneficence, freedom and autonomy, trust, sustainability, dignity, and solidarity". These principles are critical for AI projects to deliver desired outcomes to all.

Thirdly, up until now, no country has passed an AI law yet, only a small number of countries have attempted to introduce AI ethical frameworks and regulation guidelines—such as the European Union's AI ethics guidelines to inform future regulation, and the other examples include AI ethical framework attempts in Australia, Germany, Singapore, and the UK [120]. It seems to be the existing practice for most governments is adopting a "wait-and-see" approach to AI ethics and regulations [121]. Furthermore, as stated by Hagendorff [122], in most cases, the existing ethics frameworks are failing to serve their purposes as they lack any reinforcement mechanisms—in other words, there are no consequences if these ethical principles are not followed.

Next, having no regulation, at present, does not mean that the AI domain will not be regulated in the near future—where in this instance, we note the EU's recently released pioneering AI regulation [123]. It is very likely that—as happened in the sharing economy applications, e.g., Uber and AirBnB [124,125]—governments will eventually regulate the AI practice to alleviate its undesired consequences [126]. As stated by Yara et al. [87],

with the development of technology, changes are needed in the legal regulation of AI so that the consequences of its use become useful for the whole society. Market forces with their own resources will not ensure successful development for the whole population. Thus, legal regulation of AI is inevitable.

Lastly, there is a critical role for all stakeholders, e.g., public and private sectors, academia and the public, to play to make sure that the forthcoming AI plans, ethics, and regulations are to also bring efficiency, sustainability, and equity perspectives to the technology domain that will support achieving SDGs [127,128]. This renewed green AI approach and capacity will also consolidate the efforts made to transform our cities into smart ones and support the smart and sustainable development of our cities and communities [129]. In other words, as also indicated by Fisher [130], we need to put our best effort into making AI an efficient, sustainable, and equitable technology for establishing smart cities and sustainable futures [131].

Acknowledgements

This chapter, with permission from the copyright holder, is a reproduced version of the following journal article: Yigitcanlar, T., Mehmood, R., & Corchado, J. (2021).

Green artificial intelligence: Towards an efficient, sustainable and equitable technology for smart cities and futures. *Sustainability*, 13(16), 8952.

References

1. Morrar, R., Arman, H., Mousa, S. (2017). The fourth industrial revolution (Industry 4.0). *Technology Innovation Management Review*, 7(11), 12–20.
2. Lee, M., Yun, J., Pyka, A., Won, D., Kodama, F., Schiuma, G., … Zhao, X. (2018). How to respond to the fourth industrial revolution, or the second information technology revolution? *Journal of Open Innovation: Technology, Market, and Complexity*, 4, 21.
3. Kirwan, C., Fu, Z. (2020). *Smart Cities and Artificial Intelligence*. Elsevier, Oxford, UK.
4. Shukla, A., Janmaijaya, M., Abraham, A., Muhuri, P. (2019). Engineering applications of artificial intelligence. *Engineering Applications of Artificial Intelligence*, 85, 517–532.
5. Cugurullo, F. (2020). Urban artificial intelligence. *Frontiers in Sustainable Cities*, 2, 1–14.
6. Singh, S., Sharma, P., Yoon, B., Shojafar, M., Cho, G., Ra, I. (2020). Convergence of blockchain and artificial intelligence in IoT network for the sustainable smart city. *Sustainable Cities and Society*, 63, 102364.
7. Mora, L., Deakin, M., Reid, A. (2019). Strategic principles for smart city development. *Technological Forecasting and Social Change*, 142, 70–97.
8. Kassens-Noor, E., Hintze, A. (2020). Cities of the future? *AI*, 1, 192–197.
9. Yigitcanlar, T., Kankanamge, N., Regona, M., Maldonado, M., Rowan, R., Ryu, A., Desouza, K., Corchado, J., Mehmood, R., Li, R. (2020a). Artificial intelligence technologies and related urban planning and development concepts. *Journal of Open Innovation*, 6, 187.
10. Yu, Y., Zhang, N. (2019). Does smart city policy improve energy efficiency? *Journal of Cleaner Production*, 229, 501–512.
11. Corchado, J., Chamoso, P., Hernández, G., Gutierrez, A., Camacho, A., González-Briones, A., … & Omatu, S. (2021). Deepint. net. *Sensors*, 21(1), 236.
12. Wang, S., Cao, J. (2021). AI and deep learning for urban computing. In: *Urban Informatics*. Springer, Singapore.
13. Ortega-Fernández, A., Martín-Rojas, R., García-Morales, V. (2020). Artificial intelligence in the urban environment. *Sustainability*, 12, 7860.
14. Gutberlet, T. (2019). Data-driven smart sustainable cities. *Geopolitics, History, and International Relations*, 11, 55–61.
15. Erkal, B., Hajjar, J. (2017). Laser-based surface damage detection and quantification using predicted surface properties. *Automation in Construction*, 83, 285–302.
16. Mohammadi, M., Watson, D., Wood, R. (2019). Deep learning-based damage detection from aerial SfM point clouds. *Drones*, 3(3), 68.
17. Nasimi, R., Moreu, F. (2021). Development and implementation of a laser camera. *Journal of Engineering Mechanics*, 147(8), 4021045.
18. Ghosh Mondal, T., Jahanshahi, M., Wu, R., Wu, Z. (2020). Deep learning-based multi-class damage detection for autonomous post-disaster reconnaissance. *Structural Control and Health Monitoring*, 27(4), e2507.
19. Faisal, A., Kamruzzaman, M., Yigitcanlar, T., Currie, G. (2019). Understanding autonomous vehicles. *Journal of Transport and Land Use*, 12, 45–72.

20. Dennis, S., Paz, A., Yigitcanlar, T. (2021). Perceptions and attitudes towards the deployment of autonomous and connected vehicles: Insights from Las Vegas, Nevada. *Journal of Urban Technology*, 28(3–4), 75–95.
21. Allam, Z., Dey, G., Jones, D. (2020). Artificial intelligence (AI) provided early detection of the coronavirus (COVID-19) in China. *AI*, 1, 156–165.
22. Tiddi, I., Bastianelli, E., Daga, E., d'Aquin, M., Motta, E. (2020). Robot–city interaction. *International Journal of Social Robotics*, 12, 299–324.
23. Ashfaq, M., Yun, J., Yu, S., Loureiro, S. (2020). I, Chatbot. *Telematics and Informatics*, 54, 101473.
24. Engin, Z., Treleaven, P. (2019). Algorithmic government. *The Computer Journal*, 62, 448–460.
25. Wirtz, B., Weyerer, J., Geyer, C. (2019). Artificial intelligence and the public sector. *International Journal of Public Administration*, 42, 596–615.
26. Yigitcanlar, T., Corchado, J., Mehmood, R., Li, R., Mossberger, K., Desouza, K. (2021). Responsible urban innovation with local government artificial intelligence. *Journal of Open Innovation*, 7, 71.
27. Sun, W., Bocchini, P., Davison, B. (2020). Applications of artificial intelligence for disaster management. *Natural Hazards*, 103, 2631–2689.
28. Desouza, K., Dawson, G., Chenok, D. (2020). Designing, developing, and deploying artificial intelligence systems. *Business Horizons*, 63, 205–213.
29. Yigitcanlar, T., Han, H., Kamruzzaman, M., Ioppolo, G., Sabatini-Marques, J. (2019). The making of smart cities. *Land Use Policy*, 88, 104187.
30. Yigitcanlar, T., Cugurullo, F. (2020). The sustainability of artificial intelligence. *Sustainability*, 12, 8548.
31. Valentine, S. (2019). Impoverished algorithms. *Fordham Urban Law Journal*, 46, 364–427.
32. Nishant, R., Kennedy, M., Corbett, J. (2020). Artificial intelligence for sustainability. *International Journal of Information Management*, 53, 102104.
33. Shin, D. (2009). Ubiquitous city. *Journal of Information Science*, 35, 515–526.
34. Yigitcanlar, T., Kamruzzaman, M. (2019). Smart cities and mobility. *Journal of Urban Technology*, 26(2), 21–46.
35. Batty, M. (2018). Artificial intelligence and smart cities. *Environment and Planning B: Urban Analytics and City Science*, 45(1), 3–6.
36. Ullah, Z., Al-Turjman, F., Mostarda, L., Gagliardi, R. (2020). Applications of artificial intelligence and machine learning in smart cities. *Computer Communications*, 154, 313–323.
37. Yigitcanlar, T., Butler, L., Windle, E., Desouza, K., Mehmood, R., Corchado, J. (2020). Can building 'artificially intelligent cities' protect humanity from natural disasters, pandemics and other catastrophes? *Sensors*, 20, 2988.
38. Zhang, Y., Geng, P., Sivaparthipan, C., Muthu, B. (2021). Big data and artificial intelligence based early risk warning system of fire hazard for smart cities. *Sustainable Energy Technologies and Assessments*, 45, 100986.
39. Yigitcanlar, T., Desouza, K., Butler, L., Roozkhosh, F. (2020). Contributions and risks of artificial intelligence (AI) in building smarter cities. *Energies*, 13, 1473.
40. Eubanks, V. (2018). *A Child Abuse Prediction Model Fails Poor Families*. Accessed from www.wired.com/story/excerpt-from-automating-inequality.
41. Cooper, Y. (2018). *Amazon Ditched AI Recruiting Tool that Favored Men for Technical Jobs*. Accessed from www.theguardian.com/technology/2018/oct/10/amazon-hiring-ai-gender-bias-recruiting-engine.

42. Ledford, H. (2019). *Millions of Black People Affected by Racial Bias in Health-care Algorithms.* Accessed from www.nature.com/articles/d41586-019-03228-6.
43. Hill, K. (2020). *The Secretive Company that Might End Privacy as We Know It.* Accessed from www.nytimes.com/2020/01/18/technology/clearview-privacy-facial-recognition.html.
44. Whiteford, P. (2020). *Robodebt was a Fiasco With a Cost We Have Yet to Fully Appreciate.* Accessed from https://theconversation.com/robodebt-was-a-fiasco-with-a-cost-we-have-yet-to-fully-appreciate-150169.
45. Pasquinelli, M. (2019). How a machine learns and fails. *Journal for Digital Cultures,* (5), 1–17.
46. Kuziemski, M., Misuraca, G. (2020). AI governance in the public sector. *Telecommunications Policy, 44*(6), 101976.
47. Allam, Z., Dhunny, Z. (2019). On big data, artificial intelligence and smart cities. *Cities,* 89, 80–91.
48. Floridi, L., Cowls, J., Beltrametti, M., Chatila, R., Chazerand, P., Dignum, V., ... & Vayena, E. (2018). AI4People. *Minds and Machines,* 28, 689–707.
49. Wearn, O., Freeman, R., Jacoby, D. (2019). Responsible AI for conservation. *Nature Machine Intelligence,* 1, 72–73.
50. Falco, G. (2019). *Participatory AI.* In: 2019 IEEE International Conference on Computational Science and Engineering and IEEE International Conference on Embedded and Ubiquitous Computing.
51. Metaxiotis, K., Carrillo, F., Yigitcanlar, T. (2010). *Knowledge-based Development for Cities and Societies.* IGI Global, Hersey, PA.
52. Yigitcanlar, T., Kamruzzaman, M. (2015). Planning, development and management of sustainable cities. *Sustainability,* 7, 14677–14688.
53. Dizdaroglu, D., Yigitcanlar, T. (2016). Integrating urban ecosystem sustainability assessment into policy-making. *Journal of Environmental Planning and Management,* 59, 1982–2006.
54. Hunter, A., Hewson, J. (2020). *There are 10 Catastrophic Threats Facing Humans Right Now, and Coronavirus is Only One of Them.* Accessed from https://theconversation.com/there-are-10-catastrophic-threats-facing-humans-right-now-and-coronavirus-is-only-one-of-them-136854.
55. Copland, S. (2020). Anti-politics and global climate inaction. *Critical Sociology,* 46, 623–641.
56. Hornsey, M., Fielding, K. (2020). Understanding (and reducing) inaction on climate change. *Social Issues and Policy Review,* 14, 3–35.
57. Yun, J., Lee, D., Ahn, H., Park, K., Lee, S., Yigitcanlar, T. (2016). Not deep learning but autonomous learning of open innovation for sustainable artificial intelligence. *Sustainability,* 8, 797.
58. Sharma, G., Yadav, A., Chopra, R. (2020). Artificial intelligence and effective governance. *Sustainable Futures,* 2, 100004.
59. Mortoja, M., Yigitcanlar, T. (2020). Local drivers of anthropogenic climate change. *Remote Sensing,* 12, 2270.
60. Shockley, K. (2018). The great decoupling. *Journal of Agricultural and Environmental Ethics,* 31, 429–442.
61. Stahl, B., Andreou, A., Brey, P., Hatzakis, T., Kirichenko, A., Macnish, K., ... & Wright, D. (2021). Artificial intelligence for human flourishing. *Journal of Business Research,* 124, 374–388.

62. Vinuesa, R., Azizpour, H., Leite, I., Balaam, M., Dignum, V., Domisch, S., ... & Nerini, F. (2020). The role of artificial intelligence in achieving the sustainable development goals. *Nature Communications*, 11, 1–10.

63. Gupta, S., Langhans, S., Domisch, S., Fuso-Nerini, F., Felländer, A., Battaglini, M., ... & Vinuesa, R. (2021). Assessing whether artificial intelligence is an enabler or an inhibitor of sustainability at indicator level. *Transportation Engineering*, 4, 100064.

64. Goralski, M., Tan, T. (2020). Artificial intelligence and sustainable development. *International Journal of Management Education*, 18, 100330.

65. Dwivedi, Y., Hughes, L., Ismagilova, E., Aarts, G., Coombs, C., Crick, T., ... & Williams, M. (2019). Artificial intelligence. *International Journal of Information Management*, 57, 101994.

66. Wamba, S., Bawack, R., Guthrie, C., Queiroz, M., Carillo, K. (2021). Are we preparing for a good AI society? *Technological Forecasting and Social Change*, 164, 120482.

67. Ye, Z., Yang, J., Zhong, N., Tu, X., Jia, J., Wang, J. (2020). Tackling environmental challenges in pollution controls using artificial intelligence. *Science of the Total Environment*, 699, 134279.

68. Zhao, L., Dai, T., Qiao, Z., Sun, P., Hao, J., Yang, Y. (2020). Application of artificial intelligence to wastewater treatment. *Process Safety and Environmental Protection*, 133, 169–182.

69. Jothiswaran, V., Velumani, T., Jayaraman, R. (2020). Application of artificial intelligence in fisheries and aquaculture. *Biotica Research Today*, 2, 499–502.

70. Corcoran, E., Denman, S., Hamilton, G. (2021). Evaluating new technology for biodiversity monitoring: Are drone surveys biased? *Ecology and Evolution*, *11*(11), 6649–6656.

71. Huntingford, C., Jeffers, E., Bonsall, M., Christensen, H., Lees, T., Yang, H. (2019). Machine learning and artificial intelligence to aid climate change research and preparedness. *Environmental Research Letters*, 14, 124007.

72. Pelorosso, R., Gobattoni, F., Geri, F., Leone, A. (2017). PANDORA 3.0 plugin. *Ecosystem Services*, 26, 476–482.

73. Haupt, S., Pasini, A., Marzban, C. (2008). *Artificial Intelligence Methods in the Environmental Sciences*. Springer.

74. United Nations (2015). *The 17 Goals, Sustainable Development*. Accessed from https://sdgs.un.org/goals.

75. Bjørlo, L., Moen, Ø., Pasquine, M. (2021). The role of consumer autonomy in developing sustainable AI. *Sustainability*, 13, 2332.

76. Jin, L., Duan, K., Tang, X. (2018). What is the relationship between technological innovation and energy consumption? *Sustainability*, 10, 145.

77. MacCarthy, M., Kenneth, K. (2021). *Machines Learn that Brussels Writes the Rules*. Accessed from www.brookings.edu/blog/techtank/2021/05/04/machines-learn-that-brussels-writes-the-rules-the-eus-new-ai-regulation.

78. Unwin, T. (2020). *Digital Technologies are Part of the Climate Change Problem*. Accessed from www.ictworks.org/digital-technologies-climate-change-problem/#.YJDJ9S0RpYs.

79. Ritchie, H., Roser, M. (2017). *Technology Adoption*. Accessed from https://ourworldindata.org/technology-adoption.

80. Cuen, L. (2021). *The Debate about Cryptocurrency and Energy Consumption*. Accessed from https://techcrunch.com/2021/03/21/the-debate-about-cryptocurrency-and-energy-consumption.

81. Song, M., Cao, S., Wang, S. (2019). The impact of knowledge trade on sustainable development and environment-biased technical progress. *Technological Forecasting and Social Change*, 144, 512–523.
82. Dhar, P. (2020). The carbon impact of artificial intelligence. *Nature Machine Intelligence*, 2, 423–425.
83. Schwartz, R., Dodge, J., Smith, N., Etzioni, O. (2020). Green AI. *Communications of the ACM*, 63, 54–63.
84. Yang, X., Hua, S., Shi, Y., Wang, H., Zhang, J., Letaief, K. (2020). Sparse optimization for green edge AI inference. *Journal of Communications and Information Networks*, 5, 1–15.
85. Candelieri, A., Perego, R., Archetti, F. (2021). Green machine learning via augmented Gaussian processes and multi-information source optimization. *Soft Computing*, 25, 12591–12603.
86. Dobbe, R., Whittaker, M. (2019). *AI and Climate Change*. Accessed from https://med ium.com/@AINowInstitute/ai-and-climate-change-how-theyre-connected-and-what-we-can-do-about-it-6aa8d0f5b32c.
87. Yara, O., Brazheyev, A., Golovko, L., Bashkatova, V. (2021). Legal regulation of the use of artificial intelligence. *European Journal of Sustainable Development*, 10, 281–281.
88. Gould, S. (2020). *Green AI*. Accessed from www2.deloitte.com/uk/en/blog/experie nce-analytics/2020/green-ai-how-can-ai-solve-sustainability-challenges.html.
89. Yigitcanlar, T., Foth, M., Kamruzzaman, M. (2019). Towards post-anthropocentric cities. *Journal of Urban Technology*, 26, 147–152.
90. Alotaibi, S., Mehmood, R., Katib, I., Rana, O., Albeshri, A. (2020). Sehaa. *Applied Sciences*, 10, 1398.
91. Holst, A. (2021). *IoT Connected Devices Worldwide 2019–2030*. Accessed from www. statista.com/statistics/1183457/iot-connected-devices-worldwide.
92. Lee, S., Yigitcanlar, T., Han, J., Leem, Y. (2008). Ubiquitous urban infrastructure. *Innovation*, 10, 282–292.
93. Bibri, S.E. (2018). The IoT for smart sustainable cities of the future. *Sustainable Cities and Society*, 38, 230–253.
94. Alomari, E., Katib, I., Albeshri, A., Yigitcanlar, T., Mehmood, R. (2021). Iktishaf. *Sensors*, 21, 2993.
95. Trettin, C., Lăzăroiu, G., Grecu, I., Grecu, G. (2019). The social sustainability of citizen-centered urban governance networks. *Geopolitics, History and International Relations*, 11, 27–33.
96. Arshad, R., Zahoor, S., Shah, M., Wahid, A., Yu, H. (2017). Green IoT. *IEEE Access*, 5, 15667–15681.
97. Garcia-Retuerta, D., Chamoso, P., Hernández, G., Guzmán, A., Yigitcanlar, T., Corchado, J. M. (2021). An efficient management platform for developing smart cities. *Electronics*, *10*(7), 765.
98. Wang, S., Paul, M., Dredze, M. (2015). Social media as a sensor of air quality and public response in China. *Journal of Medical Internet Research*, *17*(3), e22.
99. Hayes, J., Britt, B., Evans, W., Rush, S., Towery, N., Adamson, A. (2021). Can social media listening platforms' artificial intelligence be trusted? *Journal of Advertising*, *50*(1), 81–91.
100. Gupta, V., Tripathi, S., De, S. (2020). Green sensing and communication. *Journal of the Indian Institute of Science*, 100, 383–398.
101. Gabrys, J. (2016). *Program Earth*. University of Minnesota Press.

102. Kumar, N., Rodrigues, J., Guizani, M., Choo, K., Lu, R., Verikoukis, C., Zhong, Z. (2018). Achieving energy efficiency and sustainability in edge/fog deployment. *IEEE Communications Magazine*, 56, 20–21.

103. Janbi, N., Katib, I., Albeshri, A., Mehmood, R. (2020). Distributed artificial intelligence-as-a-service for smarter IoE and 6G environments. *Sensors*, 20, 5796.

104. Mohammed, T., Albeshri, A., Katib, I., Mehmood, R. (2020). UbiPriSEQ. *Applied Sciences*, 10, 7120.

105. Latva-aho, M., Leppänen, K., Clazzer, F., Munari, A. (2020). *Key Drivers and Research Challenges for 6G Ubiquitous Wireless Intelligence*. Accessed from https://elib.dlr.de/133477.

106. Giordani, M., Polese, M., Mezzavilla, M., Rangan, S., Zorzi, M. (2020). Towards 6G networks: use cases and technologies. *IEEE Communications Magazine*, 58, 55–61.

107. Docomo, N. (2021). *5G Evolution and 6G*. Accessed from www.nttdocomo.co.jp/nglish/binary/pdf/corporate/technology/whitepaper_6g/DOCOMO_6G_White_PaperEN_v3.0.pdf.

108. Zhang, Z., Xiao, Y., Ma, Z., Xiao, M., Ding, Z., Lei, X., ... & Fan, P. (2019). 6G wireless networks. *IEEE Vehicular Technology Magazine*, 14, 28–41.

109. Letaief, K., Chen, W., Shi, Y., Zhang, J., Zhang, Y. (2019). The roadmap to 6G. *IEEE Communications Magazine*, 57, 84–90.

110. Gui, G., Liu, M., Tang, F., Kato, N., Adachi, F. (2020). 6G. *IEEE Wireless Communications*, 27, 126–132.

111. Khan, L., Yaqoob, I., Imran, M., Han, Z., Hong, C. (2020). 6G wireless systems. *IEEE Access*, 8, 147029–147044.

112. Usman, S., Mehmood, R., Katib, I., Albeshri, A., Altowaijri, S.M. (2019). ZAKI. *Mobile Networks and Applications*, https://doi.org/10.1007/s11036-019-01318-3.

113. Lauterbach, A. (2019). Artificial intelligence and policy. *Digital Policy, Regulation and Governance*, 21, 238–263.

114. Camillus, J., Baker, J., Daunt, A., Jang, J. (2020). Strategies for transcending the chaos of societal disruptions. *Vilakshan–XIMB Journal of Management*, 17, 5–14.

115. Girasa, R. (2020). *Artificial Intelligence as a Disruptive Technology*. Springer, Singapore.

116. Smuha, N. (2021). From a 'race to AI' to a 'race to AI regulation'. *Law, Innovation and Technology*, 13, 57–84.

117. Toll, D., Lindgren, I., Melin, U., Madsen, C. (2020). Values, benefits, considerations and risks of AI in government. *eJournal of eDemocracy and Open Government*, 12(1), 40–60.

118. Margetts, H., Dorobantu, C. (2019). Rethink government with AI. *Nature* 568, 163–165.

119. Jobin, A., Ienca, M., Vayena, E. (2019). The global landscape of AI ethics guidelines. *Nature Machine Intelligence*, 1, 389–399.

120. Floridi, L. (2019). Establishing the rules for building trustworthy AI. *Nature Machine Intelligence*, 1, 261–262.

121. Walch, K. (2020). *AI Laws are Coming*. Accessed from www.forbes.com/sites/cogniti veworld/2020/02/20/ai-laws-are-coming/?sh=2a12fe00a2b4.

122. Hagendorff, T. (2020). The ethics of AI ethics. *Minds and Machines*, 30, 99–120.

123. McNally, A. (2020). *Creating Trustworthy AI for the Environment*. Accessed from www.scu.edu/environmental-ethics/resources/creating-trustworthy-ai-for-the-envi ronment-transparency-bias-and-beneficial-use.

124. Leshinsky, R., Schatz, L. (2018). I don't think my landlord will find out. *Urban Policy and Research*, 36, 417–428.

125. Stein, E., Head, B. (2020). Uber in Queensland. *Australian Journal of Public Administration*, 79, 462–479.
126. de Almeida, P. G. R., dos Santos, C. D., Farias, J. S. (2021). Artificial intelligence regulation: a framework for governance. *Ethics and Information Technology*, *23*(3), 505–525.
127. Di Vaio, A., Palladino, R., Hassan, R., Escobar, O. (2020). Artificial intelligence and business models in the sustainable development goals perspective. *Journal of Business Research*, 121, 283–314.
128. Fatima, S., Desouza, K., Dawson, G., Denford, J. (2021). *Analyzing Artificial Intelligence Plans in 34 Countries*. Accessed from www.brookings.edu/blog/techtank/2021/05/13/analyzing-artificial-intelligence-plans-in-34-countries.
129. Zhou, Y., Kankanhalli, A. (2021). AI regulation for smart cities. In: *Smart Cities and Smart Governance: Towards the 22nd Century Sustainable City*. Springer.
130. Fisher, D. (2011). Computing and AI for a sustainable future. *IEEE Intelligent Systems*, *26*(6), 14–18.
131. Yigitcanlar, T., Mehmood, R., Corchado, J. (2021). Green artificial intelligence: Towards an efficient, sustainable and equitable technology for smart cities and futures. *Sustainability*, 13(16), 8952.

8 Smart Urban Mobility

8.1 Introduction

The ongoing COVID-19 pandemic has given many cities an astonishing view of the effects of private vehicle travel [1]. Road transportation is a leading cause of air pollution. Hence, as people adhered to social distancing, worked from home, and travelled less for recreational purposes, cities saw dramatic increases in air quality. In fact, as smog and haze cleared due to reduced travel, many used social media to share images of blue skies and uninterrupted views of mountains and other landmarks [2].

Nevertheless, the impact of the private vehicle does not end at air quality [3]. From an environmental perspective, transportation-related emissions are also linked to climate change, forest decline, eutrophication, and decreased soil and water quality. Furthermore, private vehicle travel contributes to urban sprawl, which leads to habitat fragmentation, wildlife loss, and problems associated with the urban heat island effect [4]. Urban sprawl also contributes to economic and social impacts including increased infrastructure costs, energy inefficiencies, unequal distribution of property values, transportation disadvantage, and social exclusion [5].

The concept of smart urban mobility has been introduced in recent years to address a broad range of needs including limiting the negative consequences of private vehicles on our cities, societies, and the environment [6]. A "smarter" transportation system is one where the environmental, economic, and social effects of mobility are balanced to produce a more sustainable transport system [7]. Hence, whereas smart urban mobility is commonly used to describe the various technological developments in the field of urban transportation, it should be considered an overarching concept that seeks to improve the urban transportation system as a whole, including land use integration [8] and sustainable infrastructure development [9].

This is an important distinction because each generation brings new innovations that could lead to "smarter" (or dumber) urban transportation outcomes. These innovations could include direct technological advances, such as the internal combustion engine (ICE), or they could involve new approaches to managing transportation, which in turn give way to new business models and ways of looking

DOI: 10.1201/9781003403630-10

at the world of transportation. These approaches could introduce new mobility stakeholders beyond the traditional public transportation operators, private vehicle owners, and manufacturers [10–11].

Transport innovations, therefore, represent one of the driving forces to achieve a sustainable transport system with other coordinated strategies—including encouraging more active, public and shared transport, telecommuting, and better use of existing road capacity—used to address key concerns such as vehicular emissions, transportation cost, travel time, congestion, safety, accessibility, and social equity [12–14]. Still, given the rapid technological advances in the transportation sector, there is a growing need to provide an overarching view of the most common smart urban mobility innovations discussed in the literature. Furthermore, given the goal of achieving a more sustainable transportation system, there is a need to evaluate these innovations against sustainability criteria and provide specific policy recommendations based on these findings.

Against this premise, the primary aim of this research is to identify and describe the various innovations in urban transport as identified in smart mobility literature. In a continuation on the sustainability theme of smart mobility, the secondary aim of the research is to evaluate the sustainability of the identified smart mobility innovations.

8.2 Methodology

For this study, a two-stage technical review and evaluation method was developed based on the two basic elements identified by Noh et al. [15] as the core components of any evaluation model. These elements involved asking two basic questions: (1) What technology do we evaluate? and (2) How do we evaluate the technology [15]?

Stage 1 of the research methodology involved searching relevant smart mobility articles to identify the primary urban transportation innovations currently being discussed in the literature. To identify these innovations a search was conducted using a library search engine with access to almost 400 academic databases. The term "smart mobility" was used to search the abstracts and titles of articles that were available online. These articles (n=292) were then filtered to remove duplicates, articles not in English, not peer-reviewed, and those without "smart mobility" as a key word.

The remaining 49 articles were then analysed to determine the main smart mobility innovations mentioned in the literature. For this stage, a conventional content analysis method was applied to derive coding categories directly from the articles consulted [16]. Firstly, Nvivo software was used to manually scan and code all transportation innovations mentioned in the selected literature. This initial list of innovations was then refined to six broad groups using a process of pattern matching and with reference similar groups and themes identified in the literature and also assisted by SAE International [97,100,106] and Perallos et al. [10]. The final categories determined from this review were: (a) intelligent transport systems; (b) driving automation systems; (c) alternative fuel systems; (d) shared mobility services; (e) demand-responsive transport; and (f) integrated mobility systems.

Stage 2 involved the actual evaluation of the sustainability of the innovations. A framework was selected based on a highly cited article [17] which identified five criteria for assessing transport sustainability: (a) safety; (b) congestion; (c) energy consumption; (d) environmental impacts; and (e) accessibility [17]. Other articles were consulted, such as [18] and [19], however, the selected framework was preferred as it included a concise package of priority, near-term impacts that could be addressed with immediate policy invention. A brief description of these indicators is provided in Table 8.1.

Based on this framework a qualitative analysis of the previously identified literature was undertaken using a directed content analysis method, where coding categories were determined based on the framework criteria [16]. Pattern matching was utilised to identify opportunities and risks associated with the five criteria for assessing transport sustainability within the selected literature—in addition to

Table 8.1 Sustainability evaluation criteria

Criteria	Description
Safety	Safety is a critical component to ensure the sustainability of a transport system. Key factors which influence the safety of a passenger transportation system include human error, vehicle, and infrastructure design and operations [17,20]
Congestion	The demand for road space is primarily influenced by the need to travel. In addition, more time spent in traffic can result in increased consumption and exacerbate environmental impacts. Similarly, it can result in increased fuel costs creating a follow-on effect that reduces transport accessibility [17]
Energy consumption	Energy consumption relates to the amount of fuel consumed per passenger. Increased energy consumption can have both economic and environmental impacts. Key factors which influence consumption include vehicle kilometres travelled (VKT) and fuel economy. Energy consumption can also have a follow-on effect resulting in environmental impacts [17]
Environment	Environment impacts in the context of transportation relate to both the direct impacts of transport (e.g. emissions), and indirect impacts (e.g. urban sprawl, loss of habitat, reduced soil quality, and climate change). Key factors with which transport impacts the environment include VKT, congestion, and energy consumption. Environmental impacts can also have a follow-on effect resulting in safety concerns associated with emissions and possible health impacts [17]
Accessibility	Accessibility refers to the ability for users to access transport. The ability to access transportation has been shown to be a contributing factor to maintain standard of living, and ensuring equitable access to employment, education, and other recreational activities. Key factors include physical accessibility, cost of transport, digital divide, and land use which could influence the spatial distribution and frequency of services [17,21]

Table 8.2 Smart mobility innovations mentioned in the literature

Smart mobility innovations	Literature
Intelligent transport systems	[12,14,21–49]
Driving automation systems	[14,21,24,26,30,33,39,44,45,48,50–56]
Alternative fuel systems	[12,21,23,26,28-30,36,44,46,47,51,52,57–60]
Shared mobility services	[12,21,26,29,30,32,33,35,38,39,44,52,54,56–58,60–63]
Demand responsive transport	[21,26,33,45,52,63–65]
Integrated mobility systems	[11,12,21,30,33,39,41,44,45,52,56,59,61–66]

relevant articles obtained using the process of backward snowballing. Opportunities were identified as factors that would increase the sustainability of the transport system, with risks identified as factors reducing sustainability. During this process additional articles were consulted to support findings and provide a contextual background to the research.

It is important to note that these criteria are based on the consequences of transport innovations and there is some overlap between the influential factors that lead to these consequences. For instance, increased VKT is likely to impact most criteria. Similarly, criteria groups also contain some significant overlaps. For instance, increased energy consumption is likely to result in more emissions and lead to increased environmental impact. In addition, increased congestion leads to increased time spent in traffic, which can in turn influence consumption—and consequently emissions and environmental impact [17]. Smart mobility innovations and relevant literature are presented in Table 8.2

8.3 Intelligent Transportation Systems

Intelligent transport systems (ITSs) utilise the latest computing, and information and communication technologies (ICT)s to improve the overall efficiency and safety of the transportation system. Originally introduced as a way of controlling traffic via route guidance [67,68] ITS also includes wider applications within public transport, private travel, shared mobility [69], advanced analytics and traffic safety [70], and smart infrastructure [71]. In fact, as interest in smart mobility has grown in sync with rapid technological advances, the use of ITS has become commonplace as cities strive to use new technology as a way of managing and developing a more holistic view of the transportation system [10,26]. ITS has been applied to a wide range of areas relating to the management, control, and operation of the transportation system. A summary of these areas is shown in Table 8.3.

Given the importance of data sharing and communication, the innovations such as 5G, Internet of Things (IoT), cloud computing, artificial intelligence (AI), blockchain, and connected and wearable devices are becoming critical, which will assist in the performance of ITS [21]. A summary of each of these supporting technologies is shown in Table 8.4.

Table 8.3 Summary of intelligent transport system areas

Area	Literature
Automatic traffic management systems	[12,26,36,72]
Automatic traffic control systems	[23,26,29,34,72]
Advanced traveller information systems	[73–76]
Public transport information systems	[42,74,77,78]
Driver assistance systems	[9,79]
Fleet management systems	[80,81]
Cooperative communication systems	[82–84]

Table 8.4 Technology to support intelligent transport systems

Technology	Literature
5G networks	[47,85]
IoT	[9,36,61,65,86,87]
Cloud computing	[47,88]
AI	[21,36,89,90]
Blockchain	[91]

8.4 Alternative Fuel Systems

Alternative fuel systems refer to a range of vehicle types which utilise fuel sources that do not necessarily rely on the use of fossil fuels [21]. Smart mobility articles generally focus on alternative fuel vehicles which operate on battery-power—electric vehicles (EV)—and use charging stations fuelled by the power grid, hydrogen, or solar energy [26,30,48,55,92].

EV are not a new technology—early prototypes were developed concurrently with ICEV—however, the recent developments in lithium-ion batteries have increased the practicality of using EV for everyday transportation needs. There are three main types of EV: "battery EV" (BEV); "hybrid EV" (HEV); and "fuel cell EV" (FCEV) [93]. A brief description of these types of vehicles is provided in Table 8.5.

Advances in battery-powered technology have also led to an increase in the use of powered micromobility devices (PMDs). PMDs are a type of vehicle used for transporting single commuters over short distances and are typically designed for off-road use (e.g. footpaths or bikeways). They are operated on battery power, or the battery is used to assist physical effort. They are quick to charge and make short distance travel easier and quicker without the need for physical effort. Their small size makes them easy to store and transfer between modes [97].

PMDs have been identified as a potential way to bridge the "first and last mile" gap between home and public transport and work. Some examples include: (a)

Table 8.5 Types of electric vehicles

Technology	Literature
Battery electric vehicles	[94]
Hybrid electric vehicles	[95,96]
Fuel cell electric vehicles	[93,96]

e-bikes; (b) powered non-self-balancing boards (e.g. e-skateboards); (c) powered self-balancing boards (e.g. segways, e-unicycles); (d) powered skates; (e) powered seated scooters, and; (f) powered standing scooters [98]. These vehicles have become a central part of the transportation strategy for many cities, to reduce private vehicle travel, particularly through the implementation of free-floating shared schemes in high-density areas [97].

8.5 Driving Automation Systems

Autonomous vehicles (AVs), also known as automated vehicles, self-driving vehicles, driverless vehicles, or robotic vehicles, refer to any vehicle—e.g. automobile, trucks, buses, trains, and drones —that can sense their environment and drive without human input for all or part of their journey [55]. These vehicles are considered one of the most cutting-edge innovations in the smart mobility realm and are representative of the substantial developments driving automation systems have made in recent years [99].

Various types of driving automation systems have been in use for several years providing some cross over with ITS and driver assistance systems such as cruise control, automatic braking, and parking assistance. To provide a distinction between fully AV and vehicles with partial automation, the Society of Automotive Engineers International (SAE) has developed a five-level classification system to measure vehicle automation levels. This classification is widely considered to have become industry standard and is often cited in academic literature [55,99,100]. The levels of automation range from Level 0 (where all tasks are controlled by the driver) to Levels 4 and 5 (where the vehicle is considered fully autonomous). The SAE five-level classification is shown in Table 8.6 [101].

Due to rapid advances and significant interest in AV, many cities throughout the world have implemented, or are in the process of implementing, pilot programs for trialling their use. Many of these trials relate to how AVs can be incorporated into the public transport system. In fact, autonomous buses trialled as part of ProjectCAVForth started carrying fare-paying customers between Fife and Edinburgh, Scotland, in 2023 [102,103]. In addition, both tech and traditional vehicle manufacturing companies are investing heavily in AVs. Some of these companies include Amazon, Audi, BMW, Mercedes-Benz, Google, Nissan, Tesla, and Uber [99]. Rapid interest in AVs from both the public and private sectors has led researchers to predict that AVs will start to become commonplace in the next

Table 8.6 SAE Level 5 classification system for autonomous vehicles

Level	Automation	Description
Driver completes most tasks with some help from automated systems		
0	Zero	All tasks are controlled by the driver
1	Assistance	Most tasks are controlled by the driver. Driver assistance systems may assist with single tasks, e.g. cruise control
2	Partial	Most tasks are controlled by the driver. Driver assistance systems may assist with one or more tasks, e.g. adaptive cruise control, or automated parking
Automated system completes most tasks with some help from driver.		
3	Conditional	All tasks are automated, but the driver must remain alert and ready to take over control of the vehicle if notified
4	High	All tasks are automated but only under certain conditions, e.g. within a defined geographic area or under certain weather conditions
5	Full	All tasks are automated in all conditions

10 to 30 years. In fact, it has been forecast that at least 50% of all vehicles will be autonomous by 2050 [92,104].

Nevertheless, the future development and implementation of Avs is likely to be reliant on parallel developments in ITS. Commonly referred to as "connected Avs" (CAVs), vehicles will be enhanced by advances in cooperative communication technology to assist with communication between vehicles, infrastructure, and broader traffic management systems [105,99]. As such, vehicles will no longer respond only to directly preceding vehicles, but also will be able to respond to preceding vehicles and broader network issues [55,104]. This will be particularly advantageous to ensure the safety and efficiency of the network in instances where AVs are required to operate in the same space as manually operated vehicles [106].

8.6 Shared Mobility Systems

Shared mobility system is a broad term used to describe a number of different transportation services where vehicles are either shared at different times (i.e. car, scooter, and bikesharing), or vehicles are shared with other riders, for all, or part, of the duration of the trip (i.e. ridesharing and ridesourcing). Shared mobility has existed in some form for many years. For example, taxis, public transport, and carpooling are all forms of ridesharing. Similarly, car or bike rental services are a form of car or bikesharing [69]. A summary shared mobility term related to passenger transportation and derived from SAE International [107] is shown in Table 8.7.

The movement towards shared mobility is being enabled by rapid advances in ITS, ICT, GPS, and the use of smart phones [29]. While the prevalence of ridesourcing, bikesharing, and scootersharing schemes has become commonplace

Table 8.7 Summary of shared mobility definitions

Terminology	Description
Alternative transport services	Shared services that include shared shuttles, microtransit (a dynamic or fixed route service that offers services on-demand and can be either publicly or privately operated) and paratransit (a form of community transport that utilises flexible route planning based on-demand to service specific disadvantaged groups). Generally, vehicles are smaller capacity than traditional public transport which facilities greater accessibility (particularly on lower order roadways) and flexibility. In the context of smart mobility and urban transport is commonly referred to as DRT [69,107,108]
Pedicabs	A type of vehicle where passengers sit in a compartment transported by a cyclist. A similar example is a rickshaw where passengers are transported by a person on-foot [107]
Personal vehicle sharing	A type of service which facilities the sharing of privately owned vehicles between consumers. Services can be shared peer-to-peer (P2P), business-to-consumer (B2C) [29], a hybrid of the two, or through fractional (or shared/pooled) ownership. Modern sharing services typically rely on users to book trips using smart phone apps that connect them with nearby drivers or available vehicles and consequently provide some overlap with ridesourcing [107,108]
Ridesharing	A formal or informal pairing of commuters with similar origins and destinations (e.g. vanpooling and carpooling). Responsibility for vehicle and driving may be shared between commuters [107]. Apps such BlaBlaCar have been developed to connect drivers with potential passengers looking for a vehicle. When offered through an app payment is typically arranged to share fuel costs with a small percentage going to the app developer [58]
Ridesourcing	A type of vehicle-sharing service that is differentiated from ridesharing in that it: (a) relies on the use of technology such as a smartphone to link up potential drivers (or passengers) on-demand [26,112]; and (b) drivers are compensated for both fuel and operational costs—like a taxi service [107,108]. However, unlike traditional taxi service many ridesourcing apps provide the option to share trips (e.g. UberPool) and cars are typically owned by the driver. The development of these schemes has been enabled by significant investment from the private sector (e.g. Uber, Lyft, and Didi) [64]
Carsharing	Carsharing services provide on-demand access to a vehicle. Carsharing services differ from traditional rental services in that users are often only charged per minute and, in the case of free-floating schemes, are not necessarily required to return the vehicle to a specific location but rather can leave the vehicle anywhere within a defined service area. Prominent companies offering these services include Streetcar, Zipcar, and DriveMyCar [61,107,109]
Scootersharing and bikesharing	Enabled by rapid advances in ICT, ITS, GPS, and the availability of PMDs these services provide on-demand access to a range of smaller vehicles—such as e-bicycles and e-scooters. They are commonly offered as pay-per-minute, free-floating schemes whereby users can pick-up and return vehicles at any location within a defined service area [61,100,107]

in large cities, the schemes continue to be identified as a potential solution to the first- and last-mile problem associated with accessing public transport and to reduce private vehicle ownership and travel [26,52,108]. As such, shared mobility is commonly identified as a central component of smart mobility and the development of smarter cities. It is hoped that moving towards a shared economy will lead to decreased private vehicle ownership and reduced VKT, consequently improving the environmental, social, and economic impacts of the transportation system [100,109].

8.7 Demand Responsive Transport

DRT, otherwise referred to as alternative transport services or on-demand services, is a type of service where vehicles can change either routes or schedules (or both) depending on user demand. DRT services generally use low-capacity vehicles such as small buses, shuttles, vans, or taxis, and charge per-passenger (as opposed to per-vehicle). Passengers are collected and returned to specific locations according to their needs [110,111].

DRT was promoted as far back as the 1970s, primarily as a replacement for low-occupancy public transport services that were not cost-effective. Initially, users would pre-book trips using the telephone with the service operators then planning routes and schedules based on the daily demand—commonly referred to as dial-a-ride. Nowadays, advances in ICT and the prevalence of smart phones mean users can book online, usually via a smart phone app, and much of the routing is automated. [111,113].

The primary advantage of DRT relates to its ability to provide greater service coverage and flexibility than regular public transport. It has been identified as a potential feeder system to connect low-density and rural areas with major public transport hubs, potentially improving the attractiveness of public transport and reducing reliance on private vehicles [111,113]. DRT either works to replace underutilised public transport systems or support these systems by providing divergent routing or schedules in less-accessible or lower occupancy areas. Areas of operation are typically defined with the range of flexibility, dependent on regional needs and resources [110]. DRT systems can be classified into four distinct areas (see Table 8.8).

Advances in ICT, ITS, and other technologies such as AI present an opportunity for DRT systems to operate more efficiently [114]. In fact, the ability to automate data collection, sharing, and analysis can significantly improve the efficiency and effectiveness of decision-making, ticketing, scheduling, and selection of vehicles [115]. These developments increase the opportunity to develop a "real-time FTS" where services can respond dynamically to user needs and increase flexibility, closer to that of the private vehicle [116]. The introduction of AVs, or "autonomous DRT" (ADRT) would also be beneficial because, without drivers, cost will be reduced and the viability of services in low-occupancy areas increased [117,118].

Table 8.8 Types of demand-responsive transport

Type	Description
Fixed route	Vehicles have fixed routes and stops along a single corridor but may only operate if there is demand [110]
Semi-fixed route	Vehicles follow a central corridor and can diverge from this route when pre-booked and within the defined service area. Fixed start, end, and intermediate stops must be met [110]
Flexible route	Vehicles either follow a central corridor or a defined service area with fixed stops at the start and/or end of the route. All other stops must be pre-booked [110]
Virtual flexible route	Vehicles have no fixed route, only a defined service area. All stops are determined by demand [110]

8.8 Integrated Mobility Systems

Integrated mobility systems utilise advances in ICT and the proliferation of smart phone technology to present multimodal transportation options to users via a single online platform or app [52]. A simple incarnation of these systems includes online journey planners that are able to plan commuter journeys across a city using a range of transport options under the control of multiple mobility providers [52,65]. More advanced versions may integrate ticketing systems or harness the power of ITS to monitor transport conditions, manage demand accordingly [30] and provide real-time information to customers regarding delays, traffic, patronage, parking, weather, and other relevant information [12,43].

Commonly referred to as mobility-as-a-service (MaaS) [44,63,64] the purpose of these systems is to provide seamless multi-modal integration and increase accessibility to transport modes other than PMVs [61]. They represent a way of providing a seamless travel experience to commuters by offering a wide range of shared transportation modes—including public transport—via a single online interface or app [12,59,61]. The primary purpose being to make accessing modes other than PMVs easier by combining journey planning, vehicle selection, ticketing, and payment [33]. Critical to the success of these systems is the ability, and desire, for mobility providers to share data [11].

MaaS is like DRT as users can book journeys on-demand, however, unlike DRT, users have access to a wider range of transportation options and can subscribe similarly to a streaming service like Netflix [52]—however pay-as-you-go or pre-pay options should still be permitted [119]. Given the centralised nature of the MaaS system, there is also the opportunity for MaaS operators to collect precise details on user behaviour and preferences that can be used to further improve services. Furthermore, given that MaaS could control large fleets of vehicles, there is also the opportunity to introduce mass innovations including ITS, EVs, and AVs into the market, or promote more sustainable modes—such as active or public transport [120,121].

8.9 Sustainability Evaluation

The following section evaluates the six identified smart mobility innovations against five sustainability evaluation criteria: (a) safety; (b) congestion; (c) energy consumption; (d) environmental impact; and (e) accessibility [17]. A summary of the findings is provided in Table 8.9.

8.9.1 Safety

When looking at the safety of the transportation system, the primary opportunities of smart urban mobility innovations relate to: (a) improvements in the way transport systems are able to monitor and respond to incidents; and (b) improvements in in-vehicle assistance systems which can remove driver distraction and reduce human error. However, there are risks associated with: (a) risk to data privacy and cybercrime; and (b) automated decision-making in AVs.

Firstly, ITS can be used to monitor the transport system for accidents and other obstacles and adjust the system to address these issues. This can have a positive effect on the safety of vehicles manoeuvring around these obstacles, and the safety of vehicles and individuals involved in or near accidents [22,36,88]. Furthermore, the real-time distribution of traffic and transport system data can ensure the efficient distribution of information related to transport incidents to the closest and most suitable respondent—i.e. police, ambulance, fire, etc. [29]. Similarly, licence plate detection can be used to ensure unlicensed or prohibited drivers are identified and potentially unsafe drivers removed from roads [29].

Secondly, from an in-vehicle perspective, use of ITS components such as voice activation could reduce possible distractions associated with operating smart devices and other car appliances and therefore lead to fewer accidents [50]. Furthermore, driver assistance systems, particularly in AVs, have been shown to reduce the risk of driver error by improving perception of the environment and automating many tasks previously reliant on human drivers [21,42]. Together with improved merging, platooning, vehicle dispersion, lane changing, and lane keeping this could lead to a reduction of accidents [47,55,98]. In fact, researchers have calculated that Avs have the potential to reduce vehicle accidents by 80–90% [98,115].

Considering 3,000 people die and 30,000 people are injured on roads every day [122], a total reduction in the amount of accidents would provide significant alleviation of a major public health issue [12]. Furthermore, from an economic perspective some calculations show that accident reduction of AVs could result in economic benefits of over US$1,000 per vehicle, per year. When factoring other costs, including those associated with insurance, congestion, and parking, the economic benefit could be as high as US$3,000–4,000 per vehicle, per year [112].

However, smart mobility innovations also bring safety concerns. Most of the systems discussed in this chapter rely on ICT, smart phones, and other personal devices for operation. This brings issues related to cyberterrorism, grid failure, faulty or bias data, and information security—including the tracking of individuals and fleets, and loss or theft of personal information [21,52]. These concerns may

Table 8.9 Summary of sustainability evaluation of smart mobility

Criteria	Opportunities	Constraints
Safety	(+) Redirects traffic flow around incidents (+) Improves response to incidents (+) Improves identification of prohibited and unsafe drivers (+) Reduces accident risk associated with driver distraction (+) Reduces accident risk associated with human error (+) Door-to-door transport could reduce risk of street crime	(−) Increases risks related to cyberterrorism, grid failure, faulty and bias data (−) Increases risks associated with data security and theft of personal information (−) Poses risks associated with unethical decision-making in automated systems (−) Could increase exposure to criminal activity and transmittable diseases on shared transport
Congestion	(+) Improves traffic flow in response to incidents (+) Improves traffic flow due to adaptive journey planning and increasing availability of modes (+) Reduces number of vehicles per passenger (+) Improves road capacity due to more efficient operation of vehicless	(−) Increases number of vehicles due to preference for lower occupancy vehicles (−) Increases number of vehicles due to improved accessibility (−) Decreases road capacity due to more pick-up and drop-off areas
Energy consumption	(+) Improves efficiency of vehicles due to smoother traffic flow, driving automation and battery electric vehicles (+) Promotes use of sustainable transport through integrated systems	(−) Continues use of fossil fuels (−) Increases VKT resulting in more consumption (−) Inability to manage grid capacity effectively
Environment	(+) Reduces GHG emissions due to more efficient traffic flow and vehicle operation (+) Reduces GHG emissions due to more efficient use of vehicles (+) Reduces direct vehicular emissions due to use of alternative fuels (+) Increases land availability and reduced road capacity and parking demand	(−) Increases demand for smart infrastructure (−) Increases urban sprawl due to longer travel distances and preference for suburban living
Accessibility	(+) Improves physical access by better matching vehicles with user needs (+) Improves physical access and ability to drive independently via driving automation systems (+) Simplifying user's ability to connect to a wide range of transport providers (+) Reduces transportation costs (+) Improves coverage and flexibility of services using shared modes, DRT, and integrating mobility	(−) Inability to access services due to digital divide (−) High upfront costs may create social equity issues (−) Need for subsidies in areas with low occupancy or long travel distances (−) Changing land use resulting in reduced job accessibility

discourage new users from using smart mobility [26,61], particularly where online payment is required [119]. It is therefore important to maintain a secure wireless network [36] with particular focus on the privacy and anonymisation of personal data [26].

In addition, AVs will also be required to make complicated, often split-second, decisions regarding safety of pedestrians, occupants, and other road users [123]. Furthermore, there are concerns that system failure in AVs [99], and operation of PMDs in spaces shared with pedestrians [97] could lead to accidents or other incidents resulting in physical harm. Ethical guidelines and regulations are therefore essential to ensure that decision-making best represents societal values and potential impacts of vehicles are minimised [55,99].

Finally, though not specifically discussed within the literature selected for this study, there could be additional safety benefits associated with DRT, shared mobility, and other door-to-door services particularly at night, in areas with high crime rates, and where public transport is not readily accessible or has low occupancy rates [124]. Conversely, while ITS systems can be used to improve surveillance and response rates, sharing space with other users opens legitimate safety concerns associated with exposure to crime or transmission of disease (e.g., COVID-19) [125,126].

8.9.2 Congestion

When looking at issues related to congestion, the primary opportunities of smart urban mobility innovations relate to: (a) improvements in the way transport systems are able to respond to incidents and redirect traffic; (b) promotion of shared mobility as a way to reduce number of vehicles per passenger; and (c) the operational improvements leading to increased road capacity. However, there are risks associated with: (a) potential increase in vehicles due to the preference for lower occupancy vehicles; (b) decreased road capacity due to increased requirement for pick-up and drop-off stops; and (c) increased number of vehicles due to improved accessibility, increased value of time, and more instances of dead runs.

Firstly, through connected infrastructure and systems which utilise roadside surveillance sensors and smart devices, vehicles, users, and traffic management systems could use available data to make better real-time decisions based on a much broader analysis of the transport network [34,36,40]. This could have significant impacts and contribute to a more efficient operation of the system, particularly where traffic flow is improved by redirecting traffic to more accessible routes, configuring traffic lights [27,43,88,104], prioritising public transport [23], or redirecting cyclists to quicker routes [62]. Similarly, integrated mobility systems such as MaaS can use congestion monitoring to recommend different modes based on user or system needs [119].

Secondly, the move towards shared mobility means that on average there could be more passengers per vehicle, or in the case of systems that promote PMDs or active transport, less commuters on roadways. In fact, some research suggests that for every shared vehicle around 10–15 PMVs could be replaced [39]. Fewer vehicles per passenger would improve road congestion based on the assumption that there would be less vehicles on the road [39]. However, an increase in shared mobility—such low-capacity minibuses or ridesourcing—may encourage a move away from high-capacity public transport and result in a total VKT increase which in turn could result in more vehicles and greater congestion issues [40]. Similarly, shared modes would require more road space for pick-up and drop-off areas, further impacting road capacity [26].

Thirdly, improved operation associated with driver assistance and driving automation systems can result in freeing up of road capacity, as cars may be able to drive closer together and require less space to safely manoeuvre [98]. Similarly, the use of autonomous drones for point-to-point passenger transportation would further increase road capacity [123]—though the use of drones is likely to bring further regulatory issues surrounding air safety, the safety of occupants, and potential impact of accidents on the ground [124,127].

Nevertheless, there is also a risk that AVs will increase congestion. The ability to automate the operation of single-occupancy vehicles means that those who were previously unable to drive now have access to a vehicle—leading to increased vehicles on the road and therefore increased congestion [55,105,128]. Combined with an increase in dead-runs where vehicles operate without a human occupant [112] and increased travel distances due to increased value of time and the ability to complete other tasks while driving [99], there is a possibility that AVs would actually exacerbate issues associated with traffic congestion.

8.9.3 Energy Consumption

When looking at issues related to energy consumption, the primary opportunities of smart urban mobility innovations relate to: (a) improved efficiency resulting from better traffic flow; (b) improve efficiency resulting from automation of vehicle operation; (c) improved efficiency of alternative fuel engines; and (d) the use of integrated systems to promote sustainable transport. However, there are risks associated with: (a) continued use of fossil fuels; (b) increasing VKT; and (c) managing grid capacity.

Firstly, reducing congestion using smart mobility innovations would increase fuel efficiency for most vehicles by enabling a smoother flow of traffic with increased average travel speeds, and less braking [26,36,43]. In addition, other ITS initiatives such as providing drivers with real-time information regarding fuel efficiency, implementing variable speed limits depending on traffic conditions, and congestion charging has been shown to reduce fuel consumption by 2.9%, 2%, and 14%, respectively [26].

Secondly, when analysing the operation of vehicles, driving automation systems are also able to improve fuel efficiency by controlling acceleration and braking. In fact, modelling of AVs has shown that energy consumption could be reduced by up to 45% when a full fleet shift towards AVs has occurred [99]. Nonetheless, the advantages of this improved efficiency are unlikely to be realised if AVs result in increased VKT. In fact, when factoring in dramatic VKT increases as a result of improved accessibility and increased number of trips (including unmanned trips associated with self-parking, fuelling, and dead-runs between customers) some estimates suggest energy use could increase by up to 300% [111]. A move towards SAV fleets would help keep VKT low, with some modelling showing an 80% reduction in energy use—particularly where enabled by ITS to automate ridesharing and reduce the instances of dead-runs [112].

Thirdly, despite the energy gains resulting from operational adjustments to ICEV, researchers argue that critical for long-term improvements in emission levels is the prevalence of alternative fuel systems such as BEV [105]. Even when factoring electric grids that are powered by coal, BEV have been shown to be more energy efficient than ICEV [100,105]. Nevertheless, there are issues associated with maintaining grid capacity—especially with regards to mass charging of vehicles and in low-density and rural areas where transmission distances are longer, and infrastructure may be lacking [21]. Shared fleets, and integrated systems, can help as charging can be staggered to avoid overloading the electrical network [128], as can investments in decentralised solar-generated charging stations [48,99]. Conversely, when factoring a fully decarbonised grid and full EV fleet some predictions suggest up to 70% reductions in GHG when factoring in both the transportation and the electrical generation sector [92].

Finally, integrated mobility systems such as MaaS can be used to provide incentives such as free public transport or promote more sustainable transport means—such as shared or active transport [26,41,64]. This could lead to users favouring active transport means such as walking and bicycles for shorter trips and lead to cultural shifts—particularly in areas with an ingrained culture associated with private vehicle ownership. Even when not fully replacing PMVs in urban networks, MaaS has been identified as a potential replacement for households' second vehicles [64].

8.9.4 Environmental Impact

When looking at the environmental impacts of smart mobility innovations it is important to note the significant overlaps between the previously discussed criteria. Firstly, increased road congestion can lead to increased energy consumption, which in turn can result in increased environmental impact through direct vehicular emissions. Similarly, increased road consumption places increased demand on road space, resulting in increased demand for land allocated for transport uses including parking. Furthermore, improvement in the efficiency of vehicles, as discussed in the previous section, is likely to have a follow-on effect resulting in reduced emissions (whether direct vehicular emissions, or those resulting from the electrical grid), and potential reduction of fossil fuel consumption even in cases where the primary source of power is non-renewable.

Given these overlaps, the primary opportunities relating to smart urban mobility's environmental impact are: (a) reduced emissions and (b) increased land availability as a result of improved road capacity and reduced parking. Nonetheless, there are also risks associated with: (a) infrastructure requirements for ICT and (b) increased urban sprawl as a result of longer travel distances.

Firstly, as previously discussed, improvements in energy consumption—whether through improving traffic flow and congestion, improving efficiency of vehicles, or promoting sustainability transport—will likely result in vehicles producing less GHG emissions [43]. Given that transportation accounts for around one-third of all GHGs in developed and 80% in developing countries [14,29], even small improvements associated with VKT and vehicle efficiency are likely to have significant environmental impacts and contribute to improved climate change mitigation efforts [26]. Smaller vehicles used in DRT systems will also contribute and are likely to have lower emissions than greater public transport, particularly at times when occupancy is low [115]. Furthermore, increased use of BEVs and FCEVs will have significant environmental and health benefits as neither of these vehicles emit ozone precursors (such as nitrogen oxide or volatile organic compounds) nor do they emit particulate matter which is linked to respiratory illness [112].

Nevertheless, given that most smart mobility innovations will require access to ICT, alternative fuel systems require charging stations, and use of active transport and PMDs is likely to rely on access to good-quality infrastructure, there is likely to be an initial environmental impact associated with building, establishing, and powering the required infrastructure to support smart mobility innovations [40,48,58]. This is important because, given the advantage of smart mobility, poor access to the required infrastructure could be a major barrier to its adoption [26,29].

Secondly, redesign of road spaces due to less demand and redistribution of parking spaces is likely to have a significant impact on urban areas. Road networks occupy around 25–35% of total land in urban areas with on-road parking spaces accounting for a significant portion of this space [55]. ITS systems have the potential to improve the efficiency of parking by managing supply and demand more effectively [36,40]. This could help drivers find parking spaces easier and reduce VKT associated with cruising for spaces—further reducing congestion and emission levels [26]. Furthermore, with shared mobility and Avs, the requirements for parking are likely to be significantly reduced—particularly in the case of SAVs where some modelling predicts a reduction of around 90% [99,128]. Reduced parking demand, in addition to reduced requirements for infrastructure such as petrol stations, is likely to free up large amounts of land for other uses. In growing cities, newly available land could be used to manage population growth through infill development, or alternatively provide opportunities for other community-based development—such as recreation spaces, increased cycling and walking infrastructure, or collection points for online shopping [55,105].

Lastly, given that AVs could encourage long travel distances, commuters may be drawn to rural and suburban areas for lifestyle and economic reasons, leading to increased development in urban fringe and rural areas [55,105]. Furthermore, increased ownership of AVs could also lead to increased demand for parking [55]. Therefore, land use policies to promote transit-oriented and infill development remain an important component of any future smart mobility solutions [26,105].

8.9.5 Accessibility

When looking at issues related to accessibility, the primary opportunities related to smart urban mobility innovations include: (a) improved physical access to vehicle; (b) reduced transportation costs; (c) improving coverage and flexibility of services; and (d) improved accessibility to employment and services. However, there are risks associated with: (a) inability to access service due to digital divide; (b) high upfront costs associated with new technology; (c) need to subsidise areas with low occupancy rates; and (d) reduced job accessibility and increased commuting time.

Firstly, smart mobility innovations are likely to improve accessibility for those people who are unable to operate a vehicle or physically access certain vehicles. Integrated mobility systems such as MaaS can help by linking users with vehicles specific to their need and providing more opportunities for door-to-door transport using dynamic route services and other shared mobility modes [21]. In addition, the use of driving automation systems will allow users who previously were not able to operate a vehicle the chance to travel independently, thus improving freedom of movement and increasing opportunities and access to essential services [55,99,112].

However, given the reliance on ICT and smart technology there is a risk that some users will be excluded due to issues associated with the digital divide [21,52]. The digital divide is related to the barriers associated with accessing and using ICT and not only includes the spatial distribution of infrastructure but also the fact that many individuals with less experience with smart devices may struggle to access the services which rely on them [21,61,116]. Simplifying the process for accessing various transport modes through integrated mobility systems can help reduce this complexity [21].

Secondly, smart mobility innovations that aim to replace PMVs are likely to reduce total transportation costs [21]. Cost savings associated with more efficient system operation, including reduced costs associated with AVs and the lack of a human driver could be passed on to customers and could be used to promote shared and integrated mobility systems over PMVs [21,99]. Furthermore, when replacing PMV ownership with shared modes there are significant cost reductions associated with the purchase of the vehicle, fuel costs, insurance, and storage [21,99]. In fact, some research has shown that in comparison to PMVs, SAVs are likely to reduce total costs by 80% [100].

Yet, initial upfront costs may exclude certain members of the community from accessing new technology—creating socioeconomic disparities between those who can access the benefits of new innovations, and those who cannot [3,61]. For example, while electric vehicles are currently available and many urban areas contain the required infrastructure for charging, the cost of the vehicles remains so high that only a very low percentage of urban fleets contain this technology [57]. These issues could therefore further exacerbate tensions associated with transport disadvantage, further entrenching existing inequalities in service provision [61,29].

Thirdly, there is potential to utilise the benefits of shared mobility, DRT, and integrated mobility to better fill the gaps in existing public transport networks—thus improving the coverage of public transport in low-density and rural areas [115]. Mobility services which integrate on-demand service providers, ridesourcing apps, vehicle sharing, and more traditional services such as taxis and community transport can utilise ITS and other technology to better match supply and demand and match users to available transport providers. These systems can then act as a feeder to major public transport nodes, a solution which may be more economical than establishing the required fixed-route public transport infrastructure in areas which may have low demand for such services [21,119].

Nonetheless, areas with low occupancy rates, that are further from public transport nodes, or those with less access to a wide range of transport modes, are likely to require significant government subsidies to ensure equal access of services [21]. While SAVs will help with reduced costs [112] cross subsidisation may also be useful to use profits in high-occupancy areas to subsidise equal access to services in low-occupancy areas [21].

Finally, improving transport accessibility, whether by increasing physical access, reducing costs, or improving coverage or services, is likely to improve accessibility to employment and other services, particularly for those living in low-density residential and rural communities [21,99]. From an employment perspective, and notwithstanding the significant impact AVs will likely have on employment demand [130,131], some single-mode innovation could improve the ability for commuters to travel longer distances, thus giving better access to employment opportunities.

Nevertheless, while the literature discusses the risk of urban sprawl as a result of increased travel distance [26,55,104], there is also a risk that employers could take advantage of this and relocate their business to lower cost land on the outskirts of cities. This is likely to further exclude those who are unable to access or afford the required travel modes or travel long distances [55]. Furthermore, even in AVs where the ability to complete other tasks while driving has added benefits such as productivity and more recreational and relaxation time [55,99], increasing commuting time will result in more time away from home, potentially impacting families and households and resulting in increased congestion, with follow-on effects associated with increased energy consumption and environmental impacts.

8.10 Policy Recommendations

Based on this review, the following policy recommendations relevant to the implementation of smart urban mobility have been identified (Figure 8.1).

Establish communication networks: As smart urban mobility becomes increasingly reliant on ICT and the use of smart devices, it is critical for decision-makers to invest in high-speed communication networks to ensure adequate coverage over all areas where transportation services are required. Furthermore, decision-makers should look to 5G networks to establish high-speed internet in rural and remote areas to ensure social equity issues associated with accessing the new transportation technology are not further exacerbated by geographical disadvantage. Establishing

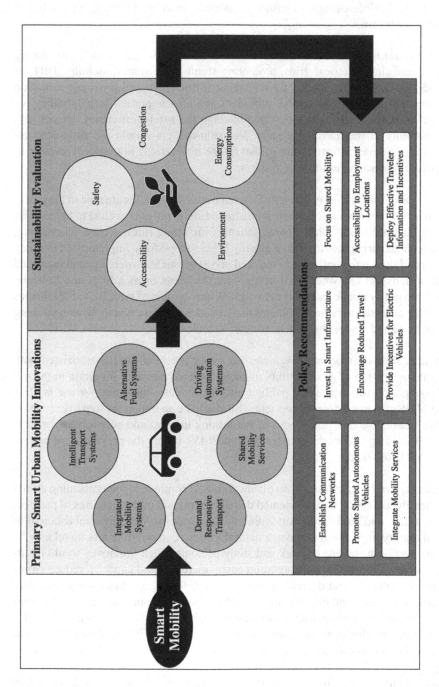

Figure 8.1 Policy recommendations for smart urban mobility innovations.

security standards is paramount to ensure the safety of these networks. Standards should be flexible enough to ensure measures can adapt to changing needs and maintain user trust.

Invest in smart infrastructure: Whether maintaining the status quo, introducing AVs, managing electrical grids, promoting stand-alone shared mobility, DRT, or MaaS, the advantages of ITS for managing traffic flow, and providing real-time information to users and service providers, remains important to help policy- or decision-makers monitor, control, and manage the safety, efficiency, impact, and accessibility of the transport system. Decision-makers should therefore consider investing in smart infrastructure so that future innovations in transport are able to harness the advantages of these systems.

Focus on shared mobility: given that shared mobility vehicles are able to maximise the use of limited resources, their implementation in cities is critical to the success of any smart mobility plan. Shared schemes including ridesourcing, bikesharing, and scootersharing schemes have already been successfully implemented in many cities and shown to contribute to reduced private vehicle ownership, and increased public transport use when used in high-density areas or as a first- and last-mile feeder to major public transport networks. When combined with BEV, ST schemes have the potential to reduce problems associated with grid capacity by encouraging large fleets and staggering the charging of vehicles.

Promote shared autonomous vehicles: to avoid potential pitfalls associated with private ownership of Avs, mobility managers should consider investing in the use of automation for shared and public transport modes—including for use in DRT and MaaS systems where appropriate. This could be an important step to encourage more sustainable transport modes by harnessing the cost and accessibility benefits of AVs, leading to a modal shift away from PMVs before the prevalence of private AVs has taken hold.

Encourage reduced travel: Urban planners should continue to focus planning efforts on density, diversity, transit-oriented development, and other measures to promote more active and public transport within the community. With the establishment of good-quality high-speed internet, a natural initiative to promote less travel may be to encourage those able to work and study at home. Such initiatives would naturally decrease individual transportation costs, increase road capacity, reduce environmental impacts, and decrease geographic disadvantage—particularly regarding access to employment opportunities. Furthermore, risks such as exposure to criminal activity and transmission of disease on public and shared transport will also be minimised. Residents will have more time to spend with family and friends or engage in other recreational activities.

Accessibility to employment locations: Critical to encourage reduced travel and improve social equity is to ensure accessibility to employment remains a high priority. Commercial, industry, and other business opportunities should be encouraged, through appropriate land use inventions, to be located as close as possible to major public transport hubs. This further reinforces the need for well-planned transit-oriented development solutions that do not only focus on residential interests.

Integrated mobility services: Integrated mobility systems such as MaaS should be explored as a way to simplify the ability for users to access and pay for various mobility options. The focus of these schemes should be on providing a range of modes so that users can explore options relative to their needs and circumstances. Access and use of the platforms should be kept as simple and intuitive as possible to reduce issues associated with the digital divide. As such, decision-makers may need to take measures to reduce consumer confusion by restricting the development of competing integrated mobility services and ensuring mobility providers have equal access to the service.

Provide incentives for electric vehicles: as demonstrated in this review, EVs, whether BEVs or FCEVs, generally operate more efficiently than ICEVs. Measures should therefore be put in place to provide incentives for individuals and companies looking to make the move to EVs. This could come in the form of tax incentives, free public charging facilities, or funding of charging infrastructure to improve the coverage of these vehicles.

Deploy effective traveller information and incentives: transport system performance is highly dependent on travellers' decision, which can be influenced by a combination of information and incentives to guide or improve performance. There are many travel information strategies and incentives that combined can significantly contribute to directing the traffic system towards less congestion, emissions, energy consumption, crashes, and other negative externalities.

8.11 Conclusion

This technology review and evaluation chapter has analysed primary transportation innovations associated with smart urban mobility and evaluated the opportunities and risks associated with their impact on the sustainability of transport. Smart mobility is of growing interest in academic literature as researchers look for ways to use the latest innovations in transportation to improve the sustainability of cities and reduce the effects of private vehicle travel. Based on the findings of this review, nine policy recommendations have been proposed to guide and assist decision-makers to manage the implementation of smart urban mobility innovations.

Given the fast-paced nature of these technological changes, further research should continue to analyse the effects of smart urban mobility innovations on urban areas, including further refinement of transport modelling, understanding consumer preferences, policy barriers, and the implementation and analysis of pilot programmes and trials [132].

Acknowledgements

This chapter, with permission from the copyright holder, is a reproduced version of the following journal article: Yigitcanlar, T., Mehmood, R., & Corchado, J. (2021). Green artificial intelligence: Towards an efficient, sustainable and equitable technology for smart cities and futures. *Sustainability*, 13(16), 8952.

References

1. Lai, K. Y., Webster, C., Kumari, S., and Sarkar, C. (2020) The nature of cities and the Covid-19 pandemic. *Current Opinion in Environmental Sustainability*, 46, 27–31.
2. Cohan, D. (2020) COVID-19 shutdowns are clearing the air, but pollution will return as economies reopen. *The Conversation*, 8 May 2020, Available: https://theconversation.com/covid-19-shutdowns-are-clearing-the-air-but-pollution-will-return-as-economies-reopen-134610.
3. Kamruzzaman, M., Hine, J., and Yigitcanlar, T. (2015) Investigating the link between carbon dioxide emissions and transport-related social exclusion in rural Northern Ireland. *International Journal of Environmental Science and Technology*, 12(11): 3463–3478.
4. Kamruzzaman, M., Deilami, K., and Yigitcanlar, T. (2018) Investigating the urban heat island effect of transit-oriented development in Brisbane. *Journal of Transport Geography*, 66: 116–124.
5. Yigitcanlar, T. (2016) *Technology and the City*. London, UK: Routledge.
6. Golbabaei, F., Yigitcanlar, T., and Bunker, J. (2021) The role of shared autonomous vehicle systems in delivering smart urban mobility: A systematic review of the literature. *International Journal of Sustainable Transportation*, 15(10), 731–748.
7. Paz, A., Maheshwari, P., Kachroo, P., and Ahmad, S. (2013) Estimation of performance indices for the planning of sustainable transportation systems. *Advances in Fuzzy Systems*, 2013: 601468.
8. Dur, F., and Yigitcanlar, T. (2015) Assessing land-use and transport integration via a spatial composite indexing model. *International Journal of Environmental Science and Technology*, 12(3): 803–816.
9. Yigitcanlar, T. (2010) *Sustainable Urban and Regional Infrastructure*. Hershey, PA.: Information Science Reference.
10. Perallos, A., Henandez-Jayo, U., Onieva, E., and Zuazola, I. (2015) Foreword. In: *Intelligent Transport Systems*, A. Perallos (ed.) West Sussex, UK: Wiley.
11. Lenz, A., and Heinrichs, D. (2017) What can we learn from smart urban mobility technologies? *IEEE Pervasive Computing*, 16(2): 84–86.
12. Tomaszewska, E.J., and Florea, A. (2018) Urban smart mobility in the scientific literature. *Engineering Management in Production and Services*, 10(2): 41–56.
13. Papa, R., Gargiulo, C., and Russo, L. (2017) The evolution of smart mobility strategies and behaviors to build the smart city. In: *5th IEEE International Conference on Models and Technologies for Intelligent Transportation Systems*. Naples, Italy, pp. 409–414.
14. Yigitcanlar, T., and Kamruzzaman, M. (2019) Smart cities and mobility. *Journal of Urban Technology*, 26(2): 21–46.
15. Hsieh, H., and Shannon, S. (2018) Content analysis. In: *The SAGE Ecyclopedia of Educational Research, Measurement, and Evaluation*. B. Fray (ed.) Thousand Oaks, CA: Sage.

16. Noh, H., Seo, J., Sun Yoo, H., and Lee, S. (2018) How to improve a technology evaluation model. *Technovation*, 72–73: 1–12.

17. Richardson, B. (2018) Sustainable transport. *Journal of Transport Geography*, 13(1): 29–39.

18. Chakhtoura, C., and Pojani, D. (2016) Indicator-based evaluation of sustainable transport plans. *Transport Policy*, 50: 15–28.

19. Toth-Szabo, Z., and Várhelyi, A. (2012) Indicator framework for measuring sustainability of transport in the city. *Procedia–Social and Behavioral Sciences*, 48: 2035–2047.

20. Arteaga, C., Paz, A., and Park, J. (2020) Injury severity on traffic crashes: A text mining with an interpretable machine-learning approach. *Safety Science*, 132, 104988.

21. Butler, L., Yigitcanlar, T., and Paz, A. (2020) How can smart mobility innovations alleviate transportation disadvantage? *Applied Sciences*, 10(18): 6306.

22. Stolfi, D., and Alba, E. (2014) Red Swarm: Reducing travel times in smart cities by using bio-inspired algorithms. *Applied Soft Computing*, 24: 181–195.

23. Losa, M., Pratelli, A., and Riccardi, C. (2014) The integration of buses with a high level of service in the medium cities urban context. *WIT Transactions on the Built Environment*, 138.

24. Saponara, S., and Neri, B. (2016) Design of compact and low-power X-band Radar for mobility surveillance applications. *Computers & Electrical Engineering*, 56; 46–63.

25. Musakwa, W., and Selala, K. (2016) Mapping cycling patterns and trends using Strava Metro data in the city of Johannesburg, South Africa. *Data in Brief*, 9: 898–905.

26. Chen, Y., Ardila-Gomez, A., and Frame, G. (2017) Achieving energy savings by intelligent transportation systems investments in the context of smart cities. *Transportation Research Part D*, 54: 381–396.

27. Melo, S., Macedo, J., and Baptista, P. (2017) Guiding cities to pursue a smart mobility paradigm. *Research in Transportation Economics*, 65: 24–33.

28. Balint, A. (2017) The concept of smart mobility. *Contemporary Readings in Law and Social Justice*, 9(2): 281–286.

29. Cledou, G., Estevez, E., and Soares Barbosa, L. (2018) A taxonomy for planning and designing smart mobility services. *Government Information Quarterly*, 35(1): 61–76.

30. Noy, K., and Givoni, M. (2018) Is 'smart mobility' sustainable? *Sustainability*, 10(2): 422.

31. Lopez-Carreiro and Monzon, A. (2018) Evaluating sustainability and innovation of mobility patterns in Spanish cities. *Sustainable Cities and Society*, 38: 684–696.

32. Toutouh, J., Arellano, J., and Alba, E. (2018) BiPred. *Sensors*, 18(12).

33. Manders, T., Wieczorek, A., and Verbong, G. (2018) Understanding smart mobility experiments in the Dutch automobility system. *Futures*, 96: 90–103.

34. Lucian, M., Ilie, D., and Laurentiu, R. (2018) Smart signalization and public transport priority. *Applied Mechanics and Materials*, 880: 383–388.

35. Orlowski A., and Romanowska, P., (2019) Smart cities concept. *Cybernetics and Systems*, 50(2): 118–131.

36. Ho, G., Tsang, Y., Wu, C., Wong, W., and Choy, K. (2019) A computer vision-based roadside occupation surveillance system for intelligent transport in smart cities. *Sensors*, 19(8): 1796.

37. Fryszman, F., Carstens, D., and Da Cunha, S. (2019) Smart mobility transition. *International Journal of Urban Sustainable Development*, 11(2): 141–153.

38. Warnecke, D., Wittstock, R., and Teuteberg, F. (2019) Benchmarking of European smart cities. *Sustainability Accounting, Management and Policy Journal*, 10(4): 654–684.

39. Manders T., and Klaassen, E. (2019) Unpacking the smart mobility concept in the Dutch context based on a text mining approach. *Sustainability*, 11(23): 6583.
40. Peprah, C., Amponsah, O., and Oduro, C. (2019) A system view of smart mobility and its implications for Ghanaian cities. *Sustainable Cities and Society*, 44: 739–747.
41. Turetken, O., Grefen, P., and Gilsing, R. (2019) Service-dominant business model design for digital innovation in smart mobility. *Business & Information Systems Engineering*, 61(1): 9–29.
42. Mauri, A., et al., (2020) Deep learning for real-time 3D multi-object detection, localisation, and tracking. *Sensors*, 20: 532.
43. Villagra, A., Alba, E., and Luque, G., (2020) A better understanding on traffic light scheduling: New cellular GAs and new in-depth analysis of solutions. *Journal of Computational Science*, 41, 101085.
44. Manders, T., Cox, R., Wieczorek, A., and Verbong, G. (2020) The ultimate smart mobility combination for sustainable transport? A case study on shared electric automated mobility initiatives in the Netherlands. *Transportation Research Interdisciplinary Perspectives*, 5, 100129.
45. Mukhtar-Landgren, D., and Paulsson, A. (2020) Governing smart mobility: Policy instrumentation, technological utopianism, and the administrative quest for knowledge. *Administrative Theory & Praxis*, 43(2), 135–153.
46. Luque-Vega, L., Carlos-Mancilla, M., Payán-Quiñónez, V., and Lopez-Neri, E. (2020) Smart cities oriented project planning and evaluation methodology driven by citizen perception. *Sustainability*, 12: 7088.
47. Peralta, G., Garrido, P., Bilbao, J., Agüero, R., and Crespo, P. (2020) Fog to cloud and network coded based architecture. *Simulation Modelling Practice and Theory*, 101.
48. Zhao, D., Thakur, N., and Chen, J. (2020) Optimal design of energy storage system to buffer charging infrastructure in smart cities. *Journal of Management in Engineering*, 36(2), 04019048.
49. Paz A., and Chiu, Y. (2011) Adaptive traffic control for large-scale dynamic traffic assignment applications. *Transportation Research Record*, 2263: 103–112.
50. Fukui, M., Watanabe, T., and Kanazawa, M. (2018) Sound source separation for plural passenger speech recognition in smart mobility system. *IEEE Transactions on Consumer Electronics*, 64(3): 399–405.
51. Tung, V., Cheong, T., and To, S. (2019) Tourism management in the era of smart mobility. *Tourism Review*, 75(1): 283–285.
52. Golub, A., Satterfield, V., Serritella, M., Singh, J., and Phillips, S. (2019) Assessing the barriers to equity in smart mobility systems. *Case Studies on Transport Policy*, 7(4): 689–697.
53. Putnam, D., Kovacova, M., Valaskova, K., and Stehel, V. (2019) The algorithmic governance of smart mobility. *Contemporary Readings in Law and Social Justice*, 11(1): 21–26.
54. Chen, C. (2019) Factors affecting the decision to use autonomous shuttle services. *Transportation Research Part F*, 67: 195–204.
55. Yigitcanlar, T., Wilson, M., and Kamruzzaman, M. (2019) Disruptive impacts of automated driving systems on the built environment and land use. *Journal of Open Innovation*, 5(2): 24.
56. van Oers, L., de Hoop, E., Jolivet, E., Marvin, S., Späth, P., and Raven, R. (2020) The politics of smart expectations: Interrogating the knowledge claims of smart mobility. *Futures*, 122, 102604.

57. Pinna, F., Masala, F., and Garau, C. (2017) Urban policies and mobility trends in Italian smart cities. *Sustainability*, 9(4): 494.
58. Dell'Era, A., Altuna, N., and Verganti, R. (2018) Designing radical innovations of meanings for society. *Creativity and Innovation Management*, 27(4): 387–400.
59. Del Vecchio, P., Secundo, G., Maruccia, Y., and Passiante, G. (2019) A system dynamic approach for the smart mobility of people: Implications in the age of big data. *Technological Forecasting and Social Change*, *149*, 119771.
60. Corradini, F., De Angelis, F., Polini, A., Castagnari, C., de Berardinis, J., and Forcina, G. (2020) Tangramob: an agent-based simulation framework for validating urban smart mobility solutions. *Journal of Intelligent Systems*, 29(1): 1188–1201.
61. Groth, S. (2019) Multimodal divide. *Transportation Research Part A*, 125: 56–71.
62. Nikolaeva, A., Te Brömmelstroet, M., Raven, R., and Ranson, J. (2019) Smart cycling futures: Charting a new terrain and moving towards a research agenda. *Journal of Transport Geography*, *79*, 102486.
63. Slavulj, M., Tomašić, D., Ćosić, M., and Šojat, D. (2020) State of developing mobility as a service in the city of Zagreb. *Tehnički vjesnik*, 27(4): 1345–1350.
64. Casey, T., Ali-Vehmas, T., and Valovirta, V. (2017) Evolution toward an open value system for smart mobility services. *Competition and Regulation in Network Industries*, 18(1–2): 44–70.
65. Porru, S., Misso, F., Pani, F., and Repetto, C., (2020) Smart mobility and public transport. *Journal of Traffic and Transportation Engineering*, 7(1): 88–97.
66. Longo, A., Zappatore, M., and Navathe, S. (2019) The unified chart of mobility services. *Journal of Parallel and Distributed Computing*, *127*: 118–133.
67. Paz, A., and Peeta, S. (2009) Behavior-consistent real-time traffic routing under information provision. *Transportation Research Part C*, 17(6): 642–661.
68. Paz, A., and Peeta, S. (2007) Information-based traffic control strategies consistent with estimated driver behavior. *Transport Research Part B*, 43(1): 73–96.
69. Contreras, S., and Paz, A. (2018) The effects of ride-hailing companies on the taxicab industry in Las Vegas, Nevada. *Transportation Research Part A*, *115*: 63–70.
70. Veeramisti, N., Paz, A., and Baker, J. (2020) A framework for corridor-level traffic safety network screening and its implementation using Business Intelligence. *Safety Science*, *121*; 100–110.
71. Merrill, S., and Paz, A. (2020) *Automated rumble strip assembly*. U.S. Patent 15 892 659.
72. Amador, A., Dias, R., Dias, T., and Canas, T. (2015) Traffic management systems. In: *Intelligent Transport Systems*, A. Perallos (ed.) West Sussex, UK: Wiley.
73. Hensher, D. (2007) Some insights into the key influences on trip-chaining activity and PT use of seniors and the elderly. *International Journal of Sustainable Transportation*, 1(1): 53–68.
74. Moreno, A., Salaberria, I., and López-de-Ipiña, D. (2015) New approaches in user services development for multimodal trip planning. In: *Intelligent Transport Systems*, A. Perallos (ed.) West Sussex, UK: Wiley.
75. Paz, A., and Peeta, S. (2009) Paradigms to deploy a behavior-consistent approach for information-based real-time traffic routing. *Networks and Spatial Economics*, 9(2): 217–241.
76. Bauer, J., Bedsole, L., Snyder, K., Neuner, M., and Smith, M. C. (2018) *Expanding Traveler Choices Through the Use of Incentives: A Compendium of Examples* (No. FHWA-HOP-18-071). United States. Federal Highway Administration.

77. Caulfield, A., and O'Mahony, M. (2007) An examination of the PT information requirements of users. *IEEE Transactions on Intelligent Transportation Systems*, 8(1): 21–30.

78. Evans, G., Guo, A. W., Blythe, P., and Burden, M. (2015) Integrated smartcard solutions. *Transportation Planning and Technology*, 38(5): 534–551.

79. Pérez, J., Gonzalez, D., and Milanés, V. (2015) Vehicle control in ADAS application. In: *Intelligent Transport Systems*, A. Perallos (ed.) West Sussex, UK: Wiley.

80. McLeod, S., Scheurer, J., and Curtis, C. (2017) Urban PT. *Journal of Planning Literature*, 32(3): 223–239.

81. Hu, Y., Chiu, Y., Hsu, C., and Chang, Y. (2015) Identifying key factors for introducing GPS-based fleet management systems to the logistics industry. *Mathematical Problems in Engineering*, 2015.

82. Eloranta, P., and Sukuvaara, T. (2015) Wireless communications in vehicular environments. In: *Intelligent Transport Systems*, A. Perallos (ed.) West Sussex, UK: Wiley.

83. Mandžuka, S., Ivanjko, E., Vujić, M., Škorput, P., and Gregurić, M. (2015) The use of cooperative ITS in urban traffic management. In: *Intelligent Transport Systems*, A. Perallos (ed.) West Sussex, UK: Wiley.

84. Knorr, F., Baselt, D., Schreckenberg, M., and Mauve, M. (2012) Reducing traffic jams via VANETs. *IEEE Transactions on Intelligent Transportation Systems*, 61(8): 3490–3498.

85. Ndashimye, E., Ray, S., Sarkar, N. I., and Gutiérrez, J. (2017) Vehicle-to-infrastructure communication over multi-tier heterogeneous networks. *Computer Networks*, 112: 144–166.

86. Levina, A., Dubgorn, A., and Iliashenko, O. (2017) Internet of things within the service architecture of intelligent transport systems. In: *2017 European Conference on Electrical Engineering and Computer Science*, 351–355.

87. Machek, E., Frazier, J., Ingles, A., and Morton, T. (2016) *Wearable sensors in transportation-exploratory advanced research program initial stage investigation* (No. FHWA-HRT-16-034). United States. Federal Highway Administration. Office of Corporate Research, Technology, and Innovation.

88. Bitam, S., and Mellouk, A. (2012) ITS-Cloud. In: *IEEE Global Telecommunications Conference*, 2054–2059.

89. Yigitcanlar, T., Desouza, K., Butler, L., and Roozkhosh, F. (2020) Contributions and risks of artificial intelligence (AI) in building smarter cities. *Energies*, 13(6): 1473.

90. Yigitcanlar, T., and Cugurullo, F. (2020) The sustainability of artificial intelligence. *Sustainability,* 12(20): 8548.

91. Yuan, Y., and Wang, F. (2016) Towards blockchain-based intelligent transportation systems. In: *2016 IEEE 19th International Conference on Intelligent Transportation Systems*, pp. 2663–2668.

92. Nunes, P., Figueiredo, R., and Brito, M. (2016) The use of parking lots to solar-charge electric vehicles. *Renewable and Sustainable Energy Reviews*, 66: 679–693.

93. Helmers, E., and Marx, P. (2012) Electric cars. *Environmental Sciences Europe*, 24(1).

94. Del Pero, F., Delogu, M., and Pierini, M. (2018) Life cycle assessment in the automotive sector. *Procedia Structural Integrity*, 12: 521–537.

95. Emadi, A., Lee, Y., and Rajashekara, K. (2008) Power electronics and motor drives in electric, hybrid electric, and plug-in hybrid electric vehicles. *IEEE Transactions on Industrial Electronics*, 55(6): 2237–2245.

96. Cardoso, S., Fael, P., and Espírito-Santo, A. (2020) A review of micro and mild hybrid systems. *Energy Reports*, 6(s1): 385–390.

97. Dowling, R. (2018) Smart mobility. In: *Governance of the Smart Mobility Transition*. Bingley, UK: Emerald, pp. 51–64.

98. SAE International, (2019) *Taxonomy and Classification of Powered Micromobility Vehicles*. SAE Standard J3194.

99. Faisal, A., Yigitcanlar, T., Kamruzzaman, M., and Currie, G. (2019) Understanding autonomous vehicles. *Journal of Transport and Land Use*, 12(1): 45–72.

100. Axsen, J., and Sovacool, B. (2019) The roles of users in electric, shared and automated mobility transitions. *Transportation Research Part D*, 71: 1–21.

101. SAE International, (2018) *Taxonomy and Definitions for Terms Related to Driving Automation Systems for On-Road Motor Vehicles*. SAE Standard J3016.

102. iMove Australia, (2020) *Smart mobility projects and trials across the world*. Available: https://imoveaustralia.com/smart-mobility-projects-trials-list/, Accessed May 20, 2020.

103. Yigitcanlar, T., Butler, L., Windle, E., Desouza, K., Mehmood, R., and Corchado, J. (2020) Can building 'artificially intelligent cities' safeguard humanity from natural disasters, pandemics and other catastrophes? *Sensors*, 20(2988).

104. Yang, C., Ozbay, K., and Ban, X. (2017) Developments in connected and automated vehicles. *Journal of Intelligent Transportation Systems*, 21(4): 251–254.

105. Kane, M., and Whitehead, J. (2018) How to ride transport disruption. *Australian Planner*, 54(2): 177–185.

106. Campos, M. S., Olabarrieta, I., and Torre, A. (2015) Reference ITS Architectures in Europe. In: *Intelligent Transport Systems*, A. Perallos (ed.) West Sussex, UK: Wiley.

107. SAE International, (2018) *Taxonomy and Definitions for Terms Related to Shared Mobility and Enabling Technologies*. SAE Standard J3163.

108. Shaheen, S., Cohen, A., and Zohdy, I. (2016) *Shared Mobility*. US Department of Transportation. Washington, DC, USA, Tech Rep. FHWA-HOP-16022.

109. Machado, C. A. S., de Salles Hue, N. P. M., Berssaneti, F. T., Quintanilha, J. A. (2018). An overview of shared mobility. *Sustainability*, 10(12), 4342.

110. Mageean, J., and Nelson, J. (2003) The evaluation of demand responsive transport services in Europe. *Journal of Transport Geography*, 11(4): 255–270.

111. Davison, L., Enoch, M., Ryley, T., Quddus, M., and Wang, C. (2014) A survey of demand responsive transport in Great Britain. *Transport Policy*, 31: 47–54.

112. Greenblatt, J., and Shaheen, S. (2015) Automated vehicles, on-demand mobility, and environmental impacts. *Current Sustainable/Renewable Energy Reports*, 2(3): 74–81.

113. Graham, H., Bell, S., Flemming, K., Sowden, A., White, P., and Wright, K. (2018) The experiences of everyday travel for older people in rural areas. *Journal of Transport & Health*, 11: 141–152.

114. Yigitcanlar, T., Kankanamge, N., and Vella, K. (2021) How are smart city concepts and technologies perceived and utilized? A systematic geo-Twitter analysis of smart cities in Australia. *Journal of Urban Technology*, 28(1), 135–154.

115. Mulley, A., and Nelson, J. (2009) Flexible transport services. *Research in Transportation Economics*, 25(1): 39–45.

116. Velaga, N., Beecroft, M., Nelson, J., Corsar, D., and Edwards, P. (2012) Transport poverty meets the digital divide. *Journal of Transport Geography*, 21: 102–112.

117. Velaga, N., Rotstein, N., Oren, N., Nelson, J., Norman, T., and Wright, S. (2012) Development of an integrated flexible transport systems platform for rural areas using argumentation theory. *Research in Transportation Business & Management*, 3: 62–70.

118. Faisal, A., Yigitcanlar, T., Kamruzzaman, M., and Paz, A. (2021) Mapping two decades of autonomous vehicle research: A systematic scientometric analysis. *Journal of Urban Technology*, 28(3–4), 45–74.

119. Jittrapirom, P., Caiati, V., Feneri, A., Ebrahimigharehbaghi, S., Alonso-González, M., and Narayan, J. (2017) Mobility as a service. *Urban Planning*, 2(2): 13–25.

120. Arias-Molinares, A., and García-Palomares, J. (2020) The Ws of MaaS. *IATSS Research*.

121. Smith, A., and Hensher, D. (2020) Towards a framework for Mobility-as-a-Service policies. *Transport Policy*, 89: 54–65.

122. Mohammed, A., Ambak, K., Mosa, A., and Syamsunur, D. (2019) A review of traffic accidents and related practices worldwide. *The Open Transportation Journal*, 14: 65–83.

123. Kellermann, R., Biehle, T., and Fischer, L. (2020) Drones for parcel and passenger transportation. *Transportation Research Interdisciplinary Perspectives*, 4, 100088.

124. Nelson, J., and Phonphitakchai, T. (2012) An evaluation of the user characteristics of an open access DRT service. *Research in Transportation Economics*, 34(1): 54–65.

125. Litman, T. (2020) Pandemic-resilient community planning. *Victoria Transport Planning Institute*. Available at: https://www.vtpi.org/PRCP.pdf.

126. Gardner, N., Cui, J., and Coiacetto, E. (2017) Harassment on public transport and its impact on women's travel behaviour. *Australian Planner*, 54(1): 8–15.

127. Kellermann, R., Biehle, T., and Fischer, L. (2020) Drones for parcel and passenger transportation. *Transportation Research Interdisciplinary Perspectives*, 4: 100088.

128. Iacobucci, R., McLellan, B., and Tezuka, T. (2018) Modeling shared autonomous electric vehicles. *Energy*, 158: 148–163.

129. Kamruzzaman, M., Yigitcanlar, T., Yang, J., and Mohamed, M. A. (2016) Measures of transport-related social exclusion: A critical review of the literature. *Sustainability*, 8(7), 696.

130. Beede, D., Powers, R., and Ingram, C. (2017) The employment impact of autonomous vehicles. *SSRN*. Available: https://papers.ssrn.com/sol3/papers.cfm?abstract_id=3022818.

131. Golbabaei, F., Yigitcanlar, T., Paz, A., and Bunker, J. (2020) Individual predictors of autonomous vehicle public acceptance and intention to use. *Journal of Open Innovation*, 6(4): 106.

132. Yigitcanlar, T., Mehmood, R., Corchado, J. (2021). Green artificial intelligence: Towards an efficient, sustainable and equitable technology for smart cities and futures. *Sustainability*, 13(16), 8952.

Part 3

Smart City Platform

This part of the book concentrates on providing a clear understanding on the platforms that help in operationalising smart city functions. These platforms include mobile energy as a service, mobility as a service, urban management platform, and city as a platform.

DOI: 10.1201/9781003403630-11

9 Mobile Energy as a Service

9.1 Introduction

The climate change crisis arising from increasing greenhouse gas (GHG) emissions from all sectors of the economy, including energy and transport, demands decisive action towards sustainability and smooth transition to cleaner energy sources [1,2]. After the recent UN Climate Change Conference (COP-26), several governments and businesses in the industrialised countries are beginning to show a paradigm shift in addressing these challenges [3]. As road transport is a significant contributor to GHG emissions [4, 5], the uptake of electric vehicles (EVs) in large numbers has been touted as one of the pathways to lower the carbon footprint from the transport sector [6]. Accordingly, the world's major automotive industries have pledged to phase out internal combustion engines (ICEs) and replace them with the EV technology. For example, the designated timelines for this conversion are Volvo in 2030, Mazda in 2030, GM in 2035, and Nissan in the early 2030s [7].

EVs form the spine of electromobility [8]; where the term electromobility is defined as "a set of activities related to the use of EVs, as well as technical and operational EV solutions, technologies and charging infrastructure, as well as social, economic and legal issues pertaining to the designing, manufacturing, purchasing and using EVs" [9, (p. 1)]. There are many challenges in establishing electromobility in cities. These range from EV costs and charging station availability and accessibility, from charging speed and battery capacity and cost to purchasing power and government incentives, from cost of electricity to vehicle to grid adoption and consumer awareness on green technologies [10–13].

In many countries, EVs are expected to proliferate over the coming decade [14]. Based on Bloomberg New Energy Financial predictions, after a tipping point in ICE/EV comparative costs in coming years, 60% of cars will be fully electric, and the rest will have the plug-in capacity by 2040. Globally, more than seven million EVs were sold in 2021 alone, indicating the serious market penetration [7]. Although EVs have significant environmental benefits, given the potential to use renewable power for charging purposes, widespread adoption is limited due to the lack of available charging infrastructure and the capability of the existing electricity distribution network to handle cumulative peak demand [15–17]. In developing a comprehensive EV charging regime, the locations, including customer premises,

DOI: 10.1201/9781003403630-12

workplaces, public stations, online charging on-route, and car parks, are critical [18,19].

In the absence of any smart charging facilities, uncoordinated and erratic bidirectional charging (charge and discharge) of EVs will hamper the stability of the electricity grid. Based on [20], most customers tend to connect their EVs to the grid immediately after returning home from work between 6:00 p.m. to 10:00 p.m. For instance, a study in the Netherlands reported that uncoordinated charging with just 30% EVs penetration leads to a 54% increase in peak demand [21]. A similar study in Western Australia reported a 62% EV penetration rate will result in a 2.57-fold increase in electricity loading [22]. Hence, large-scale uncoordinated EV penetration will lead to excessive feeder overloading and poor power quality [23,24]. The existing power quality issues, that are primarily over-voltage problems, owing to the large numbers of rooftop photovoltaics (PVs) in the distribution grids [25–28] will worsen due to the uncoordinated integration of EVs.

Therefore, there is a need to develop an intelligent scheduling and control mechanism that encourages EV owners to relieve the overloading issue in the electricity grid. In addition, optimal placements of EV charging infrastructures considering transport and urban real-estate constraints are paramount to alleviate the electricity loading constraints. Moreover, an incentive-based market mechanism where EV owners are rewarded for their bidirectional charging behaviour between EVs and grid [vehicle-to-grid (V2G) and grid-to-vehicle (G2V)] helping the electricity grid is necessary. Additionally, the bidirectional power flow could also be used to provide high-quality ancillary services such as voltage and frequency regulation, peak power management, and improvement of the load factor [29–32]. This should be combined with appropriate market research where the public acceptability of this mechanism is evaluated. Furthermore, treating EVs as mobile energy sources has created the concept of mobile energy internet [33].

This chapter introduces a novel concept of Mobile-Energy-as-a-Service (MEaaS), a well-planned mechanism incorporating transport, power, and urban infrastructure aspects of mobile energy for EVs and the flexible incentive-based pricing schemes to handle challenges introduced by the upcoming wave of EVs. Provided that this mechanism is planned well, challenges due to widespread EV uptake on urban power systems could be handled via rapidly advancing mobile energy technology [34–37]. In other words, EV batteries could serve as mobile energy sources to compensate for the pressures on the grid during peak times. Nevertheless, this requires a careful system design for large metropolitan cities that can accommodate a MEaaS system.

One of the attractive features is that MEaaS creates a platform for EV users to trade energy in an established market which can be operated via an app in smartphones. Using the arbitrage market (i.e., power price differential during peak and off-peak hours), EV owners could cover not only the costs of running their vehicles but even profit from it. The other advantage is convenience, timesaving, reliability of electricity supply to EVs, and the opportunity to be connected to a market on a 24/7 basis. Therefore, this new technology adds extra value to the rapidly emerging process of prosumaging—Prosumage is a term used for PROroduction, conSUMption, and storAGE [38]. The rollout of MEaaS should further accelerate the uptake of EVs, increase the number of prosumagers, lead to an increase in renewable energy driven by market forces [39], lower prices, and reduce GHG emissions from the transport sector. In this sense, MEaaS provides an opportunity where large numbers of EVs, with their batteries, form a giant battery when aggregated. The batteries not only will take pressure off the grid, but their mobility provides an opportunity for energy to be delivered to consumers on-demand, both to households as well as EV users in areas where shortages exist.

In this chapter, we introduce a novel MEaaS system approach and offer a discussion around the issues of: (a) measuring optimal real-time power grid operability; (b) utilising transport, power, and urban infrastructures; (c) establishing a flexible incentive-based price mechanism; and (d) gauging the public acceptability of MEaaS based on its desired attributes. All statements in this chapter are based on a thorough review of the current literature, research, developments, trends, and applications.

9.2 Mobile Energy and Transport

Smart bidirectional EV chargers can regulate the grid frequency by charging and discharging EV batteries [40]. Using the arbitrage market, EVs can be financially attractive to potential owners, covering EVs' running costs to make a profit. For example, one study reports that an EV-owner can gain between $3,777 to $4,000 per year by sharing an EV's power reserve with the power grid with a regulating power of 10–15 kW [41].

Load-levelling and peak-shaving are other potential benefits of G2V and V2G applications [42, 43]. With the help of V2G, it is possible to discharge the extra power of EV batteries to the grid during daily peak demand (peak-shaving). On the other hand, with the help of G2V, EVs can be charged during off-peak hours, improving the load profile during the day (load-levelling). According to [44], if New York City's EV population is approximately 100,000, representing a 50% penetration level, up to 10% of the peak power can be provided by EV batteries—valued at $110 million per year.

In addition, the renewable energy sector can benefit from the presence of G2V and V2G charging. Due to the intermittent nature of RERs, it is possible to use EV batteries as storage units during periods of high peak generation and discharge them during peak demand. Such a market will lead to an inevitable further increase in the uptake of rooftop PVs and EVs, and at the same time reduce the stress on the grid. Increasing amounts of renewable energy generated, through an increased number of PVs, will eventually lead to lower electricity prices even during peak hours, replacing fossil fuel-based generation, leading to an eventual decrease in GHG emissions.

On the other hand, smart bidirectional charging makes it possible to determine the charging time. This coordinated system can help decrease daily electricity costs, transformer and conductor current ratings, and flatten the power profile of the grid. The authors in [45] report that a 50% peak load increase can be avoided at a 10% EV penetration rate with a coordinated bidirectional charging strategy for the US power grid. Adopting a coordinated mechanism requires specialised equipment such as sensors and communication devices and related policies that can encourage customers to adopt EVs and adhere to associated bi-directional charging protocols. Some policies incentivise customers to purchase EVs in tax credits/ rebates and subsidise charging installation or discount in-building parking [46].

For instance, in the case of Australia, limited policies that exist at the state level look surprisingly more proactive than those at the federal level. For example, the states of Queensland and South Australia offer up-front financial incentive programmes for EV buyers and subsidies for EV bidirectional charging stations. On the other hand, some policies involve bidirectional charging scheduling strategies. In the context of coordinated bidirectional charging algorithms, most policies are based on multi-level pricing that are established using power demand and RER generation to encourage customers to shift to off-peak power demand. Several countries are lagging other developed countries in terms of coordinated scheduling with no clear framework in place to set state and federal initiatives [7]. Policymakers need to consider numerous local and national factors, including the existing infrastructure; types of bidirectional charging stations and their locations; the EV penetration rate, customer mobility profiles, convenience, preferences, and acceptability.

Urban planning is another aspect that can be significantly affected by integrating EVs to the power grid [47–49]. Public bidirectional charging stations that are optimally located and easily accessible are critical in boosting the adoption of EVs. Moreover, range anxiety is a prohibitive concern for the rapid growth of EVs. Many studies have been dedicated to maximising the satisfaction level with respect to charging demand and limited budgets [50,51]. Nevertheless, optimisation of EV bidirectional charging locations must be expanded to encompass traffic concerns, equitable distribution of stations, the capacity of roads/cities, and existing infrastructure limitations. Furthermore, the current public charger locating strategies do not consider the impact of having household chargers, which may lead to the excessive location of public chargers in residential areas.

An increasing number of studies indicate that the number of EVs on our roads will rise as they are preferred as personalised transport given the environmentally friendly benefits and the acceptance of autonomous driving technology [52]. The uptake of autonomous driving will also revolutionise smart urban mobility, where electrification of such vehicles is also a desired outcome [53]. The levels of EVs on roads and their changing environmental roles globally in recent years indicate that EVs will be the future of personalised transport, especially where autonomous EV technology is concerned [54,55].

Although it is expected that 28% of total sold vehicles will be battery-powered by 2030, little work has been done to estimate the required infrastructure and the corresponding budget to meet this growing demand. The practicability of constructing a complex infrastructure across a country requires time, deep analysis of the issues, and considerable financial expenditure. Since the rapid growth of EV numbers has already started, analysis of the current grid system is essential to ensure that grid resilience is not jeopardised. Although extra headroom for facilities is considered when the power grid is constructed to account for future power demand increases, it is unlikely to be sufficient once the EV fleet is integrated into the transport system. Thus, system augmentation is inevitable, and potential flaws must be identified.

In addition, the increasing number of EVs as public transport necessitates new bidirectional charging stations with appropriate technologies for public stations, which is different from household stations. A substantial investment is required to develop the needed technology, and significant financing is necessary to install and operate these stations. Due to the complexity of the cost estimation and its dependency on the local and national parameters, so far, no comprehensive analysis has been carried out to estimate the expected investment and the gained profit for many countries. Internationally, only two scenarios have been widely investigated for charging infrastructure requirements [56].

The first is based on bulky battery packages that can guarantee the daily driven distance of an ordinary individual. The EV is charged at night using a moderate power transmission rate in this strategy. From an investment perspective, this approach requires a low investment cost at the household level since most installed infrastructures in houses can tolerate the required power transmission based on existing ratings of the installed wires. However, the main concerns of this approach are the lack of providing the required ancillary services during the daytime and the increasing power demand across residential area feeders at night [57].

The second strategy is based on the constant charging and discharging of the EVs with a small battery-package volume which would be feasible with the help of new emerging charging technologies such as "wireless power transfer systems" (WPTS), which can charge EVs on-road. Although the continuous drive option might be an ambitious and appealing target, it requires a significant modification in both electrical and roadway infrastructures, and therefore an unjustifiable expense, particularly for low-population-density regions. In general, commercialised bidirectional chargers can be classified as Level 2 chargers (~5–10 kW) and Level 3 chargers (fast chargers, ~50 kW) [58]. The former suffers from slow bidirectional charging time, making it more suitable for household applications. Level 3 chargers can substantially increase power flows during peak power usage periods, making it more convenient for public stations.

Ideally, the adopted bidirectional charging facilities should not be restricted to a single technology. Thus, analyses related to EV infrastructure and corresponding impacts need to be expanded to encompass various bidirectional charging options. For example, so far, the investigated business models of bidirectional charger stations have been focused only on a single technology across a system (i.e., only Level 2 or only Level 3 is adopted) while the cost optimisation of hybrid bidirectional charging facilities (including Level 2, Level 3, and on-route bidirectional chargers) has not been investigated (Figure 9.1). Furthermore, how EVs as mobile energy carriers would affect the electricity grid power quality and stability and the way the electricity and transport networks are interwound have not been comprehensively investigated.

Thus, this chapter is concerned with how the variability of electricity unit price from RERs will influence the state-of-the-art stationery and dynamic bidirectional

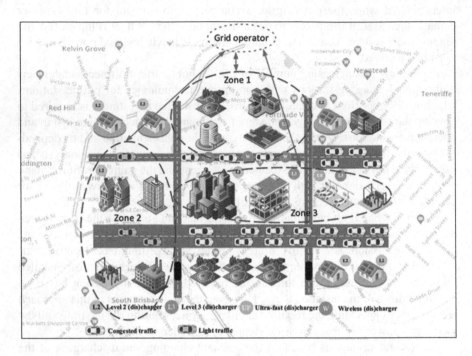

Figure 9.1 Bidirectional EV charging technologies and their interactions with power and transport grids.

charging costs and related operating expenses. In this way, a generic model for large metropolitan cities can be developed to offer the optimal combination of bidirectional chargers for the public (including on-route and stationary chargers) and household applications.

From an urban planning perspective, there are limited but growing studies concerning the location of EV charging stations [59]. In the urban planning literature, integration of land use and transport has been widely covered [60], whereas the inclusion of power infrastructure is rather new. The existing literature on the location of charging stations does not adequately factor in power, transport, and urban planning aspects [61–63]. Moreover, while there are studies on wireless power transfer with one-directional charging consideration [64–66], there are, to our knowledge, no comprehensive studies conducted to determine the optimal location of bidirectional charging stations or infrastructure.

So far, accessibility has been the main factor in determining public EVs' location bidirectional chargers. As a result, parking lots are assumed to be a reasonable location for the installation of such stations [67–69]. Nevertheless, factors such as balancing the power generation from RER and EV charging power demand at each urban locality (e.g., suburbs or neighbourhoods); system augmentation; the impact of household chargers; traffic-related concerns; the capacity of the civil infrastructure; and the change in the behaviour of drivers on the face of potential charging/discharging incentivising schemes have not been covered systematically in the literature [70].

Despite a growing literature in this domain, it only covers limited aspects in identifying optimal locations for bidirectional charging infrastructure [71]. Additionally, while MEaaS provides a system approach to urban mobility including EVs [72], there is no comprehensive and system-level approach to EVs and bidirectional charging infrastructure in the context of metropolitan cities.

Against this backdrop, this chapter advocates a system thinking to pinpoint and address the negative externalities of EVs on the power grid of our cities. Hence, in the next section, the chapter coins and conceptualises a novel concept of MEaaS to operationalise energy, transport, and urban infrastructures for establishing sustainable electromobility in large metropolitan cities.

9.3 Mobile-Energy-as-a-Service

Accordingly, this chapter aims to provide a multidisciplinary perspective—of power and transport engineering, urban planning, and social science—for the smooth transition from the grid in its present form to a network that can support a dominance of EVs on roads via MEaaS. Furthermore, this research intends to analyse the effect of the power system when EVs act as sources of mobile energy. Such mobile energy sources can be utilised to supply energy to specific areas that experience energy deprivation at any given time or absorb energy from certain areas that experience energy surplus. Thus, with proper forecasting of the mobility over the transport network, EVs can be used as dynamic energy sources to alleviate power system operational issues using bidirectional charging. This shows the symbiotic relationship between transport and energy networks that can be managed to be economically optimised.

In essence, MEaaS presents how an operational framework can manage such mobile energy sources to benefit EV owners and urban transport and energy networks, particularly in large metropolitan cities. As the geographical context of MEaaS, the primary implementation target is naturally the large metropolitan cities (cities offering increased urban socioeconomic activities, density and population, and diverse and advanced infrastructure and smart mobility options) [73–75]. Moreover, urban administrations of some global cities (also branded as knowledge or smart cities), particularly in developed nations, have the capability and interest to be the leader in urban innovation [76].

This chapter advocates the identification of appropriate charging systems for domestic requirements and for addressing some of the current shortcomings of systems. Such broad scope and the multidisciplinary research perspective also include a public preference/acceptability study to assist researchers in comprehensively investigating and developing a charging system that tracks the influence of optimisation in one aspect over the other (Figure 9.2).

This chapter proposes MEaaS as a novel concept to address some of the undesired externalities that EVs will create on urban electricity power grids.

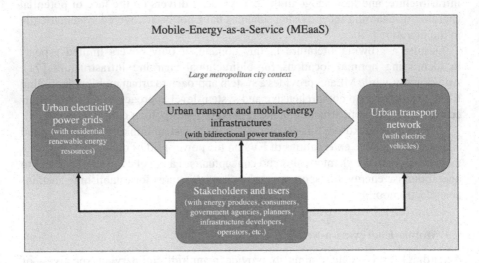

Figure 9.2 The MEaaS concept.

Turning the MEaaS concept into reality will require thorough investigations despite this benefit. Four critical ones are listed below and elaborated in the following subsections.

- Identification of optimal real-time power grid operationality when incorporating MEaaS (where this involves, inter alia, a reliability analysis of the existing urban power grid with respect to the future uptake of EVs and RERs) (further details are presented in Section 3.1).
- Determination of the structure of MEaaS in the large metropolitan city context through smart urban infrastructure design guidelines encompassing transport, power, and civil engineering aspects (where this involves analysis of the urban topography and urban form and designating the optimal locations for public charging stations) (further details are presented in Section 3.2).
- Development of the flexible incentive-based pricing mechanisms for MEaaS (where this involves optimal bidirectional charging through V2X/X2V of mobile/stationary EVs) (further details are presented in Section 3.3).
- Assessment of public acceptability of MEaaS and identifying its salient attributes under which the system could be widely deployed (where this involves public technology adoption surveys and interviews) (further details are presented in Section 3.4).

9.3.1 Measuring Optimal Real-Time Power Grid Operationality for MEaaS

The impact of EVs on the operations of electricity network utilities must be investigated to avoid imposing an unprecedented burden leading to the degradation of power quality, high-stress levels on local transformers or cables, and poor system reliability. This involves identifying optimal real-time power grid power flows incorporating MEaaS—that is, a reliability analysis of the existing power grid with respect to the future uptake of EVs and RERs. Researchers have investigated the impact on electricity grid power flows from EV charging purely from a supply point of view [77]. However, the dynamic spatio-temporal electricity demand distribution and its interaction with RERs have been overlooked. A recent report from Energeia [78] indicates the likely significant variance in cumulative EV uptake over the next decade with respect to the government intervention level and how it can significantly impact the power grid performance in large metropolitan cities.

We suggest the following procedures to measure optimal real-time power grid operationality for MEaaS involving EVs and the advanced bidirectional charging infrastructures. First, the electricity network should be categorised into several modelling zones, which in turn are defined in terms of the electricity distribution system and the local statistical areas. Electricity grids are represented by several substation zones based on local statistical areas, whereas transport networks consider several statistical areas based on socioeconomic characteristics. This needs to be amalgamated to determine the impact of EVs on the power grid. The worst-case condition in each zone, in terms of the required power consumption, can be estimated as Eq. 1:

$$P_{tot,EV} = \sum N_i P_{nom,i} \qquad \text{(Eq. 1)}$$

where the subscript "i" designates the adopted bidirectional charging technology, N_i is the number of users of the i-th technology in each zone, and $P_{nom,\epsilon}$ is the nominal power of the bidirectional charger, which is a known value for different technologies (the influence of private and public charging stations is accounted here). N_i represents private users, which can be approximated from the historical census records of each zone ($N_i = \alpha_i * N_h$ where N_h is the number of houses in each zone and α_i is the penetration rate of EV in each zone). Poisson distribution can be used to estimate the worst-case scenario of the number of public station users at a specific timeslot [20].

With the help of Poisson distribution, the probability of the customers of public stations (including the stationary and dynamic bidirectional chargers) can be determined to estimate the corresponding power consumption/generation from Eq. 1.

Customer behaviour regarding the bidirectional charging operation is influenced by several factors: electricity price, mobility trip purpose (work/recreational/ shopping), time (day/week/month), and customer convenience. The different electricity demand scenarios should be modelled considering the aforementioned factors, and Eq. 1 should be solved for different times of the day. This analysis adjusts the current/projected daily load curve by incorporating each zone's RER generation distribution and demand scenarios from the available power grid database. It should determine the limitations of the existing power grid in each zone and the need for corresponding network augmentation.

9.3.2 Transport, Power, and Urban Engineering Aspects of MEaaS

Integration of a large EV fleet into the power grid requires a placement strategy that can justify the financial outlay and consideration of urban-related issues such as congestion and social welfare. Moreover, the applications and implications of EVs are overshadowed by the uncertainties and potential consequences for the operation of the existing power grid and urban infrastructures. Regarding the placement strategies for bidirectional chargers, several critical factors such as travel anxiety level, the required time to charge with respect to the adopted technology, and fair access to these facilities must be considered. The power grid infrastructure limitations such as the power system transformer ratings must also be taken into consideration.

In addition, the advent of modern technologies such as wireless powered bidirectional chargers provides a unique opportunity for on-the-go bidirectional charging to be employed. Although the required technology for on-route bidirectional charging is more expensive than stationary chargers [64], it offers valuable features such as reducing the waiting time in queues and the requirement for the EV battery size [79].

Furthermore, in locations with sufficient traffic, the revenue generated from cars using bidirectional charging on the route can meet the investment expenses. There is limited research on developing frameworks for identifying the most suitable locations for public chargers in locations such as shopping centres and parking lots [50,56,66]. Nonetheless, most drivers were shown to prefer mobility rather than profitability and indicated social welfare, grid augmentation, and urban planning-related concerns. Noticeably, the simultaneous impact of more than one technology is not considered [80].

The grid augmentation and economic viability concerns should be conducted in parallel with the grid modelling. In terms of various available bidirectional charging options and the topography of the city, there is a clear gap in the quantitative evaluation of the placement of these stations with respect to urban planning and transport operational constraints.

Access to the strategic transport demand model and relevant socioeconomic and land use data is necessary as this provides an opportunity to demonstrate the applicability of the research on a real network and establish evidence-based findings. The research should consider spatio-temporal travel patterns, and the recent advancements in artificial intelligence and machine learning techniques (such as non-negative matrix factorisation) on the transport data can be explored for accurate and reliable modelling of base case transport patterns.

Different scenarios specified by MEaaS should be considered to model EV customer profiles with respect to the adoption of EVs. The profiling should consider different types of EV customers and their socioeconomic characteristics. Different modelling scenarios based on technology-enthusiastic early adopters should be used to assess the price sensitivity where there is mass ownership of EVs. A structured review of the emerging international findings on EV and similar technology adoptions should provide a strong foundation for the design of scenarios.

Based on the MEaaS scenarios, the charging location of EVs should be optimised considering various factors such as spatio-temporal demand distribution, temporal vehicle trip distribution, driving behaviour (on the face of incentivising schemes), power grid impact, and other technical factors related to charging type (e.g., fast/ slow, wireless/plug-in, reverse).

Different multi-objective mathematical function formulations (Z) for the objective function should be considered. In general, Z is defined as a function of the traffic delay on the network (Tg) and impact on power grid (Pg) as represented by Eq. 2. The sensitivity and stability of the different formulations should be thoroughly tested systematically. The values will be based on the simulation using the strategic transport model and the power grid simulator.

$$Z = f(Tg, Pg, other\ constraints) \qquad \text{(Eq. 2)}$$

Potential algorithms that can be considered for optimisation include simulated annealing, advanced meta-heuristic algorithms, gradient descent and its variations, evolutionary computation, hybridised algorithms, and reinforcement learning.

The optimisation protocol should take the following factors (not limited to) into account: (a) spatio-temporal distribution of mobile energy; (b) travel patterns; (c) strategic transport model; (d) customer profiling with respect to the adoption of EVs; (e) various urban scenarios; and (f) optimisation for charging infrastructure location with respect to different technology types.

To accomplish a public placement bidirectional charger plan, a MEaaS feasibility/optimisation study—looking into transport, power, and urban engineering aspects of MEaaS—should utilise a zone-based geographic partitioning technique to predict electricity generation and demand at each zone. Given the available local data and the type of land used (e.g., residential/commercial/industrial/recreational), one can forecast the behaviour and demand of users in each zone. The strategy should be based on optimal placement of the public bidirectional charging stations (Level 3) in areas with the low RER and high-power demand (such as apartment zones) where household bidirectional chargers (Level 2) are more effective. Given the traffic flow at each zone, the modelling should pinpoint those areas where there is potential for application of ultra-fast and wireless bidirectional chargers.

The interaction between the price of electricity for selling or buying, user decision to choose the travel route, and the capacity of roads to accommodate the number of EVs, generates a coupled equilibrium in power and transportation.

Such an optimisation study could learn from [50] the interaction between the price of electricity and destination choice of EV users, and the optimised profit for both the stations and users with respect to the optimal location of the stations. To this end, a combined distribution and assignment model should describe the user destination choices based on the price of charging and price paid for the purchase of excess electricity by charging stations. Research can be further extended to model the effect of vehicle discharging on traveller behaviour and road capacity, not considered in the study by [50].

9.3.3 Flexible Incentive-Based Pricing Mechanisms for MEaaS

The EV charging behaviour of users can significantly impact the power grid performance [79]. Currently, the charging infrastructure is limited to specific locations such as workplaces, residential, commercial, and recreational premises. The existing charging pattern and its impact on the grid are primarily governed by user convenience and the cost associated with existing tariffs (pay-per-kWh and pay-for-time). Such patterns are not system optimal and significantly impact the power grid.

With the advancement of technologies, users would actively participate in vehicle-to-everything or everything-to-vehicle (V2X/X2V) mechanisms through bidirectional charging and associated smart/IT/apps/technologically based solutions. Although consequential system augmentation is inevitable to some extent, adopting a reasonable policy or pricing mechanism to incentivise users should result in optimal capital investments in power, transport, and urban infrastructures.

Furthermore, due to the high penetration of RERs in some nations, such as Australia, and the lack of synchronous generators (low inertia), as pointed out in the introduction, the grid is prone to instability, and the connection of EVs to the grid could be a beneficial alternative if managed competently. Thus, there is a unique opportunity for many national electricity utilities (grid and retail) and charging station operators to benefit from the optimal integration of EVs. Nevertheless, there are neither mechanisms nor incentives for EV owners at this stage. Several studies offer guidelines for the economic operation of charging stations, ignoring the multiple options for charging EVs. Furthermore, the literature has rarely modelled strategies regarding the discharging process and sharing stored electricity of EVs with the power grid [81].

Therefore, it is imperative to incorporate multiple bidirectional charging technologies connected to the electricity grid, charging stations, and other energy storage facilities with a flexible incentive-based pricing scheme for the optimal operation of MEaaS. Such a mechanism should consider many priorities, including the RERs' generation profile, demand, and generation of power (supply) within each geographic zone and to capture the sensitiveness of buyers and sellers of electricity to changes in price to make the market dynamic.

It should be noted here that this system should be highly flexible, incentive-based, and entirely dependent on the existing demand and supply of electricity at any given time and location. Strategically, the operating system automatically, for example, increases (decreases) the sale price during peak (off-peak) demand to discourage (encourage) customers to charge (discharge) them to sell (buy) to (from) the grid, charging stations, EVs, and other storage devices. Also, it should be able to provide a travel plan for EV drivers depending on their battery capacity where possible economically beneficial pathways for them can be identified in terms of charging/discharging during travel.

Accordingly, the peak-load demands of the grid can be minimised, leading to more optimal usage of the infrastructure. One potential pricing mechanism that can be considered for the MEaaS is an improvement/variant of, for example, Australia's existing wholesale spot market pricing scheme which is operated by the Australian Energy Market Operator (AEMO), where the electricity supply and demand is "matched" simultaneously using a real-time spot market dispatched every five minutes [82].

The AEMO-operated spot market pricing scheme is not accessible to the public to directly purchase electricity from generators. Nonetheless, given the technology involved with MEaaS and because it operates within defined zones, it is argued here that the spot market for mobile energy should be instantaneous because such pricing could be arranged on a zone-by-zone basis, as shown in Figure 9.1, to reach market equilibrium prices. Markets clear when quantity demanded (Q_d) equals quantity supplied (Q_s), as represented in Eq. 3:

$$Q_d = Q_s \qquad\qquad\qquad\qquad \text{(Eq. 3)}$$

where Q_d and Q_s are quantities of electricity demanded and supplied, respectively. Using primary and secondary data, it is possible to solve for equilibrium prices and quantities. Once the price is settled in each zone, the price is instantaneously made available to all system users (buyers and sellers) via an app. The main merit of this strategy is that the price of electricity is instantaneously determined locally. Thus, with respect to RER generation, EV users can decide to charge/discharge (bidirectional charging) in a zone based on the prevailing price. Furthermore, since providing the ancillary services is crucial for grid operators, they can offer further incentives for EV users to participate in the market through V2X/X2V mechanisms. It is advocated that a fully flexible, highly incentivised pricing system that affords the opportunity to arbitrage is a key determinant of success for the uptake of the MEaaS system.

9.3.4 Public Acceptability of and Appropriate Business Models for MEaaS

Creating a dynamic pricing system for arbitrage is one of the key essentials for the success of MEaaS. Another key determinant for the uptake of this emerging technology hinges on public acceptability of mobile energy as a realistic product with the desired attributes linked to its use. For public acceptability, it is imperative to showcase the key attributes of the technology. These include the costs, monetary gains from the use of the technology, convenience, reliability, and the inclusion of renewable energy and uptake of EVs instead of ICEs.

For this purpose, a common approach is to conduct a consumer choice model, where the most desired attributes mentioned above could be tested, and consumer preferences ranked and highlighted. It is also possible to test whether consumers are willing to adopt the change, under what circumstances they would do so or whether they would prefer the status quo. In this case ICEs or EVs minus the MEaaS system. It is also possible to rank consumers' acceptability for each attribute in monetary terms. The choice modelling is usually embedded in a survey of consumers where the technology is most likely to be adopted.

A consumer choice model assumes that a consumer reveals his/her preference. Here the consumer selects the alternative that provides the highest utility [83], say between ICE and EV with MEaaS technology. That is, a consumer n selects choice i if $U_i > U_j$, $_j Î C_n$, $i \neq j$ where U_i is decomposed into a deterministic (observed), V_{nj}, and random (unobserved) part, ε_{nj}, as represented in Eq. 4:

$$U_i = V_i + \varepsilon_i \qquad \text{(Eq. 4)}$$

where V_i is a deterministic component and ε_i is a random error component which captures any influences on individual choices that are unobservable to the researcher. The deterministic component, V_i is the function of the MEaaS attributes and socio-economic characteristics of the consumer, and can be expressed as represented in Eq. 5:

$$V_i = \beta_0 + \beta_1 X_1 + \beta_2 X_2 + \ldots + \beta_n X_n + \beta_a S_1 + \beta_b S_2 + \ldots \beta_m S_k \qquad \text{(Eq. 5)}$$

where β_0 is the alternative specific constant, X_1 to X_n are the attributes, S_1 to S_k are the social, economic, and attitudinal characteristics of the consumer, and β_1 to β_n and β_a to β_m are attached to the vectors of attributes and vectors of the consumer characteristics, both of which influence utility. Models such as multinomial logit (MNL), random parameter logit (RPL), and other models can be used to analyse the choice data [84,85].

Researchers have used choice experiments to test consumers' acceptability of autonomous vehicles and one of the studies that provides before and after provision of information about the emerging technologies is [86]. These experiments which gather socioeconomic (including income, education, and gender) and attitudinal data on surveyed residents provide numerous indications, including which groups are likely to adopt such technology and those who are unlikely. This is to say, identifying key determinants of such technology is vital for technology developers, policy planners, and investors. Such modelling can also indicate barriers and identify the most preferred attributes and provides an excellent basis to measure the strengths of these markets and to what extent and under what conditions consumers are likely to embrace such technology.

In sum, choice surveys, if well-executed, could elicit critical data that will enable the planning and execution of a business model that considers customer preferences, costs, and benefits. This exercise will also provide valuable insights into the pricing mechanisms (including the development of relevant apps) that need to be put in place and obtain an understanding of the challenges and opportunities that MEaaS provides the various stakeholders.

9.4 Conclusion

The increasing urban population and their energy and mobility needs have created major energy and transport sustainability problems for particularly large metropolitan cities [87–89]. In this chapter, we argued the need for MEaaS to operationalise energy, transport, and urban infrastructures for establishing sustainable electromobility in large metropolitan cities to address the energy and transport sustainability problems. Prospective studies on MEaaS are needed as they provide numerous benefits, some of which are elaborated as below.

Prospective studies on MEaaS will disclose new knowledge and scientific outcomes: The chief specific outcome of prospective research on MEaaS will be new scientific knowledge as the MEaaS concept is the first comprehensive attempt to investigate future urban energy systems for sustainable electromobility in large metropolitan cities, where many of them today describe themselves as smart cities. These investigations will generate critical knowledge and an evidence base that will enable government agencies to follow pathways in adopting appropriate urban energy systems for sustainable electromobility.

Prospective studies on MEaaS will generate economic returns flowing from scientific outcomes: There are likely to be significant economic returns flowing from such scientific outcomes. These investigations will be of direct benefit to government agencies, and many others internationally—as these research studies will unveil new knowledge on adopting appropriate urban energy systems for sustainable electromobility. The large-scale commercialisation of these MEaaS will generate an economic return.

Prospective studies on MEaaS will provide social and environmental returns flowing from scientific outcomes: The flow-on benefits will not just be economical; there will be significant societal and environmental benefits, as these studies will identify socio-spatial negative externalities of urban mobility and prescribe responsible solutions for government agencies to address the adverse effects on communities and the environment. The MEaaS system, with its financial and other benefits, will accelerate the uptake of EVs, thus reducing the use of fossil-based fuels. These investigations will also reduce the strain imposed on the existing power grid.

Prospective studies on MEaaS will support informed urban, transport, and energy policy and debate: These studies, throughout their investigation phase, will generate research outcomes, which will be communicated regularly to inform urban, transport, and energy policy and debate, thereby raising the awareness of governments and the public regarding the importance of MEaaS solutions.

Future research will inform urban, transport, and energy policy circles and the research community by leading a public discourse on urban energy systems that foster sustainable electromobility in large metropolitan cities. Our research team will also continue to embark on different facets of MEaaS and complimentary aspects of future urban, transport and power technologies. The following conceptual framework for MEaaS, presented in Figure 9.3, could assist prospective studies.

We conclude this chapter by quoting [90],

> the electricity grid with a high penetration of renewable energy can enable travellers to travel free of emissions using state-of-the-art EVs. Extensive EV demands at the peak-times, and an increase in electricity consumption due to

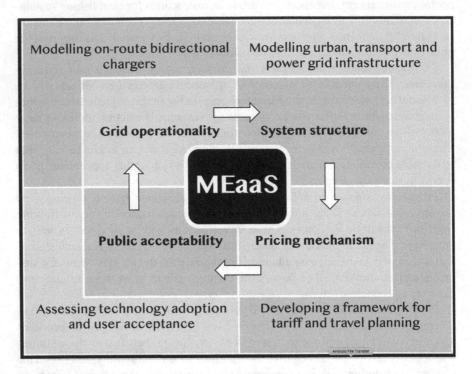

Figure 9.3 Conceptual framework of MEaaS.

population growth, have led to higher utility infrastructure investments. Mobile energy systems can be used as an innovative demand-side management solution to reduce long-term utility infrastructure investments. They can store and release electricity to the grid based on consumer demand.

(p. 1)

However, a scientific planning approach for grid integration has been overlooked where our study in this chapter offers a new conceptualisation of such a system integration with MEaaS [91].

Acknowledgements

This chapter, with permission from the copyright holder, is a reproduced version of the following journal article: Vilathgamuwa, M., Mishra, Y., Yigitcanlar, T., Bhaskar, A., & Wilson, C. (2022). Mobile-Energy-as-a-Service (MEaaS): Sustainable Electromobility via Integrated Energy–Transport–Urban Infrastructure. *Sustainability*, 14(5), 2796.

References

1. Nuttall, W. J., and Manz, D. L. (2008) A new energy security paradigm for the twenty-first century. *Technological Forecasting and Social Change*, 75(8), 1247–1259.
2. Webb, J., Silva, H., and Wilson, C. (2020) The future of coal and renewable power generation in Australia. *Economic Analysis and Policy* 68: 363–378.
3. Yilmaz, M., and Krein, P. (2013) Review of the impact of vehicle-to-grid technologies on distribution systems and utility interfaces. *IEEE Transactions on Power Electronics* 28: 5673–5689.
4. Holz-Rau, C., and Scheiner, J. (2019) Land-use and transport planning. *Transport Policy* 74: 127–137.
5. Mahbub, P., Goonetilleke, A., Ayoko, G., Egodawatta, P., and Yigitcanlar, T. (2011) Analysis of build-up of heavy metals and volatile organics on urban roads in Gold Coast, Australia. *Water Sci. Technol.*, 63: 2077–1085.
6. Li, F., Ou, R., Xiao, X., Zhou, K., Xie, W., Ma, D., et al., (2019) Regional comparison of electric vehicle adoption and emission reduction effects in China. *Resources, Conservation and Recycling, 149*: 714–726.
7. Editor, E. (2021) *Global EV sales set to smash records with 7 million cars in 2021 while crossing 10% annual threshold.* www.ecogeneration.com.au.
8. Yigitcanlar, T. (2022) Towards Smart and Sustainable Urban Electromobility: An Editorial Commentary. *Sustainability*, 14(4), 2264.
9. Macioszek, E. (2019) E-mobility infrastructure in the Górnośląsko-Zagłębiowska Metropolis, Poland, and potential for development. In: *Proceedings of the 5th World Congress on New Technologies (NewTech'19), Lisbon, Portugal* (pp. 18–20).
10. Szczuraszek, T., and Chmielewski, J. (2020) Planning spatial development of a city from the perspective of its residents' mobility needs. In: *Smart and Green Solutions for Transport Systems, Cham*, pp. 3–12.
11. Ling, Z., Cherry, C., and Wen, Y. (2021) Determining the factors that influence electric vehicle adoption. *Sustainability*, 13: 11719.
12. Coffman, M., Bernstein, P., and Wee, S. (2017) Electric vehicles revisited: a review of factors that affect adoption. *Transport Reviews*, 37: 79–93.
13. Chen, C., Zarazua de Rubens, G., Noel, L., Kester, J., and Sovacool, B. K. (2020) Assessing the socio-demographic, technical, economic and behavioral factors. *Renewable and Sustainable Energy Reviews, 121*: 109692.
14. Rietmann, N., Hügler, B., and Lieven, T. (2020) Forecasting the trajectory of electric vehicle sales and the consequences for worldwide CO_2 emissions. *Journal of Cleaner Production, 261*: 121038.
15. Buekers, J., Holderbeke, M., Bierkens, J., and Int Panis, L. (2014) Health and environmental benefits related to electric vehicle introduction in EU countries. *Transportation Research Part D: Transport and Environment*, 33: 26–38.
16. Hannan, M., Hoque, M., Mohamed, A., and Ayob, A. (2017) Review of energy storage systems for electric vehicle applications. *Renewable and Sustainable Energy Reviews*, 69: 771–789.
17. Un-Noor, F., Padmanaban, S., Mihet-Popa, L., Mollah, M. N., and Hossain, E. (2017) A comprehensive study of key electric vehicle (EV) components, technologies, challenges, impacts, and future direction of development. *Energies*, 10(8), 1217.
18. Hardman, S., Jenn, A., Tal, G., Axsen, J., Beard, G., Daina, N., et al., (2018) A review of consumer preferences of and interactions with electric vehicle charging infrastructure. *Transportation Research Part D: Transport and Environment*, 62: 508–523.

19. Pagany, R., Ramirez Camargo, L., and Dorner, W. (2019) A review of spatial localization methodologies for the electric vehicle charging infrastructure. *International Journal of Sustainable Transportation*, 13: 433–449.

20. Jarvis, R., and Moses, P. (2019) Smart grid congestion caused by plug-in electric vehicle charging. In: *2019 IEEE Texas Power and Energy Conference*, pp. 1–5.

21. Vliet, O., Brouwer, A., Kuramochi, T., Broek, M., and Faaij, A. (2011) Energy use, cost and CO_2 emissions of electric cars. *Journal of Power Sources*, *196*: 2298–2310.

22. Moses, P., Masoum, M., and Hajforoosh, S. (2012) Overloading of distribution transformers in smart grid due to uncoordinated charging of plug-in electric vehicles. In: *2012 IEEE PES Innovative Smart Grid Technologies*, pp. 1–6.

23. Khan, W., Ahmad, A., Ahmad, F., and Saad Alam, M. (2018) A comprehensive review of fast charging infrastructure for electric vehicles. *Smart Science*, *6*: 256–270.

24. Dubarry, M., Devie, A., and McKenzie, K. (2017) Durability and reliability of electric vehicle batteries under electric utility grid operations. *Journal of Power Sources*, *358*: 39–49.

25. Kharrazi, A., Sreeram, V., and Mishra, Y. (2020) Assessment techniques of the impact of grid-tied rooftop photovoltaic generation on the power quality of low voltage distribution network. *Renewable and Sustainable Energy Reviews*, *120*: 109643.

26. Hung, D., and Mishra, Y. (2018) Impacts of single-phase PV injection on voltage quality in 3-phase 4-wire distribution systems. In: *2018 IEEE Power & Energy Society General Meeting*, pp. 1–5.

27. Mishra, S., and Mishra, Y. (2017) Decoupled controller for single-phase grid connected rooftop PV systems to improve voltage profile in residential distribution systems. *IET Renewable Power Generation*, 11(2): 370–377.

28. Esplin, R., and Nelson, T. (2022) Redirecting solar feed in tariffs to residential battery storage. *Economic Analysis and Policy*, *73*: 373–389.

29. Ahmadian, A., Sedghi, M., Mohammadi-ivatloo, B., Elkamel, A., Golkar, M. A., and Fowler, M. (2018) Cost–benefit analysis of V2G implementation in distribution networks considering PEVs battery degradation. *IEEE Transactions on Sustainable Energy*, *9*: 961–970.

30. Lam, A., Leung, K., and Li, V. (2016) Capacity estimation for vehicle-to-grid frequency regulation services with smart charging mechanism. *IEEE Transactions on Smart Grid*, *7*: 156–166.

31. Zhang, Z., Mishra, Y., Yue, D., Dou, C., Zhang, B., and Tian, Y. (2021) Delay-tolerant predictive pPower compensation control for photovoltaic voltage regulation. *IEEE Transactions on Industrial Informatics*, 17: 4545–4554.

32. Zhang, Z., Mishra, Y., Dou, C., Yue, D., Zhang, B., and Tian, Y. (2020) Steady-state voltage regulation with reduced photovoltaic power curtailment. *IEEE Journal of Photovoltaics*, 10: 1853–1863.

33. Jurdak, R., Dorri, A., and Vilathgamuwa, M. (2021) A trusted and privacy-preserving internet of mobile energy. *IEEE Communications Magazine*, 59: 89–95.

34. Yu, R., Zhong, W., Xie, S., Yuen, C., Gjessing, S., and Zhang, Y. (2016) Balancing power demand through EV mobility in vehicle-to-grid mobile energy networks. *IEEE Transactions on Industrial Informatics*, 12: 79–90.

35. Zhong, W., Yu, R., Xie, S., Zhang, Y., and Yau, D. (2018) On stability and robustness of demand response in V2G mobile energy networks. *IEEE Transactions on Smart Grid*, *9*: 3203–3212.

36. Khardenavis, A., Hewage, K., Perera, P., Shotorbani, A. M., and Sadiq, R. (2021) Mobile energy hub planning for complex urban networks. *Energy*, *235*: 121424.

37. Bozchalui, M., and Sharma, R. (2012) Analysis of electric vehicles as mobile energy storage in commercial buildings. In: *2012 IEEE Power and Energy Society General Meeting*, pp. 1–8.

38. Webb, J., Whitehead, J., and Wilson, C. (2019) Who will fuel your electric vehicle in the future? In: *Consumer, Prosumer, Prosumager*, F. Sioshansi, (ed.). Academic Press, pp. 407–429.

39. Webb, J., Wilson, C., Steinberg, T., and Stein, W. (2017) Solar grid parity and its impact on the grid. In: *Innovation and Disruption at the Grid's Edge*, F. P. Sioshansi, (ed.). Academic Press, pp. 389–408.

40. Melo, H., Trovão, J., Pereirinha, P., Jorge, H., and Antunes, C. (2018) A controllable bidirectional battery charger for electric vehicles with vehicle-to-grid capability. *IEEE Transactions on Vehicular Technology*, 67: 114–123.

41. Tomić, J., and Kempton, W. (2007) Using fleets of electric-drive vehicles for grid support. *Journal of Power Sources*, 168: 459–468.

42. Li, S., and Mi, C. (2015) Wireless power transfer for electric vehicle applications. *IEEE Journal of Emerging and Selected Topics in Power Electronics*, 3: 4–17.

43. Vilathgamuwa, M., and Sampath, J. (2015) Wireless power transfer for electric vehicles. In: *Plug In Electric Vehicles in Smart Grids: Integration Techniques*, S. Rajakaruna, F. Shahnia, and A. Ghosh, (eds.). Singapore: Springer, pp. 33–60.

44. Chakraborty, S., Shukla, S., and Thorp, J. (2012) A detailed analysis of the effective-load-carrying-capacity behavior of plug-in electric vehicles in the power grid. In: *2012 IEEE PES Innovative Smart Grid Technologies*, pp. 1–8.

45. Schneider, K., Gerkensmeyer, C., Kintner-Meyer, M., and Fletcher, R. (2008) Impact assessment of plug-in hybrid vehicles on pacific northwest distribution systems. In: *2008 IEEE Power and Energy Society General Meeting*, pp. 1–6.

46. Zhou, Y., Wang, M., Hao, H., Johnson, L., Wang, H., and Hao, H. (2015) Plug-in electric vehicle market penetration and incentives. *Mitigation and Adaptation Strategies for Global Change*, 20: 777–795.

47. Yin, X., and Zhao, X. (2016) Planning of electric vehicle charging station based on real time traffic flow. In: *2016 IEEE Vehicle Power and Propulsion Conference*, pp. 1–4.

48. Zhu, J., Li, Y., Yang, J., Li, X., Zeng, S., and Chen, Y. (2017) Planning of electric vehicle charging station based on queuing theory. *The Journal of Engineering* 2017(13): 1867–1871.

49. Cui, Q., Weng, Y., and Tan, C. (2019) Electric vehicle charging station placement method for urban areas. *IEEE Transactions on Smart Grid*, 10: 6552–6565.

50. Lin, H., Bian, C., Wang, Y., Li, H., Sun, Q., and Wallin, F. (2022) Optimal planning of intra-city public charging stations. *Energy*, 238: 121948.

51. Shaikh, P., and Mouftah, H. (2021) Intelligent charging infrastructure design for connected and autonomous electric vehicles in smart cities. In: *2021 IFIP/IEEE International Symposium on Integrated Network Management*, pp. 992–997.

52. Faisal, A., Yigitcanlar, T., Kamruzzaman, M., and Paz, A. (2021) Mapping two decades of autonomous vehicle research. *Journal of Urban Technology*, 28: 45–74.

53. Wu, J., Liao, H., Wang, J., and Chen, T. (2019) The role of environmental concern in the public acceptance of autonomous electric vehicles. *Transportation Research Part F: Traffic Psychology and Behaviour*, 60: 37–46.

54. Golbabaei, F., Yigitcanlar, T., and Bunker, J. (2021) The role of shared autonomous vehicle systems in delivering smart urban mobility. *International Journal of Sustainable Transportation*, 15: 731–748.

55. Butler, L., Yigitcanlar, T., and Paz, A. (2020) Smart urban mobility innovations. *IEEE Access*, 8: 196034–196049.
56. Márquez-Fernández, F. J., Bischoff, J., Domingues-Olavarría, G., and Alaküla, M. (2021) Assessment of future EV charging infrastructure scenarios for long-distance transport in Sweden. *IEEE Transactions on Transportation Electrification*, p. 1.
57. Nykvist, B., Sprei, F., and Nilsson, M. (2019) Assessing the progress toward lower priced long range battery electric vehicles. *Energy Policy*, 124: 144–155.
58. Lee, A. H. C. (2018) *Charging the Future*. Working Paper Series, Harvard University.
59. Villeneuve, D., Füllemann, Y., Drevon, G., Moreau, V., Vuille, F., and Kaufmann, V. (2020) Future urban charging solutions for electric vehicles. *European Journal of Transport and Infrastructure Research*, 20: 78–102.
60. Dur, F., and Yigitcanlar, T. (2014) Assessing land-use and transport integration via a spatial composite indexing model. *International Journal of Environmental Science and Technology*, 12: 803–816.
61. He, J., Yang, H., Tang, T., and Huang, H. (2018) An optimal charging station location model with the consideration of electric vehicle's driving range. *Transportation Research Part C: Emerging Technologies*, 86: 641–654.
62. Yang, J., Dong, J., and Hu, L. (2017) A data-driven optimization-based approach for siting and sizing of electric taxi charging stations. *Transportation Research Part C: Emerging Technologies*, 77; 462–477.
63. Chen, Z., He, F., and Yin, Y. (2016) Optimal deployment of charging lanes for electric vehicles in transportation networks. *Transportation Research Part B: Methodological*, 91: 344–365.
64. Ahmad, A., Alam, M., and Chabaan, R. (2018) A comprehensive review of wireless charging technologies for electric vehicles. *IEEE Transactions on Transportation Electrification*, 4: 38–63.
65. Kandasamy, K., Vilathgamuwa, M., Madawala, U., and Tseng, K. (2016) Inductively coupled modular battery system for electric vehicles. *IET Power Electronics*, 9: 600–609.
66. Zhang, S., and James, J. Q. (2021) Electric vehicle dynamic wireless charging system: Optimal placement and vehicle-to-grid scheduling. *IEEE Internet of Things Journal*, 9(8), 6047–6057.
67. Wu, H., and Niu, D. (2017) Study on influence factors of electric vehicles charging station location based on ISM and FMICMAC. *Sustainability*, 9(4), 484.
68. Csiszár, C., Csonka, B., Földes, D., Wirth, E., and Lovas, T. (2019) Urban public charging station locating method for electric vehicles based on land use approach. *Journal of Transport Geography*, 74: 173–180.
69. Mirzaei, M., Kazemi, A., and Homaee, O. (2016) A probabilistic approach to determine optimal capacity and location of electric vehicles parking lots in distribution networks. *IEEE Transactions on Industrial Informatics*, 12: 1963–1972.
70. Foley, B., Degirmenci, K., and Yigitcanlar, T. (2020) Factors affecting electric vehicle uptake: Insights from a descriptive analysis in Australia. *Urban Science*, 4(4), 57.
71. Habib, S., Khan, M., Abbas, F., and Tang, H. (2018) Assessment of electric vehicles concerning impacts, charging infrastructure with unidirectional and bidirectional chargers, and power flow comparisons. *International Journal of Energy Research*, 42: 3416–3441.
72. Butler, L., Yigitcanlar, T., and Paz, A. (2021) Barriers and risks of Mobility-as-a-Service (MaaS) adoption in cities. *Cities*, 109: 103036.
73. Yigitcanlar, T. and Bulu, M. (2015) Dubaization of Istanbul. *Environment and Planning A: Economy and Space*, 47: 89–107.

74. Sarimin, M., and Yigitcanlar, T. (2012) Towards a comprehensive and integrated knowledge-based urban development model. *International Journal of Knowledge-Based Development*, *3*: 175–192.

75. Yigitcanlar, T., Velibeyoglu, K., and Baum, S. (2008) *Creative Urban Regions*. Hershey, PA, USA: IGI Global.

76. Esmaeilpoorarabi, N., Yigitcanlar, T., and Guaralda, M. (2018) Place quality in innovation clusters. *Cities*, 74: 156–168.

77. Wang, X., Shahidehpour, M., Jiang, C., and Li, Z. (2019) Coordinated planning strategy for electric vehicle charging stations and coupled traffic-electric networks. *IEEE Transactions on Power Systems*, 34: 268–279.

78. Australian Government (2018) *Australian Electric Vehicle Market Study*. https://arena.gov.au/knowledge-bank/australian-electric-vehicle-market-study/

79. Li, X., Xiang, Y., Lyu, L., Ji, C., Zhang, Q., Teng, F., et al., (2020) Price incentive-based charging navigation strategy for electric vehicles. *IEEE Transactions on Industry Applications*, 56: 5762–5774.

80. Dorcec, L., Pevec, D., Vdovic, H., Babic, J., and Podobnik, V. (2019) How do people value electric vehicle charging service? A gamified survey approach. *Journal of Cleaner Production*, 210, 887–897.

81. Solanke, T., Ramachandaramurthy, V., Yong, J., Pasupuleti, J., Kasinathan, P., and Rajagopalan, A. (2020) A review of strategic charging–discharging control of grid-connected electric vehicles. *Journal of Energy Storage*, 28: 101193.

82. Zhang, S., Mishra, Y., and Shahidehpour, M. (2017) Utilizing distributed energy resources to support frequency regulation services. *Applied Energy*, 206: 1484–1494.

83. Hanley, N., Mourato, S., and Wright, R. (2001) Choice modelling approaches. *Journal of Economic Surveys*, 15: 435–462.

84. Lin, Z., and Greene, D. (2010) A plug-in hybrid consumer choice model with detailed market segmentation. *Transportation Research Board*, 10-1698.

85. Hensher, D., and Johnson, L. (2018) *Applied Discrete-Choice Modelling*. Routledge.

86. Webb, J., Wilson, C., and Kularatne, T. (2019) Will people accept shared autonomous electric vehicles? *Economic Analysis and Policy*, 61: 118–135.

87. Yigitcanlar, T., Dodson, J., Gleeson, B., and Sipe, N. (2007) Travel self-containment in master planned estates. *Urban Policy and Research*, 25(1): 129–149.

88. Ingrao, C., Messineo, A., Beltramo, R., Yigitcanlar, T., and Ioppolo, G. (2018) How can life cycle thinking support sustainability of buildings? *Journal of Cleaner Production*, 201: 556–569.

89. Lantz, T., Ioppolo, G., Yigitcanlar, T., and Arbolino, R. (2021) Understanding the correlation between energy transition and urbanization. *Environmental Innovation and Societal Transitions*, 40: 73–86.

90. Khardenavis, A., Hewage, K., Perera, P., Shotorbani, A., and Sadiq, R. (2021) Mobile energy hub planning for complex urban networks. *Energy*, 235: 121424.

91. Vilathgamuwa, M., Mishra, Y., Yigitcanlar, T., Bhaskar, A., and Wilson, C. (2022) Mobile-Energy-as-a-Service (MEaaS): Sustainable electromobility via integrated energy–transport–urban infrastructure. *Sustainability*, 14(5): 2796.

10   Mobility as a Service

10.1 Introduction

Pressure on transportation systems in urban areas is being intensified by worldwide urbanisation and consumer preference for private automobiles (Zhao, 2014). The appeal of owning an automobile is related to status, convenience, comfort, and independence (Redman et al., 2013). In many urban areas, residents—especially in countries with poor public transportation systems—are increasingly dependent on the ability to access a private automobile. This dependency on vehicles has contributed to a range of environmental, economic, and social effects, including urban sprawl, community severance, climate change, social exclusion, costs associated with vehicle ownership, infrastructure, congestion, loss of agricultural land, and health issues arising from accidents, pollution, and inactivity (Newman & Kenworthy, 1996). There is a growing need to develop smart mobility solutions that appeal to individual preferences while limiting the societal, economic, and environmental impacts of the automobile.

Smart mobility is a sub-theme to the concept of smart cities (Yigitcanlar & Kamruzzaman, 2019). In recent times many urban areas have developed smart city policies to take advantage of technological advancements to transform urban areas and address issues relating to prosperity, liveability, and sustainability (Yigitcanlar & Kamruzzaman, 2018; Yigitcanlar et al., 2019a). The use of smart urban technologies has the potential to transform cities and contribute to benefits, including improved infrastructure capacity, reduced consumption, reduced emissions, improved access to services, and improved access to data which can be used to improve the functionality of transportation, energy, and water systems (Yigitcanlar, 2016). With this in mind, and capitalising on the growing trend for a sharing economy and proliferation of on-demand transportation services, Mobility-as-a-Service (MaaS) has been proposed as a potential smart mobility solution which can address transportation-related issues in urban areas.

The basic concept behind MaaS, or Transportation-as-a-Service (TaaS) as it is sometimes referred to (Ho et al., 2018), is that it provides a system whereby traditional services such as public transport can be integrated with other on-demand and shared services—such as ride, bike and car sharing—and a single online interface utilised for payment, journey planning, and other traveller information.

DOI: 10.1201/9781003403630-13

Journeys can be planned out in advance, trips generated based on a range of available transportation modes, and payments made through a single account (Goodall et al., 2017). Advocates highlight the potential for MaaS to reduce private vehicle ownership and transportation costs as well as to promote less resource-intensive transportation modes such as public transport (Jittrapirom et al., 2017).

The concept of MaaS began to attract worldwide attention following the 2014 ITS Europe Congress and the successful trials of the Whim App in Helsinki, Finland, in 2016 (Goodall et al., 2017; Audouin & Finger, 2018). Encouraging reports of these early trials generated further interest and have been followed by rapid development of similar schemes throughout Europe (Hensher, 2017). In addition to continental Europe, MaaS trials have been implemented in the UK, the US, Canada, India, Taiwan, and Australia (Jittrapirom et al., 2017; Chang et al., 2020; Singh, 2020). The shift towards MaaS is partly driven by changing trends associated with the increased use of ridesourcing apps and reduced car ownership among younger populations (Casey et al., 2017).

As a result of this growing interest, the number of research articles that focus on MaaS is expanding. In such an emerging research topic, a systematic literature review is invaluable to extract insights and analyse relationships between existing research. To date, several reviews focusing on MaaS have been published in academic journals. Most recently, Arias-Molinares and Garcia-Palomares (2020) completed a bibliometric review of 57 peer-reviewed articles with a focus on defining MaaS, understanding its history, identifying the main actors, and how and why MaaS should be implemented. Other reviews have focused on real-world trials (Kamargianni et al., 2016), definitions (Jittrapirom et al., 2017), insider threat (Callegati et al., 2018), the role of transport modes (Utriainen & Pöllänen, 2018), supply-side modelling (Calderon & Miller, 2019), creating taxonomy for MaaS integration from a user perspective (Lyon et al., 2019), electric MaaS systems (Garcia et al., 2020), and its ability to deliver promises and unanticipated implications (Pangbourne et al., 2020a)

The broad aim of this research is to strengthen our understanding of MaaS, with the specific aim being to contribute to existing research by investigating the barriers to MaaS adoption in cities. In doing so it will identify potential risks associated with these barriers and highlight broad actions, which should be investigated prior to implementing MaaS in cities. From this research, a conceptual framework has been developed that outlines specific barriers and how they could be addressed in the urban mobility context. This chapter also highlights future areas of research that can assist researchers, policymakers, and planners to see beyond the rhetoric of MaaS, and better understand challenges and risks it poses to our cities and societies.

10.2 Literature Background

Smart mobility has become a growing trend within cities as a way to improve the efficiency and functionality of transportation. Smart mobility solutions aim to harness new technological advances and innovations to make better use of available capacity and influence changes in the transportation system with the view to improving the overall environmental, social, and economic outcomes of cities. Key goals associated with smart mobility include reduced congestion, reduced emissions, improved transportation efficiency, less crashes, less pollution, increased active transport, and reduced private vehicle use (Yigitcanlar et al., 2019b).

Some of the most commonly identified innovations within the smart mobility realm include: (a) flexible transport services (FTS), which have been used to provide door-to-door transportation at a higher degree of flexibility than public transport and can include demand-responsive services that utilise fixed, semi-fixed, or dynamic routing based on user demand; (b) intelligent transport systems (ITS) and infrastructure, enabled by advances in information and communication technology (ICT), big data, cloud computing, the Internet of Things (IoT), and artificial intelligence (AI), which could improve decision-making by enhancing the ability for regulators, operators, planners, and transportation users to collect, analyse, distribute, and learn from transport data; (c) autonomous vehicles (AVs), which could remove driver costs, improve overall safety, and contribute to social inclusion by enabling those currently unable to operate an automobile to travel independently (Faisal et al., 2020; Golbabaei et al., 2021); (d) shared mobility (SM), which could help reduce traffic, improve transport efficiency, and improve social interactions (Contreras & Paz, 2018); and (e) electric mobility (EM), which has the potential to reduce direct vehicular emissions and, depending on the fuel source of the grid, contribute to reduced reliance on non-renewable resources (Docherty et al., 2018; Yigitcanlar & Kamruzzaman, 2019; Yigitcanlar et al., 2019b).

While each of the abovementioned innovations represents a separate innovative approach, they also can be integrated to better achieve the aims of smart mobility. For instance, while flexible demand-responsive systems have the potential to be less costly than providing public transport in low-occupancy areas, government subsidies are often still required to cover costs (Jokinen et al., 2019). AVs could significantly reduce operational costs as no drivers will be required (Faisal et al., 2019; Yigitcanlar et al., 2019c). Furthermore, advances in technologies such as AI, Internet of Things, cloud computing, and 5G networks are helping to increase the viability of demand-responsive systems by continuing to improve the efficiency of routing and scheduling, data collection, and ticketing (Stanley & Lucas, 2014; Yigitcanlar et al., 2020).

In addition, the movement towards a shared economy and improvements in ICT systems has led to a proliferation of ride-sourcing, ride-sharing, and car-sharing within cities. These schemes, such as Uber, Lyft, and Drive My Car, harness advances in ICT to provide pay-per-minute options that offer an alternative to traditional taxi and car rental services. When used as a replacement for a private vehicle, users are no longer burdened with costs associated with fuel, insurance, storage, and purchase. Some studies have shown that in high-density areas, where trips are shorter, these schemes present a viable alternative to private vehicles, particularly among young adults (Soares Machado et al., 2018).

Intelligent sensors and tracking technology have also led to an increase in free floating car- (e.g., Zipcar and Car2Go), bike- (e.g., Mobike and Ofo), and scooter-sharing schemes (e.g., Lime and Neuron) within cities. These pay-per-minute schemes allow customers to identify and book nearby vehicles using their smart devices. Vehicles can then be dropped off at any location within the defined service areas—thus enhancing freedom of movement and improving door-to-door mobility (Soares Machado et al., 2018).

MaaS does not necessarily represent a direct technological innovation to the transport sector (Smith & Hensher, 2020), rather, it represents an innovative new way of offering transport services to users (Alexandros et al., 2017). It provides a service from which the growing options associated with smart mobility such as free-floating vehicle sharing, FTS, or SM can be provided to users in conjunction with more traditional transportation providers, such as public transport, taxis, or car rentals. It would also provide an opportunity for mobility providers to share and collect data on the transportation system and work together to improve its efficiency. Furthermore, with mobility providers controlling larger fleets of vehicles than individual ownership, mass changes in electrification and autonomy can be made quicker and more efficiently (Fuentes et al., 2019).

In this sense, MaaS systems aim to facilitate the integration of a wide range of mobility providers and help strengthen the efficiency of the transport network by looking at the system as a whole rather than individual elements working in isolation. It does not necessarily change the overall functionality of transport but rather provides opportunities for incremental changes that together can contribute to a more efficient and sustainable system (Smith & Hensher, 2020). The type of services offered, and functionality of MaaS may vary depending on the needs of the society in which it is implemented. Therefore, this chapter utilises the simple definition for MaaS offered by Smith and Hensher (2020, p.56), MaaS is "a type of service that through a joint digital channel enables users to plan, book and pay for multiple types of mobility services".

10.3 Methodology

This study has used a systematic literature review based on the three-stage methodological approach adopted by Kankanamge et al. (2019), to address the following research questions: What are the barriers related to the adoption of MaaS, and what risks are associated with these barriers?

In Stage 1 (planning), we first defined our objective as being to examine the concept of MaaS, and identify the barriers and impacts related to its implementation in cities. "Mobility-as-a-Service", "Transportation-as-a-Service", and "Transport-as-a-Service" were selected as the key words for this research. These words were then used to search the titles, abstracts, and keywords of available publications using a university search engine that has access to over 390 academic databases. As MaaS is a relatively new concept the publication date was left open-ended. Our search was conducted in August 2020 and yielded a total of 578 articles. Since this number of articles was manageable no further search parameters were required.

In Stage 2 (carrying out the review), the 578 articles yielded from the search were reviewed based on the primary inclusionary and exclusionary criteria. The titles, abstracts, and keywords of the remaining 201 articles were screened against

Table 10.1 Exclusion and inclusion criteria

Primary criteria		Secondary criteria	
Inclusionary	*Exclusionary*	*Inclusionary*	*Exclusionary*
Articles	Duplicate records	MaaS related	Not MaaS related
Peer-reviewed	Books and chapters	Relevance to	Irrelevant to research aims
Full text available	Industry reports	research aims	
online	Government reports		

Table 10.2 Criteria for category formulation

Selection criteria

Determine the key critiques relevant to MaaS using the eye-balling technique in the
   literature
Detect barriers relating to the implementation of MaaS systems in urban areas
Identify potential impacts MaaS systems will have on urban mobility
Group the identified barriers and impacts with similarities to form broader potential
   categories
Narrow down categories and check consistency against other literature
Final review of literature and analysis of shortlisted categories
Verify, classify, and finalise the creation of final categories
Distribute the selected and review literature under most relevant categories

the secondary criteria. This resulted in the number of relevant articles reducing to 123. The full texts of these articles were then read against the secondary inclusion and exclusion criteria. This resulted in a further reduction of papers to 91 articles. Primary and secondary criteria are shown in Table 10.1.

In Stage 3 (reporting), the final 91 articles were analysed using a descriptive, rather than statistical, technique. Qualitative techniques of pattern matching and explanation building were utilised, the purpose of which was to classify the selected articles into defined categories. Pattern matching, or scanning for common subjects and differences, was completed using an eye-balling technique which was considered sufficient to evaluate and structure the data. In accordance with Yigitcanlar et al. (2019b) a four-step process was then used to classify the reviewed literature into specific themes. These themes were then reconsidered, refined, and cross-checked against other literature and review studies. Finally, the selected articles were categorised under three themes, being "desired outcomes and risks" (n= 22), "supply-side barriers" (n=36), and "demand-side barriers" (n=33). The criteria for formation of the themes are presented in Table 10.2. The categorisation of selected articles is presented in Tables 10.3–10.5.

Stage 3 (reporting and disseminating) was then undertaken. This stage involved writing and presenting the results from the 91 articles analysed as part of this review. During this stage, additional publications (n=22) relevant to MaaS, which

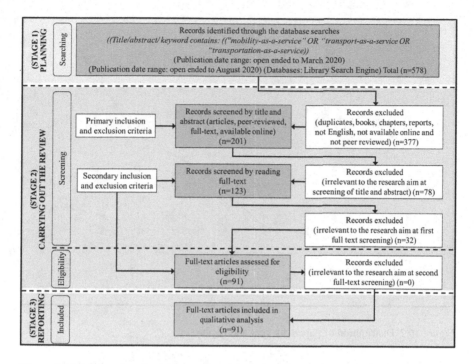

Figure 10.1 Literature selection procedure.

did not meet the aforementioned search criteria but were identified following a process of backward snowballing and personal knowledge were used to support, elaborate, and establish a contextual background for this study. A summary of the above methodology including the Boolean search phrase used is shown in Figure 10.1.

10.4 Results

10.4.1 General Observations

The publication dates for the 91 articles included in this review reflect the rapidly growing interest in MaaS as a topic among researchers, in 2015 one article was published, followed by three in 2016, five in 2017, 19 in 2018, 20 in 2019, and 43 in the first eight months of 2020. Most leading authors are affiliated with academic institutions in Europe (n=59), reflecting the significant interest in Europe where the concept was born and initial trials were implemented. Nonetheless, there is also significant interest in Australia (n=12) and North America (n=10), and Asia (n=7), with a few studies in South American (n=2) and the Middle East (n=1). A graph showing the growth of MaaS literature in relation to publication year and world region is shown in Figure 10.2.

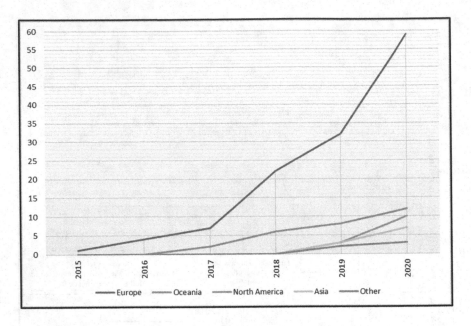

Figure 10.2 Distribution of papers by year and region.

The most common leading authors were Göran Smith (n=5), Corinne Mulley (n=4), Peraphan Jittrapirom (n=3), and Jana Sochor (n=3). Given MaaS represents a new concept in transportation it is not surprising that the majority of articles selected for the research were published in journals with a focus on transports (n= 64). Over a third of these articles were published in Transportation Research Part A (n=25) which has a focus on transportation issues and papers from a policy, planning, and governmental perspective. Of the remaining 66 articles, seven were published in Research in Transportation Business and Management, five articles each in Sustainability, Transportation, and Travel Behaviour and Society, four articles each in European Transport Research Review, IATSS Research, and Research in Transportation Economics, three articles in Transport Research Part C, and two articles each in Competition and Regulation in Network Industries, Public Management Review, Transport Reviews, and Transportation Research Record. The remaining 21 articles were published in 21 different journals, seven of which focus on urban and land use planning and policy, and six on transportation.

Regarding research methods, a large number of papers aimed to analyse stakeholder and user perception of MaaS, whether through qualitative methods such as interviews, focus groups, and workshop (n=18), quantitative methods such as surveys and questionnaires (n=12), or a mixed-method approach which combines both (n=13). While providing valuable insights into user and stakeholder perception these methods can be problematic considering MaaS is a new concept and many of the respondents may not have had much prior experience with the service. Even for studies where data were collected following MaaS trials (n=9) there can be issues as trial participants may not be representative of the general population but rather represent a segment that already has an inherent curiosity with the services and therefore is more likely to hold positive opinions. Furthermore, businesses could have a vested interest in providing specific responses.

The next most common research methods are policy and institutional analysis (n=15) and literature reviews (n=14). Of the 14 literature reviews included in this study a total of nine are focused on MaaS while the remainder look at future mobility in a more general sense. Literature reviews are a useful source for getting a good overview of a research topic and providing a knowledge base, but are limited in that they rely on previously published material. Policy and institutional analysis can help understand how existing policy and governance structure might influence or be required to change to meet new conditions imposed by innovations such as MaaS. Finally, a number of studies (n=10) have incorporated the use of statistical models (such as discrete choice models). These models provide a useful way for researchers to predict the future impact of MaaS on the transportation system. However, since MaaS is still in its infancy, further research would be helpful to better calibrate these models. The distribution of papers by type is shown in Figure 10.3.

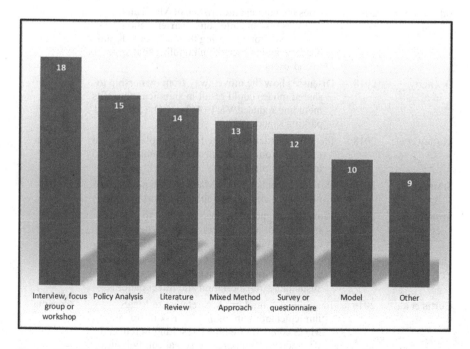

Figure 10.3 Distribution of papers by type.

10.4.2 Desired MaaS Outcomes and Risks

This section discusses some of the desired outcomes and associated risks related to MaaS implementation in cities. Based on the reviewed literature the following outcomes were identified: (a) reduction of per capita vehicle kilometres travelled (VKT) and associated externalities; (b) increase in trip awareness and planning; (c) reduction of parking spaces; (d) reduction of car ownership; and (e) improved social equity (Table 10.3).

Table 10.3 MaaS desired outcomes

Literature	Year	Relevance	Region
Sochor et al.	2016	Provides insights on customer perspectives from a real-world trial of MaaS including evidence of travel mode and behaviour change, and reduced cost	Europe
Strömberg et al.	2016	Provide insights regarding how people may adopt different travel behaviours following the introduction of MaaS	Europe
Hensher	2017	Discusses some potential impacts as a result of replacing conventional PT with MaaS particularly in low-density areas	Oceania
Jittrapirom et al.	2017	Defines the core characteristics of MaaS and provides insights into some barriers relating its implementation including the need for a digital platform and subscription bundling that appeals to end-users	Europe
Docherty et al.	2018	Discusses how the move away from ownership to shared modes could result in significant benefits including reduced VKT (44%), CO_2 (53%), and parking spaces (95%)	Europe
Mulley et al.	2018	Identifies challenges related to the implementation of MaaS from the perspective of community transportation providers	Oceania
Smith et al.	2018	Provide insights on how MaaS has the potential to negatively impact on public transport system	Europe
Strömberg et al.	2018	Provides insights into MaaS potential to change transportation mode choices, travel behaviour and car ownership	Europe
Utriainen & Pöllänen	2018	Identifies potential impacts of MaaS systems such as reduced ownership, parking, increase in sustainable transportation and travel patterns	Europe
Curtis et al.	2019	Identifies potential impacts relating to MaaS implementation including the risk of private MaaS competing with PT resulting in reduced PT ridership and potential social equity issues arising from development of transportation monopolies	Oceania

Table 10.3 (Continued)

Literature	Year	Relevance	Region
Fuentes et al.	2019	Provides insights into how sharing technologies are more efficient that single vehicle ownership	Middle East
Hawkins & Habib	2019	Provides insights into the potential social equity issues associated with MaaS, large households, and fringe areas	North America
Johansson et al.	2019	Provides insights into MaaS impact on parking, and car ownership	Europe
Segui-Gasco et al.	2019	Provides insights from simulations model regarding potential for MaaS to result in reduction in private vehicle use and bus services	Europe
Tirachini	2020	Provides insights into MaaS potential to reduce VKT and its impacts on pollution, accidents, congestion, ride hailing. Discusses implications for parking	South America
Becker et al.	2020	Provides insights into MaaS systems and transportation-related energy consumption	Europe
Franco et al.	2020	Provides insights into the impact of MaaS on private vehicle use and public transport use	Europe
Hörcher & Graham	2020	Provides interesting insights regarding the impact of private vehicle ownership of VKT	Europe
Nikitas et al.	2020	Discusses potential risks associated with MaaS	Europe
Pangbourne et al.	2020	Discusses potential for MaaS to encourage walking	Europe
Rosenblum et al.	2020	Provide insights in changes in parking following AV and MaaS implementation, and the potential role for hybrid parking structures	North America
Wong et al.	2020	Provides insights into the potential for MaaS to impact public transportation ridership, and use of road pricing to control traffic	Oceania
Wright et al.	2020	Provides insights into how MaaS systems could reduce private vehicle ownership	Europe

Firstly, researchers propose that if MaaS could increase the modal split of SM it would be able to meet the same demands while also reducing total VKT per passenger. A reduction of VKT would have a flow-on effect and lead to a per capita reduction in negative transport externalities (Tirachini, 2020), including energy consumption (Becker et al., 2020). This premise is supported by results from MaaS trials in Europe which show a reduction in private vehicle use, particularly among participants who went into the trial with the intended purpose of finding an alternative to ownership (Strömberg et al., 2018). However, these results should be viewed with caution, not least due to the predisposed intentions of trial participants, but also because many users who previously relied on private vehicle travel simply replaced this use with other single-occupancy services (Strömberg et al., 2016; Hensher, 2017; Strömberg et al., 2018). When given a choice between multiple transport options, users who typically relied on more sustainable means such as public or active transport may be attracted to the comfort and convenience of single-mode or low-occupancy transport (Jang et al., 2021; Pangbourne et al., 2020a). If this occurs issues associated with increased VKT are unlikely to be resolved. In fact, they could be exacerbated, particularly if users replace conventional public transport with car-based services (Hensher, 2017; Curtis et al., 2019; Tirachini, 2020). To overcome this issue, researchers highlight the need for MaaS systems to be designed so that car-based services complement, rather than compete with, public transport (Utriainen & Pöllänen, 2018). Furthermore, given that vehicle occupancy rates are key to improving sustainability, initiatives that promote ride pooling will be important (Tirachini, 2020; Wright et al., 2020).

Secondly, an analysis of user experiences following MaaS trials has shown that the need to coordinate trips to fit available subscription models is likely resulting in changed travel behaviour including increased trip chaining, reducing "unnecessary" trips, and increasing active, public, and shared modes (Sochor et al., 2016). Furthermore, results show that a well-designed app has the potential to make the realisation of transport choices more mentally accessible, which in turn provides a catalyst for users to make new discoveries and better reflect on current transport patterns (Sochor et al., 2016; Strömberg et al., 2016). It is theorised that as users become more active in preplanning daily trips, and are made more aware of all available options, they will realise that they are not dependent on private vehicles (Strömberg et al., 2018). However, given that many participants in these trials are likely innately curious and eager for alternatives, the results may not reflect the behaviour of the wider community (Strömberg et al., 2018). Nevertheless, researchers highlight the potential for MaaS apps to take advantage of participant's increased awareness by promoting or encouraging changed behaviour, towards more environmentally friendly or active travel modes (Utriainen & Pöllänen, 2018; Pangbourne et al., 2020a; Wright et al., 2020). Nonetheless, some researchers argue that if MaaS can be used to change behaviour there is a risk it is used for more nefarious means that are not necessarily in the best interests of the community (e.g. could journey planners be used to favour more profitable modes) (Lyon et al., 2019).

The third outcome relates to decreased parking demand. If MaaS results in more shared trips, cities could see a reduction in parking as SM service can simply move onto the next passenger after a trip is completed (Tirachini, 2020). In fact, simulation of London's transport system by Segui-Gasco et al. (2019) determined that parking could be reduced by up to 38% when factoring in a 15% shift toward low-occupancy minibuses (even when accounting for a 34% shift away from larger buses). Similarly, when you consider that AVs will require less space for parking (i.e. there is no need for a human driver and passengers can simply be dropped off prior to parking) there is potential for more significant reductions with some modelling suggesting demand could be reduced by 95% (Docherty et al., 2018).

While this would theoretically free up large amounts of land for other uses, it could create additional issues (Utriainen & Pöllänen. 2018). Firstly, cities would need to allocate more space for drop off and pick up areas and, factoring in EM, additional charging stations (Rosenblum et al., 2020). In addition, cities may see more vehicles completing dead runs—i.e. without passengers, or in the case of AVs without occupants. This would increase VKT and further contribute to the external effects of personal transportation (Segui-Gasco et al., 2019; Tirachini, 2020; Nikitas et al., 2020). In addition, removing the need to park vehicles at home could be used as an incentive for users to move away from ownership by freeing up space for storage and other uses (Webb, 2019).

The fourth identified outcome relates to car ownership. Much like streaming services have removed the need to own or rent content, the basic premise behind MaaS is that car ownership could be reduced by simplifying the process for accessing transportation and removing the need for fixed costs (Fuentes et al., 2019). Reducing car ownership will theoretically have a follow-on effect resulting in increased use of SM (Nikitas et al., 2020). However, reduced car ownership will not necessarily result in positive impacts. In fact, users may be drawn to other single-occupancy modes, or alternatively an increase in public transport numbers could lead to overcrowding and other issues leading to a boomerang effect where even more users are pushed towards less sustainable modes (Hörcher & Graham, 2020). Notwithstanding, evidence of MaaS impact on ownership is still in its infancy and the actual impact is unknown. Early research shows that it might not result in a large shift (particularly in cities where car travel is the dominant mode of transport). In fact, Wright et al. (2020) found that while 40% trial participants were willing to replace some of their trips with SM, this only amounted to a potential 1.7% reduction in car ownership. Reducing vehicle ownership is therefore likely to rely on additional motivators such as travel subsidies, parking restrictions, or zoning laws (Johansson et al., 2019; Franco et al., 2020).

The final outcome relates to improved social equity. MaaS has potential to offer disadvantaged groups (e.g., low income, aged, and disabled) greater freedom to satisfy their mobility needs using shared services and forgoing the need to rely on public transportation, which is limited by fixed schedules and routes, or private transport which typically comes at high fixed costs (Mulley et al., 2018; Utriainen & Pöllänen, 2018). The basic premise behind this improvement is that MaaS will offer users more options, which in turn gives users increased choices to satisfy their various needs (Jittrapirom et al., 2017). This, in turn, could increase accessibility in locations that traditionally rely on private vehicle travel (Jittrapirom et al., 2017; Docherty et al., 2018). The social implications of increased equity of services includes greater access to healthcare services, recreational facilities, improving social wellbeing, and support for more active communities while the economic benefits relate to greater access to employment, training, and education and improving the liveability of communities (Alexandros et al., 2017).

Increased equity is particularly important in low-density areas where public transport providers have traditionally found it difficult to provide services that meet the varying needs of the community (Hensher, 2017). Under a MaaS system, fixed route services could be replaced by a network of SM services which act as a feeder system to major public transport nodes. This network of services could be accessed by users via smartphones and would provide greater geographic coverage and flexibility than existing services, offering greater equality in transportation offerings, and including more customised service to cover the specific needs of certain sociodemographic groups (e.g., aged and disabled) (Hensher, 2017; Franco et al., 2020). However, there is a risk that under a MaaS model, low-occupancy uses that might be a necessity to a certain sociodemographic group and rely on significant government subsidies, are removed in favour of more profitable services resulting in further deterioration of public services (Hawkins & Habib, 2020; Wong et al., 2020).

10.4.3 MaaS Supply-Side Barriers

This section discusses the barriers related to the supply of MaaS services within cities. Supply-side factors refer to those affecting the operation and distribution of the service offerings. These include: (a) lack of cooperation among stakeholders; (b) lack of business interest; (c) lack of service coverage; (d) lack of a clear, shared vision; and (e) lack of data and cyber security (Table 10.4).

The first supply-side barrier relates to cooperation among stakeholders. The basic premise is that given MaaS's primary aim is to integrate transportation

Table 10.4 MaaS supply-side barriers

Literature	Year	Relevance	Region
Sochor et al.	2015	Provides insights on stakeholder perspectives from a real-world trial of MaaS regarding the importance cooperation between public and private actors, the importance of balancing user, provider and societal needs, and the development of a service concept	Europe
Alexandros et al.	2017	Describes how mobility providers fear losing relationships with clients and financial incentives are important to encourage pioneers	Europe
Casey et al.	2017	Describes the importance of open API in development of MaaS system	Europe
Audouin & Finger	2018	Generates insights into how governance systems can support the integration of key stakeholders relating to MaaS implementation including the importance of shared vision, and legislation to keep dominant players from resisting change	Europe
Callegati et al.	2018	Describes risks associated with insider threat	Europe
Eckhardt et al.	2018	Provides insights into the potential need for incentives and subsidies to entice mobility providers into rural areas	Europe

Table 10.4 (Continued)

Literature	Year	Relevance	Region
Jittrapirom et al.	2018	Discusses collaboration between actors as being the most crucial challenge facing the implementation of MaaS. Benefits include enhancing knowledge through data sharing, and offering attractive business opportunities for potential providers	Europe
Jittrapirom et al.	2020	Discusses how there is a perception among business that MaaS will bring high economic and marking costs, unnecessary risks (such as cyber security, privacy), and no short-term return. Discusses how incentives can be used to encourage stakeholder collaboration	Europe
Mulley & Kronsell	2018	Discusses the need for collaboration between operators and mobility providers. Identifies need for intermediary actors (or integrators) to bring mobility offerings to MaaS operators	Oceania
Polydoropoulou et al.	2020a	Examines stakeholder viewpoints relating to the implementation of MaaS and the need for private and public cooperation, risk of monopoly, need for business incentives, and data safety	Europe
Smith et al.	2018	Discusses the need for economic incentives and importance of collaboration among stakeholders to ensure that MaaS is able to contribute to societal goals. MaaS vision should be strong, yet adaptable and developed in collaboration with a range of important stakeholders	Europe
Sochor et al.	2018	Describes how business and political interest in MaaS scheme may benefit following successful trials	Europe
Surakka et al.	2018	Identifies policy and legislation as a significant barrier for introducing MaaS systems. Describes how there is optimism within the public and private sector in relation to the implementation of MaaS	Europe
Veeneman et al.	2018	Describes how for MaaS to succeed it needs to convince both users and mobility providers that the platform adds value. As system gets more complex a clear vision can provide a framework for which new users can build their services on	Europe
Calderón & Miller	2020	Provides insights into the use of MaaS to solve the first-mile, last mile problem, and provide thin flows, of demand-responsive transport in low density areas. Importance of AV in success of MaaS	North America

(*Continued*)

Table 10.4 (Continued)

Literature	Year	Relevance	Region
Cooper et al.	2019	Describes public private collaboration as the most significant barrier for the successful implementation of MaaS systems	Europe
Hirschhorn et al.	2019	Identifies the need for new governance frameworks which facilitate collaboration between wide range of stakeholders and guided by society values	Europe
Hoerler et al.	2019	Discusses how for innovation in transport system to occur collaboration is essential	Europe
Lyons et al.	2019	Discusses how MaaS potential to influence behaviour could be cause for concern.	Europe
Mukhtar-Landgren & Smith	2019	Describes the importance of vision and collaboration in development of MaaS policy and legislation to ensure competing interests are balanced and societal values supported	Europe
Narupiti	2019	Identifies challenges relating to stakeholder cooperation and the potential for intermediary actors to mediate	South East Asia
Pandey et al.	2019	Describes the need for regulatory frameworks to ensure MaaS is developed in a way that is fair to all stakeholders, and does not result in suboptimal outcomes	North America
Smith et al.	2019	Identifies risks associated with lack of vision and perception of existing legislation as a barrier to MaaS	Europe
Beheshtian et al.	2020	Provides insights into the use of road pricing schemes to improve transport efficiency	North America
Cottrill	2020	Provides insights in regarding MaaS and the role social networks and importance of developing customer trust	Europe
García et al.	2020	Provides insights into the role of data in MaaS and how it can enhance policy development	Europe
Karlsson et al.	2020	Describes the important of top-down governance to ensure all levels of government shared the same vision, and discusses transport subsidies in relation to MaaS	Europe
Liu et al.	2020	Discusses issues associated with implementing MaaS in rural communities	North America
Masini et al.	2020	Discusses the use of meta-surfaces to overcome issues associated with obstruction of network signals	South America
Merkert et al.	2020	Discusses the use of a broker to coordinate services in MaaS system. Highlighted issues such as conflicts between brands, data ownerships, brokers that are owned by mobility providers and whether broker is public or privately managed	North America

Table 10.4 (Continued)

Literature	Year	Relevance	Region
Meurs et al.	2020	Describes stakeholder collaboration as being a significant barrier for MaaS implementation and highlights the need for a clear vision and good governance	North America
Polydoropoulou et al.	2020b	Describes the important of policy, and identifies some potential issues arising from lack of cooperation for MaaS implementation	Europe
Sakai	2020	Provides insights into the importance of data sharing in MaaS ecosystem	East Asia
Singh	2020	Describes how MaaS planning should facilitate collaboration between stakeholder and be flexible and adaptive to changes	South Asia
Smith & Hensher	2020	Identifies coordination of mobility providers as the most disruptive aspect of MaaS, discusses how policy reform is a crucial element for MaaS and points out challenges facing rural communities	Europe
Smith et al.	2020	Determines stakeholders hopes and fears associated with the use of intermediaries who facilitate better collaboration between MaaS operators and transportation service providers	Europe
Stehlin et al.	2020	Discusses how MaaS requires a collaborative approach	North America

services within a city, a wide range of competing interests, goals, and strategies from the private and public sectors, users, and the broader society will need to be taken into consideration (Sochor et al., 2015; Hoerler et al., 2019; Cooper et al., 2019). Good collaborative efforts between both sectors, and across administrative boundaries, can help address service limitations including funding, staff, technical, and capability requirements (Liu et al., 2020; Singh, 2020; Stehlin et al., 2020), while lack of cooperation could potentially result in network inefficacies (including increased VKT), monopolisation, uncertainty (Polydoropoulou et al., 2020b) and, political and business disinterest (Eckhardt et al., 2018; Meurs et al., 2020). The problem is that few regions have experience with MaaS, researchers expect some important actors may be averse to collaboration (Jittrapirom et al., 2020), and there may be significant differences in stakeholder perspectives (Polydoropoulou et al., 2020b). Researchers therefore highlight the importance of an integrated body responsible for organising and enticing stakeholders to join MaaS, balancing competing interests, and stimulating public action when required (Mukhtar-Landgren & Smith, 2019; Merkert et al., 2020; Meurs et al., 2020; Smith et al., 2020).

A key argument relates to whether public or private actors are most suited for this role. In one sense, public actors (particularly public transport operators) are best positioned from a strategic and regulatory point of view, but may lack resources

(Narupiti, 2019; Polydoropoulou et al., 2020b). Private actors, on the other hand, would have more incentive to create profit and innovative services but less incentive to fulfil societal goals, or operate collaboratively (Narupiti, 2019; Smith & Hensher, 2020). Notwithstanding, for a fully integrated MaaS system mobility providers should be willing to allow third parties to sell tickets and access journey information (Sakai, 2020). Furthermore, given the inherent complexities related to stakeholder collaboration, cities would likely benefit from MaaS trials and pilot programs so that different methods of collaboration can be experimented with, and relationships and trust between actors developed (Smith et al., 2019; Karlsson et al., 2020). Given that many transport providers already provide services through an online platform, the integration of e-ticketing and journey planning has been identified as the natural first step in the development of these programmes (Narupti, 2019; Merkert et al., 2020).

The second identified supply-side barrier relates to the potential lack of business support for MaaS. Researchers argue that if there is no economic incentive for business, the goal of integrating mobility service into one overarching platform seems unlikely (Polydoropoulou et al., 2020a; Smith et al., 2018a; Venneman et al., 2018). MaaS is a new product and while there is a general optimism among both public and private sectors (Surakka et al., 2018), there is a perception that MaaS brings with it high economic and marketing costs (Jittrapirom et al., 2018). Furthermore, the potential for short-term return on investment is low (Jittrapirom et al., 2018; Karlsson et al., 2020), and mobility providers may be scared to lose existing relationships with customers (Alexandros et al., 2017). To overcome this barrier some researchers have highlighted the importance of providing economic incentives to create financial support for early MaaS providers (Alexandros et al, 2017; Jittrapirom et al., 2018). For larger operators, incentives could come in the form of a larger market share, increased revenue, or better access to demand data (Polydoropoulou et al., 2020a; Surakka et al., 2018). Smaller operators, while also benefiting from increased revenue, could be further enticed by the possibility of improving their marketplace visibility (Polydoropoulou et al., 2020a). However, financial incentives should be used with caution as there is a risk they may manipulate the process of pricing services and threaten the ongoing economic sustainability of MaaS (Beheshtian et al., 2020). Notwithstanding, successful trials that demonstrate how MaaS is a more sustainable transport option may help garner political support, increase public interest, and trigger business interest (Jittrapirom et al., 2018; Sochor et al., 2018).

The third supply-side barrier relates to service coverage. Coverage not only relates to bringing actual transport services into all areas within the city, but also having the necessary network coverage of which MaaS is reliant on from both a consumer (i.e. accessing resources) and a provider perspective (i.e. coordinating services) (Liu et al., 2020; Masini et al., 2020). Network coverage is not only problematic in less centralised areas but also in areas where buildings and other structures obstruct wireless signals (Masini et al., 2020). Low-density areas present further problems related to service coverage due to long travel distances, lack of existing public transport services, and less variety in available transport modes (Liu et al., 2020). Smaller administrative areas may also lack funding, staff, and general technological capabilities to support services (Liu et al., 2020). Researchers argue that to provide adequate service in these areas MaaS should use SM and other modes to act as a feeder to existing public transport nodes (Calderón & Miller, 2020). Furthermore, significant subsidies will be required to operate at a cost suitable for their residents (Eckhardt et al., 2018; Karlsson et al., 2020; Smith & Hensher, 2020). However, it is theorised that these inequalities could also be balanced via a levied charge placed on areas with high accessibility, a charge that could then be used to subsidise areas with lower accessibility (Docherty et al., 2018). Once services are established in these areas future advances in automation could lead to reduced operational costs (i.e. no need for a human driver) and lessen the need for government subsidies (Calderón & Miller, 2020). Pilot programmes and trials can also be used to gauge coverage issues (Liu et al. 2020).

The fourth supply-side barrier relates to the development of a shared vision to guide the delivery and scope of MaaS within cities. Researchers argue that if there is no common vision it can be difficult for stakeholders to align goals, which in turn creates challenges when trying to facilitate communication between stakeholders (Surakka et al., 2018; Smith et al., 2019; Meurs et al., 2020), or mediate between societal goals and business interests (Sochor et al., 2015; Veeneman et al., 2018). In fact, following trials of MaaS in Europe, a shared vision has been shown to help facilitate clearer, aligned policy goals between departments, reduce uncertainty, and conveys a message to the private sector that the public sector is supportive of its development (Karlsson et al., 2020). Further reinforcing the importance of cooperation among stakeholders, Smith et al. (2018a) note that the vision needs to be developed with representatives from a mix of governmental agencies, public and private mobility providers (including any new entrants or start-ups), and the general community. The vision should be developed in the early stages of planning, be adaptable, and can be reinforced through the implementation of policy and legislation (Surakka et al., 2018; Polydoropoulou et al., 2020b). Good policy and legislation can strengthen strategic alignments (Audouin & Finger, 2018; Karlsson et al., 2020), protect data privacy (Jittrapirom et al., 2018), reduce inefficiencies (Pandey et al., 2019), balance competing interests, and support societal values (Hirschhorn et al., 2019; Mukhtar-Landgren & Smith, 2019), and can be further enhanced through smart decision-making systems that utilise smart sensors, the IoT, and AI which can assist with data collection, sharing, and analytics (Garcia et al., 2020).

The final barrier relates to data and cyber security. The MaaS environment represents a complex array of networks involving public and private mobility providers and customers containing a large variety of data including personal information (e.g. payment details and travel logs), business data (e.g. costs, fees, service records etc.), and other open data (including timetabling and service locations) (Casey et al., 2017; Cottrill, 2020). From a user perspective there is a risk that personal and payment information will be accessed by nefarious sources (He & Chow, 2020), which could result in issues relating to both financial and personal safety (Veeneman, et al., 2018; Casadó et al., 2020). For mobility providers there are concerns that intellectual property will be breached, potentially resulting in business losing competitive advantage and concerns of insider threat (Callegati, 2018; He & Chow, 2020). Privacy regulations are therefore critical for the development of MaaS and to maintain the trust of both user and providers (Veeneman, et al., 2018; Cottrill, 2020).

10.4.4 MaaS Demand-Side Barriers

This section discusses the barriers related to the demand side of MaaS services within cities. Demand-side barriers relate to the factors affecting the consumption of MaaS within cities. These include: (a) overcoming the lack of appeal with older generations; (b) overcoming the lack of appeal with public transport users; (c) need to provide a platform that is attractive and easy to use; (d) customer willingness to pay; and I overcoming the culture of private vehicle travel (Table 10.5).

Table 10.5 MaaS demand-side barriers

Literature	Year	Relevance	Region
Kamargianni et al.	2016	Identifies benefits relating to MaaS including reduction in time and hassle to purchase a ticket, cost	Europe
Mulley	2017	Describes how culture and perceptions are one of the biggest challenges relating to the transition to MaaS	Oceania
Ho et al.	2018	Provides insights into the social challenges faced by the introduction of MaaS including the cultural shift from private vehicle ownership, acceptance from PT users and willingness to pay for MaaS subscriptions	Oceania
Keller et al.	2018	Describes how the older residents are less likely to be early adopters of integrated mobility platforms	Europe
Matyas & Kamargianni	2018	Provides insights into consumers' willingness to use alternative modes	Oceania
Esztergár-Kiss & Kerényi	2020	Provides insights into what subscription bundles are preferred by users and that they are less interested in bike sharing as an option	Europe
Fioreze et al.	2019	Provides insights into why older generation may be unlikely to take up MaaS, that PT users are the most likely to subscribe, that regular car users are likely to underestimate the cost of MaaS, and MaaS as a sole alternative to private vehicle may be unlikely	Europe
Liyanage et al.	2019	Discusses how MaaS platform and interface can encourage users, including personalised subscriptions, awards and other incentives	Oceania
Pickford & Chung	2019	Discusses socioeconomic barriers including reluctance for car users to take up MaaS, and the potential for MaaS to replace the second vehicle in households	East Asia

Table 10.5 (Continued)

Literature	Year	Relevance	Region
Sakai	2019	Describes how convenience of MaaS can replace private vehicle	East Asia
Alonso-González et al.	2020	Provides insights related to private vehicle ownership as a barrier to MaaS adoption	Europe
Caiati et al.	2020	Provides insights on user perspective and acceptance of MaaS systems. Younger generations and multimodal travellers most likely to adopt MaaS. Older generations less likely. Customers prefer subscription that bundle together unlimited PT trips	Europe
Casadó et al.	2020	Describes how young people are concerned about personal safety and not necessarily uninterested in car ownership	Europe
Chang et al.	2020	Identifies the importance of regular reviews to ensure MaaS is meeting community expectation	East Asia
Feneri et al.	2022	Demonstrates that it is not price alone that impacts on user uptake of MaaS	Europe
Guidon et al.	2020	Provides insights into ways MaaS can enhance trip experiences, subscription offerings, and reluctance towards bike sharing	Europe
Harrison et al.	2020	Demonstrate only a small modal shift from private vehicle in an area with few modal options	Europe
He & Chow	2020	Discusses issues associated with data privacy	North America
Ho et al.	2020	Provides insights into the difference in willingness-to-pay for MaaS in two geographic areas	Oceania
Hoerler et al.	2020	Discusses how public transport users are more inclined towards MaaS than private vehicle users	Europe
Jang et al.	2021	Describes how users are not inclined to use the service and more publicity may be required	Europe
Liljamo et al.	2020	Discusses how respondents were only willing to pay 64% of their current transport costs for a mobility package	Europe
Matyas	2020	Discusses ways cycling can be more attractive to MaaS users, and perception of private vehicle travel	Europe
Mulley et al.	2020	Provides unique insights into user acceptance of MaaS among older people who currently have their mobility provided by community transportation	Oceania
Pangbourne et al.	2020	Provides insights into social barriers associated with the introduction of MaaS	Europe

(Continued)

Table 10.5 (Continued)

Literature	Year	Relevance	Region
Schikofsky et al.	2020	Provides insights into why social acceptance is important for uptake of MaaS	Europe
Sjöman et al.	2020	Provides insights into the acceptance of MaaS among car owners	Europe
Sourbati & Behrendt	2020	Provides insights into older generations and the use of new technologies	Europe
Storme et al.	2020	Provides insights into the relationship between private vehicle use and MaaS	Europe
Vij et al.	2020	Discusses user willingness-to-use MaaS	Oceania
Ye et al.	2020	Discusses user willingness-to-use MaaS	East Asia

The first demand-side barrier relates to MaaS's lack of appeal with older generations (Caiati et al., 2020). Although the use of technology among older aged groups is rising (Sourbati & Behrendt, 2020), there remain strong correlations between older age groups and reluctance to use MaaS (Ho et al., 2018; Keller et al., 2018; Caiati et al., 2020; Vij et al., 2020). Researchers theorise that reluctance to use MaaS is likely due to a higher percentage of this age group having less experience with smartphones, online route planners, and ride-sharing and sourcing apps (Fioreze et al., 2019; Pangbourne et al., 2020b; Sourbati & Behrendt, 2020). Furthermore, their habitual use of private vehicles may be more psychologically ingrained (Caiati et al., 2020). Given that MaaS' integrated platform can simplify the ability for these users to access transportation that meets their needs, this reluctance to use MaaS may represent a missed opportunity to improve the equity of transport services within the city. There is therefore potential to highlight its value by providing training or engaging these groups in pilot programmes (Cottrill, 2020; Mulley et al., 2020). This can help develop positive attitudes among peers, which can significantly impact the uptake of MaaS (Schikofsky et al., 2020). An interim strategy, which can also be applied to areas with low network coverage, could be the provision of a hybrid service that does not necessarily rely on smartphones or ICT (Alonso-Gonzalez et al., 2020).

The second demand-side barrier relates to overcoming the lack of appeal among existing public transportation users. Surveys have found that despite public transport being identified as an essential part of MaaS success, its patrons are not necessarily interested in MaaS as a concept (Ho et al., 2018). However, in other studies, public transport users have been identified as the most likely to use MaaS (together with those who view car ownership as unimportant, and the environmentally and health conscious) (Fioreze et al., 2019). Researchers argue that this discrepancy may have more to do with satisfaction with existing public transport systems in specific cities, rather than a general assumption about all users (Ho et al., 2020). Furthermore, it may be more reflective of the possibility that single-mode travellers (whether they currently travel by bike, private vehicle, or public transport) are less interested in MaaS as a concept (Alonso-Gonzalez et al., 2020). Presumably because they either do not require the multimodal transportation options offered by MaaS or they may already be exposed to many of technological instruments of MaaS systems (i.e. online journey planners, e-ticketing etc.), they do not see any inherent benefit to the platform (Alonso-Gonzalez et al., 2020). A measure to help these users overcome their reluctance to use MaaS would be to highlight the additional benefits of the service by incorporating MaaS services into existing public transport smart card systems (Alonso-Gonzalez et al., 2020).

The third demand-side barrier relates to the need to provide a platform that is attractive and easy to use. In fact, to attract users to the digital platform, researchers state that it should function in a way that enhances the trip experience (Liyanage et al., 2019; Ye et al., 2020). Additional services including the ability to plan journeys over a range of modes, payment integration, and real-time updates are also important to better cater for customer expectations and create a travel experience that can compete with the comfort and convenience of private vehicle travel (Kamargianni et al., 2016; Guidon et al., 2020). However, individuals have different needs, and service providers should consider allowing users to personalise the experience (e.g., tailor trips based on personal preferences, and bespoke subscription bundling) (Guidon et al., 2020). By enhancing the trip experience and providing a service which is better, more efficient, and less costly than existing transport options it is theorised that MaaS has the potential to improve its appeal with socio-economic groups and transport users who initially may be reluctant to subscribe. Moreover, customer trust should be obtained through organisational transparency, cyber security, data security, and access to reliable and effective travel information (Cottrill, 2020) that factors customers likely response behaviour and its effects on system performance (Paz & Peeta, 2009). Finally, regular reviews are important to help ensure service packages, pricing, and availability of mobility providers meet consumer expectations (Chang et al., 2020).

The fourth demand-side barrier relates to user willingness to pay. In fact, a survey found that potential MaaS users were only willing to pay 64% of their current transport budget on MaaS (Liljamo et al., 2020). This is problematic, particularly considering users often underestimate their own transport costs (Fioreze et al., 2019) and willingness to pay for MaaS is significantly lower than the actual cost of providing the service (Mulley et al., 2018). These results present significant barriers for the adoption of MaaS, leading some to conclude discounts and subsidies will be required prior to mainstream use of MaaS (particularly where the goal of increasing public transport use is paramount) (Ho et al., 2018; Ho et al., 2020; Jang et al., 2021). However, since MaaS is a relatively unfamiliar topic among the general public, mobility needs vary based on individuals, and people tend to underestimate existing transport costs, willingness-to-pay results can often be misleading (Golbabaei et al., 2020b; Ho et al., 2020; Liljamo et al., 2020). In fact, it is likely reduced costs alone will be unable to create a behavioural shift in car users (Ho et al., 2020). Some studies have shown that potential customers are more likely to want to pay for MaaS services when it is offered via an application which is able to bundle services into a single package which manages ticketing and payments through a weekly or monthly subscription (Kamargianni et al., 2016; Feneri et al., 2022; Guidon et al., 2020). Customers would likely prefer fixed-rate subscription models that bundle unlimited public transport trips (or other modes), with car- and ride-sharing options that might allow a certain number of uses in any given period (Esztergár-Kiss & Kerényi, 2020; Caiati et al., 2020; Vij et al., 2020). The advantage of bundled services is reflected in Matyas and Kamargianni's (2018, p. 1965) study which shows "60% of respondents would be willing to try (alternative) transportation modes"—such as shared modes—if they were included in their package. However, consumers are reluctant towards including bike sharing, and prefer to keep it as a pay-as-you-go option (Esztergár-Kiss & Kerényi, 2020; Guidon et al., 2020). This may be due to safety concerns and could be improved with increased spending on cycling infrastructure (Matyas, 2020).

The final demand-side barrier is related to overcoming the tradition of private vehicle travel within cities (Mulley, 2017). A basic assumption of MaaS is that by integrating services into a single platform, SM and public transport services could become more attractive to users, resulting in fewer trips using private vehicles (Sakai, 2019). This, combined with an observed trend in younger generations which has seen an increased use of ridesourcing and sharing apps, and a reduced interest in obtaining driver's licences, has been identified for its potential role in reducing car ownership (Casey et al., 2017). However, despite these trends some question whether car ownership among young people is actually decreasing (Casadó et al., 2020). Furthermore, private vehicle users are continually identified as the least likely social group to adopt MaaS (Alonso-Gonzalez et al., 2020; Hoerler et al., 2020), with few seeking alternatives (Ho et al., 2018; Alonso-Gonzalez et al., 2020), and many perceiving private vehicle travel as the only transportation option that can satisfy their needs (Matyas, 2020; Sjöman et al., 2020).

Even when willing to reduce private vehicle travel, car users encounter great difficulties changing behaviour (particularly for leisure trips) (Storme et al., 2020). Therefore, some researchers argue that the vision of replacing private vehicle ownership with MaaS will be unlikely in the short term (Fioreze et al., 2019; Storme et al., 2020), but could be promoted as an alternative for a household's second vehicle (Pickford & Chung, 2019; Ho et al., 2020). This can help users get familiar with the new technology and potentially move away from private vehicle ownership in the long term (Alonso-Gonzalez et al., 2020). Parking restrictions in areas with high accessibility can also help though they may be only useful for new residents and unlikely to change habits (Johansson et al., 2019). As can having access to a wider range of transport alternatives (Harrison et al., 2020), and continuing to plan cities around active and shared transport nodes (Sjöman et al., 2020).

10.5 Discussion and Conclusion

10.5.1 Key Findings

The primary goal of MaaS is to develop a transportation system that can act as an alternative to driving alone. By providing a system where accessibility to alternative transportation modes—including shared, active, and public—is made easier and more attractive, the desired outcomes associated with MaaS systems include: (a) reduced VKT per capita; (b) increased trip awareness and planning; (c) reduced parking demand; (d) reduced private vehicle ownership; anI(e) improved social equity. In achieving these outcomes MaaS aims to reduce some of the environmental, economic, and social impacts associated with private vehicle dependency including emissions, congestion, crashes, infrastructure demand, social exclusion, high transportation costs, and health issues arising from accidents, pollution, and inactivity. This study focused on the question: What are the barriers related to the implementation of MaaS, and what risks are associated with these barriers? A summary of supply- and demand-side barriers, including the potential risks and actions determined from the systematic literature review, is presented in Table 10.6.

Table 10.6 Summary of key findings

Supply-side barriers	Potential risks	Potential actions	Literature
Lack of collaboration	Noncooperation Network inefficacies Monopolisation Uncertainty No support	Consider intermediary actors Integrate e-ticketing Integrate journey planning Engage stakeholders early	(Sochor et al., 2015; Eckhardt et al., 2018; Jittrapirom et al., 2020; Mulley & Kronsell, 2018; Cooper et al., 2019; Hoerler et al., 2019; Mukhtar-Landgren & Smith, 2019; Narupiti, 2019; Narupti, 2019; Smith et al., 2019; Karlsson et al., 2020; Liu et al., 2020; Merkert et al., 2020; Meurs et al., 2020; Polydoropoulou et al., 2020b; Sakai, 2020; Singh, 2020; Smith & Hensher, 2020; Smith et al., 2020; Stehlin et al., 2020)
Lack of business support	Few mobility providers Little or no profit Price manipulation	Provide subsidies and incentives Implement MaaS trials	(Alexandros et al., 2017; Jittrapirom et al., 2018; Polydoropoulou et al., 2020a; Smith et al., 2018b; Sochor et al., 2018; Surakka et al., 2018; Venneman et al., 2018; Beheshtian et al., 2020; Karlsson et al., 2020)

(Continued)

Table 10.6 (Continued)

Supply-side barriers	Potential risks	Potential actions	Literature
Lack of coverage	Social inequity	Provide subsidies and incentives Establish a feeder system to public transport Implement AV trials	(Docherty et al., 2018; Eckhardt et al., 2018; Calderón & Miller, 2020; Karlsson et al., 2020; Liu et al., 2020; Masini et al., 2020; Smith & Hensher, 2020)
Lack of shared vision	Noncooperation Uncertainty No support Network inefficacies	Engage stakeholders early Create policy and legislation	(Sochor et al., 2015; Audouin & Finger, 2018; Jittrapirom et al., 2018; Smith et al., 2018b; Surakka et al., 2018; Veeneman et al., 2018; Hirschhorn et al., 2019; Mukhtar-Landgren & Smith, 2019; Pandey et al., 2019; Smith et al., 2019; Garcia et al., 2020; Karlsson et al., 2020; Meurs et al., 2020; Polydoropoulou et al., 2020b)
Lack of security	Loss of personal information Loss of intellectual property Loss of competitive advantage Reduced personal safety Reduced financial safety	Privacy regulations	(Casey et al., 2017; Callegati, 2018; Veeneman, et al., 2018; Cottrill, 2020; Casadó et al., 2020; He & Chow, 2020)
Appeal to older generations	Social inequity Missed opportunity	Provide education and training Implement MaaS trials Hybrid service that does not rely on ICT	(Ho et al., 2018; Keller et al., 2018; Fioreze et al., 2019; Alonso-Gonzalez et al., 2020; Caiati et al., 2020; Cottrill, 2020; Mulley et al., 2020; Pangbourne et al., 2020b; Schikofsky et al., 2020; Sourbati & Behrendt, 2020; Vij et al., 2020)
Appeal to public transport users	Lack of user support	Integrate with public transport smart card	(Ho et al., 2018; Fioreze et al., 2019; Alonso-Gonzalez et al., 2020; Ho et al., 2020)

Table 10.6 (Continued)

Supply-side barriers	Potential risks	Potential actions	Literature
Appeal of platform	Lack of user support Lack of user trust	Attractive and easy to use Targeted subscription packages Provide access to reliable information	(Kamargianni et al., 2016; Liyanage et al., 2019; Chang et al., 2020; Cottrill, 2020; Guidon et al., 2020; Ye et al., 2020)
Willingness-to-pay	Lack of user support Social inequity	Targeted subscription packages Improved cycling infrastructure Provide subsidies and incentives	(Kamargianni et al., 2016; Ho et al., 2018; Matyas & Kamargianni, 2018; Mulley et al., 2018; Esztergár-Kiss & Kerényi, 2020; Fioreze et al., 2019; Caiati et al., 2020; Feneri et al., 2022; Guidon et al., 2020; Ho et al., 2020; Jang et al., 2021; Liljamo et al., 2020; Matyas, 2020; Vij et al., 2020)
Tradition of private vehicle	Lack of user support	Provide education and training Enforce parking restrictions Transit-oriented development	(Casey et al., 2017; Mulley, 2017; Ho et al., 2018; Fioreze et al., 2019; Johansson et al., 2019; Pickford & Chung, 2019; Sakai, 2019; Alonso-Gonzalez et al., 2020; Casadó et al., 2020; Harrison et al., 2020; Ho et al., 2020; Hoerler et al., 2020; Matyas, 2020; Sjöman et al., 2020; Storme et al., 2020)

Supply-side barriers identified include: (a) lack of collaboration; (b) lack of business and political interest; (c) lack of service coverage; (d) lack of shared vision; and (e) lack of security. Given that the integration of transportation modes is considered one of the essential elements for MaaS (Jittrapirom et al., 2017) collaboration between public and private stakeholders is the most important of these barriers. Collaboration is essential to foster relationships, ensure adequate service coverage, identify and develop attractive business incentives—including the possible requirement for subsidies—and develop and implement a shared vision.

Even if the business incentive is strong but relationships with the public sector are not adequate, then there is a risk that a similar model to MaaS could be developed that bypasses the public transport system, creating greater competition with private industry, and further encouraging less sustainable means of transportation. Alternatively, a MaaS model, that incorporates an already lacklustre public transport network, with limited mode choice, and lack of attractive first- and last-mile options, is unlikely to appeal to consumers. Legislation may be required to maintain governance structures and ensure that a culture of cooperation between private and public industry is maintained.

Demand-side barriers identified include: (a) lack of appeal with older generations; (b) lack of appeal with public transport users; (c) attractiveness of the digital platform; (d) willingness to pay and (e) overcoming the tradition of private vehicle use. Given the primary goal of MaaS is to reduce private vehicle travel and ultimately improve transportation sustainability, the most important of these barriers is overcoming the culture of private vehicle travel. In urban areas where private vehicle travel accounts for a small modal share of all trips, this may be an achievable goal. For instance, in many European and Asian cities (e.g., Helsinki, Gothenburg, London, Taipei, Tokyo) the private vehicle is represented in less than 25% of all trips taken (Yigitcanlar et al., 2007). MaaS could act as the "icing on the cake" to relegate private vehicle usage to hobbyists and workers, encourage more active and sustainable travel modes, and provide a simpler way to integrate transportation choices. The key challenges will likely be convincing customers of the benefits of MaaS—particularly among single-mode travellers and older generations who may not have experience using the technologies required to operate MaaS.

In lower density sprawling cities that are ubiquitous within North America and Australia, where public transport systems are under-utilised, lack sufficient coverage, and private motor vehicle travel dominates mode choice, a different model for MaaS may need to be explored. In these areas there is a greater need for business incentives, subsidies, and "out-of-the-box" thinking to ensure MaaS provides greater coverage and meets the needs of the community. The expectations of what MaaS can achieve may need to be downgraded to reflect the reality of consumer reliance on private vehicles. In this sense, it may be more suitable to look to MaaS to improve network efficiency, particularly as an alternative to low-occupancy buses in suburban areas (Hensher, 2017). Potential cost savings from improved efficiency could be passed on to the customer or used to improve existing networks with a longer-term goal to reduce private vehicle travel to a minority modal share. Moreover, because many households in automobile-dependent cities own more than one vehicle it may be more realistic to promote MaaS as an alternative to a second car rather than a replacement for all trips (Ho et al., 2020; Pickford & Chung, 2019).

10.5.2 Towards a Conceptual Framework of MaaS Implementation and Impact

Following the completion of the literature review, a conceptual framework was developed to highlight findings and help guide future research and MaaS development (Figure 10.4). The conceptual framework shows that the risks associated with MaaS in cities is dependent on the barriers encountered during the implementation process. Overcoming these risks and achieving the desired outcomes (reduced VKT, parking, ownership, and social equity) is dependent on addressing both the supply- and demand-side barriers identified. While a number of potential actions have been highlighted there is unlikely to be a "one size fits all" version of MaaS, and each city—with its own unique geographic, cultural, and stakeholder characteristics—needs to address each barrier, and apply each action with consideration of local characteristics. Even on a city-wide level, the individual needs at a suburban, neighbourhood, and household level should be considered to ensure MaaS does not result in further social or geographic disadvantage, environmental impact, and economic cost.

Moving beyond the rhetoric of MaaS as a solution to solve all passenger transportation woes is crucial to harness the potential benefits that it can bring to urban areas. Given the possibility for MaaS to fail to achieve its desired outcomes, there is a need to develop appropriate actions to ensure cities can overcome barriers and mitigate any potential risks. Actions not only need to consider the geographic and cultural aspects of a region but also any events or incidents that may impact its use.

This is reinforced by looking at the continuing global impact of the recent COVID-19 pandemic. The quick spread of the virus is showing the hidden costs and fragility of global supply chains, and has some commentators questioning whether our society is prepared to deal with the rapid spread of disease (Osterholm & Olshaker, 2020). The pandemic has also highlighted increased vulnerabilities within our public transportation systems. For instance, passengers sitting in close quarters in air-conditioned vehicles with little ventilation and overcrowding has been linked to an increased risk of cross-contamination, helping to exacerbate the spread of disease (Wong, 2020). However, Tirachini (2020) argues that more research is needed on the link between public transport and disease transmission as continued criticism without the appropriate evidence is likely to result in public transport being viewed as a problem, whether there is enough evidence to support this claim.

Much of the existing research expects public transport to be the backbone of a MaaS system. However, since public transport ridership has dramatically decreased because of COVID-19 lockdowns, there is a very real risk that as commuters return to relative normalcy, they will continue to avoid public transport due to safety fears. Further degradation of the public transport system could have disastrous effects, particularly for those residents that have no other choice and rely on it to access employment and other services (Tirachini, 2020). Given the potential impacts, planning for disease prevention and response should be at the forefront of new research into public transport. Furthermore, because public transport and other shared travel underpin the most crucial elements of MaaS, researchers should investigate whether the COVID-19 pandemic has resulted in changed attitudes regarding its safety and appeal (Butler et al., 2021).

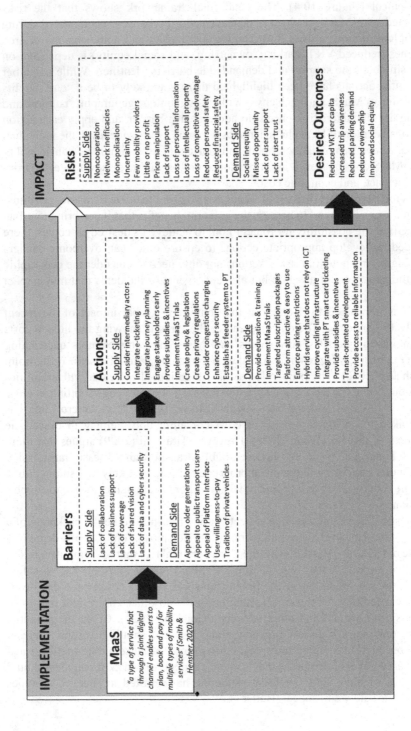

Figure 10.4 Conceptual framework of MaaS implementation and impact.

Acknowledgements

This chapter, with permission from the copyright holder, is a reproduced version of the following journal article: Butler, L., Yigitcanlar, T., & Paz, A. (2021). Barriers and risks of Mobility-as-a-Service (MaaS) adoption in cities: A systematic review of the literature. *Cities*, 109, 103036.

References

Alexandros, N., Ioannis, K., Elena, A., Eric Njoya, T. (2017). How can autonomous and connected vehicles, electromobility, BRT, hyperloop, shared use mobility and Mobility-as-a-Service shape transport futures for the context of smart cities? *Urban Science*, *1*(4), 36.

Alonso-González, M., Hoogendoorn-Lanser, S., Oort, N., Cats, O., Hoogendoorn, S. (2020). Drivers and barriers in adopting Mobility-as-a-Service. *Transportation Research Part A*, *132*, 378–401.

Arias-Molinares, D., García-Palomares, J. C. (2020). The Ws of MaaS: Understanding mobility as a service from a literature review. *IATSS Research*, *44*(3), 253–263.

Audouin, M., Finger, M. (2018). The development of mobility-as-a-service in the Helsinki metropolitan area. *Research in Transportation Business and Management*, *27*, 24–35.

Becker, H., Balac, M., Ciari, F., Axhausen, K. (2020). Assessing the welfare impacts of shared mobility and Mobility-as-a-Service. *Transportation Research Part A*, *131*, 228–243.

Beheshtian, A., Richard Geddes, R., Rouhani, O., Kockelman, K., Ockenfels, A., Cramton, P., Do, W. (2020). Bringing the efficiency of electricity market mechanisms to multi-modal mobility across congested transportation systems. *Transportation Research Part A*, *131*, 58–69.

Butler, L., Yigitcanlar, T., Paz, A. (2021). Barriers and risks of Mobility-as-a-Service (MaaS) adoption in cities: A systematic review of the literature. *Cities*, 109, 103036

Caiati, V., Rasouli, S., Timmermans, H. (2020). Bundling, pricing schemes and extra features preferences for mobility-as-a-service. *Transportation Research Part A*, *131*, 123–148.

Calderón, F., Miller, E. J. (2020). A literature review of mobility services: definitions, modelling state-of-the-art, and key considerations for a conceptual modelling framework. *Transport Reviews*, *40*(3), 312–332.

Callegati, F., Giallorenzo, S., Melis, A., Prandini, M. (2018). Cloud-of-things meets Mobility-as-a-Service. *Computers & Security*, *74*, 277–295.

Casadó, R. G., Golightly, D., Laing, K., Palacin, R., Todd, L. (2020). Children, Young people and Mobility as a Service: Opportunities and barriers for future mobility. *Transportation Research Interdisciplinary Perspectives*, *4*, 100107.

Casey, T., Ali-Vehmas, T., Valovirta, V. (2017). Evolution toward an open value system for smart mobility services. *Competition and Regulation in Network Industries*, *18*, 44–70.

Chang, S., Chen, H., Chen, H. (2020). Mobility-as-a-Service policy planning, deployments and trials in Taiwan. *IATSS Research*, *3*, 312–332.

Contreras, S., Paz, A. (2018). The effects of ride-hailing companies on the taxicab industry in Las Vegas, Nevada. *Transportation Research Part A*, *115*, 63–70.

Cooper, P., Tryfonas, T., Crick, T., Marsh, A. (2019). Electric vehicle mobility-as-a-service. *Journal of Urban Technology*, *26*, 35–56.

Cottrill, C. (2020). MaaS surveillance. *Transportation Research Part A*, *131*, 50–57.

Curtis, C., Stone, J., Legacy, C., Ashmore, D. (2019). Governance of future urban mobility. *Urban Policy and Research, 37*, 393–404.

Docherty, I., Marsden, G., Anable, J. (2018). The governance of smart mobility. *Transportation Research Part A, 115*, 114–125.

Eckhardt, J., Nykänen, L., Aapaoja, A., Niemi, P. (2018). MaaS in rural areas. *Research in Transportation Business and Management, 27*, 75–83.

Esztergár-Kiss, D., Kerényi, T. (2020). Creation of mobility packages based on the MaaS concept. *Travel Behaviour and Society, 21*, 307–317.

Faisal, A., Yigitcanlar, T., Kamruzzaman, M., Currie, G. (2019). Understanding autonomous vehicles. *Journal of Transport and Land Use, 12*, 45–72.

Faisal, A., Yigitcanlar, T., Kamruzzaman, M., Paz, A. (2021). Mapping two decades of autonomous vehicle research: A systematic scientometric analysis. *Journal of Urban Technology, 28*(3–4), 45–74.

Feneri, A. M., Rasouli, S., Timmermans, H. J. (2022). Modeling the effect of Mobility-as-a-Service on mode choice decisions. *Transportation Letters, 14*(4), 324–331.

Fioreze, T., de Gruijter, M., Geurs, K. (2019). On the likelihood of using mobility-as-a-service. *Case Studies on Transport Policy, 7*, 790–801.

Franco, P., Johnston, R., McCormick, E. (2020). Demand responsive transport. *Transportation Research Part A, 131*, 244–266.

Fuentes, R., Hunt, L. C., Lopez-Ruiz, H. G., Manzano, B. (2019). From the "iPhone effect" to the "amazon" of energy. *Network Industries Quarterly, 21*(3), 8–11.

García, J., Lenz, G., Haveman, S., Bonnema, G. (2020). State of the art of Mobility as a Service ecosystems and architectures. *World Electric Vehicle Journal, 11*, 1–10.

Golbabaei, F., Yigitcanlar, T., Bunker, J. (2021). The role of shared autonomous vehicle systems in delivering smart urban mobility: A systematic review of the literature. *International Journal of Sustainable Transportation, 15*(10), 731–748.

Golbabaei, F., Yigitcanlar, T., Paz, A., Bunker, J. (2020b). Individual predictors of autonomous vehicle public acceptance and intention to use. *Journal of Open Innovation, 6*, 106.

Goodall, W., Fishman, T., Bornstein, J., Bonthron, B. (2017) The rise of Mobility-as-a-Service. *Deloitte Review, 20*, 111–130.

Guidon, S., Wicki, M., Bernauer, T., Axhausen, K. (2020). Transportation service bundling. *Transportation Research Part A, 131*, 91–106.

Harrison, G., Gühnemann, A., Shepherd, S. (2020). The business case for a journey planning and ticketing app. *Sustainability, 12*, 4005.

Hawkins, J., Habib, K. N. (2020). Heterogeneity in marginal value of urban mobility: Evidence from a large-scale household travel survey in the Greater Toronto and Hamilton Area. *Transportation, 47*(6), 3091–3108.

He, B., Chow, J. (2020). Optimal privacy control for transport network data sharing. *Transportation Research Part C, 113*, 370–387.

Hensher, D. (2017). Future bus transport contracts under a Mobility-as-a-Service regime in the digital age. *Transportation Research Part A, 98*, 86–96.

Hirschhorn, F., Paulsson, A., Sørensen, C.H., Veeneman, W. (2019). Public transport regimes and Mobility-as-a-Service. *Transportation Research Part A, 130*, 178–191.

Ho, C., Hensher, D., Mulley, C., Wong, Y. (2018). Potential uptake and willingness-to-pay for Mobility-as-a-Service. *Transportation Research Part A, 117*, 302–318.

Ho, C., Mulley, C., Hensher, D. (2020). Public preferences for Mobility-as-a-Service. *Transportation Research Part A, 131,* 70–90.

Hoerler, R., Haerri, F., Hoppe, M. (2019). New solutions in sustainable commuting. *Social Sciences, 8,* 220.

Hoerler, R., Stünzi, A., Patt, A., Duce, A. (2020). What are the factors and needs promoting mobility-as-a-service? *European Transport Research Review, 12,* 1–16.

Hörcher, D., Graham, D. (2020). MaaS economics. *Economics of Transportation, 22,* 100167.

Jang, S., Caiati, V., Rasouli, S., Timmermans, H., Choi, K. (2021). Does MaaS contribute to sustainable transportation? A mode choice perspective. *International journal of sustainable transportation, 15*(5), 351–363.

Jittrapirom, P., Caiati, V., Feneri, A., Ebrahimigharehbaghi, S., Alonso-González, M., Narayan, J. (2017). Mobility-as-a-service. *Urban Planning, 2,* 13–25.

Jittrapirom, P., Marchau, V., Heijden, R., Meurs, H. (2018). Dynamic adaptive policymaking for implementing mobility-as-a service. *Research in Transportation Business and Management, 27,* 46–55.

Jittrapirom, P., Marchau, V., van der Heijden, R., Meurs, H. (2020). Future implementation of mobility as a service (MaaS): Results of an international Delphi study. *Travel Behaviour and Society, 21,* 281–294.

Johansson, F., Henriksson, G., Envall, P. (2019). Moving to private-car-restricted and mobility-served neighborhoods, *Sustainability, 11,* 6208.

Jokinen, J.-P., Sihvola, T., Mladenovic, M. N. (2019). Policy lessons from the flexible transport service pilot Kutsuplus in the Helsinki Capital Region. *Transport Policy, 76,* 123–133.

Kamargianni, M., Li, W., Matyas, M., Schäfer, A. (2016). A critical review of new mobility services for urban transport. *Transportation Research Procedia, 14,* 3294–3303.

Kankanamge, N., Yigitcanlar, T., Goonetilleke, A., Kamruzzaman, M. (2019). Can volunteer crowdsourcing reduce disaster risk? *International Journal of Disaster Risk Reduction, 35,* 101097.

Karlsson, I., Mukhtar-Landgren, D., Smith, G., Koglin, T., Kronsell, A., Lund, E., Sarasini, S. & Sochor, J. (2020). Development and implementation of Mobility-as-a-Service. *Transportation Research Part A, 131,* 283–295.

Keller, A., Aguilar, A., Hanss, D. (2018). Car sharers' interest in integrated multimodal mobility platforms. *Sustainability, 10,* 4689.

Liljamo, T., Liimatainen, H., Pöllänen, M., Utriainen, R. (2020). People's current mobility costs and willingness to pay for Mobility as a Service offerings. *Transportation Research Part A, 136,* 99–119.

Liu, X., Yu, J., Trisha, S., Beimborn, E. (2020). Exploring the feasibility of Mobility as a Service in small urban and rural communities. *Journal of Urban Planning and Development, 146*(3), 05020016.

Liyanage, S., Dia, H., Abduljabbar, R., Bagloee, S. A. (2019). Flexible mobility on-demand. *Sustainability, 11*(5), 1262.

Lyons, G., Hammond, P., Mackay, K. (2019). The importance of user perspective in the evolution of MaaS. *Transportation Research Part A, 121,* 22–36.

Masini, B., Silva, C., Balador, A. (2020). The use of meta-surfaces in vehicular networks. *Journal of Sensor and Actuator Networks, 9,* 15.

Matyas, M. (2020). Opportunities and barriers to multimodal cities. *European Transport Research Review, 12,* 7.

Matyas, M., Kamargianni, M. (2018). The potential of Mobility-as-a-Service bundles as a mobility management tool. *Transportation*, *46*, 1951–1968.

Merkert, R., Bushell, J., Beck, M. (2020). Collaboration as a service to fully integrate public transportation. *Transportation Research Part A*, *131*, 267–282

Meurs, H., Sharmeen, F., Marchau, V., van der Heijden, R. (2020). Organizing integrated services in Mobility-as-a-Service systems. *Transportation Research Part A*, *131*, 178–195.

Mukhtar-Landgren, D., Smith, G. (2019). Perceived action spaces for public actors in the development of Mobility-as-a-Service. *European Transport Research Review*, *11*, 1–12.

Mulley, C. (2017). Mobility-as-a-service. *Transport Reviews*, *37*, 247–251.

Mulley, C., Ho, C., Balbontin, C., Hensher, D., Stevens, L., Nelson, J.D., Wright, S. (2020). Mobility-as-a-Service in community transport in Australia. *Transportation Research Part A*, *131*, 107–122.

Mulley, C., Kronsell, A. (2018). The "uberisation" of public transport and mobility-as-a-service (MaaS). *Research in Transportation Economics*, *69*, 568–572.

Mulley, C., Nelson, J., Wright, S. (2018). Community transport meets mobility-as-a-service. *Research in Transportation Economics*, *69*, 583–591.

Narupiti, S. (2019). Exploring the possibility of MaaS service in Thailand. *IATSS Research*, *43*, 226–234.

Newman, P., Kenworthy, J. (1996). The land use-transport connection. *Land Use Policy*, *13*, 1–22.

Nikitas, A., Michalakopoulou, K., Njoya, E., Karampatzakis, D. (2020). Artificial intelligence, transport and the smart city. *Sustainability*, *12*(7), 2789.

Osterholm, M., Olshaker, M. (2020). Why we are ill prepared for an epidemic like coronavirus. Accessed from https://time.com/5777923/america-prepared-pandemic-coronavirus.

Pandey, V., Monteil, J., Gambella, C., Simonetto, A. (2019). On the needs for MaaS platforms to handle competition in ridesharing mobility. *Transportation Research Part C*, *108*, 269–288.

Pangbourne, K., Bennett, S., Baker, A. (2020a). Persuasion profiles to promote pedestrianism. *Travel, Behaviour & Society*, *20*, 300–312.

Pangbourne, K., Mladenović, M., Stead, D., Milakis, D. (2020b). Questioning mobility-as-a-service. *Transportation Research Part A*, *131*, 35–49.

Paz, A., Peeta, S. (2009). Information-based traffic control strategies consistent with estimated driver behavior. *Transportation Research Part B*, *43*, 73–96.

Pickford, A., Chung, E. (2019). The shape of MaaS. *IATSS Research*, *43*, 219–225.

Polydoropoulou, A., Pagoni, I., Tsirimpa, A. (2020a). Ready for Mobility as a Service? Insights from stakeholders and end-users. *Travel Behaviour and Society*, *21*, 295–306.

Polydoropoulou, A., Pagoni, I., Tsirimpa, A., Roumboutsos, A., Kamargianni, M., Tsouros, I. (2020b). Prototype business models for Mobility-as-a-Service. *Transportation Research Part A: Policy and Practice*, *131*, 149–162.

Redman, L., Friman, M., Gärling, T., Hartig, T. (2013). Quality attributes of public transport that attract car users. *Transport Policy*, *25*, 119–127

Rosenblum, J., Hudson, A., Ben-Joseph, E. (2020). Parking futures. *Land Use Policy*, *91*, 104054.

Sakai, K. (2019). MaaS trends and policy-level initiatives in the EU. *IATSS Research*, *43*, 207–209.

Sakai, K. (2020). Public transport promotion and Mobility-as-a-Service. *IEICE Transactions on Fundamentals of Electronics, Communications and Computer Sciences, E103A*, 226–230.

Schikofsky, J., Dannewald, T., Kowald, M. (2020). Exploring motivational mechanisms behind the intention to adopt Mobility-as-a-Service. *Transportation Research Part A, 131*, 296–312.

Segui-Gasco, P., Ballis, H., Parisi, V., Kelsall, D., North, R., Busquets, D. (2019). Simulating a rich ride-share mobility service using agent-based models. *Transportation, 46*, 2041–2062.

Singh, M. (2020). India's shift from mass transit to MaaS transit. *Transportation Research Part A, 131*, 219–227.

Sjöman, M., Ringenson, T., Kramers, A. (2020). Exploring everyday mobility in a living lab based on economic interventions. *European Transport Research Review, 12*, 5.

Smith, G., Hensher, D. (2020). Towards a framework for Mobility-as-a-Service policies. *Transport Policy, 89*, 54–65.

Smith, G., Sochor, J., Karlsson, I. (2018a). Mobility-as-a-Service. *Research in Transportation Economics, 69*, 592–599.

Smith, G., Sochor, J., Karlsson, I. (2019). Public–private innovation. *Public Management Review, 21*, 116–137.

Smith, G., Sochor, J., Karlsson, I. (2020). Intermediary MaaS integrators. *Transportation Research Part A, 131*, 163–177.

Smith, G., Sochor, J., Sarasini, S. (2018b). Mobility-as-a-Service. *Research in Transportation Business and Management, 27*, 36–45.

Soares Machado, C., Quintanilha, J. (2018). An overview of shared mobility. *Sustainability, 10*, 4342.

Sochor, J., Arby, H., Karlsson, I., Sarasini, S. (2018). A topological approach to Mobility-as-a-Service. *Research in Transportation Business and Management, 27*, 3–14.

Sochor, J., Karlsson, I., Strömberg, H. (2016). Trying out Mobility-as-a-Service experiences from a field trial and implications for understanding demand. *Transportation Research Record, 2542*, 57–64.

Sochor, J., Strömberg, H., Karlsson, I. (2015). Implementing Mobility-as-a-Service challenges in integrating user, commercial, and societal perspectives. *Transportation Research Record, 2536*, 1–9.

Sourbati, M., Behrendt, F. (2021). Smart mobility, age and data justice. *New Media & Society, 23*(6), 1398–1414.

Stanley, J., Lucas, K. (2014). Delivering sustainable public transport. *Research in Transportation Economics, 48*, 315–322.

Stehlin, J., Hodson, M., McMeekin, A. (2020). Platform mobilities and the production of urban space: Toward a typology of platformization trajectories. *Environment and Planning A: Economy and Space, 52*(7), 1250–1268.

Storme, T., De Vos, J., De Paepe, L., Witlox, F. (2020). Limitations to the car-substitution effect of MaaS. *Transportation Research Part A, 131*, 196–205.

Strömberg, H., Karlsson, I., Sochor, J. (2018). Inviting travelers to the smorgasbord of sustainable urban transport. *Transportation, 45*, 1655–1670.

Strömberg, H., Rexfelt, O., Karlsson, I., Sochor, J. (2016). Trying on change. *Travel Behaviour and Society, 4*, 60–68.

Surakka, T., Härri, F., Haahtela, T., Horila, A., Michl, T. (2018). Regulation and governance supporting systemic MaaS innovations. *Research in Transportation Business and Management, 27*, 56–66.

Tirachini, A. (2020). Ride-hailing, travel behaviour and sustainable mobility: an international review. *Transportation, 47*(4), 2011–2047.

Utriainen, R., Pöllänen, M. (2018). Review on Mobility-as-a-Service in scientific publications. *Research in Transportation Business and Management, 27*, 15–23.

Veeneman, W., van Der Voort, H., Hirschhorn, F., Steenhuisen, B., Klievink, B. (2018). PETRA. *Research in Transportation Economics, 69*, 420–429.

Vij, A., Ryan, S., Sampson, S., Harris, S. (2020). Consumer preferences for Mobility-as-a-Service in Australia. *Transportation Research Part C, 117*, 102699.

Webb, J. (2019). The future of transport. *Economic Analysis and Policy, 61*, 1–6.

Wong, Y. Z. (2020). To limit coronavirus risks on public transport, here's what we can learn from efforts overseas. Accessed from https://theconversation.com/to-limit-coronavirus-risks-on-public-transport-heres-what-we-can-learn-from-efforts-overseas-133764

Wong, Y. Z., Hensher, D., Mulley, C. (2020). Mobility-as-a-Service (MaaS). *Transportation Research Part A, 131*, 5–19.

Wright, S., Nelson, J., Cottrill, C. (2020). MaaS for the suburban market. *Transportation Research Part A, 131*, 206–218.

Ye, J., Zheng, J., Yi, F. (2020). A study on users' willingness to accept mobility as a service based on UTAUT model. *Technological Forecasting & Social Change, 157*, 120066.

Yigitcanlar, T. (2016). *Technology and the city.* Routledge, New York.

Yigitcanlar, T., Desouza, K., Butler, L., Roozkhosh, F. (2020). Contributions and risks of artificial intelligence (AI) in building smarter cities. *Energies, 13*, 1473.

Yigitcanlar, T., Dodson, J., Gleeson, B., Sipe, N. (2007). Travel self-containment in master planned estates. *Urban Policy and Research, 25*, 129–149.

Yigitcanlar, T., Han, H., Kamruzzaman, M., Ioppolo, G., Sabatini-Marques, J. (2019a). The making of smart cities. *Land Use Policy, 88*, 104187.

Yigitcanlar, T., Kamruzzaman, M. (2018). Does smart city policy lead to sustainability of cities? *Land Use Policy, 73*, 49–58.

Yigitcanlar, T., Kamruzzaman, M. (2019). Smart cities and mobility. *Journal of Urban Technology, 26*, 21–46.

Yigitcanlar, T., Kamruzzaman, M., Foth, M., Sabatini-Marques, J., Da Costa, E., Ioppolo, G. (2019b). Can cities become smart without being sustainable? *Sustainable Cities and Society, 45*, 348–365.

Yigitcanlar, T., Wilson, M., Kamruzzaman, M. (2019c). Disruptive impacts of automated driving systems on the built environment and land use. *Journal of Open Innovation, 5*, 24.

Zhao, P. (2014). Private motorised urban mobility in China's large cities. *Journal of Transport Geography, 40*, 53–63.

11 Urban Management Platform

11.1 Introduction

A smart city is an environment that uses innovative technologies to make networks and services more flexible, effective, and sustainable with the use of information, digital, and telecommunication technologies, improving the city operations for the benefit of its citizens. However, where does the concept of smart cities and smart territories stand currently? The United Nations Educational, Scientific and Cultural Organization (UNESCO) gives us a fairly accurate view on this situation: "All the cities and territories who claim the smart city status are merely patchworks of opportunistic modernization, which is not always coherent and is sometimes juxtaposed without any real unity of function or meaning" (UNESCO, 2019). This proposal has been fully developed based on this statement and the PIs have accordingly guided the choice of the concepts to be developed in this project.

It is estimated that in 2030, the population density will increase by 30% in most cities, 60% of world's population will live in cities, and there will be 43 megacities; these metropolitan zones will have more than 10 million residents. Most experts agree on the fact that such population densities promote sustainable economic growth, which explains the increased mobility of the population from rural to urban areas. The downside of these advantages is the rise of uncontrollable sociological phenomena, such as urban violence and unhealthy crowding. Most cities face these issues, regardless of their political or economic regime. To counteract negative consequences, the emerging smart cities must adapt measures that will guarantee their economic attractiveness, and most importantly, they must meet the population's high expectations regarding the quality of life.

Contrary to the initial smart city concept, which favoured the modernisation of leading cities in developed countries, the new trend consists in deploying smart micro-territories (or villages) within megacities and in their neighbouring regions, serving as smart satellites. The ideas presented in this proposal follow this smart city deployment policy. Most smart city projects aim to achieve sustainability and control economic growth by avoiding the loss of the already invested resources, by maintaining an ecology-friendly environment and by striving towards social equity. However, in reality this turns out to be very utopian, and several worldwide experiences show that this theoretical balance has never been successful at the

DOI: 10.1201/9781003403630-14

practical level. As a result, smart city development tends to be geared towards only one of these objectives, failing to adapt a comprehensive approach.

We conceive the smart city concept as a smart, realistic, and technically balanced combination of the objectives and values described above. A smart city should be thought out and deployed following the principles of modular design, where each module is implemented, tested, and deployed independently, so that it can be easily modified, replaced, or exchanged. Thus, modules are defined as dynamic and evolutionary. Each module is dedicated to a particular task within the smart city, such as transportation control, logistics planning, traffic control, crowd management, e-health, etc. All modules interact and exchange the information collected within the smart city through a centralised management platform. Deepint.net is the platform presented in this chapter that can work independently and/or in collaboration with other (existing) smart city platforms/IoT systems. Furthermore, this platform is equipped with most of the required connectors, facilitating its integration.

Such is the added value of the data that not only cities/territories but also users and companies in all sectors have been interested in AI-based data analysis and visualisation methodologies. This is because they are fully aware of the benefits of those processes. As a result, the artificial intelligence sector has enjoyed high demand in recent years.

In this research, a platform has been developed that can apply the most well-known techniques within the data analysis sector in a way that is simple and user-friendly. The platform's design makes it fully prepared for the management of smart cities and territories, regardless of the size of the territories and the origin of the data. Deepint.net not only processes data, but also automates its intake, visualisation, and integration with any other platform and dashboard.

This platform is easy to use and does not require specialists in artificial intelligence, edge computing, or machine learning. Deepint.net has been designed to provide managers with tools for data analysis and to help them generate models efficiently with no need for specialised data analysts or developers.

The platform aids the data analysis process at different levels: (a) it gives computer support so that cities do not have to invest in infrastructure; (b) it offers mechanisms for the ingestion of data from different sources (relational and non-relational databases, files, repositories based on CKAN, streaming data, multifunctional IoT sensors, social networks, etc.) and in different formats; (c) it offers data-processing mechanisms to all users who do not have knowledge of programming (information fusion, data filtering, etc.); (d) it offers information representation techniques based on interactive graphics to help understand data, the results of analysis and rapid decision-making; and (e) it helps select the methodologies that can be applied to the data provided by the user and automatically searches for the configuration that provides the best results (through cross-validation), so that the user does not have to configure anything at all. The data management flow can be found in Figure 11.1.

The platform, therefore, includes signal-processing methods capable of transforming and using data (even real-time data) from any given source: IoT

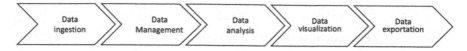

Figure 11.1 Data management flow in Deepint.net.

sensors, advanced multi-functional sensors, smart edge nodes, next-generation networks, etc., or even the data from relational and non-relational databases. The platform helps the users select and use the most adequate combination of mathematical models; dynamic data assimilation and neurosymbolic artificial intelligence systems can work with knowledge and data; they adapt to new time constraints and can explain why a certain decision has been taken. Research into the creation of explainable adaptive mixtures of expert systems is the key innovation of this project, together with its application in the smart logistics field.

The platform has been used to develop several smart territory projects in the cities of Santa Marta and Carbajosa (Spain), in Caldas (Colombia), in Panama City, in Istanbul (Turkey), and other cities across the globe.

11.2 Smart Territory Platforms and the Edge Computing Approach

It is expected that the global population will reach 9.7 billion in 2050. By then, two-thirds of the population will live in urban environments (UNESCO, 2019). The United Nations estimates that by 2030 there will be 43 megacities (defined as metropolitan areas with a population greater than 10 million), most of them in developing countries. Critical social and ecological challenges that cities will face may include urban violence, inequality, discrimination, unemployment, poverty, unsustainable energy and water use, epidemics, pollution, environmental degradation, and increased risk of natural disasters.

The concept of smart cities, which emerged in the early 2000s, attempts to provide solutions to these challenges by implementing information and communication technologies, improving the socio-ecological network of urban areas and the quality of life of its citizens. The initial concept of smart cities focused on the modernisation of megacities. However, most of the so-called smart cities are just cities with several smart projects (UNESCO, 2019). The main reason for this is that existing cities are difficult to modernise, mostly because buildings are too old to renovate, or they are heritage-listed buildings (due to their historical value), so they cannot be rebuilt or demolished. To overcome these limitations, different approaches have been proposed. The most promising trend is the creation of smart micro-territories, defined as hi-tech small towns, districts, or satellite towns near megacities (UNESCO, 2019). Real-life examples include Songdo City; a satellite village near Seoul, or Cyberabad District in Hyderabad (India). This chapter presents Deepint.net as a platform for the efficient and dynamic management of smart territories.

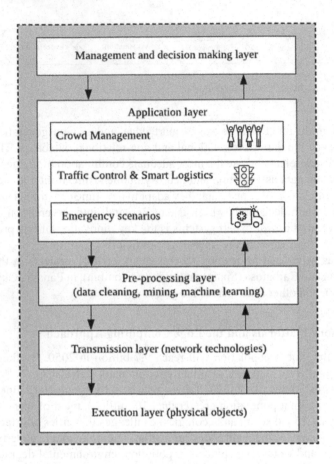

Figure 11.2 Smart city management architecture.

Given the availability of large amounts of data, the challenge is to identify intelligent and adaptive ways of combining the information to create valuable knowledge (Silva et al., 2018). However, the implementation of smart cities still poses several challenges, such as design and operational costs, sustainability, or information security. Thus, over the last few years, platforms have been designed and developed to provide innovative solutions to these problems. These platforms combine the data collected by electronic devices (sensors and actuators) with the data that have been generated by citizens and are stored on different types of databases.

In general, smart city management platforms focus on one or several of the following dimensions: crowd management, traffic control, and smart logistics, or resource prioritisation in emergency scenarios, etc. These modules interact and exchange information among them. Figure 11.2 illustrates an architecture that is typical of these platforms, which normally work independently and/or in collaboration with other existing platforms and IoT systems.

Smart mobility is generally considered one of the main dimensions of smart cities. With the rapid population growth and its high concentration in urban environments, urban traffic congestion (which significantly lengthens waiting times) has a significant impact on citizens' daily life. To monitor and manage the state of road traffic, sensors are employed on road intersections and public transport vehicles, measuring location, speed, and density. Aimed at supporting local authorities in traffic control, recent studies propose different systems and platforms which improve the safety and security of the commuter (Latif et al., 2018; Ning et al., 2019; Pan et al., 2019; Rehena & Janssen, 2018; Yao et al., 2019; Kapser & Abdelrahman, 2020). Another important aspect of smart mobility is last-mile delivery. With the exponential growth of e-commerce, the logistics sector is experiencing efficiency difficulties. Technologies such as the Internet of Things or autonomous delivery vehicles are expected to have a positive impact on this industry (Luo et al., 2020).

In a smart transportation system, crowd management is a key variable, not only during commutes and regular travel, but also when an event takes place. Major events with large crowd gatherings (sport events, concerts, protests, etc.) are celebrated in urban areas every year. Overcrowding and the poor management of crowds can lead to threatening and unsafe situations, such as injuries, stampedes, and crushing. Therefore, effective crowd management is a crucial task. Crowd management systems have been developed to support services and infrastructures devoted to managing and controlling crowds at any time, so that in the case of emergency situations, crowds are well managed, while the dangers and risks are minimised. Current studies focus on crowd counting and monitoring models (Luo et al., 2020) and algorithms (Kumar et al., 2018), and crowd flow prediction architectures (Zhao et al., 2019), their aim is to provide the government and local authorities with valuable information on large crowds (Solmaz et al., 2019).

The objective of many smart city projects is to prioritise the efficient use of resources: irrigation systems, energy consumption, or dealing with emergency scenarios, such as the one provoked by the COVID-19 pandemic. Thousands of people have lost their lives in epidemics, pandemics, natural disasters (hurricanes, floods, fires), and human-induced disasters (stampedes, terrorist attacks, or communicable diseases), and it is believed that a reasonable number of these fatalities are associated with the poor management of crowds and slow response to accidents. One of the key challenges involved in managing an emergency is minimising the time it takes for personnel and supplies to arrive at the scenario. Emergency services, such as health services, police, and fire departments, are expected to make critical decisions and to correctly prioritise the use of resources, using limited time and information. To facilitate this task, several systems have been proposed in recent years. Rego et al. (2018) introduced an IoT-based platform that modifies the routes of normal and emergency road traffic to reduce the time it takes for resources to arrive at the scenario of an emergency. Rajak and Kushwaha (2019) propose a framework capable of creating a "Green Corridor" for emergency vehicles. Ranga and Sumi (2018) present a traffic management system that helps ambulances and fire trucks find the shortest routes.

Social media data could be of much value when responding to an emergency. Alkhatib et al. (2019) propose a novel framework for the management of incidents in smart cities by using social media data; Perez and Zeadally (2019) present a communication architecture for crowd management in disruptive emergency scenarios; and Kousiouris et al. (2018) propose a tracking and monitoring system that identifies events of interest for Twitter users.

Statistics from the Department of Economic and Social Affairs of the United Nations (DESAP) indicate that 68% of the world's population will live in cities or urban areas by 2050 (2019), which means rapid and even uncontrolled growth with consequent challenges for governments, for example: pollution; limited mobility due to traffic and congestion; high cost of housing, food and basic services; as well as security problems (Liu et al., 2019).

To address this growth, the smart city concept emerged as the integration of the urban environment with information and communication technologies (ICTs), attracting the interest of all major sectors (governments, universities, research centres, etc.) in presenting solutions or developments that would make up a smart city (Ullah et al., 2020). The objective of this paradigm is the effective management of the challenges associated with the growth of urban areas through the adoption of ICTs in developments, solutions, applications, services, or even in the design of state policies (Chamoso et al., 2020).

Currently, the term smart city is widely used, for example, in the systematic reviews of the literature there are more than 36 definitions that address different dimensions of the urban environment such as: mobility, technology, public services, economy, environment, quality of life, or governance (Laufs et al., 2020). One of the most widely used definitions is the one proposed by Elmaghraby and Losavio (2014): "an intelligent city is one that incorporates information and communication technologies to increase operational efficiency, shares information independently within the system and improves the overall effectiveness of services and the well-being of citizens". However, the growth of the Internet of Things and of devices permanently connected to the Internet has led to growing interest in data management (Chamoso et al., 2020) and security (Kitchin & Dodge, 2019) as new urban management challenges emerge.

Ensuring the security of information, devices, infrastructure, and users in an environment where large volumes of data are managed in real time is the objective of state-of-the-art research, because it is a critical element of any solution aimed at smart cities/territories (O'Dwyer et al., 2019). This challenge has generated a research trend: edge computing and its integration with the IoT, which is reflected in statistics and in the interest of large corporations in research, development, and implementation opportunities in smart territory scenarios, so that they can increase their profits and market shares (Khan et al., 2020; Jia et al., 2017; Premsankar et al., 2018; Schneider et al., 2017; Taleb et al., 2017; Hussain et al., 2019; Gheisari et al., 2020). Table 11.1 lists the studies that have employed edge computing in different smart city scenarios. These proposals evidence the interest in this technology.

In this context, most cities are not prepared and do not have the policies required to understand and ensure the confidentiality of a huge amount of data, as well as

Table 11.1 Edge computing applied in smart city/territory environments

Field	Solution	Literature
Mobility	The study considered an SC/territory scenario where vehicles ran applications that take data from the environment and send them to edge computing servers through roadside units	Premsankar et al., (2018)
	The authors conducted a case study on the fog and edge computing requirements of the intelligent traffic light management system	Hussain et al., (2019)
Tourism	Mobile edge computing potential in making cities/territories smarter	Taleb et al., (2017)
Industry and augmented reality	Proposes the use of edge computing to enable intelligent management of industrial tasks	Schenider et al., (2017)
Smart district (manhole cover)	Edge computing servers interact with corresponding management personnel through mobile devices based on the collected information. A demo application of the proposed IMCS in the Xiasha District of Hangzhou, China, showed its high efficiency	Jia et al., (2017)

their correct processing and storage. Another important factor is the application of artificial intelligence techniques for the extraction of information which facilitates the management of key infrastructures, systems, and devices in a district, making them functional and efficient. However, rapid response time is fundamental for the functioning of a smart territory. In addition, the large volume of data that is sent from a smart territory directly to the cloud has high associated and variable costs, forcing cities to seek solutions that reduce the cost of using cloud services, energy, and bandwidth.

In a smart territory scenario, the proposed architecture should be capable of managing the heterogeneity of IoT devices to ensure the management system's safety and efficiency. Although there are many proposals in the state of the art, Figure 11.3 represents a general model of most architectures, where blockchain technology may be implemented to preserve the safety and reliability of the sensitive data generated by IoT devices at the edge of the network. Edge nodes are also included in architectures of this type, using artificial intelligence and deep learning algorithms for filtering, real-time data processing, and low latency (Sittón-Candanedo et al., 2019a).

Figure 11.3 shows a basic schema of an edge computing architecture with edge nodes that allow user application processes to be executed closer to the data sources (Sittón-Candanedo et al., 2019b). The edge nodes perform computing tasks such as filtering, processing, caching, load balancing, requesting services and information, and reducing the amount of data that is sent to or received from the cloud.

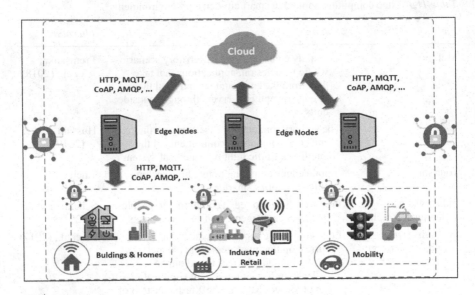

Figure 11.3 Edge computing for smart cities (Sittón-Candanedo et al., 2019a).

11.2.1 Smart City Vertical Markets and Tools

The development of a smart city involves a series of phases, from planning to the selection of the most suitable tools. Both citizens and the private sector have to be involved in the development of a smart city, resulting in a connected, innovative, digital, and successful city.

The projects that constitute a smart city can be classified as follows: smart governance, smart economy, smart mobility, smart environment, smart people, and smart living. Based on these indicators, a number of rankings classify the most advanced smart cities, which are the fruit of governance oriented towards innovation and digital inclusion. The highest scores have been obtained by London, Singapore, Seoul, New York, and Helsinki. It should be noted that these cities also stand out for having one of the best open data portals, another smart city pillar that favours innovation. In particular, the high quality of data available in several US cities has led to a number of data science competitions on the Kaggle platform to predict future demand for city bikes.

In addition, Europe's profits from the use of AI-based software are expected to reach a value of more than $1.5 billion by 2025, five times the amount obtained in 2020. Several companies have presented proposals related to smart city platforms and architectures, highlighting the Huawei Horizon@City, Toyota, and NTT smart city platform and IBM City Operations Platform reference architecture proposals. The Deepint.net tool has been created as the starting point for the solution to these problems, facilitating the rapid and efficient development of the infrastructure that

Table 11.2 The vertical markets and domains of smart cities

Vertical markets	Domain
Smart governance	Participation
	Social services
	Transparency
Smart economy	Innovation
	Productivity
	Entrepreneurship
	Flexible labour market
Smart mobility	Connected public transport
	Multimodality
	Logistics
	Accessibility
Smart environment	Environmental protection
	Resources management
	Energy efficiency
Smart people	Digital education
	Creativity
	Inclusive society
Smart living	Tourism
	Security
	Healthcare
	Culture

any smart city requires. Smart city vertical markets and their domains can be found in Table 11.2.

11.3 Deepint.net: A Platform for Smart Territories

Today, cities/territories are the largest data producers, and all major sectors can extract knowledge and benefit considerably from data analyses. Thanks to advances in computing such as distributed processing techniques, improved processing capabilities, and cheaper technology, current artificial intelligence techniques can be applied to large volumes of data at a very fast pace; this would have been unthinkable less than a decade ago.

As a result, large investments are being made in the information and computing sector, either through the acquisition of technology that allows for the recovery and processing of information, or by investing in hiring highly qualified scientists to carry out precise studies. Such staff is not always easy to find due to the scientific complexity involved and the peculiarities of the problem domain.

Deepint.net is a platform that seeks to cover the current "gap" between the need to create smart territories and the large expenses that this normally entails in terms of tools and data scientists. This platform has been created for the managers of intelligent cities/territories, facilitating all aspects of data management, processing, and visualisation.

Deepint.net is a platform deployed in a self-adapting cloud environment, which enables users to apply artificial intelligence methodologies to their data using the most widespread techniques (random forest, neural networks, etc.), even if they lack knowledge of their operation/configuration, or even programming skills. Deepint.net facilitates the construction of models for data processing, guiding the user through the process. It indicates how to ingest data, work with the data, visualise the information, apply a model, and finally, obtain, evaluate, interpret, and use the results. The platform incorporates a wizard that automates the process, it is even able to select the configuration for the artificial intelligence methodology that will provide the best solution to the problem the user is trying to solve.

Furthermore, additional features enable users to exploit all the results through dynamic, reusable dashboards that can be shared and used by other smart city tools. Moreover, the results can be exported in different formats for simple integration, for example, in a report. Figure 11.4 shows elements and tools that can be used along the process of data management, from data intake to the creation of scorecards or data exploitation.

Deepint.net is a platform created for managing and interpreting data in an efficient and simple way. It has been structured in five different functional layers as shown in Figure 11.4. Figure 11.5 presents the elements of the data ingestion layer of Deepint.net.

On Deepint.net, both static and dynamic data may be incorporated in the tool. Dynamic data are constantly updated. The data are stored as "data sources",

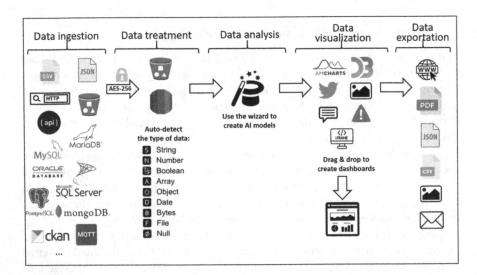

Figure 11.4 Data analysis flow and elements.

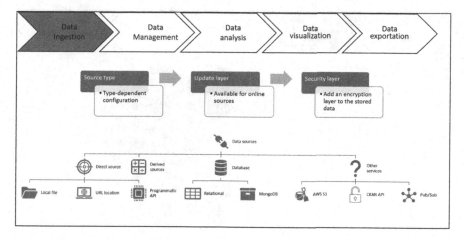

Figure 11.5 Data ingestion layer description.

as presented in Figure 11.5. The data sources on Deepint.net are elementary because they are the starting point of the rest of the functions that can be applied. To create a data source from data that are available elsewhere, the wizard asks the user to specify the type of media in which the original data are found, and the configuration associated with that type of media. For example, if it is a database, the user must indicate the host, username, password, database name, and the SQL query to be executed. After indicating the configuration of the data source, the wizard requests information on the data update frequency in the case of dynamic data. Finally, it is possible to encrypt the data in a data source on Deepint.net. This option slightly slows down all operations, as the user is asked to perform a decryption operation every time they want to make use of the data. Nevertheless, it provides an extra layer of security that other tools on the market do not offer.

Regarding the type of support in which the original data are found, the following are allowed: (i) direct sources: CSV or JSON files containing the data to be imported from local files, URLs, or calls to existing endpoints; (ii) derived sources: new data sources obtained from existing data sources (very useful for the next step of the flow, data management); (iii) databases: both relational and NoSQL databases; and (iv) other services: for data coming from well-known services such as AWS S3, CKAN, or data streaming (such as MQTT).

Deepint.net offers multiple functionalities to users for the management of the information contained in data sources (Figure 11.6). To begin with, the system automatically detects the type of data and the format (for decimal data or dates), thus, the user does not have to spend time on specifying it. However, in the case of certain graphs or models it may be important to specify the type of data and Deepint.net allows users to specify it manually or change the type that has been

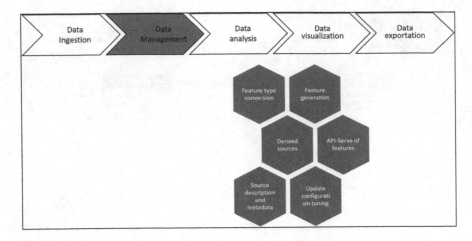

Figure 11.6 Data management layer.

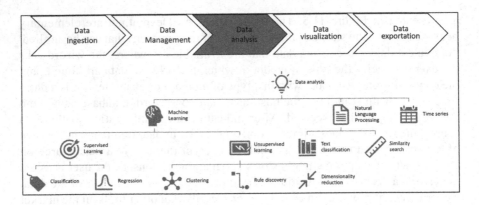

Figure 11.7 Data analysis layer.

detected automatically. It also allows the user to generate features from existing fields using user-defined expressions. At this point in the flow, the creation of derived data sources from existing data sources is possible, as discussed in the previous section. More specifically, different types of operations may be performed on the different data sources, such as filters on records or parameters in a data source, merging two data sources with the same parameters, and much more. The tool also offers the possibility of working with data sources from an API to edit them programmatically.

The platform provides tools for knowledge extraction within the context of various learning methodologies, as shown in Figure 11.7. We can find in it multiple supervised learning methodologies, both for classification and regression problems, using algorithms such as decision tree, random forest, gradient boosting, extreme gradient boosting, naive Bayes, support vector machines, and linear and logistic regressions. In all of these cases, the configuration of the algorithms can be adjusted to achieve better performance. Additionally, there are unsupervised learning techniques available, including clustering methods (k-means, DBSCAN, and others), as well as association rule learning or dimensionality reduction techniques, for example, principal component analysis (PCA).

Another field of application of the platform is natural language processing, which involves processes such as text classification, text clustering, and similarity-based retrieval.

The tool offers a wizard that facilitates the process of creating dynamic and interactive graphs. It only takes a few simple steps, as presented in Figure 11.8. In the first step, the user is asked to specify the data source they want to use to create the visualisation. They can create as many visualisations of a data source as they wish. In the same step, the source can be filtered to represent a subset that meets the conditions specified by the user (conditions can be nested with AND and OR operations). Similarly, the user can select a subset of the sample, which is ordered randomly or by the user in situations where large volumes of data are represented with pivot charts which may slow down the user's computer (since these are pivot charts developed in JavaScript, the processing power is provided by the client). The next step that the user must do is to select the type of chart they want and configure it. The configuration depends specifically on each of the types of graphs and there are more than 30 different graphs. Likewise, the information to be represented can be configured, and the style (title, legend, series, colours, etc.) can be easily set using the wizard.

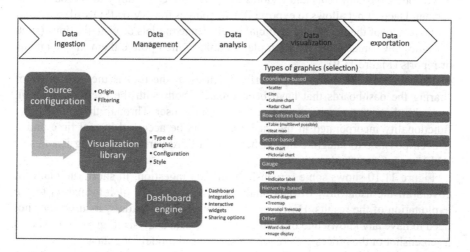

Figure 11.8 Data visualisation layer.

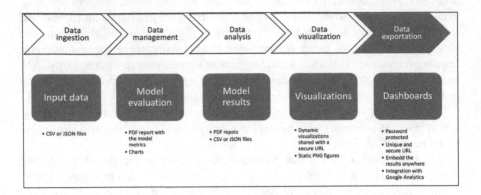

Figure 11.9 Data exportation layer.

Once the visualisations are created, they can be added to interactive dashboards and placed in the positions that the user wants by means of drag and drop. Different forms can be added with which the user can interact to filter the information that is represented (a second level of filtering in addition to the filtering performed when creating the visualisation). This offers multiple benefits when it comes to controlling cities and monitoring only the information that is relevant at any given time. The user can also add other elements to the dashboards, such as the results of the machine learning models, iframes, images, or content through WYSIWYG editors, among many other possibilities.

A very important aspect of data analysis is being able to export the obtained results, as well as the data used as input. This feature facilitates, for example, the use of other types of tools and enables the scientific community to reproduce the system. Deepint.net allows to export all data sources to CSV or JSON files, as well as the results of the developed artificial intelligence models or visualisations (such as static PNG images) to, for example, be able to incorporate them in documents or reports (Figure 11.9).

However, one of the most powerful features of the tool is the possibility of sharing the dashboards that have been created, both with the users of the tool, and with those that receive a unique link from the user. Through this link, all the functionality incorporated in the dashboards can be accessed in real time and it is even possible to integrate the dashboards in third-party tools using iframes or WebViews, for example.

Figure 11.10 shows some screenshots of data ingestion. In short, the platform covers all the usual flow of data analysis from the intake of information to the exploitation of the results. However, unlike other existing tools, its user does not need to have any knowledge of programming or data analysis. Figure 11.11 shows a screenshot of the process of creating a supervised model for data analysis.

Deepint.net offers mechanisms for the management of all the information provided by the user, enabling the creation of different projects. Figure 11.12 shows

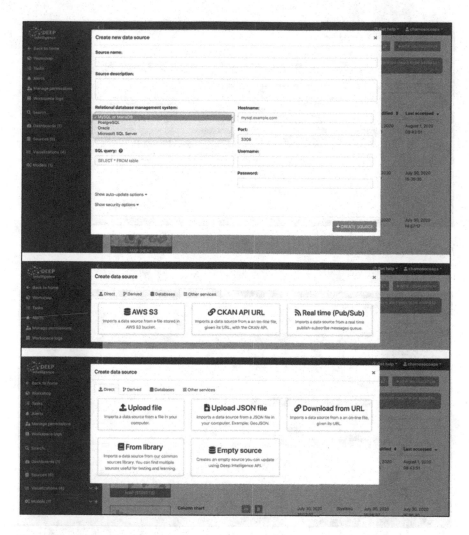

Figure 11.10 Data ingestion.

a screenshot of the process of creating a model for data visualisation, which as you can see, is extremely simple, since it consists of selecting the type of model to display the data, the dataset, and the selected parameters. Figure 11.13 gives a screenshot of the dashboards created for the visualisation of city information [Panama (top) and Istanbul (bottom)]. Similarly, the creation of users and permissions is allowed so that all the group members/employees can exploit the results of the analysis, displaying them on dynamic and interactive dashboards. Deepint.net is a versatile, multipurpose platform, whose utility for smart territory or city management is of special interest.

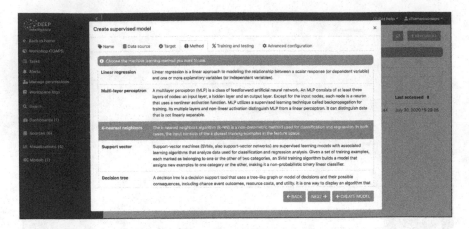

Figure 11.11 Intelligent model selection.

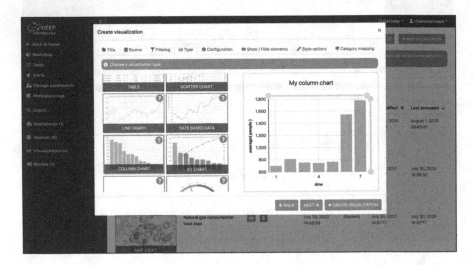

Figure 11.12 Screenshot of the process of creating visualisation models.

These are some of the functionalities of Deepint.net:

- User management functionality which offers plans that are customised to the needs of the cities.
- Integration of multi-source data, prioritising the most common sources: formatted local and internet (CSV/JSON) files, databases (NoSQL and SQL), streaming data (MQTT, among others), CKAN-based repositories, etc.
- Automatic detection of the data type to facilitate analysis and representation.

Figure 11.13 Creation of dashboards: Panama (top) and Istanbul (bottom).

- Mechanisms for data processing (filtering records according to a criterion, eliminating fields, merging sources, creating compound fields, etc.).
- Guided mechanisms that facilitate the representation of the information provided by the user.
- Mechanisms for the guided creation of data analysis models, suggesting the best configuration to the users while allowing advanced users to carry out this process themselves if they wish.
- Simple evaluation of the results of the model according to different metrics.
- Dashboard definition by inserting created visualisations, model results, etc. through "drag and drop" so that users can customise how they want to work with the tool.

- Structuring the user's projects so that with one account the tool can be used in different areas or for different clients.
- Creation of city users with different roles so that all employees can use the platform as specified by the administrator.
- Exportation of results for easy integration in reports, etc.
- Possibility to deploy the system in a commercial cloud environment (AWS) that allows to provide services on demand to all users, in a way that is adapted to their needs, with high performance and high availability.

Compared to its competitors, one of the main advantages of this platform is wizards. Users just need to learn how to use them, which does not require any advanced knowledge, to integrate the results of machine learning tools, the monitoring tools, and the visualisation of results. The data accuracy of all data science tasks depends directly on the input and the selected algorithms. The accuracy of both generic and specific algorithms is considered constant, independently of the platform. The volume of data that the platform can manage depends on its architecture, which is introduced in the section that follows.

11.3.1 Platform Architecture

The platform architecture can be deployed in an on-premise environment or in a commercial cloud environment.

The on-premise solution has been designed for situations in which it is not possible to process information in the infrastructures of third-party companies due to, for example, restrictive data protection policies.

Nevertheless, the solutions advertised on the platform web page are all hosted in commercial cloud environments (other solutions require a custom study and deployment).

Figure 11.14 provides a high-level representation of the architecture to be deployed in AWS (Amazon Web Services). Clients can connect to the application through the internet, available on app.deepint.net. The load balancer redirects the traffic to the corresponding EC2 instance. The users of the free version share resources, while the users of the paid version have private EC2 instances and do not share resources, which always guarantees a good processing capacity.

In each EC2 there is a web server and task workers, which are managed by a Redis server for event management on the platform (for the cache and the pub/sub system).

These resources access the serverless systems when they stop dealing with information. For the processing of information on Deepint, a relational database is used, in this case an Aurora DB as it is the serverless relational system of AWS. In addition, the system uses the storage system S3 to deploy all the data sources which the users upload on the system. The deployment can be encrypted with AES-256 if the user specifies it.

As the cloud environment of AWS is used, there is no limit on the volume of data and the response times depend directly on the type of EC2 chosen by the

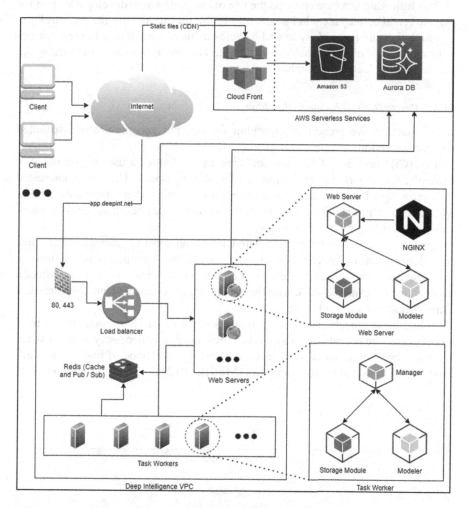

Figure 11.14 High-level representation of the platform architecture.

client. In case the client needs to improve the response times, they can increase their expenditure on resources or migrate to an on-premise solution.

The main technical challenges considered during the platform design are: parallelisation aspects, availability of on-demand resources, and a serverless solution which allows the user to work on with no size restrictions.

11.4 Case Study

This platform can be adapted for the development of vertical markets, as part of smart city management. In general, vertical markets are associated with mobility, security, pollution, etc.

The following is a case study on the use of the platform to develop a system for bicycle rental management in Paris. It allows the user to identify the areas of Paris in which they are more likely to find bicycles using historical data to predict areas with the highest bicycle density in real time. The process is carried out using the Pareto optimal location algorithm.

11.4.1 Pareto Optimal Location Algorithm

In this section, we present an algorithm for optimal geographically distributed resource selection.

Let $\{C_i\}$I be a set of locations offering the resources a user is seeking. For example, the resources might be public bike-sharing stands. The user is interested in borrowing a bike, but they risk arriving at a location where there are no bikes available. The probability of one of those resources can be modelled as a set of functions $\{p_i(t)\}$i, where t is the time.

Such functions can be approximated using an existing dataset, where further dependence on other variables is allowed. For example, a set of models $\{p_i(\text{weekday,hour,weather})\}$I can be built using machine learning prediction algorithms. An example made with the Vélib dataset, available from the open data Paris portal, is shown in Figure 11.15.

While these models can be used to suggest the resource locations to the user, to maximise the probability of satisfying their need, it is necessary to address the interplay between distance to the resource and the likelihood of finding an available bike. A notion of Pareto optimality (Morris, 2012) can be introduced to reduce

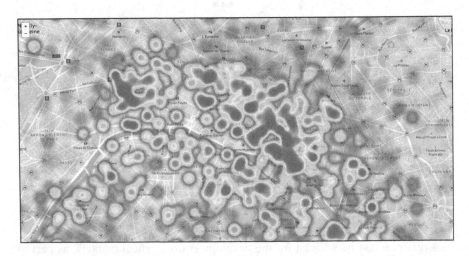

Figure 11.15 The heat map of a probability model for the availability of bikes in the city of Paris.

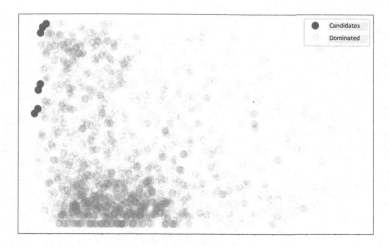

Figure 11.16 Pareto optimal points on the time–probability plane.

the choice to a smaller set of points. A resource location j dominates another one I if the following conditions apply:

$$\{(d(x,Ci) \geq d(x,Cj)pi(t+d(x,Ci)) \leq pj(t+d(x,Cj)))\} \Leftrightarrow Ci \leq Cj \qquad (1)$$

where d is the estimated time to arrive at a given location, x is the user's location, and, in the right-hand-side, a notation for this domination condition has been introduced. A location Ci in a set $\{Ci\}(i \in I)$, Pareto is optimal if there is no other point dominating it, i.e.,

$$\exists j \in I : j \neq i, Ci \leq Cj \qquad (2)$$

A natural approximation for simplifying the model assumes the variations of probability are negligible on the time scale of displacement, i.e.,

$$pi(t+d(x,Ci)) \approx pi(t) \qquad (3)$$

This allows to reduce the notion to a regular Pareto condition on the plane (d(x,Ci),pi). An example is shown in Figure 11.16, where optimal points are found in the upper left corner.

A representation of the points in terms of real-world coordinates is shown in Figure 11.17.

Finally, an ordered list of recommendations can be provided to the user by introducing a risk-aversion parameter $\omega \in R$, so

$$vi = pi - d(x,Ci)\omega \qquad (4)$$

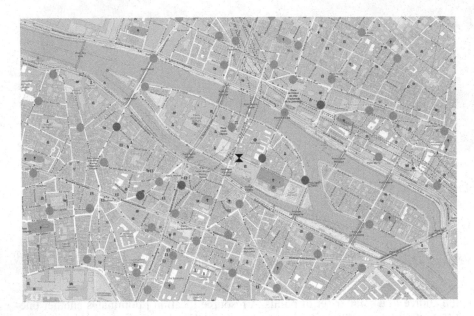

Figure 11.17 Real-world coordinates of the Pareto optimal points. The location of the user
is shown as the black cross. Pareto-optimal choices are shown as blue dots,
while sub-optimal locations are shown in orange.

defines a metric which serves to order the Pareto optimal points. Users with
higher risk aversion (larger ω) tend to choose options with greater probabilities,
while users with higher risk tolerance (smaller ω) tend to choose the closest
resources. The choice of reasonable values for ω is scale-dependent and can be
tuned by presenting sets of Pareto optimal points to the user and asking for their
preference.

11.4.2 Implementation with Deepint.net

The algorithm described in the previous section was implemented using the
Deepint.net platform, as well as specific deployments. An outline of the process is
described in this section.

Firstly, a prediction algorithm was built using tabulated historical data. A simple
example of such data is shown in Figure 11.18. These data could be used to predict the probability of availability (ratio) as a function of the station, the weather conditions, and the date (here only distinguishing weekdays and weekends for
simplicity).

Regressors were built using these data with the assistance of the platform's
online wizard. Figure 11.19 shows a random forest model, including a predicted-
observed diagram and an interactive form to invoke the model.

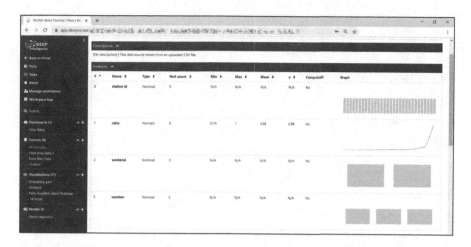

Figure 11.18 Data uploaded on Deepint.net to build a prediction model.

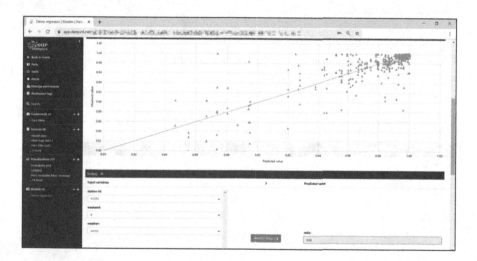

Figure 11.19 Prediction model built on Deepint.net.

Finally, a specially designed mobile application used the Deepint.net API (Figure 11.20) to retrieve the model predictions. This information was used to perform the Pareto optimisation as described in the previous section, providing the user with an interactive map where they could choose their preferred option.

The integration of the platform was completed with the construction of a set of dashboards which allowed to monitor the information, as shown in Figure 11.21.

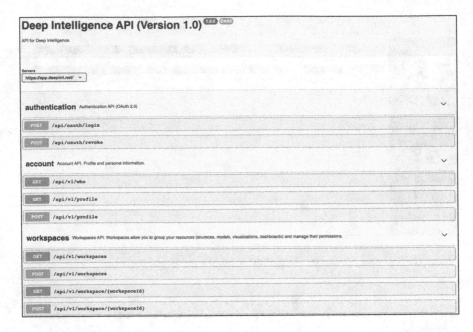

Figure 11.20 Online documentation of the Deepint.net API.

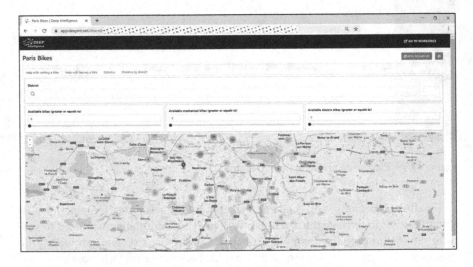

Figure 11.21 System dashboard built using the Deepint.net platform.

11.5 Conclusion

Deepint.net is a platform that facilitates knowledge management and the creation of intelligent systems for managing territories efficiently. The platform facilitates the use of centralised intelligence and edge architectures, with intelligent nodes, allowing for both decentralised and centralised analyses.

The implementation of a smart territory management systems involves a reduction in costs associated with maintenance and resource management. Depending on its application, the platform can facilitate traffic optimisation, create systems for analysing the opinions citizens on social networks, or help assess and prevent pollution, and so on.

In general, the use of a platform of this type, which allows for the use of any cloud, reduces the initial investment needs. Normally, costly infrastructures are required to analyse medium and large volumes, since the cost can be very high if 1 GB is exceeded. This cost would be significantly reduced by processing the data in a remote cloud-based infrastructure tailored to the needs of each territory. The use of commercial infrastructures also reduces risks and increases the security of data management. Moreover, it is possible to scale the infrastructure to the needs of each moment. The platform is designed to ingest and manage any type of infrastructure, such as intelligent nodes, facilitating the decentralisation of intelligence and the creation of intelligent models distributed in edge computing mode.

Similarly, the territories or cities in which this platform would be used would not need to have staff with programming or data analysis knowledge. Instead, they would only need to have knowledge of the information owned by their company. The user takes on the role of a data analysis expert; they work with the data and understand if the obtained results are satisfactory or not. This allows to focus on the result and not on the development costs, which would be negligible thanks to the proposed system.

The system may be operated in real time by any user in the city. Users with no computer knowledge would only display the information on a real-time dashboard while managers would oversee monitoring the general performance of the company. All city stakeholders can benefit.

The wizards offered by Deepint.net for the integration of data sources, creation of visualisations, dashboards, and modelling, cover the entire ecosystem within the data analysis life cycle. This proposal is advantageous over other commercial data analysis solutions which are much more limited in functionality and usability.

The development process of this platform has been made efficient thanks to the use of Deepint.net. The platform also facilitated the carrying out of the case study in the city of Paris. Moreover, Deepint.net is highly versatile and is currently undergoing further development in order to incorporate new functionalities which can adapt to a wider range of smart territories, eventually aiming to become a comprehensive agent capable of speeding up the development of any smart city. Furthermore, in-depth research is being carried out on the many technologies which form deepint.net and the findings will be shared with the scientific community in future studies (Corchado et al., 2021).

Acknowledgements

This chapter, with permission from the copyright holder, is a reproduced version of the following journal article: Corchado, J., Chamoso, P., Hernandez, G., Gutierrez, A., Camacho, A., Briones, A., Santos, F., Goyenechea, E., Retuerta, D., Miguel, M., Hernandez, B., Villaverde, B., Verdejo, M., Martinez, P., Pérez, M., Garcia, S., Alonso, R., Vara, R., Tejedor, J., Prieta, F., Gonzalez, S., Dominguez, J., Mohamad, M., Trabelsi, S., Plaza, E., Coria, J., Yigitcanlar, T., Novais, P., & Omatu, S., (2021). Deepint. net: A rapid deployment platform for smart territories. *Sensors*, 21(1), 236.

References

Alkhatib, M., El Barachi, M., Shaalan, K. (2019). An Arabic social media based framework for incidents and events monitoring in smart cities. *Journal of Cleaner Production*, *220*, 771–785.

Chamoso, P., González-Briones, A., De La Prieta, F., Venyagamoorthy, G., Corchado, J. (2020). Smart city as a distributed platform. *Computer Communications*, *152*, 323–332.

Corchado, J., Chamoso, P., Hernandez, G., Gutierrez, A., Camacho, A., Briones, A., Santos, F., Goyenechea, E., Retuerta, D., Miguel, M., Hernandez, B., Villaverde, B., Verdejo, M., Martinez, P., Pérez, M., Garcia, S., Alonso, R., Vara, R., Tejedor, J., Prieta, F., Gonzalez, S., Dominguez, J., Mohamad, M., Trabelsi, S., Plaza, E., Coria, J., Yigitcanlar, T., Novais, P., Omatu, S., (2021). Deepint. net: A rapid deployment platform for smart territories. *Sensors*, 21(1), 236.

Elmaghraby, A., Losavio, M. (2014). Cyber security challenges in Smart Cities. *Journal of Advanced Research*, *5*(4), 491–497.

Gheisari, M., Wang, G., Chen, S. (2020). An edge computing-enhanced internet of things framework for privacy-preserving in smart city. *Computers & Electrical Engineering*, *81*, 106504.

Hussain, M., Alam, M., Beg, M. (2019). Fog computing model for evolving smart transportation applications. *Fog and Edge Computing*, *22*(4), 347–372.

Jia, G., Han, G., Rao, H., Shu, L. (2017). Edge computing-based intelligent manhole cover management system for smart cities. *IEEE Internet of Things Journal*, *5*(3), 1648–1656.

Kapser, S., Abdelrahman, M. (2020). Acceptance of autonomous delivery vehicles for last-mile delivery in Germany. *Transportation Research Part C*, *111*, 210–225.

Khan, L., Yaqoob, I., Tran, N., Kazmi, S., Dang, T., Hong, C. (2020). Edge-computing-enabled smart cities. *IEEE Internet of Things Journal*, *7*(10), 10200–10232.

Kitchin, R., Dodge, M. (2019). The (in)security of smart cities. *Journal of Urban Technology*, *26*(2), 47–65.

Kousiouris, G., Akbar, A., Sancho, J., Ta-Shma, P., Psychas, A., Kyriazis, D., Varvarigou, T. (2018). An integrated information lifecycle management framework for exploiting social network data to identify dynamic large crowd concentration events in smart cities applications. *Future Generation Computer Systems*, *78*, 516–530.

Kumar, S., Datta, D., Singh, S., Sangaiah, A. (2018). An intelligent decision computing paradigm for crowd monitoring in the smart city. *Journal of Parallel and Distributed Computing*, *118*, 344–358.

Latif, S., Afzaal, H., Zafar, N. (2018). Intelligent traffic monitoring and guidance system for smart city. In: *Proceedings of the International Conference on Computing, Mathematics and Engineering Technologies.*

Laufs, J., Borrion, H., Bradford, B. (2020). Security and the smart city. *Sustainable Cities and Society, 55,* 102023.

Liu, Y., Yang, C., Jiang, L., Xie, S., Zhang, Y. (2019). Intelligent edge computing for IoT-based energy management in smart cities. *IEEE Network, 33*(2), 111–117.

Luo, A., Yang, F., Li, X., Nie, D., Jiao, Z., Zhou, S., Cheng, H. (2020). Hybrid graph neural networks for crowd counting. In *Proceedings of the AAAI Conference on Artificial Intelligence.*

Morris, P. (2012). *Introduction to Game Theory.* Springer.

Ning, Z., Huang, J., Wang, X. (2019). Vehicular fog computing. *IEEE Wireless Communications, 26*(1), 87–93.

O'Dwyer, E., Pan, I., Acha, S., Shah, N. (2019). Smart energy systems for sustainable smart cities. *Applied Energy, 237,* 581–597.

Pan, X., Zhou, W., Lu, Y., Sun, N. (2019). Prediction of Network Traffic of Smart Cities Based on DE-BP Neural Network. *IEEE Access, 7,* 55807–55816

Perez, A., Zeadally, S. (2019). A communication architecture for crowd management in emergency and disruptive scenarios. *IEEE Communications Magazine, 57*(4), 54–60.

Premsankar, G., Ghaddar, B., Di Francesco, M., Verago, R. (2018). Efficient placement of edge computing devices for vehicular applications in smart cities. In: *Network Operations and Management Symposium.* IEEE.

Rajak, B., Kushwaha, D. (2019). Traffic control and management over IoT for clearance of emergency vehicle in smart cities. In: *Information and Communication Technology for Competitive Strategies.* Springer, Singapore.

Rego, A., Garcia, L., Sendra, S., Lloret, J. (2018). Software defined network-based control system for an efficient traffic management for emergency situations in smart cities. *Future Generation Computer Systems, 88,* 243–253.

Rehena, Z., Janssen, M. (2018). Towards a framework for context-aware intelligent traffic management system in smart cities. In: *Proceedings of the Companion Web Conference,* Lyon, France.

Schneider, M., Rambach, J., Stricker, D. (2017). Augmented reality based on edge computing using the example of remote live support. In: *Proceedings of 2017 IEEE International Conference on Industrial Technology.* IEEE.

Silva, B., Khan, M., Han, K. (2018). Towards sustainable smart cities. *Sustainable Cities and Society, 38,* 697–713.

Sittón-Candanedo, I., Alonso, R., Corchado, J., Rodríguez-González, S., Casado-Vara, R. (2019b). A review of edge computing reference architectures and a new global edge proposal. *Future Generation Computer Systems, 99,* 278–294.

Sittón-Candanedo, I., Alonso, R., García, Ó., Muñoz, L., Rodríguez-González, S. (2019a). Edge computing, IoT and social computing in smart energy scenarios. *Sensors, 19*(15), 3353.

Solmaz, G., Wu, F., Cirillo, F., Kovacs, E., Santana, J., Sánchez, L., Sotres, P., Munoz, L., (2019). Toward understanding crowd mobility in smart cities through the internet of things. *IEEE Communications Magazine, 57*(4), 40–46.

Sumi, L., Ranga, V. (2018). Intelligent traffic management system for prioritizing emergency vehicles in a smart city. *International Journal of Engineering, 31*(2), 278–283.

Taleb, T., Dutta, S., Ksentini, A., Iqbal, M., Flinck, H. (2017). Mobile edge computing potential in making cities smarter. *IEEE Communications Magazine*, *55*(3), 38–43.

Ullah, Z., Al-Turjman, F., Mostarda, L., Gagliardi, R. (2020). Applications of artificial intelligence and machine learning in smart cities. *Computer Communications*, *154*, 313–323.

UNESCO (2019). *Smart cities*. UNESCO. Paris.

Yao, H., Gao, P., Wang, J., Zhang, P., Jiang, C., Han, Z. (2019). Capsule network assisted IoT traffic classification mechanism for smart cities. *IEEE Internet of Things Journal*, *6*(5), 7515–7525.

Zhao, L., Wang, J., Liu, J., Kato, N. (2019). Routing for crowd management in smart cities. *IEEE Communications Magazine*, *57*(4), 88–93.

12 City as a Platform

12.1 Introduction

Statistics from the Department of Economic and Social Affairs of the United Nations (DESAP) indicate that 68% of the world's population will live in cities or urban areas by 2050 (Yigitcanlar et al., 2019), which means rapid and even uncontrolled growth with consequent challenges for governments, for example: pollution; problems of travel due to traffic and congestion; high costs of housing, food and basic services; as well as security problems (Perveen et al., 2017). Noise pollution is becoming a growing concern as it is the second most important pollutant after air—it has been discovered to have great effects in both the health of adults (Basner et al., 2014) and children (Lercher et al., 2003).

To address the above-mentioned problems, the smart city concept emerged over recent years, which refers to the integration of the urban environment with the information and communication technologies (ICTs). This concept has attracted the interest of all sectors (governments, universities, research centres, etc.) to present solutions or developments to achieve a smart city (Edvardsson et al., 2016). The objective of the smart city paradigm is the effective management of challenges related to the growth of urban areas through the adoption of ICTs in developments, solutions, applications, services, or even in the design of state policies (Chamoso et al., 2020).

Modern models of municipal governance promote the creation of public value through articulated initiatives involving citizens. In this context, the generation of useful information for citizens is essential, and citizens are increasingly demanding that it be accessible via the Internet. Making data open and mobilising collective knowledge are increasingly important to enable the creation of sustainable solutions for cities. It is in this context that the concept of city-as-platform emerges, which is associated with the movement for open government and the application of digital technologies to expand the possibilities for the co-production of public services (Repette et al., 2021). The city-as-platform is the technological and governmental infrastructure that enables society to play a direct and broader role in the life of cities. Digital technologies are applied to promote an open space for collaboration and democratisation of information and knowledge, which requires governance that is consensual, transparent, responsive,

DOI: 10.1201/9781003403630-15

efficient, effective, equitable, and inclusive. To promote this type of initiative, it is essential to have tools such as the one presented in this chapter, in order to have dynamic, efficient, and fast mechanisms to facilitate the analysis of information and to provide it to citizens. This platform makes it easy to capture data from IoT platforms, open data, etc. and process them using artificial intelligence techniques, augmented reality, etc.

Currently, smart city is a broadly used term, for example, in systematic reviews of the literature more than 36 definitions have been identified that address different dimensions of the urban environment such as: mobility, technology, public services, economy, environment, quality of life, or governance (Butler et al., 2020; D'Amico et al., 2020; Yigitcanlar et al., 2022; Ramaprasad et al., 2020). One of the most widely used definitions is the one proposed by Elmaghraby and Losavio (2014): "an intelligent city is one that incorporates information and communication technologies to increase operational efficiency, shares information independently within the system and improves the overall effectiveness of services and the well-being of citizens". However, the growth of the Internet of Things since 2017 has led to many devices being permanently connected to the Internet. This has led to increased interest in overcoming the challenges posed to effective data management and security and opened a debate regarding their importance in urban management and in the wellbeing of the population (Kitchin et al., 2019; Pancholi et al., 2019; Yigitcanlar et al., 2017).

Security is a very important element in cities, it is vital to guaranteeing a safe environment for both the citizens and the data that are generated. Any city must implement security measures to ensure full protection of citizens' data, and the data generated by the urban infrastructure and sensors, etc. Given the seriousness of the COVID-19 pandemic, it is also important to facilitate compliance with security measures that protect citizens and that, for example, they maintain an adequate social distance. For this reason, imaginative systems that allow us to identify those areas where there is a lower density of pedestrians can be of great interest, for example to facilitate the leisure of families who want to go out and enjoy the city. Smart cities need a secure and flexible platform for managing data coming from city sensors, service providers, citizens, etc. (Yigitcanlar et al., 2016). Data come from real-time sensors, smart nodes, and relational or non-relational databases. Especially small to medium-sized cities or territories need scalable platforms, that are easy to deploy and manage and that do not require specialised data analysts, which they do not generally have (Yigitcanlar et al., 2015). The construction of a smart city is a dynamic process, and the management platforms must be ready not just for real-time data ingestion but also for the inclusion of data from different sources, to manage such data, to analyse it, to create different visualisation models, and to integrate different datasets. It is also of great relevance to exploit the data, to be able to develop classification, optimisation, prediction, etc. models and to develop secure dashboards that can be integrated in the control system of a city or county council or any other entity responsible for the management of the smart city. All these challenges must be tackled while developing a smart city, therefore slowing down the process and creating several problems for the developers. How does one accelerate the development of smart cities, while reducing costs, time, and difficulties?

This chapter presents the deepin.net platform (Corchado et al., 2021) and how it has been used to implement a model that facilitates the maintenance of social distancing when walking around a city. Many cities have cameras to guarantee security and/or facilitate decision-making with respect to, for example, traffic, frequency of cleaning, etc. In this case we show how a model with a facial recognition algorithm has been implemented on images captured in real time and another regressive one. This collects images from security cameras and identifies the number of pedestrians on a street, calculates the density, and using historical data predicts what the density of pedestrians will be in the future. The HOG (Histogram of Oriented Gradients) algorithm is used to detect pedestrians and calculate their density on a street. The XGBoost algorithm (Chen, 2016) is used to predict the future. The facility that deepint.net must incorporate sensor data, in this case from camera images, and to implement these algorithms makes it very simple to build mechanisms for automated decision-making processes. With this information, citizens will be able to plan their walks, know the density of pedestrians on a street at a given time, and also what is likely to happen in the future.

One of the main advantages of deepint.net compared with similar platforms is its serverless design, based on the cloud environment of AWS. This results in no volume restrictions for the data and response times corresponding to the AWS machine chosen by the client. Moreover, its ease-of-use makes it possible for anyone with basic knowledge to take part in the development of a smart city, greatly speeding up the developing and deployment phases.

11.2 Literature Background

Cities are constantly evolving and regardless of their size they are seeking solutions to improve the quality of life of their citizens, to be more efficient and to optimise their resources. Information and communication technology (ICT) is a basic element in the development of intelligent cities and numerous projects have been launched to create information management systems especially adapted to the needs of cities (Repette et al., 2021).

In all these developments it is essential to consider aspects that are closely related to the citizens, such as human capital/education, social and relational capital, the environment, etc. For smart city models to be useful and progress together with their citizens it is necessary for them to be efficient, flexible, easy and rapid to implement, and to integrate with other smart city tools or technologies (Chamoso et al., 2020; Cardullo & Kitchin, 2019). Many countries are making considerable efforts to develop a "smart" urban growth strategy in their metropolitan areas (Cardullo & Kitchin, 2019). The Intelligent Community Forum conducts research on the local effects of ICTs that are now available worldwide.

The role of innovation in the ICT sector is fundamental in the development of the infrastructure that provides a city with intelligence and of tools for the sustainable, citizen-oriented, realistic, and coherent management that is required (Peris-Ortiz et al., 2017). The scope of research is extraordinarily broad in this field and there are numerous options for the implementation of intelligent cities. It is therefore important to know all of them and make the right choices. Interesting options have been presented for smart cities in the fields of wireless sensor networks (Hashim et al., 2018; Toutouh & Alba, 2017), agriculture (González-Briones et al., 2018a; González-Briones et al., 2018b), energy optimisation (González-Briones et al., 2018d; Chamoso et al., 2018a; González-Briones et al., 2018e; González-Briones et al., 2018f), optimal resource allocation (Enayet et al., 2018), risks and challenges of EV adoption (Potdar et al., 2018), vehicle networks (Rivas et al., 2018; Toutouh & Alba, 2018), and route optimisation (González-Briones et al., 2018g; Chamoso et al., 2018b; González-Briones et al., 2018c).

The Internet of Things is a basic element in the development of intelligent cities (Chamoso et al., 2020; Arasteh et al., 2016). City data, especially if accessible in real time, can be used to effectively transform and manage the city and promote urban planning and development (Garcia et al., 2019). Appropriate real-time solutions and systems capable of making decisions to solve run-time problems are elements that can improve the efficiency of smart cities (Chatterjee et al., 2018). This chapter provides an example of how the data extracted from real-time images can be used to identify areas where pedestrians can walk, maintaining an adequate social distance.

Any platform for smart city management must have a robust system to acquire and process data from multiple data sources (databases, trackers, third-party applications, sensors, intelligent nodes). Architectures require flexible and scalable computing power to process large volumes of data. Today, thanks to technological advances and lower storage and sensor prices, the amount of generated and stored data is huge and growing exponentially. Multicore processing [in the form of symmetric multiprocessing (SMP) and asymmetric multiprocessing (AMP)] is becoming common, with embedded multicore CPUs expected to grow by a factor of ×6 in the coming years (Venture Development Corporation). In addition, field programmable gate arrays (FPGAs) have grown in capacity and decreased in cost, providing the high-speed functionality that could only be achieved with application-specific integrated circuits (ASICs) (Trimberger, 2018). In addition, virtualisation is driving the development of large scalable systems and blurring the connection between hardware and software by allowing multiple operating systems to run on a single processor.

There are numerous platforms for the management of smart cities, which facilitate both massive and secure data intake and processing. These platforms have mechanisms for information analysis, data transmission, information fusion, preprocessing, etc. In addition, these platforms must be prepared for integration with other platforms, with information management systems, etc. Some of the platforms used for the management of smart cities are presented in Table 12.1.

Although much research is being done on smart cities, a compact system is still needed that is efficient and scalable, and easy to implement and integrate with other platforms. The platforms presented in the previous tables offer many options and some of them are quite flexible for data management. They all have been analysed

Table 12.1 Main platforms used for the management of smart cities

Platform name	Description	Key features
Deepint.net	Platform for data acquisition, integration, preprocessing, and modelling. Incorporates a complete suite of artificial intelligence techniques for data analysis: clustering, forecasting, optimisation, etc. It is scalable and easy to implement	Scalable, ease-to-use, versatile, smart city development focus
ICOS	An open repository of solutions for smart cities, offering a set of existing applications and projects that can be reused for application creation	Open-source, active forum, re-usable solutions
Webinos	Web application platform that allows developers to access native resources through APIs. Webinos makes it easy to connect any IoT device	Open-source, independent software components
Sofia2	Middleware that enables interoperability between multiple systems and devices, offering a semantic platform that makes real-world information available to smart, mainly IoT-oriented applications	IoT focus, interoperability among systems
Kaa	An initiative that defines an open and efficient cloud platform to provide IoT solutions. Among the most common solutions is the connection of all types of sensors that can be found or deployed in a smart city	Focus on road infrastructure, public service facilities, and smart buildings
Altair SmartWorks	PaaS-type platform designated for IoT and M2M. It can be used to connect the information-providing infrastructure to a smart city. However, the platform remains at this level, without offering user-oriented services, a layer that would have to be created independently of the platform	PaaS platform, good IoT protocols support
FIWARE	A platform that provides a series of APIs for the development and deployment of Internet applications, targeting a number of verticals. Many of these sectors are responsible for providing a variety of smart city services	Open-source, powerful APIs, strong ecosystem

and some are more efficient in modelling data, others are better at acquiring data from sensors but the most interesting one, with the greatest potential, is deepint.net (Corchado et al., 2021).

Deepint.net offers all the necessary elements to build a system for collecting and managing data using all the power of artificial intelligence. Deepint.net simplifies the development of the management systems of a smart city and offers the possibility of integrating data from any source.

Deepint.net offers user-centred services and facilitates the creation of intelligent dashboards without the need for knowledge of intelligent systems, as it has an intelligent tutor that guides experts in city management to develop their own models. The platform is ready to integrate new management models and facilitates the composition of intelligent hybrid or expert mixing systems, so that different algorithms work together to obtain results from integrated or heterogeneous data sources.

Moreover, one of the main characteristics of smart cities is the heterogeneity of all their components (Paskaleva, 2011), both in the final applications and in the technology used in the deployed infrastructure. For example, within the IoT sector, there are many manufacturers, protocols and communication technologies (Ferraris et al., 2019; Sandulli et al., 2017). As detailed below, one of the main advantages of the platform presented in this chapter is that it is compatible with any technology or manufacturer.

Deepint.net incorporates the elements required for the management of any smart city without the need for ICT professionals or expert data analysts, and it has been developed under the concept of "Smart City as a Platform". The platform includes artificial intelligence techniques for the extraction of information that is useful in the management of infrastructures, systems, and devices, making the city functional and efficient. Moreover, maintaining a rapid response time is fundamental for the functioning of a smart city. Without deepint.net, the large volume of data collected from a smart city is normally sent directly to the cloud; this has high associated and variable costs, forcing cities to seek solutions that reduce the costs of payments to cloud service providers, as well as energy and bandwidth consumption. Deepint.net is a scalable, easy to use, and dynamic platform that has a fast response time, and that is capable of satisfying the immediate needs of any city or territory.

The development of a smart city must be based on certain foundations, which range from a well-defined planification phase to the selection of the most suitable tools (Yigitcanlar et al., 2020). In many cases, key aspects such as an in-depth review of the human factors of the city or the validation of market-ready technologies, have been left out. This can result in slow adoption of new systems and unsuccessful smart city projects. Vertical markets and tools for smart cities are

Table 12.2 Verticals and domains of smart cities

Verticals	Domains
Smart governance	Social services, participation, transparency…
Smart economy	Innovation, productivity, entrepreneurship, flexible labour market…
Smart mobility	Connected public transport, multimodality, logistics, accessibility…
Smart environment	Environmental protection, resources management, anergy efficiency…
Smart people	Digital education, creativity, inclusive society…
Smart living	Tourism, security, healthcare, culture…

often classified following the principles outlined in Table 12.2, which provide a solid structure upon which a smart city must be built.

11.3 A Novel Platform for Smart Cities

Today, all sectors can extract knowledge and benefit considerably from data analysis, with cities or territories being the largest producers of data that exist today. Thanks to advances in computing such as distributed processing techniques, improved processing capabilities, and cheaper technology, artificial intelligence techniques can now be applied to large volumes of data, offering rapid results, which was unthinkable less than a decade ago.

Deepint.net offers functionalities that cover the entire data analysis flow: a wizard for data ingestion from multiple sources and in multiple formats, a wizard for data management (pre-processing, filtering, etc.), a wizard for applying proprietary data analysis methodologies with the advantage that no algorithm needs to be programmed or configured, a wizard for creating fully customised dynamic visualisations and dashboards using drag and drop techniques, and finally, mechanisms for exporting data and visualisation results, allowing, for example, for the interactive sharing of analyses with any Internet user. The architecture of the platform includes five different layers, as described in Figure 12.1.

Deepint.net is a platform that can be used to create data collection and management systems for members efficiently and without the need for data scientists, which is difficult to find nowadays, as it includes many data analysis algorithms created with artificial intelligence techniques. It is a platform created for the managers of smart cities, and it facilitates all the aspects related to data management, processing, and visualisation.

Deepint.net is a platform deployed in a self-adapting cloud environment, which allows users to apply artificial intelligence methodologies to their data, using the most widespread techniques (random forest, neural networks, etc.). The user does not have to know how these techniques work, nor how to configure them, it is not even necessary to have programming skills. Deepint.net facilitates the construction of models for data processing in a guided and clear way, indicating how to ingest data, work with the data, visualise the information to understand the data, apply a model and, finally, obtain, evaluate, interpret, and use the results. The platform incorporates a wizard that automates the process, selecting the configuration for the artificial intelligence methodology that provides the best solution to the problem the user is addressing.

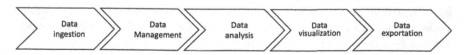

Figure 12.1 Deepint.net architecture layers.

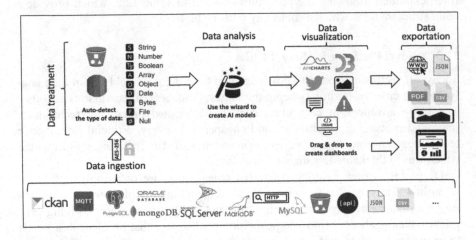

Figure 12.2 Flow and elements of data analysis.

Figure 12.2 shows which elements and tools can be used throughout the data and information management process, from data entry to the creation of dashboards or data exploitation at the end. Deepint.net allows users to exploit all results through dynamic, reusable dashboards that can be shared and used within other tools available to the city, such as exporting results in different formats for easy reporting, for example.

It is a platform that covers all the usual flow of data analysis from the intake of information to the exploitation of the results, but unlike other existing tools, the user has no knowledge of programming or data analysis but is only an expert in smart cities (Corchado et al., 2021).

Some of the most outstanding features of this platform are related to its plans tailored to the needs of cities, its ability to integrate datasets from different sources, prioritising the most common: formatted files (CSV/JSON) both local and available on the Internet, databases (NoSQL and SQL), streaming data (MQTT, among others), repositories based on CKAN, etc., the inclusion of models for the automatic detection of the type of data, the use of automatic mechanisms for data processing (filtering records according to a criterion, eliminating fields, merging sources, creating compound fields, etc.), guided mechanisms that facilitate the representation of the information provided by the user, mechanisms for the creation of data analysis models in a guided manner, and suggesting the best configuration to users. Meanwhile, the platform has advanced features which can be used by users who have knowledge of data analysis; the use of metrics that allow the model results to be evaluated in a simple manner, the definition of dashboards by inserting created visualisations, model results, etc. by means of "drag & drop" so that users can personalise how they want to work with the tool, etc.

In addition, deepint.net allows users to create different roles, structure user projects in such a way that with one account the tool can be used in different environments or for different clients, exploit results for the creation of reports, etc., and deploy the system in a commercial cloud environment (i.e., AWS) that allows all users to be served in a way that is adapted to their needs, on demand, with high performance and high availability.

12.4 Case Study: Melbourne

In this section, a model is presented for real-time crowd detection and future crowd prediction using video surveillance footage. The use case is set in the city of Melbourne and focuses on the ability to detect the most crowded streets of the city and the streets which have the lowest number of pedestrians. This information is of critical importance to both government institutions and citizens, especially during the current COVID-19 pandemic. Crowds may contribute to the spread of the Coronavirus if the social distancing among people is not adequate, and maintaining such distance can be rather difficult. The information generated by the presented model may help citizens and city authorities in making decisions.

The method allows the user to identify the areas of Melbourne in which crowds will appear using historical and real-time data from the video surveillance cameras of the city. The process is carried out using a hybrid algorithm with two modules: a face recognition unit and a regression unit.

12.4.1 Input Data

The method is designed in such a way that constant image flow is the only required input. Camera footage is analysed every 2 minutes by the face recognition unit and the number of detected faces is fed to the regressor unit, which is re-trained once a month. This creates a well-labelled dataset and provides real-time insight to the users. To test both units separately, the use case presented in this chapter uses independent data for each unit.

The regressor unit has been trained using a dataset which contains hourly pedestrian counts since 5 January 2009, to 31 October 2020, from pedestrian sensor devices located across the city of Melbourne (the link is provided in the Data Availability Statement). It is formed by 3,391,523 data instances and contains information about each sensor's location, the time of the measurement and the number of pedestrian hourly counts. The data are considered reliable, up-to-date, and publicly available.

As for the face recognition unit, data protection laws do not permit the publishing of open datasets of street surveillance footage without blurring the faces of the people involved. This obstacle has been overcome by using a well-tested algorithm which provided a good performance in a vast variety of datasets (Dadi et al., 2016; Dalal et al., 2005; Huang et al., 2007)

An example of the data used is shown in Table 12.3.

Table 12.3 The face recognition algorithm applied to a frame of a crowd at a country fair. The average number of faces detected per frame is used to estimate the people density in the area

Year	Month	M date	Day	Time	Sensor_ID	Hourly_Counts	Latitude	Longitude
2019	September	20	Friday	2	57	16	-37.8164124	144.9558028
2017	March	9	Thursday	2	40	6	-37.8150015	144.95226225
2014	October	8	Wednesday	14	9	507	-37.818124	144.953581
2011	February	9	Wednesday	12	3	2.297	-37.81000274999995	144.9625943689245
2013	June	16	Sunday	8	12	64	-37.8145826	144.9422374
2018	January	4	Thursday	11	33	182	-37.8217763	144.9519159

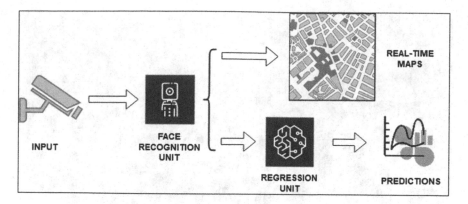

Figure 12.3 Flow and elements of the crowd detection method.

12.4.2 Crowd Detection Method

The goal of this solution is to accurately describe and predict the locations of crowds in any developed smart city. To achieve this, security camera footage is processed using a face recognition algorithm which calculates the number of individuals in each frame. This process is carried out every 2 minutes and the obtained number is extrapolated to estimate the people density surrounding the considered sensor. The obtained information is useful for monitoring crowd behaviours and creating a training dataset. An output describing the areas of the city by "low, medium, or high density of pedestrians" is generated.

Afterwards, a machine learning algorithm is trained with the labelled dataset and used for predicting the behaviour of crowds in the near future. An output describing the density of pedestrians in the different areas of the city is generated after 1 hour and 2 hours.

The overall process is described in Figure 12.3.

12.4.3 Face Recognition Unit

The main aim of this module is to transform the input, which consists of camera images, into a consistent dataset of people density. To achieve this, the number of faces in each frame is obtained and the average number of people over a period is calculated. This results in a dataset of people density in the location of each camera, which is used for training a regression unit.

This unit makes usage of the HOG (Histogram of Oriented Gradients) algorithm due to its good performance for human face image detection. This algorithm obtains a near-perfect separation on the original MIT pedestrian database and an 89% accuracy in other more complex datasets (Dalal et al., 2005).

Figure 12.4 The face recognition algorithm applied to a frame of a crowd at a country fair.

The face recognition process is as follows (Figure 12.4):

- Convert the image to greyscale and calculate the gradient of each pixel. This creates a common ground for all images. Changes in brightness do not affect the algorithm anymore.
- The gradients are stored in an array, divided into 16×16 pixel squares and the direction of the greatest gradients of each square is selected.
- A trained linear support vector machine (SVM) is used to find face patterns.

The algorithm produces a series of locations within the image which contain people's faces. A visual example of the output of the algorithm is shown in Figure 12.5. The accuracy of the algorithm reaches 99.38% on the Labelled Faces in the Wild benchmark (Huang et al., 2008).

12.4.4 Regression Unit

The regression unit in this case makes use of the XGBoost algorithm. This method stands out as it has shown very powerful performance and accuracy, and it has good interpretability. The goal is to model the previously obtained dataset and use it to predict future crowds as well as to monitor current ones (Figure 12.5).

XGBoost is an optimisation method which makes use of regularisation and a loss function as described in Chen et al. (2016). It addresses the problem of traditional Euclidean space optimisation methods and achieves a gradient tree boosting method. The (simplified) objective function is defined as:

$$\Lambda^{(t)} = \sum_{i=1}^{n} l\left(y_i, \overline{y}_i^{(t-1)} + f_t(x_i)\right) + \Omega(f_t) \tag{1}$$

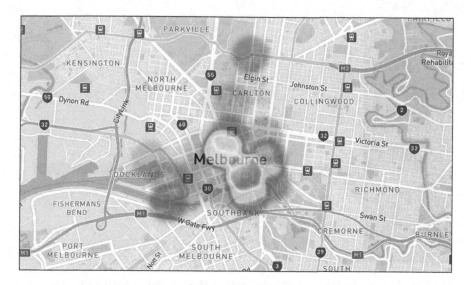

Figure 12.5 The heat map of a probability model of crowds in the city of Melbourne.

where l is the loss function, y_i is the real observed value, $\overline{y}_i^{(t-1)}$ is the previously predicted value, $f_t(x_i)$ is the function to optimise in step I, and $\Omega(f_t)$ is the regurgitation factor of the function.

This is defined as a computational-enhanced version of the Tailor Theorem which, in addition, can apply Euclidean space optimisation techniques.

Similarly, if we consider the second-order Taylor approximation, we obtain the truly used goal function:

$$\Lambda^{(t)} = \sum_{i=1}^{n} \frac{1}{2} h_i \left(f_i(x_i) - \frac{g_i}{h_i} \right)^2 + \Omega(f_t) + C \qquad (2)$$

where $g_i = \dfrac{\partial l\left(I, \overline{y}_i^{(t-1)}\right)}{\partial \overline{y}_i^{(t-1)}}$ and $h_i = \dfrac{\partial^2 l\left(I_i, \overline{y}_i^{(t-1)}\right)}{\partial \left(\overline{y}_i^{(t-1)}\right)^2}$ are the first- and second-order

gradient statistics of the loss function and C is a constant.

The usage of this function results in a lower computational complexity as compared to random forest and traditional tree ensemble models.

12.4.5 Using Deepint.net to Construct a Solution

The previously described algorithm has been implemented on deepint.net and its deployed version has been tested. An overview of the process is presented in this section.

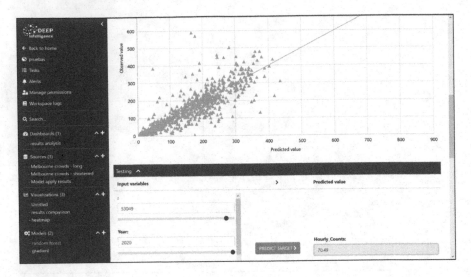

Figure 12.6 Predicted-observed diagram of the trained model and wizard for interactive predictions.

All the data analysis is made using wizards on deepint.net. The user must only select the data source and the model to be used, and the platform will automatically look for the best hyper-parameters and configurations. The performance of the created model can be directly observed in predicted-observed diagrams and other ways to interact with the model. For example, predictions of arbitrary dates and other types of data input can be made (Figure 12.6).

The ease-of-use is a key feature of the design of the platform. In just a few basic steps, a model can be created and there are several visualisations available to analyse its behaviour, performance, and accuracy, and to interact with the model. The basics of all the available options are described in detail in the dialogue boxes, the user just has to select the wished-for configuration. Furthermore, advanced data scientists can fine-tune the parameters manually if they wish, while using the functionalities of deepint.net via an API REST.

After the models have been created and connected within the smart territory, the design of the platform allows the user to create a set of dashboards for real-time monitoring of the sensors (Figure 12.7). Furthermore, heatmaps as shown in Figure 12.5 can be added to new dashboards.

12.5 Results

Deepint.net is a platform which eases the development and monitoring of intelligent systems in smart territories while providing robust results. The developed applications can be operated in real time by any user in the city: both a pedestrian who wants to plan a quiet walking route and a manager who has to decide where

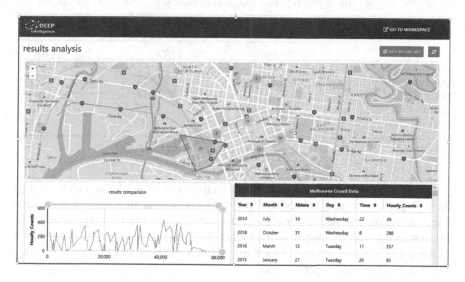

Figure 12.7 System dashboard for real-time monitoring of crowds, created using deepint. net.

to reinforce the street cleaning routines. Moreover, during the current COVID-19 pandemic it would allow pedestrians to keep a safe distance between themselves, as well as help authorities maintain a lower infection rate within their territory. All city stakeholders can therefore benefit.

The wizards offered by deepint.net for the integration of data sources, creation of visualisations, dashboards, and modelling, cover the entire ecosystem within the data analysis life cycle. This proposal has this key advantage over other commercial data analysis solutions which are more limited in functionality and usability.

The algorithm used for prediction was XGBoost as it is an optimised distributed gradient boosting library designed to be highly efficient, flexible, and portable. It implements machine learning algorithms under the Gradient Boosting framework, which provides fast and accurate results for most data science problems. It is widely used nowadays as it has achieved a better accuracy than other tree ensemble algorithms and even outperformed newer algorithms such as LightGBM (Liang et al., 2020). The discussed use case, designed as a mock-up version to test the platform's possibilities, has used a reduced version of the dataset (first 57,000 instances out of the 2,281,353 total instances) and obtained a mean relative error of 0.314. As can be seen in Figure 12.7, most values can be found near the predicted-observed line, with only a small amount of them far away. This performance corresponds with the basic results obtained when the platform automatically configures all the parameters, equivalent to a beginner user without any experience using it. For more advanced users, the wizards make it possible to boost this performance by manually fine-tuning the parameters and testing multiple configurations.

Table 12.4 Comparison of different face recognition algorithms (Adouani et al., 2019)

Metrics	Methods		
	HAAR	*HOG*	*LBP*
Detected frames	653,484	772,954	503,516
Detected faces	652,451	772,954	503,350
TPR (%)	78.23	92.68	60.37
FNR (%)	21.76	7.31	39.64

The face recognition algorithm applied in the use case has been selected due to its high performance, accuracy, and popularity; resulting in a trust-worthy algorithm. A comparison with other algorithms is shown in Table 12.4. The HOG algorithm stands out as the one with the higher detection rate, and it has been shown to work well with subsequent algorithms within a complex task (Dadi et al., 2016; Dalal et al., 2005; Huang et al., 2008).

Limitations: The proposed system assumes that the cameras used for crowd detection are located in relevant locations with a suitable angle to capture pedestrians—a camera facing a wall could confuse the classifier and distort the heatmaps. Furthermore, the model trained in this use case is designed to emulate the process performed by the most basic user. If a model is to be used in a real-world scenario, it will need to be fine-tuned by a data scientist.

12.6 Conclusion

The proposed model makes use of advanced machine learning algorithms for face recognition and an ensemble learning method that successfully predicts the present and future locations of crowds within cities, as evidenced by the results. The developed platform is the cornerstone of smart territory development, enabling any user to achieve equivalent results seamlessly and to implement them in real-life scenarios, facilitating the entire development process. Deepint.net made the creation of an advanced crowd detection dashboard possible and greatly reduced the development time—a few working days as opposed to the typical months of R&D for creating a system from the ground up. Most methods are based on well-established Python libraries, providing a high degree of reliability to any developed system.

The platform has much greater potential than specialised tools with regards to providing strong, resilient models to a wider public, without a drop in performance. As the number of smart cities around the world continues to increase, such advancements are needed more than ever. Deepint.net can reduce the costs associated with maintenance and resource management in smart territories while accelerating their development.

Current technological advantages are changing our cities from many different perspectives, and an efficient data management model is required. Such changes constitute a key challenge to any smart city, and they constantly make platforms become obsolete and full of limitations. As a result, deepint.net and any other such platform must include constant upgrades and incorporate new, promising ideas and algorithms.

The concept of "City-as-a-Platform" has been successfully introduced and is driving the development of smart cities, efficient in the use of data and boosting the development of smart applications. In this sense, it is not sufficient to have mechanisms for data processing and solution development; it is necessary to have platforms that allow for the construction of these systems in an efficient, fast, and secure way. The availability of "open-data" platforms, sensors capable of providing secure and continuous data, and the demand for solutions for each of the verticals identified by the many smart cities under development. It seems clear that what impedes municipal governments from undergoing a definitive and disruptive transformation is the use of inappropriate platforms. This hindrance has been addressed in this chapter, by demonstrating that deepint.net is a platform with great potential for information capture, visualisation, management, modelling, and representation. Municipal governance implies a systematic and definitive boost in the use of technologies such as those presented in this chapter. The presented user-friendly platform employs AI to manage data originating from IoT architectures (Garcia-Retuerta et al., 2021).

Acknowledgements

This chapter, with permission from the copyright holder, is a reproduced version of the following journal article: Garcia-Retuerta, D., Chamoso, P., Hernández, G., Guzmán, A., Yigitcanlar, T., & Corchado, J. (2021). An efficient management platform for developing smart cities: solution for real-time and future crowd detection. *Electronics*, 10(7), 765.

References

Adouani, A., Henia, W., Lachiri, Z. (2019). Comparison of Haar-like, HOG and LBP approaches for face detection in video sequences. In: *Proceedings of 2019 16th International Multi-Conference on Systems, Signals & Devices*, IEEE.

Arasteh, H., Hosseinnezhad, V., Loia, V., Tommasetti, A., Troisi, O., Shafie-khah, M., Siano, P. (2016). IoT-based smart cities. In: *Proceedings of 2016 IEEE 16th International Conference on Environment and Electrical Engineering*. IEEE.

Basner, M., Babisch, W., Davis, A., Brink, M., Clark, C., Janssen, S., Stansfeld, S. (2014). Auditory and non-auditory effects of noise on health. *The Lancet, 383*(9925), 1325–1332.

Butler, L., Yigitcanlar, T., Paz, A. (2020). Smart urban mobility innovations: A comprehensive review and evaluation. *IEEE Access, 8*, 196034–196049.

Cardullo, P., Kitchin, R. (2019). Smart urbanism and smart citizenship. *Environment and Planning C, 37*(5), 813–830.

Chamoso, P., González-Briones, A., Prieta, F., Venyagamoorthy, G., Corchado, J. (2020). Smart city as a distributed platform. *Computer Communications*, *152*, 323–332.

Chamoso, P., González-Briones, A., Rivas, A., Bueno De Mata, F., Corchado, J. (2018a). The use of drones in Spain. *Sensors*, *18*(5), 1416.

Chamoso, P., González-Briones, A., Rodríguez, S., Corchado, J. (2018b). Tendencies of technologies and platforms in smart cities. *Wireless Communications and Mobile Computing*, *3086854*, 1–17.

Chatterjee, S., Kar, A., Gupta, M. (2018). Success of IoT in smart cities of India. *Government Information Quarterly*, *35*(3), 349–361.

Chen, T., Guestrin, C. (2016). Xgboost. In: *Proceedings of International Conference on Knowledge Discovery and Data Mining*.

Corchado, J., Chamoso, P., Hernández, G., Gutierrez, A., Camacho, A., González-Briones, A., ... Omatu, S. (2021). Deepint. net. *Sensors*, *21*(1), 236.

D'Amico, G., L'Abbate, P., Liao, W., Yigitcanlar, T., Ioppolo, G. (2020). Understanding sensor cities: Insights from technology giant company driven smart urbanism practices. *Sensors*, *20*(16), 4391.

Dadi, H., Pillutla, G. (2016). Improved face recognition rate using HOG features and SVM classifier. *IOSR Journal of Electronics and Communication Engineering*, *11*(04), 34–44.

Dalal, N., Triggs, B. (2005). Histograms of oriented gradients for human detection. In: *Proceedings of Computer Society Conference on Computer Vision and Pattern Recognition*. IEEE.

Edvardsson, I. R., Yigitcanlar, T., Pancholi, S. (2016). Knowledge city research and practice under the microscope: A review of empirical findings. *Knowledge Management Research & Practice*, *14*(4), 537–564.

Elmaghraby, A. S., Losavio, M. M. (2014). Cyber security challenges in Smart Cities: Safety, security and privacy. *Journal of Advanced Research*, *5*(4), 491–497.

Enayet, A., Razzaque, M., Hassan, M., Alamri, A., Fortino, G. (2018). A mobility-aware optimal resource allocation architecture for big data task execution on mobile cloud in smart cities. *IEEE Communications Magazine*, *56*(2), 110–117.

Ferraris, A., Erhardt, N., Bresciani, S. (2019). Ambidextrous work in smart city project alliances. *International Journal of Human Resource Management*, *30*(4), 680–701.

Garcia-Retuerta, D., Chamoso, P., Hernández, G., Guzmán, A., Yigitcanlar, T., Corchado, J. (2021). An efficient management platform for developing smart cities: Solution for real- time and future crowd detection. *Electronics*, *10*(7), 765.

González-Briones, A., Castellanos-Garzón, J., Mezquita Martín, Y., Prieto, J., Corchado, J. (2018a). A framework for knowledge discovery from wireless sensor networks in rural environments. *Wireless Communications and Mobile Computing*, 1–14.

González-Briones, A., Chamoso, P., De La Prieta, F., Demazeau, Y., Corchado, J. (2018b). Agreement technologies for energy optimization at home. *Sensors*, *18*(5), 1633.

González-Briones, A., Chamoso, P., Rivas, A., Rodríguez, S., De La Prieta, F., Prieto, J., Corchado, J. (2018c). Use of gamification techniques to encourage garbage recycling. In: *Proceedings of International Conference on Knowledge Management in Organizations*, Springer.

González-Briones, A., De La Prieta, F., Mohamad, M., Omatu, S., Corchado, J. (2018d). Multi-agent systems applications in energy optimization problems. *Energies*, *11*(8), 1928.

González-Briones, A., Prieto, J., Corchado, J., Demazeau, Y. (2018e). EnerVMAS. In: *International Conference on Hybrid Artificial Intelligence Systems*, Springer.

González-Briones, A., Prieto, J., De La Prieta, F., Herrera-Viedma, E., Corchado, J. (2018f). Energy optimization using a case-based reasoning strategy. *Sensors, 18*(3), 865.

González-Briones, P. Chamoso, H. Yoe, J. Corchado (2018g) Greenvmas, *Sensors, 18*(3), 861–897.

González García, C., Núñez Valdéz, E., García Díaz, V., Pelayo García-Bustelo, B., Cueva Lovelle, J. (2019). A review of artificial intelligence in the internet of things. *International Journal of Interactive Multimedia and Artificial Intelligence*, 5.

Hashim Raza Bukhari, S., Siraj, S., Husain Rehmani, M. (2018). Wireless sensor networks in smart cities: applications of channel bonding to meet data communication requirements. *Transportation and Power Grid in Smart Cities*, 247–268.

Huang, G., Mattar, M., Berg, T., Learned-Miller, E. (2008). Labeled faces in the wild. In: *Workshop on Faces in 'Real-Life' Images: Detection, Alignment, and Recognition*.

Huang, G., Ramesh, M., Berg, T., Learned-Miller, E. (2007). Faces in the wild. *Technical Report*, 7–49.

Lercher, P., Evans, G., Meis, M. (2003). Ambient noise and cognitive processes among primary schoolchildren. *Environment and Behavior, 35*(6), 725–735.

Liang, W., Luo, S., Zhao, G., Wu, H. (2020). Predicting hard rock pillar stability using GBDT, XGBoost, and LightGBM algorithms. *Mathematics, 8*(5), 765.

Pancholi, S., Yigitcanlar, T., Guaralda, M. (2019). Place making for innovation and knowledge-intensive activities: The Australian experience. *Technological Forecasting and Social Change, 146*, 616–625.

Paskaleva, K. (2011). The smart city. *Intelligent Buildings International, 3*(3), 153–171.

Peris-Ortiz, M., Bennett, D., Yábar, D. (2017). Sustainable smart cities. *Innovation, Technology, and Knowledge Management*. Cham: Springer.

Perveen, S., Kamruzzaman, M., Yigitcanlar, T. (2017). Developing policy scenarios for sustainable urban growth management: A Delphi approach. *Sustainability, 9*(10), 1787.

Potdar, V., Batool, S., Krishna, A. (2018). Risks and challenges of adopting electric vehicles in smart cities. In: *Smart Cities*. Cham: Springer.

Repette, P., Sabatini-Marques, J., Yigitcanlar, T., Sell, D., Costa, E. (2021). The Evolution of City-as-a-Platform. *Land, 10*(1), 33.

Rivas, A., Chamoso, P., González-Briones, A., Corchado, J. (2018). Detection of cattle using drones and convolutional neural networks. *Sensors, 18*(7), 2048.

Sandulli, F., Ferraris, A., Bresciani, S. (2017). How to select the right public partner in smart city projects. *R&D Management, 47*(4), 607–619.

Toutouh, J., Alba, E. (2017). Parallel multi-objective metaheuristics for smart communications in vehicular networks. *Soft Computing, 21*(8), 1949–1961.

Toutouh, J., Alba, E. (2018). A swarm algorithm for collaborative traffic in vehicular networks. *Vehicular Communications, 12*, 127–137.

Trimberger, S. (2018). Three Ages of FPGAs. *IEEE Solid-State Circuits Magazine, 10*(2), 16–29.

Yigitcanlar, T., Degirmenci, K., Butler, L., Desouza, K. C. (2022). What are the key factors affecting smart city transformation readiness? Evidence from Australian cities. *Cities, 120*, 103434.

Yigitcanlar, T., Edvardsson, I. R., Johannesson, H., Kamruzzaman, M., Ioppolo, G., Pancholi, S. (2017). Knowledge-based development dynamics in less favoured regions: insights from Australian and Icelandic university towns. *European Planning Studies, 25*(12), 2272–2292.

Yigitcanlar, T., Guaralda, M., Taboada, M., Pancholi, S. (2016). Place making for knowledge generation and innovation: Planning and branding Brisbane's knowledge community precincts. *Journal of Urban Technology, 23*(1), 115–146.

Yigitcanlar, T., Inkinen, T., Makkonen, T. (2015). Does size matter? Knowledge-based development of second-order city-regions in Finland. *disP-The Planning Review, 51*(3), 62–77.

Yigitcanlar, T., Kankanamge, N., Regona, M., Maldonado, A., Rowan, B., Ryu, A., ... Li, R. (2020). Artificial intelligence technologies and related urban planning and development concepts. *Journal of Open Innovation, 6*(4), 187.

Index

Printed in the United States
by Baker & Taylor Publisher Services